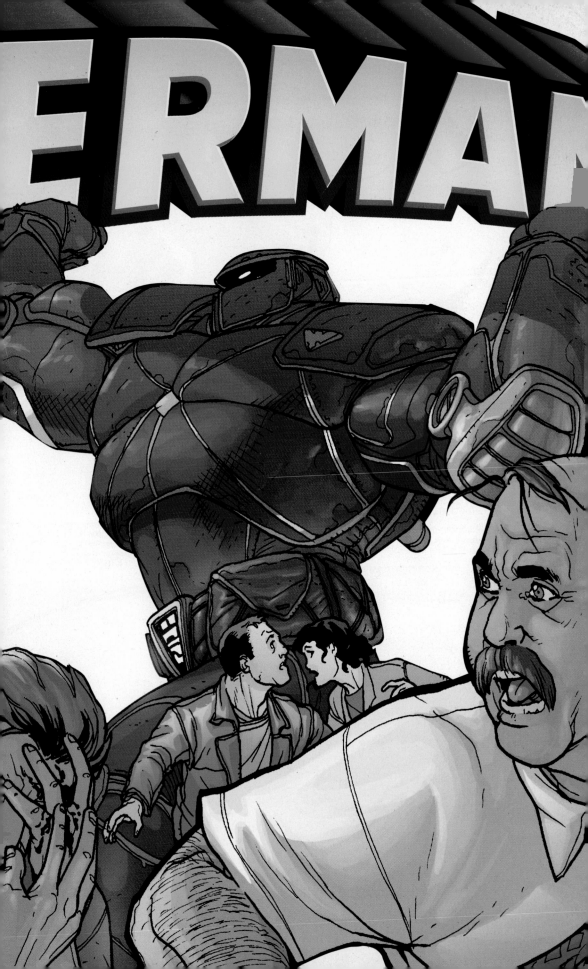

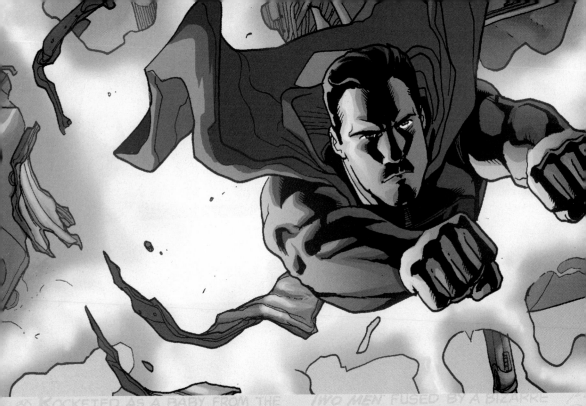

Dan DiDio Senior VP-Executive Editor   **Matt Idelson Julius Schwartz** Editors-original series   **Nachie Castro** Associate editor-original series
Bob Harras Group Editor-collected edition   **Robbin Brosterman** Senior Art Director   **Louis Prandi** Art Director   **Paul Levitz** President & Publisher
Georg Brewer VP-Design & DC Direct Creative   **Richard Bruning** Senior VP-Creative Director   **Patrick Caldon** Executive VP-Finance & Operations
Chris Caramalis VP-Finance   **John Cunningham** VP-Marketing   **Terri Cunningham** VP-Managing Editor   **Stephanie Fierman** Senior VP-Sales & Marketing
Alison Gill VP-Manufacturing   **Hank Kanalz** VP-General Manager, WildStorm   **Jim Lee** Editorial Director-WildStorm
Paula Lowitt Senior VP-Business & Legal Affairs   **MaryEllen McLaughlin** VP-Advertising & Custom Publishing
John Nee VP-Business Development   **Gregory Noveck** Senior VP-Creative Affairs   **Cheryl Rubin** Senior VP-Brand Management
Jeff Trojan VP-Business Development, DC Direct   **Bob Wayne** VP-Sales

Cover illustration by **Dave Gibbons**
Color reconstruction on DC COMICS PRESENTS 4, 17 and 24 by **Dave Tanguay**

SUPERMAN: BACK IN ACTION   Published by DC Comics. Cover, introductions and compilation copyright © 2007 DC Comics. All Rights Reserved. Originally
published in single magazine form in DC COMICS PRESENTS 4, 17, 24 and ACTION COMICS 841-843 Copyright © 1978, 1980, 2006 DC Comics. All Rights
Reserved. All characters, their distinctive likenesses and related elements featured in this publication are trademarks of DC Comics. The stories, characters and
incidents featured in this publication are entirely fictional. DC Comics does not read or accept unsolicited submissions of ideas, stories or artwork. DC Comics, 1700
Broadway, New York, NY 10019. A Warner Bros. Entertainment Company. Printed in Canada. First Printing. ISBN:1-4012-1263-8. ISBN 13: 978-1-4012-1263-6

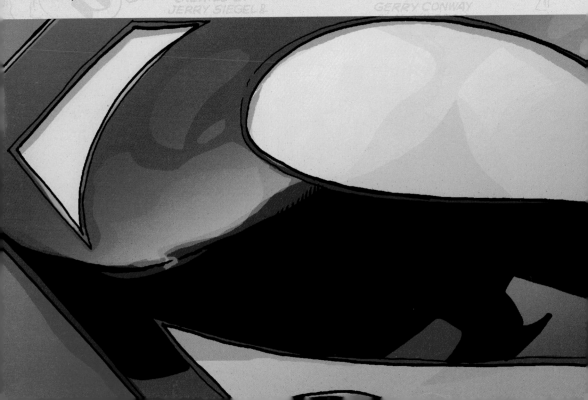

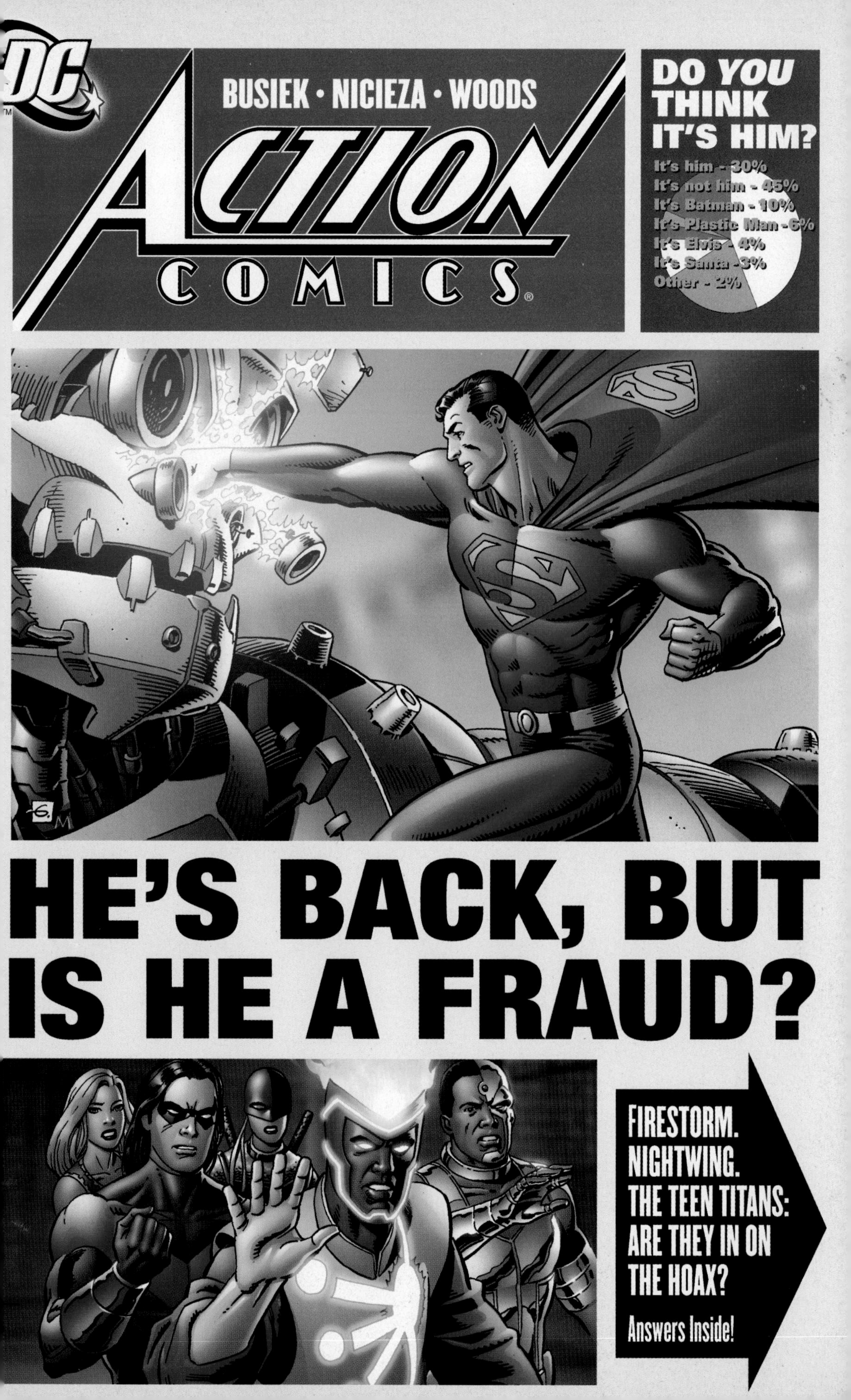

DC
BUSIEK • NICIEZA • WOODS
ACTION COMICS
DO YOU THINK IT'S HIM?
It's him - 30%
It's not him - 45%
It's Batman - 10%
It's Plastic Man - 6%
It's Elvis - 4%
It's Santa - 3%
Other - 2%
HE'S BACK, BUT IS HE A FRAUD?
FIRESTORM. NIGHTWING. THE TEEN TITANS: ARE THEY IN ON THE HOAX?
Answers Inside!

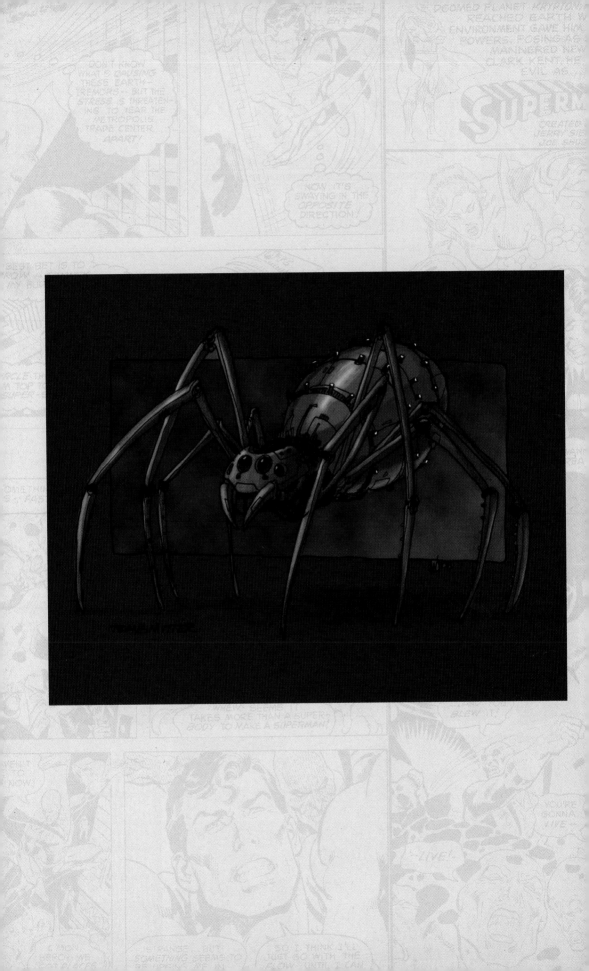

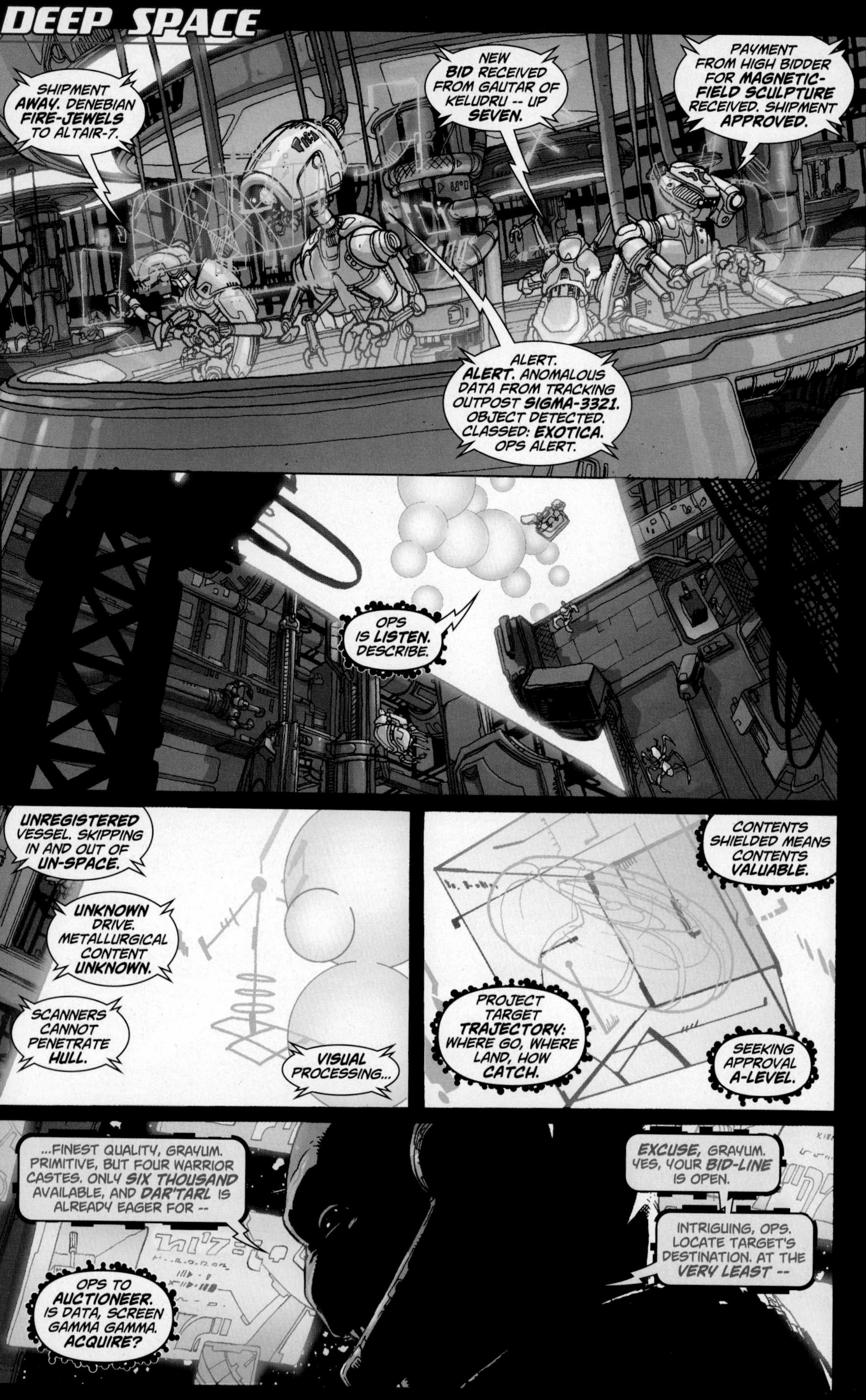
DEEP SPACE
SHIPMENT AWAY. DENEBIAN FIRE-JEWELS TO ALTAIR-7.
NEW BID RECEIVED FROM GAUTAR OF KELUDRU -- UP SEVEN.
PAYMENT FROM HIGH BIDDER FOR MAGNETIC-FIELD SCULPTURE RECEIVED. SHIPMENT APPROVED.
ALERT. ALERT. ANOMALOUS DATA FROM TRACKING OUTPOST SIGMA-3321. OBJECT DETECTED. CLASSED: EXOTICA. OPS ALERT.
OPS IS LISTEN. DESCRIBE.
UNREGISTERED VESSEL. SKIPPING IN AND OUT OF UN-SPACE.
UNKNOWN DRIVE. METALLURGICAL CONTENT UNKNOWN.
SCANNERS CANNOT PENETRATE HULL.
VISUAL PROCESSING...
CONTENTS SHIELDED MEANS CONTENTS VALUABLE.
PROJECT TARGET TRAJECTORY: WHERE GO, WHERE LAND, HOW CATCH.
SEEKING APPROVAL A-LEVEL.
...FINEST QUALITY, GRAYUM. PRIMITIVE, BUT FOUR WARRIOR CASTES. ONLY SIX THOUSAND AVAILABLE, AND DAR'TARL IS ALREADY EAGER FOR --
OPS TO AUCTIONEER. IS DATA, SCREEN GAMMA GAMMA. ACQUIRE?
EXCUSE, GRAYUM. YES, YOUR BID-LINE IS OPEN.
INTRIGUING, OPS. LOCATE TARGET'S DESTINATION. AT THE VERY LEAST --

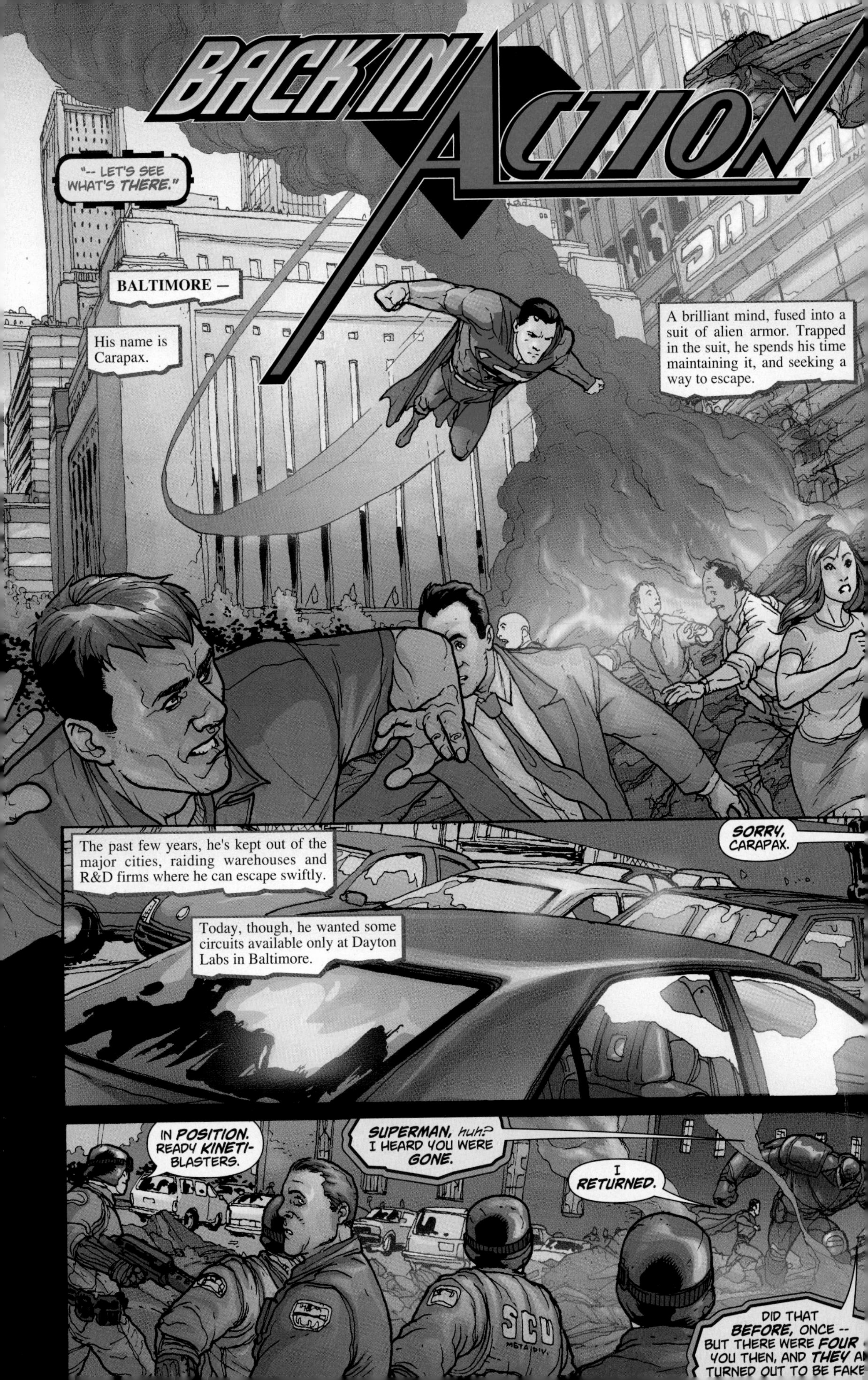
BACK IN ACTION
"-- LET'S SEE WHAT'S THERE."
BALTIMORE --
His name is Carapax.
A brilliant mind, fused into a suit of alien armor. Trapped in the suit, he spends his time maintaining it, and seeking a way to escape.
The past few years, he's kept out of the major cities, raiding warehouses and R&D firms where he can escape swiftly.
Today, though, he wanted some circuits available only at Dayton Labs in Baltimore.
SORRY, CARAPAX.
IN POSITION. READY KINETI-BLASTERS.
SUPERMAN, huh? I HEARD YOU WERE GONE.
I RETURNED.
DID THAT BEFORE, ONCE -- BUT THERE WERE FOUR YOU THEN, AND THEY A TURNED OUT TO BE FAKE
SCU

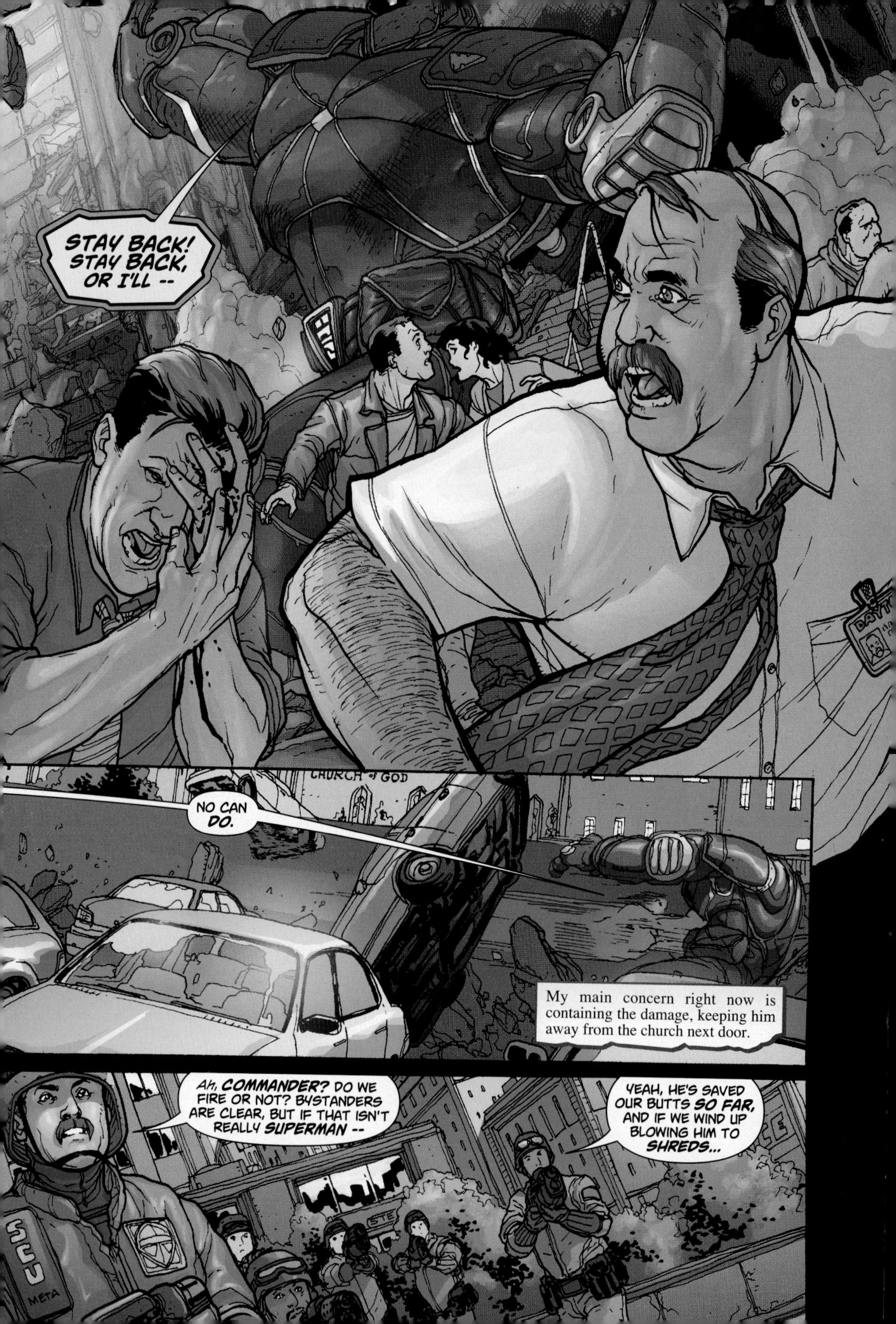
STAY BACK! STAY BACK, OR I'LL --
CHURCH of GOD
NO CAN DO.
My main concern right now is containing the damage, keeping him away from the church next door.
Ah, COMMANDER? DO WE FIRE OR NOT? BYSTANDERS ARE CLEAR, BUT IF THAT ISN'T REALLY SUPERMAN --
YEAH, HE'S SAVED OUR BUTTS SO FAR, AND IF WE WIND UP BLOWING HIM TO SHREDS...
SCU
META

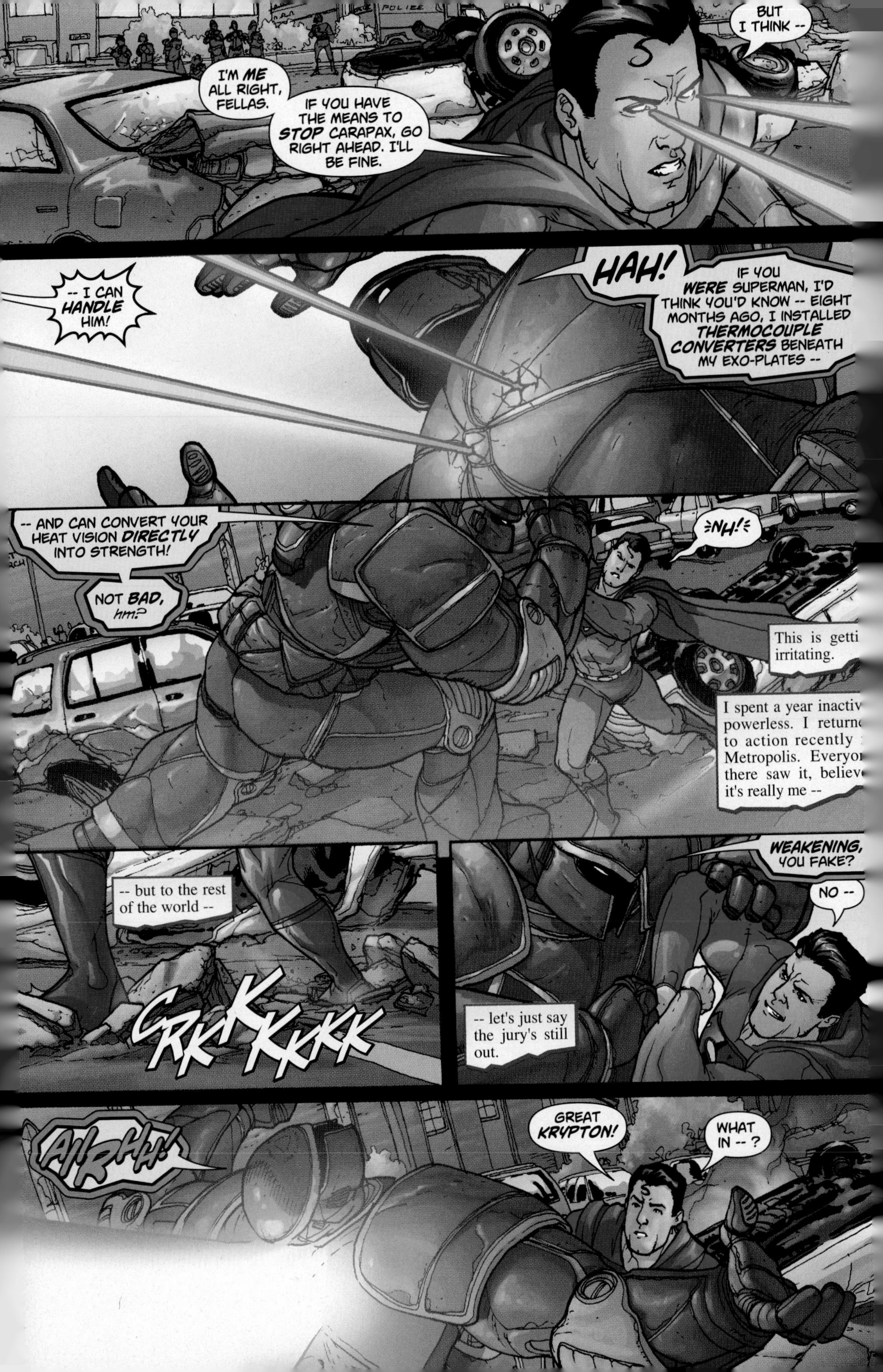
I'M ME ALL RIGHT, FELLAS.
IF YOU HAVE THE MEANS TO STOP CARAPAX, GO RIGHT AHEAD. I'LL BE FINE.
BUT I THINK --
-- I CAN HANDLE HIM!
HAH!
IF YOU WERE SUPERMAN, I'D THINK YOU'D KNOW -- EIGHT MONTHS AGO, I INSTALLED THERMOCOUPLE CONVERTERS BENEATH MY EXO-PLATES --
-- AND CAN CONVERT YOUR HEAT VISION DIRECTLY INTO STRENGTH!
NOT BAD, hm?
NH!
This is getti irritating.
I spent a year inactiv powerless. I returne to action recently Metropolis. Everyor there saw it, believ it's really me --
-- but to the rest of the world --
CRKKKKKK
WEAKENING, YOU FAKE?
NO --
-- let's just say the jury's still out.
AIRHH!
GREAT KRYPTON!
WHAT IN -- ?

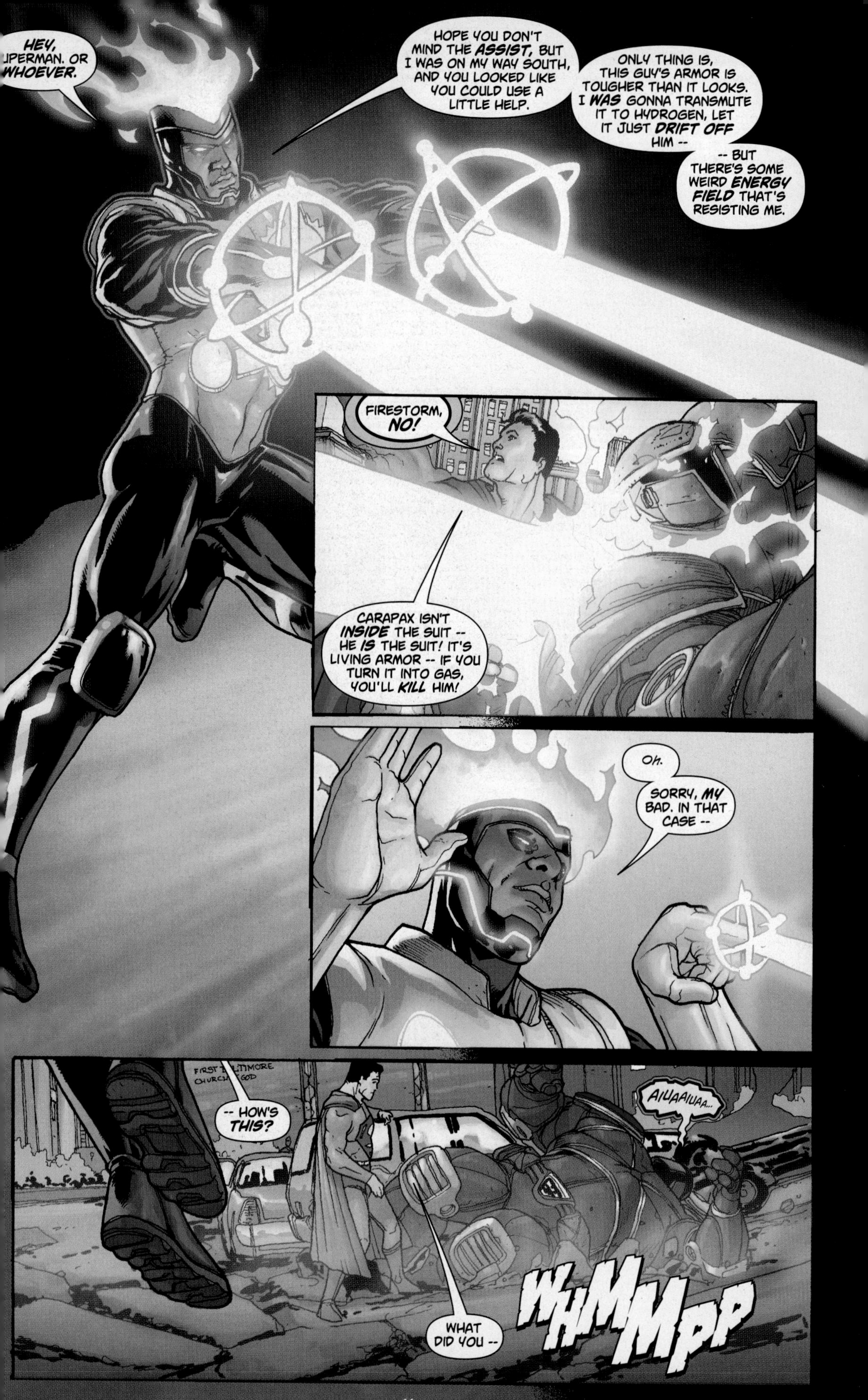
HEY, SUPERMAN. OR WHOEVER.
HOPE YOU DON'T MIND THE ASSIST, BUT I WAS ON MY WAY SOUTH, AND YOU LOOKED LIKE YOU COULD USE A LITTLE HELP.
ONLY THING IS, THIS GUY'S ARMOR IS TOUGHER THAN IT LOOKS. I WAS GONNA TRANSMUTE IT TO HYDROGEN, LET IT JUST DRIFT OFF HIM --
-- BUT THERE'S SOME WEIRD ENERGY FIELD THAT'S RESISTING ME.
FIRESTORM, NO!
CARAPAX ISN'T INSIDE THE SUIT -- HE IS THE SUIT! IT'S LIVING ARMOR -- IF YOU TURN IT INTO GAS, YOU'LL KILL HIM!
Oh.
SORRY, MY BAD. IN THAT CASE --
-- HOW'S THIS?
AIUAAIUAA...
WHAT DID YOU --
WHMMPP

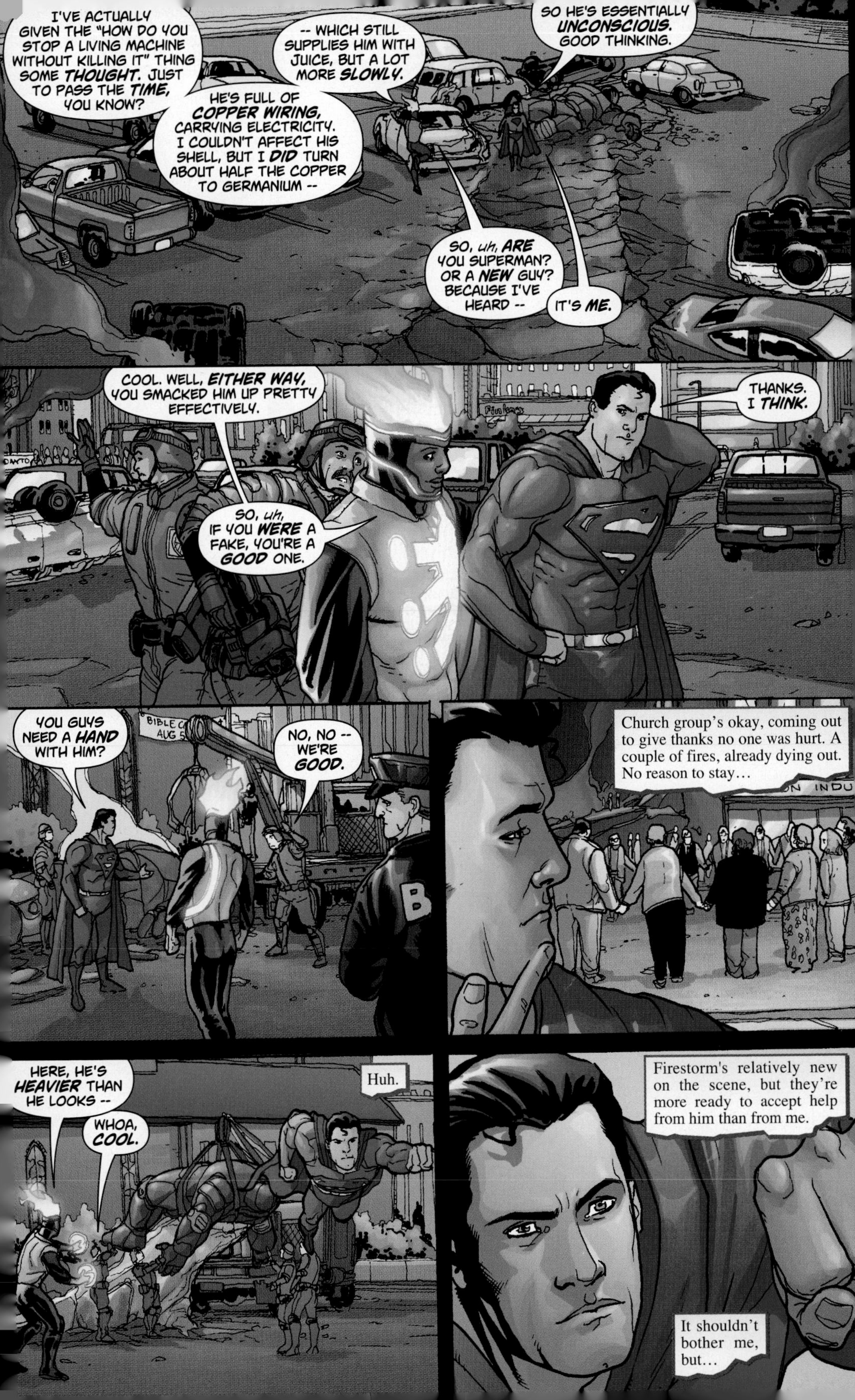
I'VE ACTUALLY GIVEN THE "HOW DO YOU STOP A LIVING MACHINE WITHOUT KILLING IT" THING SOME THOUGHT. JUST TO PASS THE TIME, YOU KNOW?
HE'S FULL OF COPPER WIRING, CARRYING ELECTRICITY. I COULDN'T AFFECT HIS SHELL, BUT I DID TURN ABOUT HALF THE COPPER TO GERMANIUM --
-- WHICH STILL SUPPLIES HIM WITH JUICE, BUT A LOT MORE SLOWLY.
SO HE'S ESSENTIALLY UNCONSCIOUS. GOOD THINKING.
SO, uh, ARE YOU SUPERMAN? OR A NEW GUY? BECAUSE I'VE HEARD --
IT'S ME.
COOL. WELL, EITHER WAY, YOU SMACKED HIM UP PRETTY EFFECTIVELY.
SO, uh, IF YOU WERE A FAKE, YOU'RE A GOOD ONE.
THANKS. I THINK.
YOU GUYS NEED A HAND WITH HIM?
NO, NO -- WE'RE GOOD.
Church group's okay, coming out to give thanks no one was hurt. A couple of fires, already dying out. No reason to stay…
HERE, HE'S HEAVIER THAN HE LOOKS --
WHOA, COOL.
Huh.
Firestorm's relatively new on the scene, but they're more ready to accept help from him than from me.
It shouldn't bother me, but…

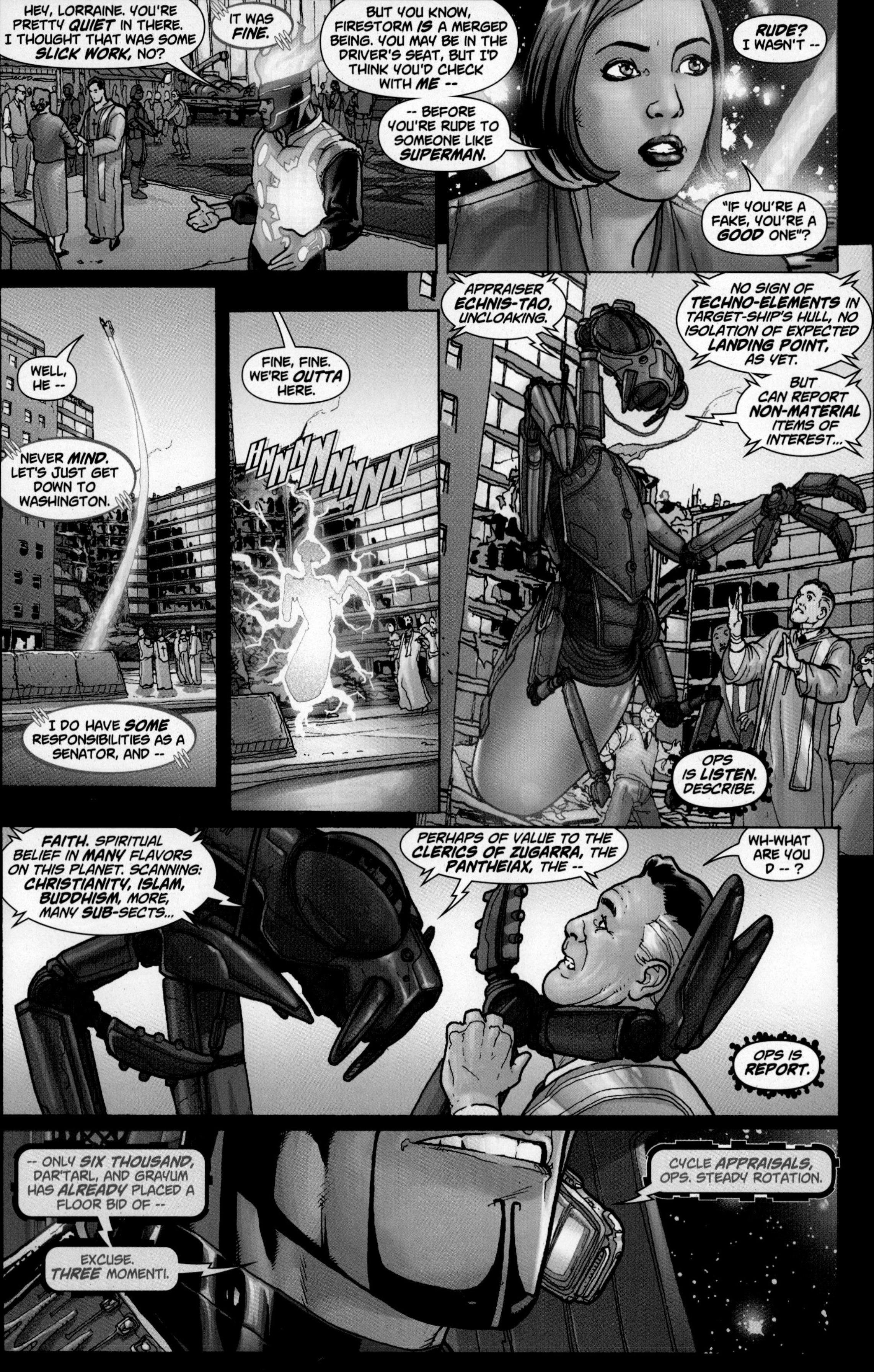
HEY, LORRAINE. YOU'RE PRETTY QUIET IN THERE. I THOUGHT THAT WAS SOME SLICK WORK, NO?
IT WAS FINE.
BUT YOU KNOW, FIRESTORM IS A MERGED BEING. YOU MAY BE IN THE DRIVER'S SEAT, BUT I'D THINK YOU'D CHECK WITH ME --
-- BEFORE YOU'RE RUDE TO SOMEONE LIKE SUPERMAN.
RUDE? I WASN'T --
"IF YOU'RE A FAKE, YOU'RE A GOOD ONE"?
WELL, HE --
NEVER MIND. LET'S JUST GET DOWN TO WASHINGTON.
I DO HAVE SOME RESPONSIBILITIES AS A SENATOR, AND --
FINE, FINE. WE'RE OUTTA HERE.
HNNNNNNNN
APPRAISER ECHNIS-TAO, UNCLOAKING.
NO SIGN OF TECHNO-ELEMENTS IN TARGET-SHIP'S HULL, NO ISOLATION OF EXPECTED LANDING POINT, AS YET.
BUT CAN REPORT NON-MATERIAL ITEMS OF INTEREST...
OPS IS LISTEN. DESCRIBE.
FAITH. SPIRITUAL BELIEF IN MANY FLAVORS ON THIS PLANET. SCANNING: CHRISTIANITY, ISLAM, BUDDHISM, MORE, MANY SUB-SECTS...
PERHAPS OF VALUE TO THE CLERICS OF ZUGARRA, THE PANTHEIAX, THE --
WH-WHAT ARE YOU D -- ?
OPS IS REPORT.
-- ONLY SIX THOUSAND, DAR'TARL, AND GRAYUM HAS ALREADY PLACED A FLOOR BID OF --
EXCUSE. THREE MOMENTI.
CYCLE APPRAISALS, OPS. STEADY ROTATION.

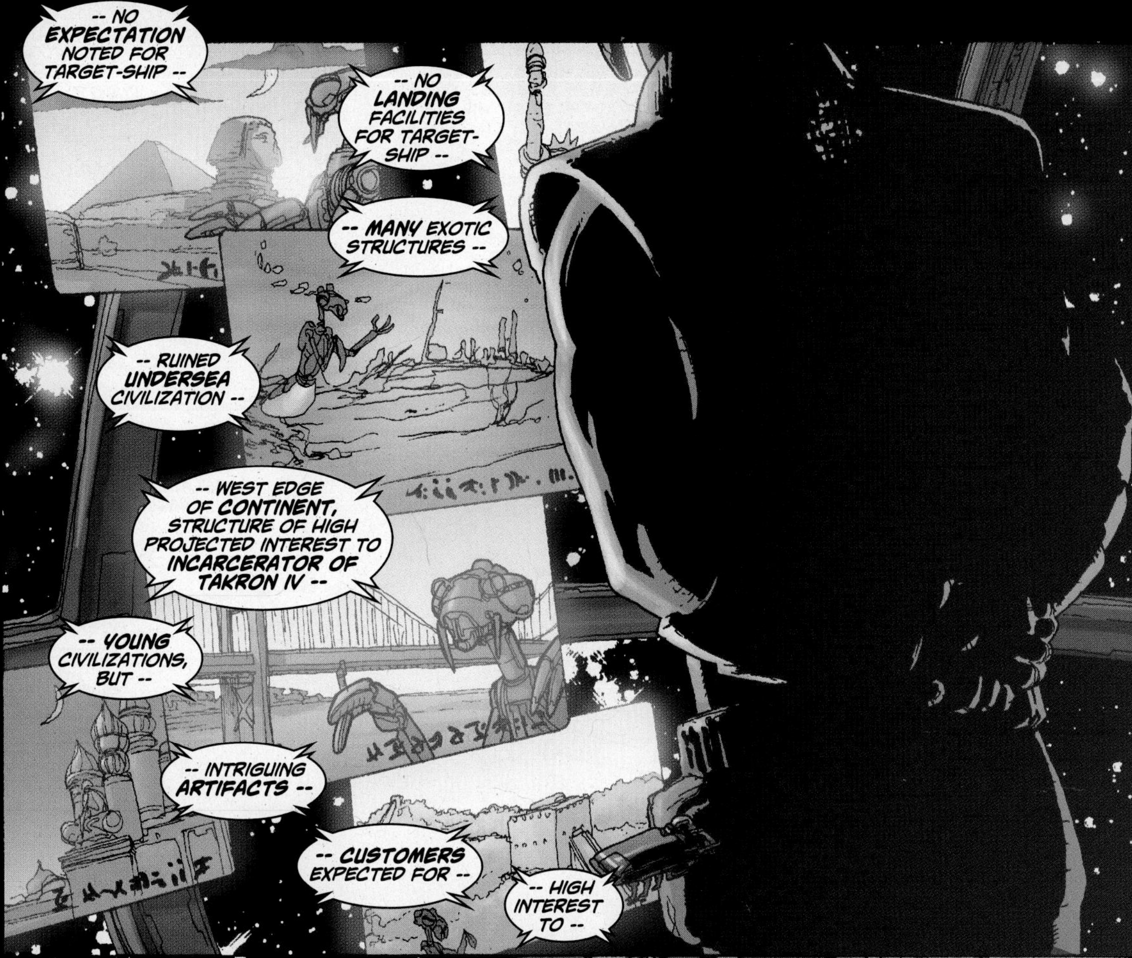
-- NO EXPECTATION NOTED FOR TARGET-SHIP --
-- NO LANDING FACILITIES FOR TARGET-SHIP --
-- MANY EXOTIC STRUCTURES --
-- RUINED UNDERSEA CIVILIZATION --
-- WEST EDGE OF CONTINENT, STRUCTURE OF HIGH PROJECTED INTEREST TO INCARCERATOR OF TAKRON IV --
-- YOUNG CIVILIZATIONS, BUT --
-- INTRIGUING ARTIFACTS --
-- CUSTOMERS EXPECTED FOR --
-- HIGH INTEREST TO --

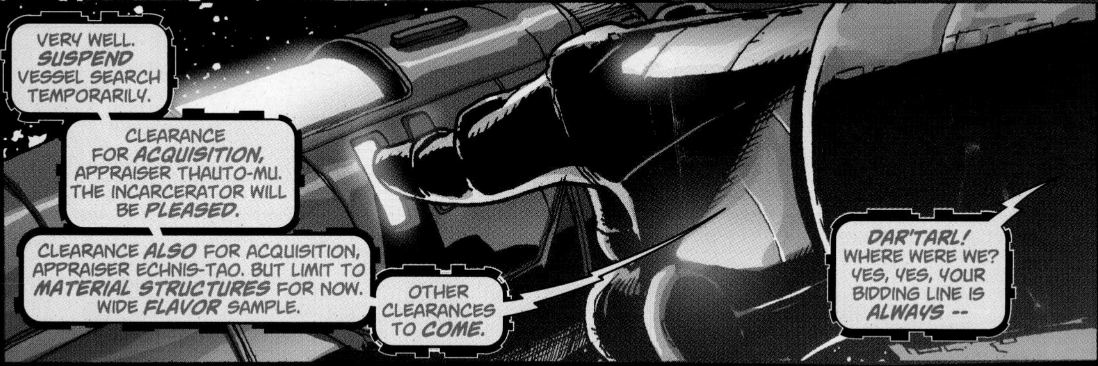
VERY WELL. SUSPEND VESSEL SEARCH TEMPORARILY.
CLEARANCE FOR ACQUISITION, APPRAISER THAUTO-MU. THE INCARCERATOR WILL BE PLEASED.
CLEARANCE ALSO FOR ACQUISITION, APPRAISER ECHNIS-TAO. BUT LIMIT TO MATERIAL STRUCTURES FOR NOW. WIDE FLAVOR SAMPLE.
OTHER CLEARANCES TO COME.
DAR'TARL! WHERE WERE WE? YES, YES, YOUR BIDDING LINE IS ALWAYS --

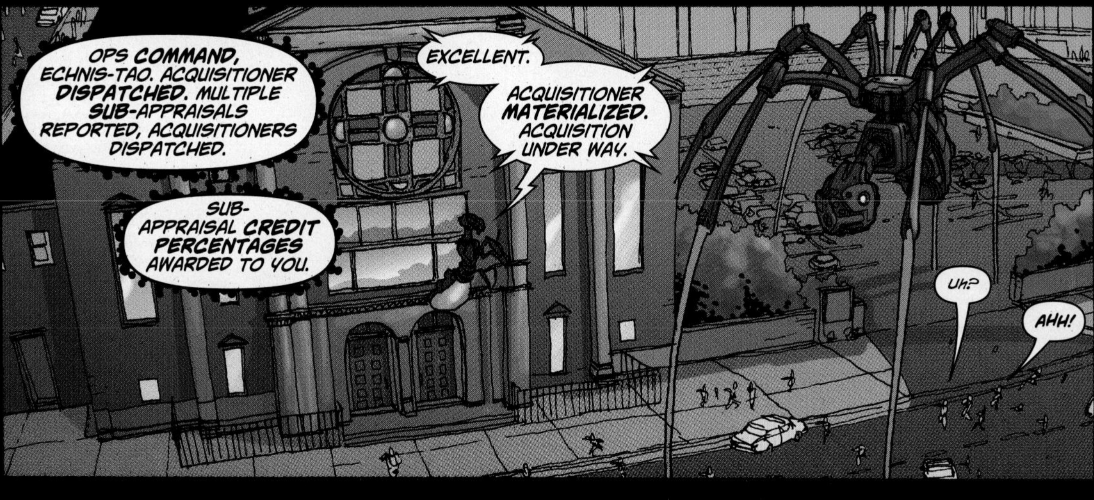
OPS COMMAND, ECHNIS-TAO. ACQUISITIONER DISPATCHED. MULTIPLE SUB-APPRAISALS REPORTED, ACQUISITIONERS DISPATCHED.
EXCELLENT.
ACQUISITIONER MATERIALIZED. ACQUISITION UNDER WAY.
SUB-APPRAISAL CREDIT PERCENTAGES AWARDED TO YOU.
UH?
AHH!

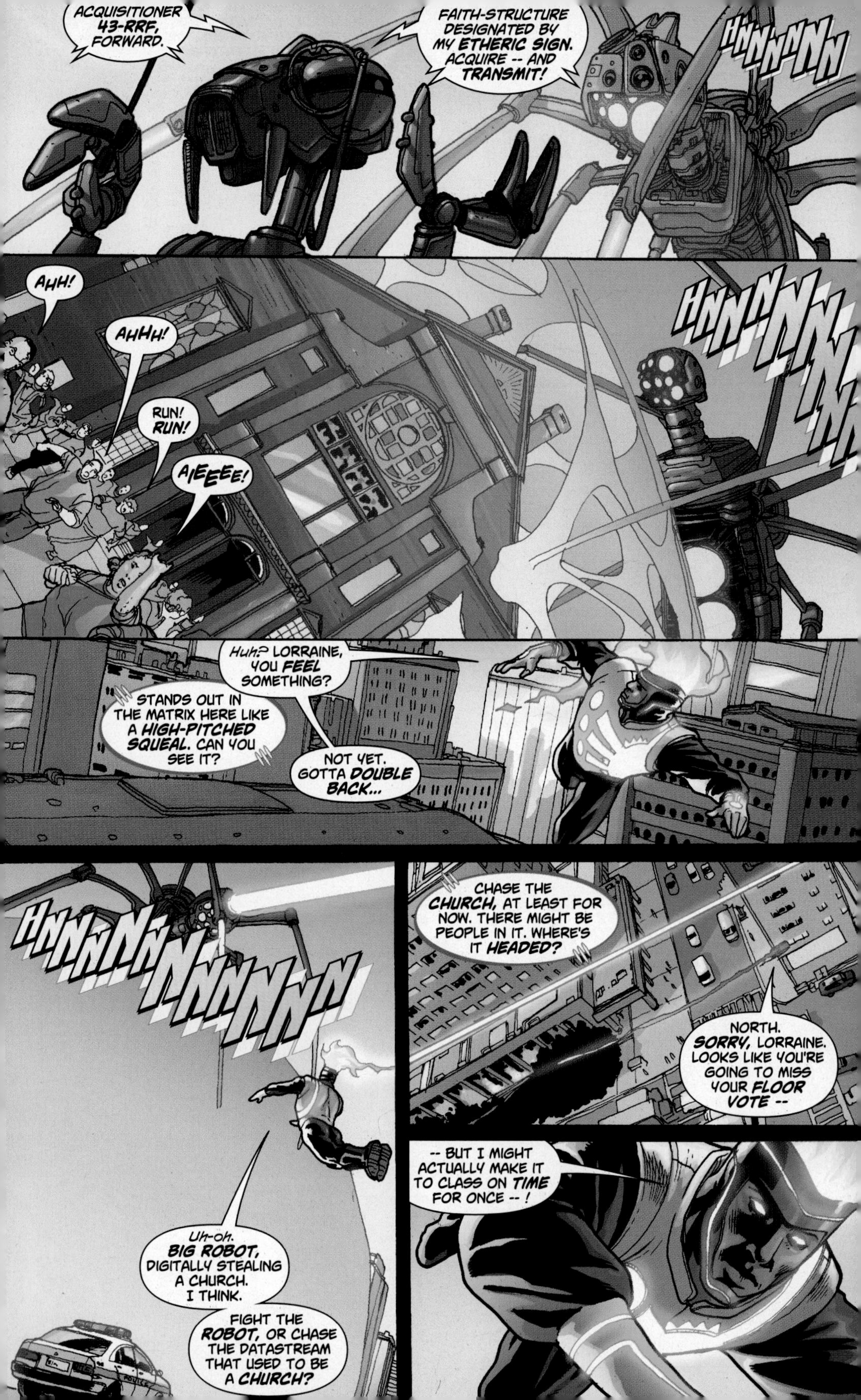
ACQUISITIONER 43-RRF, FORWARD.
FAITH-STRUCTURE DESIGNATED BY MY ETHERIC SIGN. ACQUIRE -- AND TRANSMIT!
HNNNNNN
AHH!
AHHH!
RUN! RUN!
AIEEEE!
HNNNNNNNNN
Huh? LORRAINE, YOU FEEL SOMETHING?
STANDS OUT IN THE MATRIX HERE LIKE A HIGH-PITCHED SQUEAL. CAN YOU SEE IT?
NOT YET. GOTTA DOUBLE BACK...
HNNNNNNNNNNNNN
Uh-oh. BIG ROBOT, DIGITALLY STEALING A CHURCH. I THINK.
FIGHT THE ROBOT, OR CHASE THE DATASTREAM THAT USED TO BE A CHURCH?
CHASE THE CHURCH, AT LEAST FOR NOW. THERE MIGHT BE PEOPLE IN IT. WHERE'S IT HEADED?
NORTH. SORRY, LORRAINE. LOOKS LIKE YOU'RE GOING TO MISS YOUR FLOOR VOTE --
-- BUT I MIGHT ACTUALLY MAKE IT TO CLASS ON TIME FOR ONCE -- !

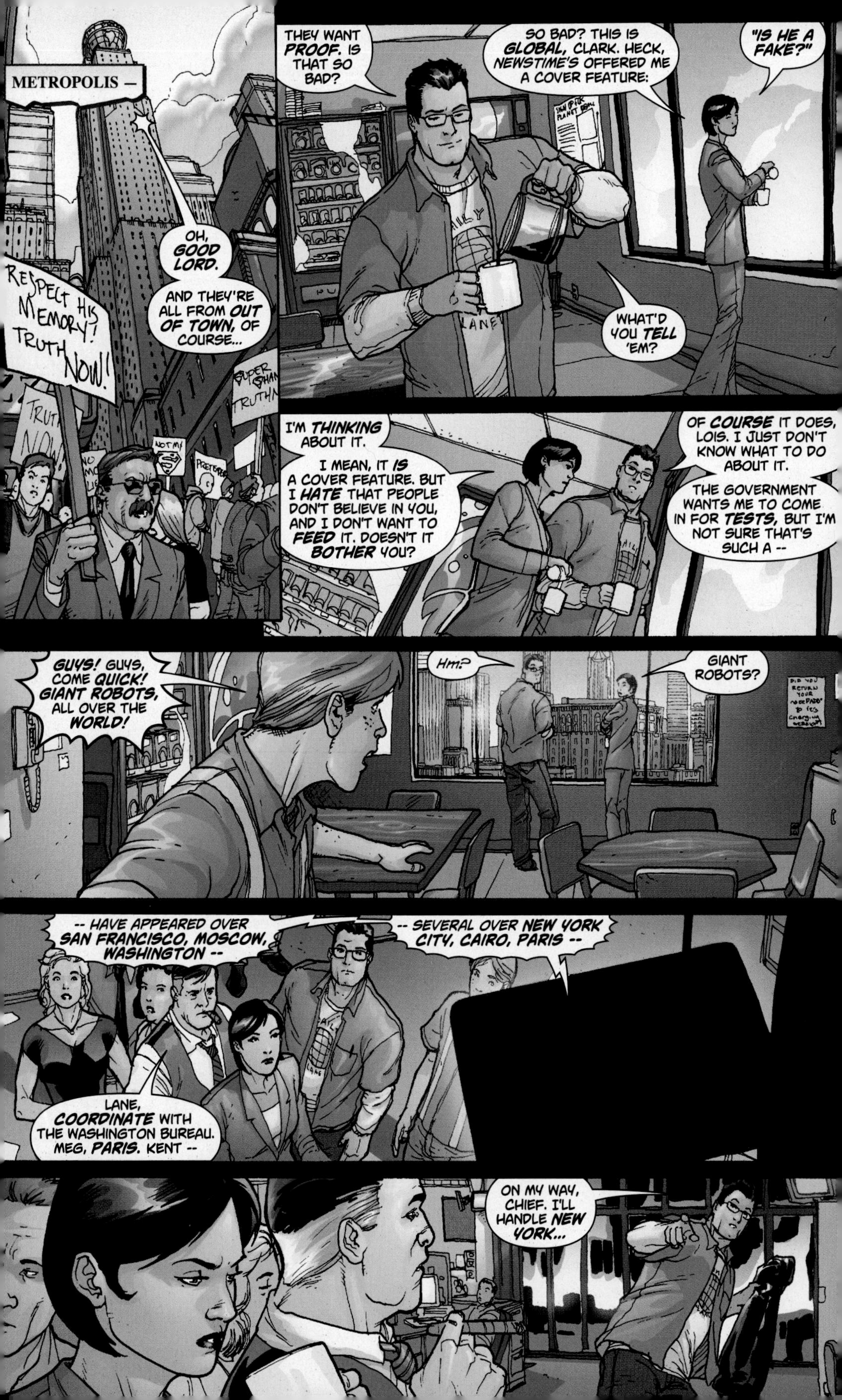
METROPOLIS —
OH, GOOD LORD.
AND THEY'RE ALL FROM OUT OF TOWN, OF COURSE...
RESPECT HIS MEMORY! TRUTH NOW!
NOT MY
THEY WANT PROOF. IS THAT SO BAD?
SO BAD? THIS IS GLOBAL, CLARK. HECK, NEWSTIME'S OFFERED ME A COVER FEATURE:
"IS HE A FAKE?"
WHAT'D YOU TELL 'EM?
I'M THINKING ABOUT IT.
I MEAN, IT IS A COVER FEATURE. BUT I HATE THAT PEOPLE DON'T BELIEVE IN YOU, AND I DON'T WANT TO FEED IT. DOESN'T IT BOTHER YOU?
OF COURSE IT DOES, LOIS. I JUST DON'T KNOW WHAT TO DO ABOUT IT.
THE GOVERNMENT WANTS ME TO COME IN FOR TESTS, BUT I'M NOT SURE THAT'S SUCH A --
GUYS! GUYS, COME QUICK! GIANT ROBOTS, ALL OVER THE WORLD!
Hm?
GIANT ROBOTS?
-- HAVE APPEARED OVER SAN FRANCISCO, MOSCOW, WASHINGTON --
-- SEVERAL OVER NEW YORK CITY, CAIRO, PARIS --
LANE, COORDINATE WITH THE WASHINGTON BUREAU. MEG, PARIS. KENT --
ON MY WAY, CHIEF. I'LL HANDLE NEW YORK...

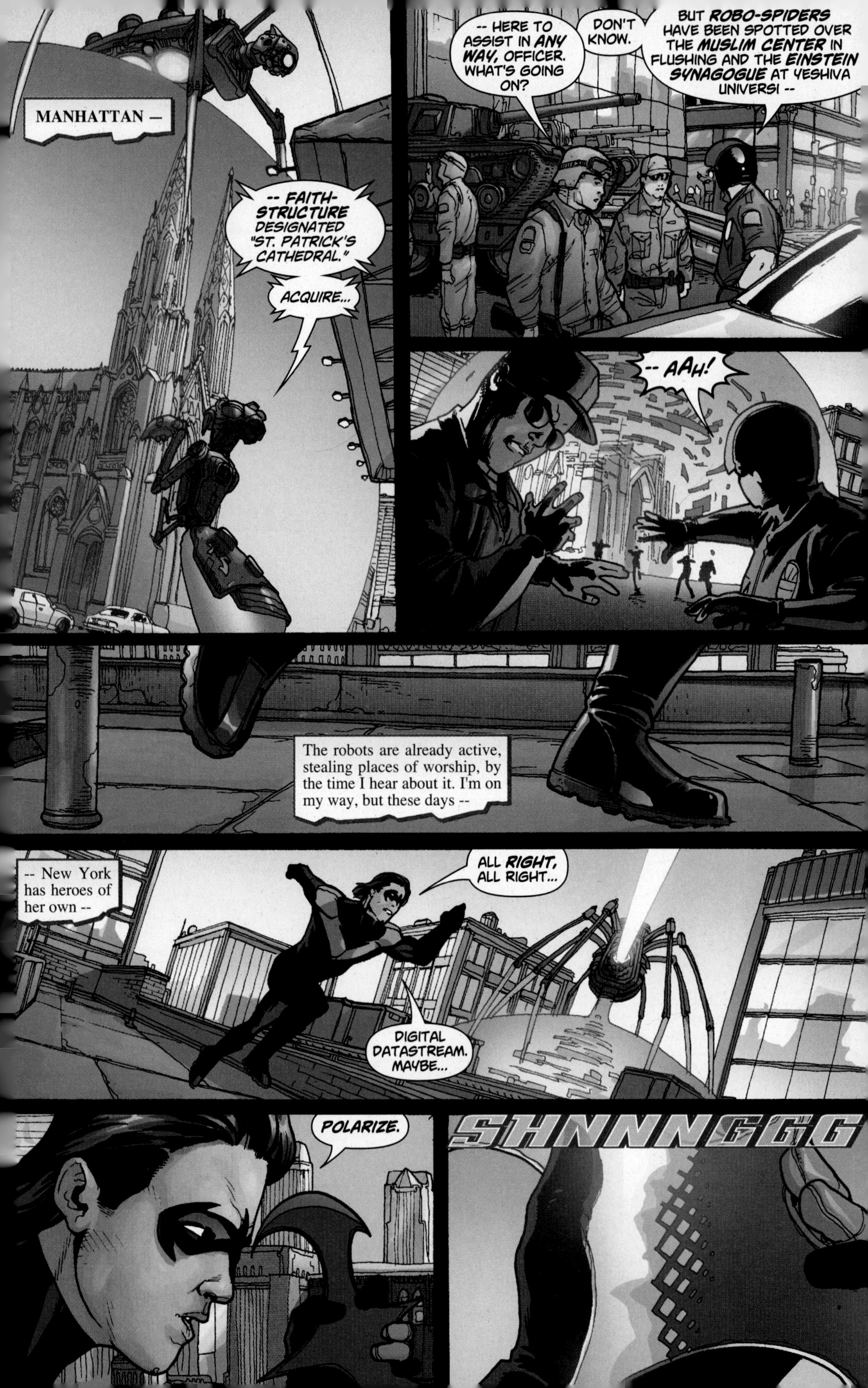
MANHATTAN --
-- FAITH-STRUCTURE DESIGNATED "ST. PATRICK'S CATHEDRAL."
ACQUIRE...
-- HERE TO ASSIST IN ANY WAY, OFFICER. WHAT'S GOING ON?
DON'T KNOW.
BUT ROBO-SPIDERS HAVE BEEN SPOTTED OVER THE MUSLIM CENTER IN FLUSHING AND THE EINSTEIN SYNAGOGUE AT YESHIVA UNIVERSI --
-- AAH!
The robots are already active, stealing places of worship, by the time I hear about it. I'm on my way, but these days --
-- New York has heroes of her own --
ALL RIGHT, ALL RIGHT...
DIGITAL DATASTREAM. MAYBE...
POLARIZE.
SHNNNNGGG

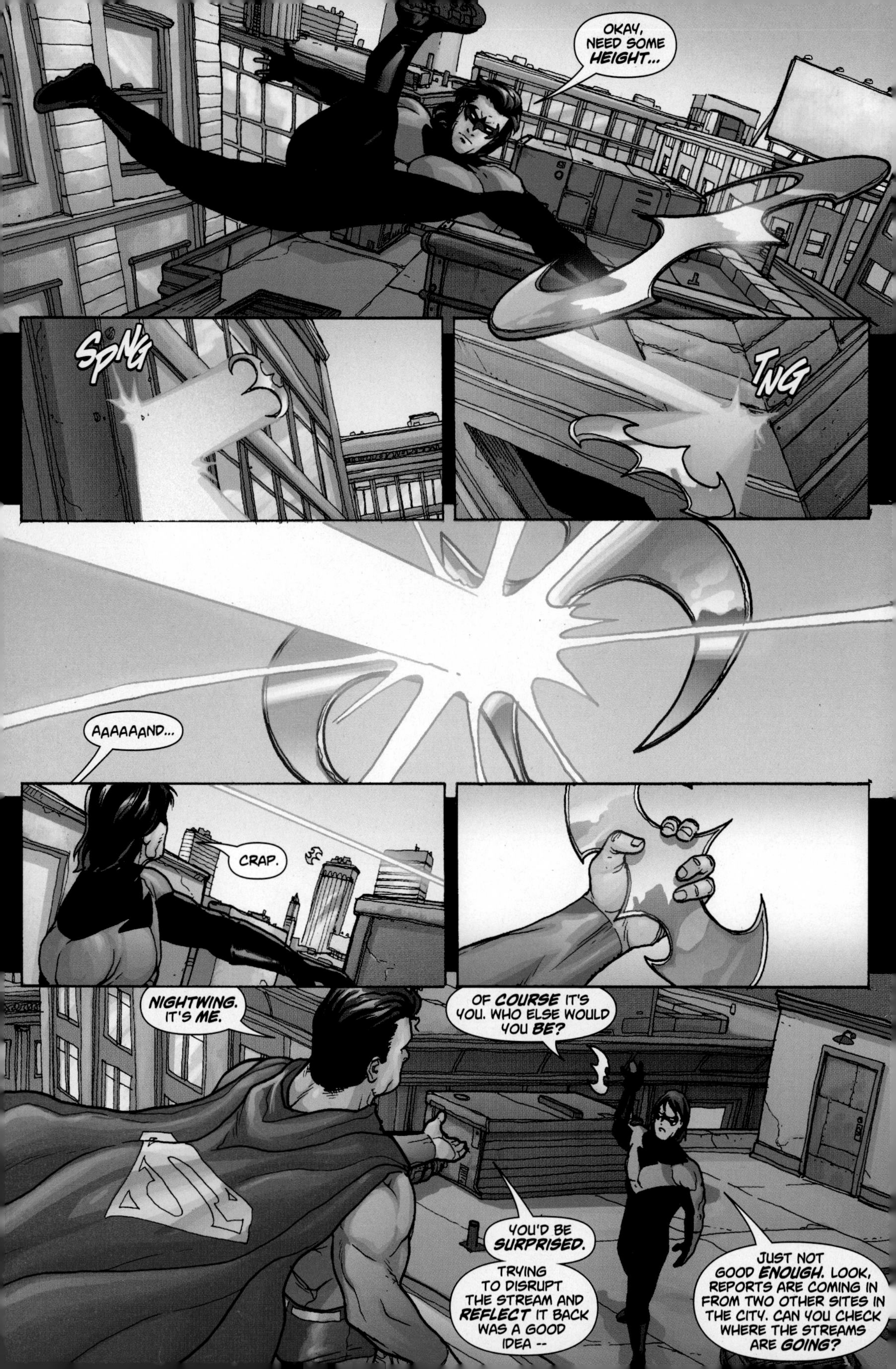
OKAY, NEED SOME HEIGHT...
SPNG
TNG
AAAAAAND...
CRAP.
NIGHTWING. IT'S ME.
OF COURSE IT'S YOU. WHO ELSE WOULD YOU BE?
YOU'D BE SURPRISED.
TRYING TO DISRUPT THE STREAM AND REFLECT IT BACK WAS A GOOD IDEA --
JUST NOT GOOD ENOUGH. LOOK, REPORTS ARE COMING IN FROM TWO OTHER SITES IN THE CITY. CAN YOU CHECK WHERE THE STREAMS ARE GOING?

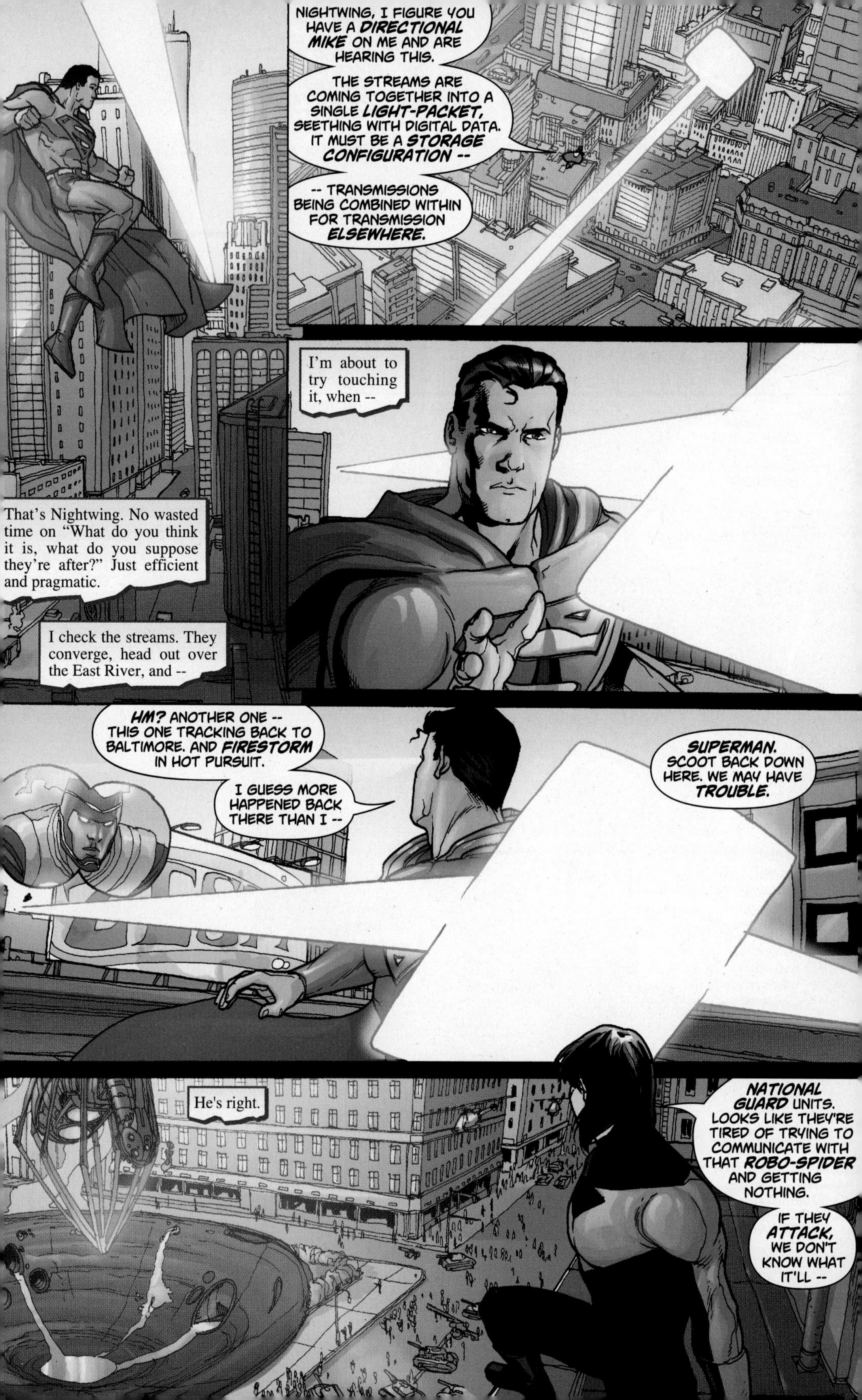
NIGHTWING, I FIGURE YOU HAVE A DIRECTIONAL MIKE ON ME AND ARE HEARING THIS.
THE STREAMS ARE COMING TOGETHER INTO A SINGLE LIGHT-PACKET, SEETHING WITH DIGITAL DATA. IT MUST BE A STORAGE CONFIGURATION --
-- TRANSMISSIONS BEING COMBINED WITHIN FOR TRANSMISSION ELSEWHERE.
That's Nightwing. No wasted time on "What do you think it is, what do you suppose they're after?" Just efficient and pragmatic.
I check the streams. They converge, head out over the East River, and --
I'm about to try touching it, when --
HM? ANOTHER ONE -- THIS ONE TRACKING BACK TO BALTIMORE. AND FIRESTORM IN HOT PURSUIT.
I GUESS MORE HAPPENED BACK THERE THAN I --
SUPERMAN. SCOOT BACK DOWN HERE. WE MAY HAVE TROUBLE.
He's right.
NATIONAL GUARD UNITS. LOOKS LIKE THEY'RE TIRED OF TRYING TO COMMUNICATE WITH THAT ROBO-SPIDER AND GETTING NOTHING.
IF THEY ATTACK, WE DON'T KNOW WHAT IT'LL --

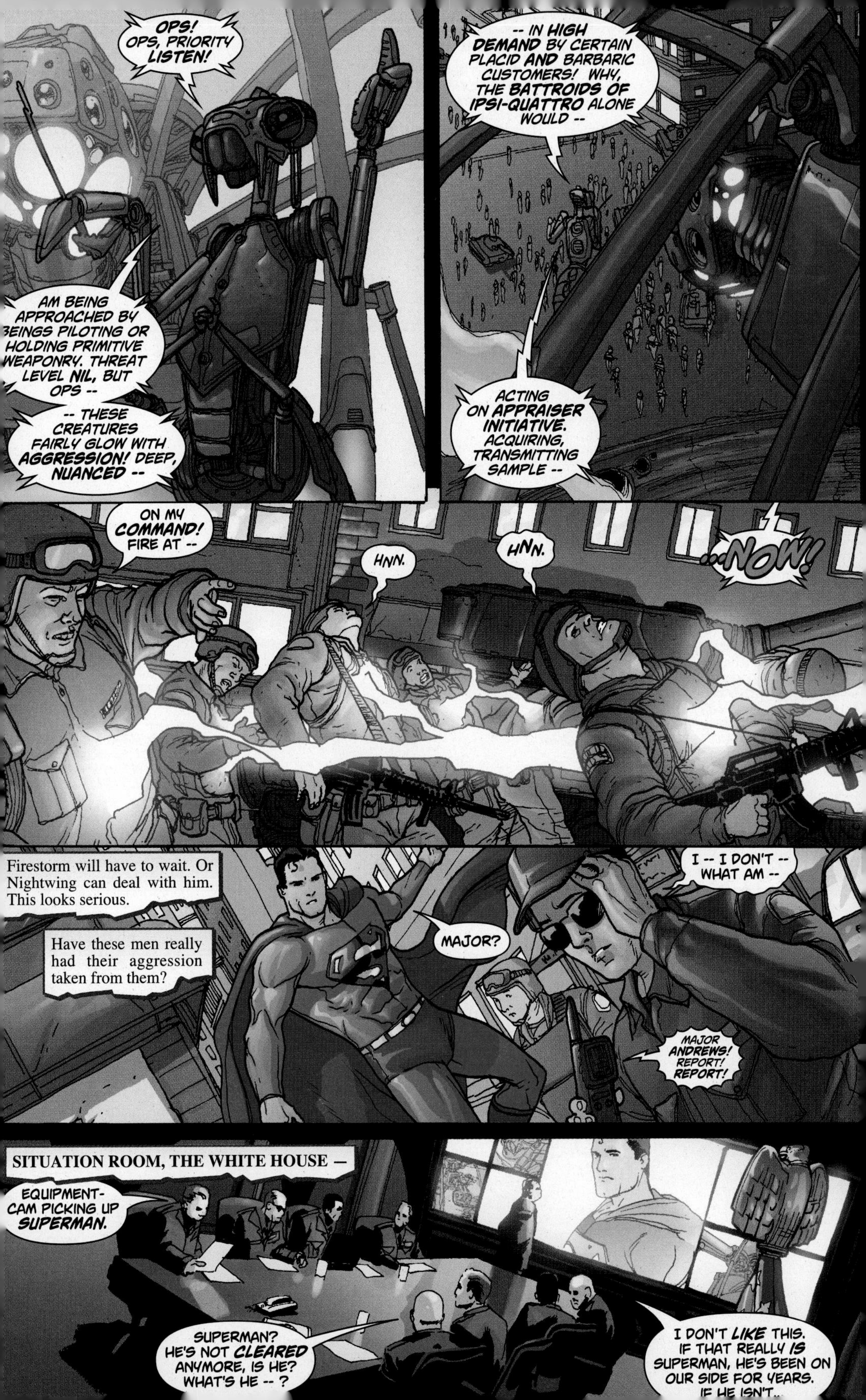
OPS! OPS, PRIORITY LISTEN!
AM BEING APPROACHED BY BEINGS PILOTING OR HOLDING PRIMITIVE WEAPONRY. THREAT LEVEL NIL, BUT OPS --
-- THESE CREATURES FAIRLY GLOW WITH AGGRESSION! DEEP, NUANCED --
-- IN HIGH DEMAND BY CERTAIN PLACID AND BARBARIC CUSTOMERS! WHY, THE BATTROIDS OF IPSI-QUATTRO ALONE WOULD --
ACTING ON APPRAISER INITIATIVE. ACQUIRING, TRANSMITTING SAMPLE --
ON MY COMMAND! FIRE AT --
HNN.
HNN.
...NOW!
Firestorm will have to wait. Or Nightwing can deal with him. This looks serious.
Have these men really had their aggression taken from them?
MAJOR?
I -- I DON'T -- WHAT AM --
MAJOR ANDREWS! REPORT! REPORT!
SITUATION ROOM, THE WHITE HOUSE —
EQUIPMENT-CAM PICKING UP SUPERMAN.
SUPERMAN? HE'S NOT CLEARED ANYMORE, IS HE? WHAT'S HE -- ?
I DON'T LIKE THIS. IF THAT REALLY IS SUPERMAN, HE'S BEEN ON OUR SIDE FOR YEARS. IF HE ISN'T..

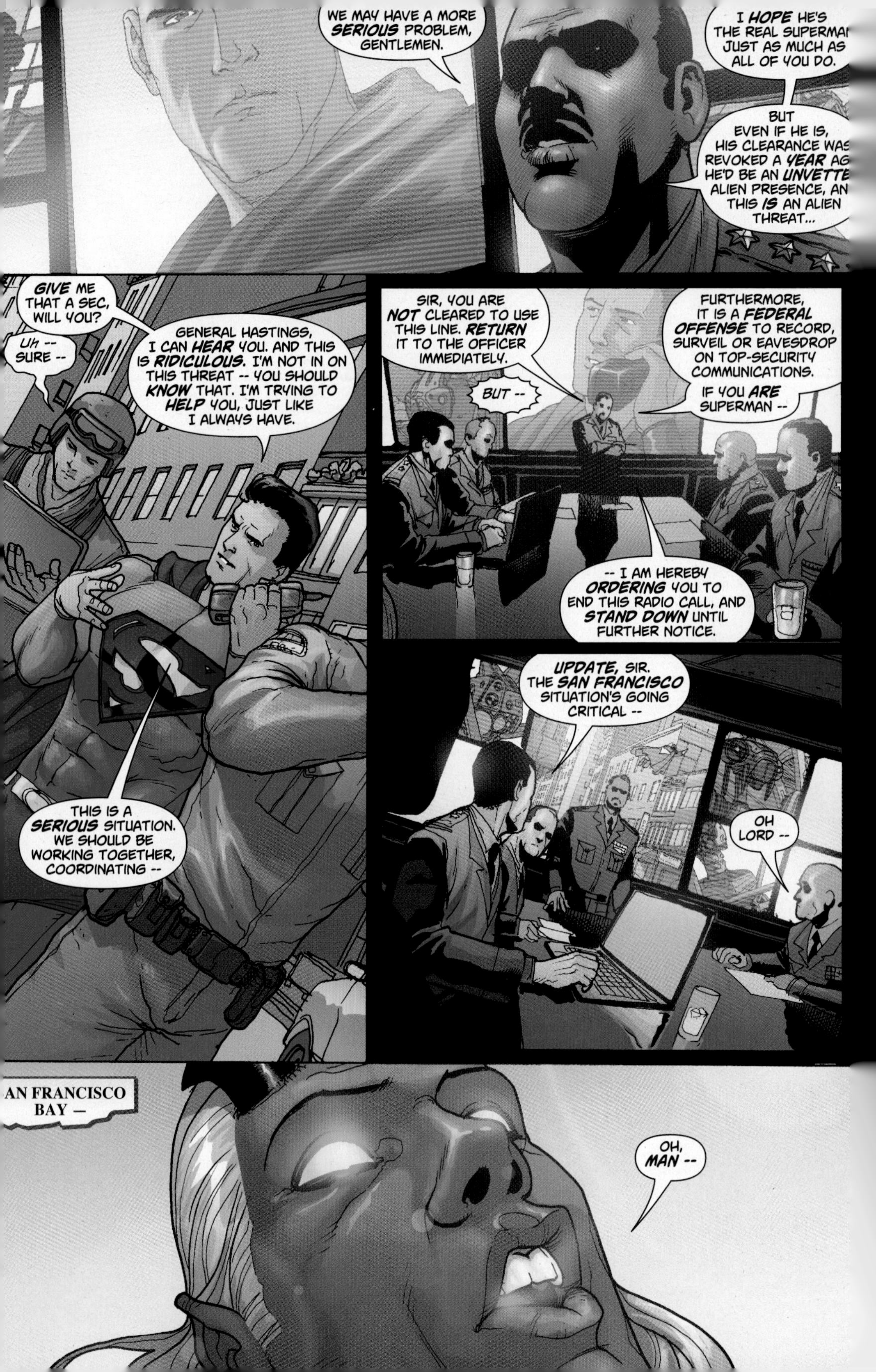

WE MAY HAVE A MORE SERIOUS PROBLEM, GENTLEMEN.
I HOPE HE'S THE REAL SUPERMA JUST AS MUCH AS ALL OF YOU DO.
BUT EVEN IF HE IS, HIS CLEARANCE WAS REVOKED A YEAR AG HE'D BE AN UNVETTE ALIEN PRESENCE, AN THIS IS AN ALIEN THREAT...
GIVE ME THAT A SEC, WILL YOU?
Uh -- SURE --
GENERAL HASTINGS, I CAN HEAR YOU. AND THIS IS RIDICULOUS. I'M NOT IN ON THIS THREAT -- YOU SHOULD KNOW THAT. I'M TRYING TO HELP YOU, JUST LIKE I ALWAYS HAVE.
THIS IS A SERIOUS SITUATION. WE SHOULD BE WORKING TOGETHER, COORDINATING --
SIR, YOU ARE NOT CLEARED TO USE THIS LINE. RETURN IT TO THE OFFICER IMMEDIATELY.
BUT --
FURTHERMORE, IT IS A FEDERAL OFFENSE TO RECORD, SURVEIL OR EAVESDROP ON TOP-SECURITY COMMUNICATIONS.
IF YOU ARE SUPERMAN --
-- I AM HEREBY ORDERING YOU TO END THIS RADIO CALL, AND STAND DOWN UNTIL FURTHER NOTICE.
UPDATE, SIR. THE SAN FRANCISCO SITUATION'S GOING CRITICAL --
OH LORD --
AN FRANCISCO BAY —
OH, MAN --

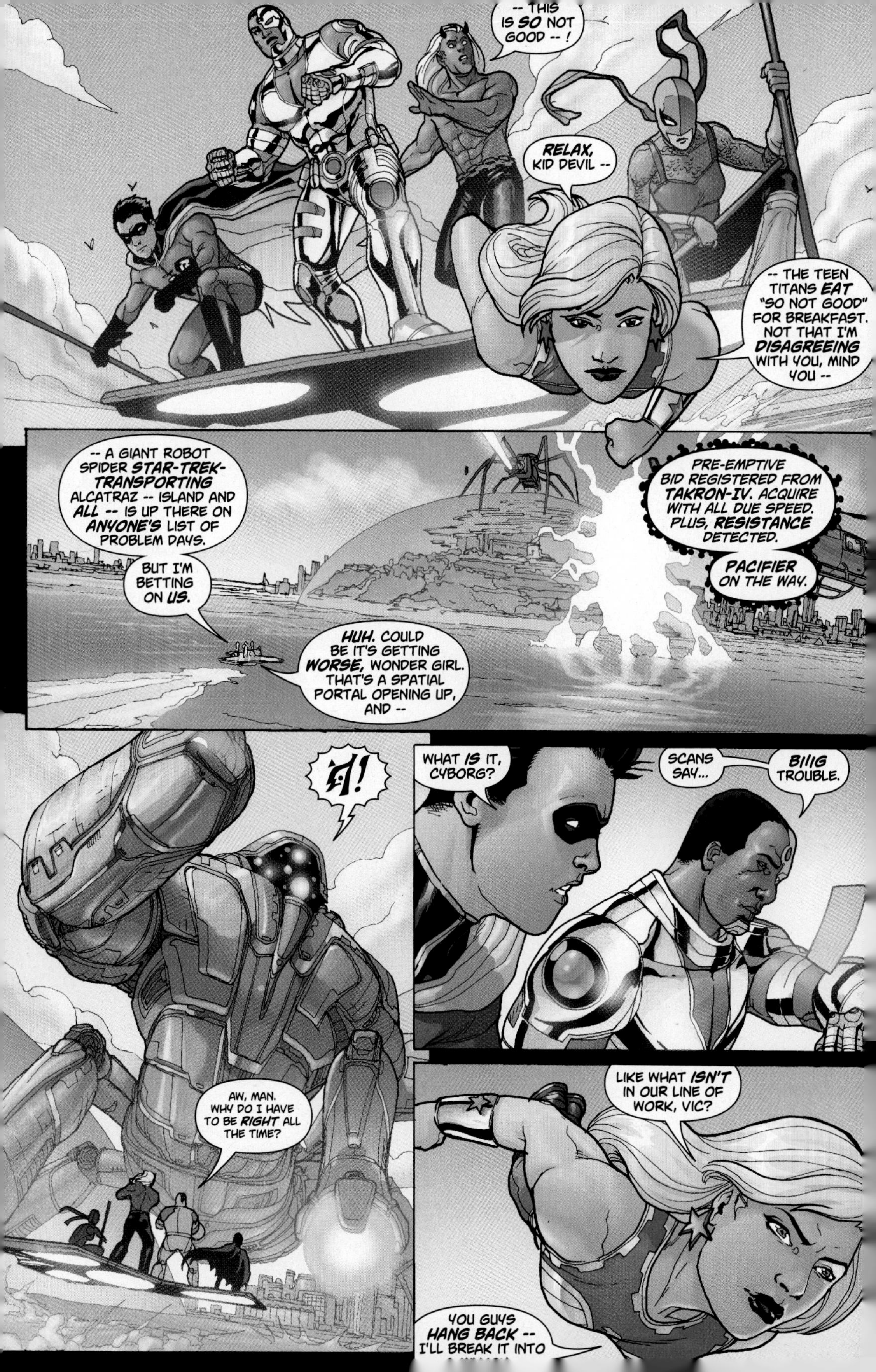

-- THIS IS SO NOT GOOD -- !
RELAX, KID DEVIL --
-- THE TEEN TITANS EAT "SO NOT GOOD" FOR BREAKFAST. NOT THAT I'M DISAGREEING WITH YOU, MIND YOU --
-- A GIANT ROBOT SPIDER STAR-TREK-TRANSPORTING ALCATRAZ -- ISLAND AND ALL -- IS UP THERE ON ANYONE'S LIST OF PROBLEM DAYS.
BUT I'M BETTING ON US.
HUH. COULD BE IT'S GETTING WORSE, WONDER GIRL. THAT'S A SPATIAL PORTAL OPENING UP, AND --
PRE-EMPTIVE BID REGISTERED FROM TAKRON-IV. ACQUIRE WITH ALL DUE SPEED. PLUS, RESISTANCE DETECTED.
PACIFIER ON THE WAY.
AW, MAN. WHY DO I HAVE TO BE RIGHT ALL THE TIME?
WHAT IS IT, CYBORG?
SCANS SAY...
BIIIG TROUBLE.
LIKE WHAT ISN'T IN OUR LINE OF WORK, VIC?
YOU GUYS HANG BACK -- I'LL BREAK IT INTO

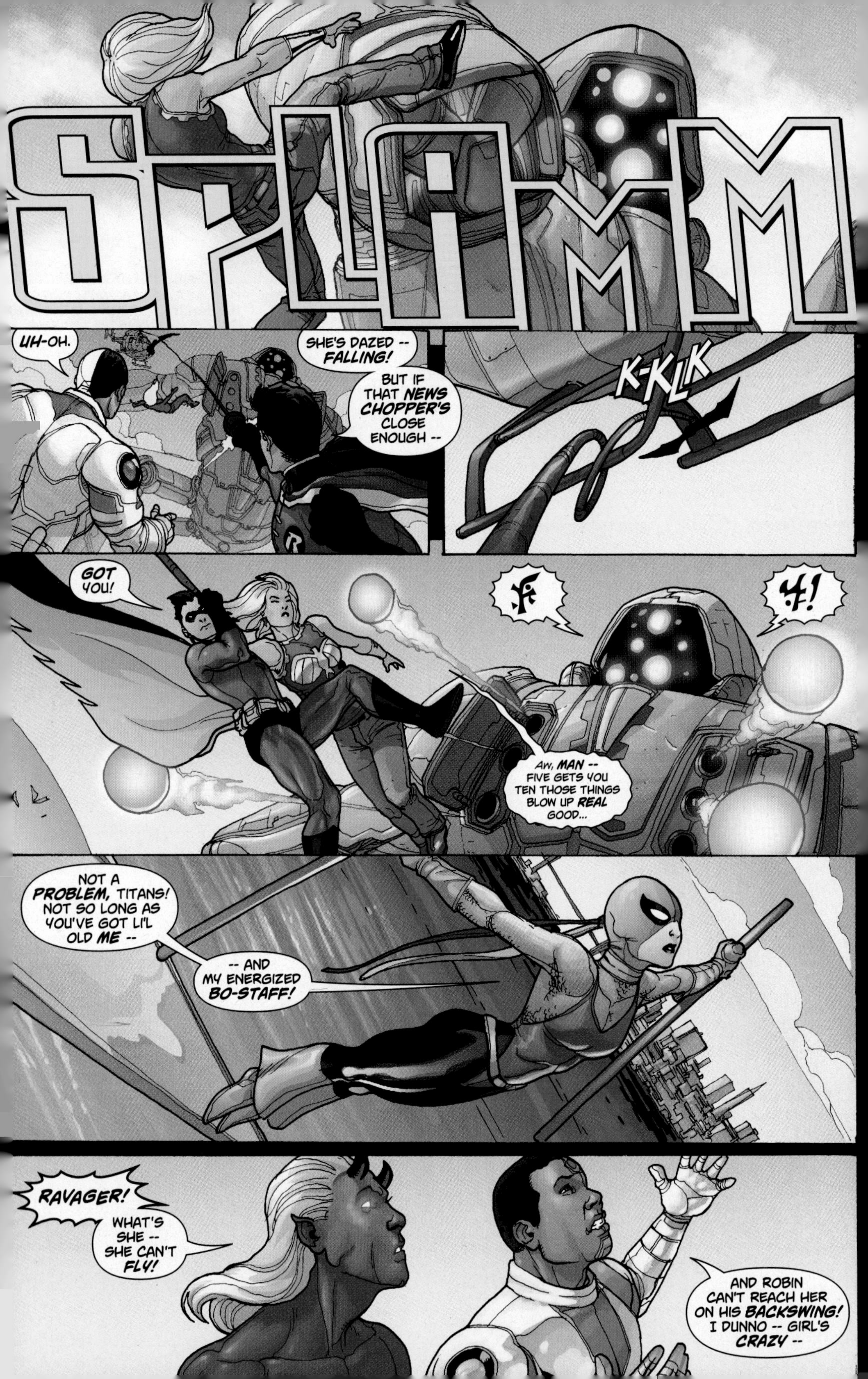
SPLAMM
UH-OH.
SHE'S DAZED -- FALLING!
BUT IF THAT NEWS CHOPPER'S CLOSE ENOUGH --
K-KLK
GOT YOU!
AW, MAN -- FIVE GETS YOU TEN THOSE THINGS BLOW UP REAL GOOD...
NOT A PROBLEM, TITANS! NOT SO LONG AS YOU'VE GOT LI'L OLD ME --
-- AND MY ENERGIZED BO-STAFF!
RAVAGER!
WHAT'S SHE -- SHE CAN'T FLY!
AND ROBIN CAN'T REACH HER ON HIS BACKSWING! I DUNNO -- GIRL'S CRAZY --

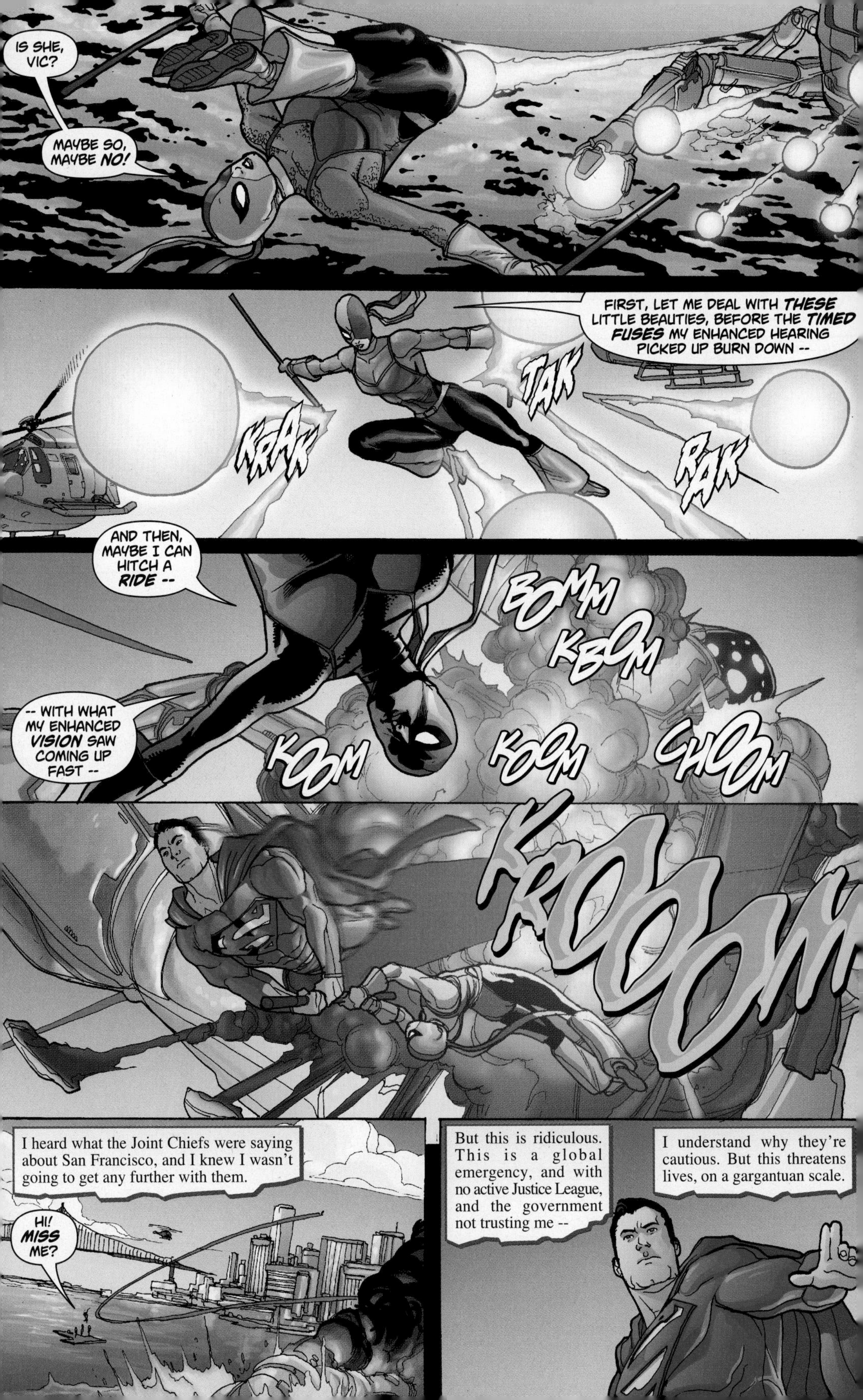

IS SHE, VIC?
MAYBE SO, MAYBE NO!
FIRST, LET ME DEAL WITH THESE LITTLE BEAUTIES, BEFORE THE TIMED FUSES MY ENHANCED HEARING PICKED UP BURN DOWN --
KRAK
TAK
RAK
AND THEN, MAYBE I CAN HITCH A RIDE --
BOMM
KBOOM
-- WITH WHAT MY ENHANCED VISION SAW COMING UP FAST --
KOOM
KOOM
CHOOM
KROOOM
I heard what the Joint Chiefs were saying about San Francisco, and I knew I wasn't going to get any further with them.
HI! MISS ME?
But this is ridiculous. This is a global emergency, and with no active Justice League, and the government not trusting me --
I understand why they're cautious. But this threatens lives, on a gargantuan scale.

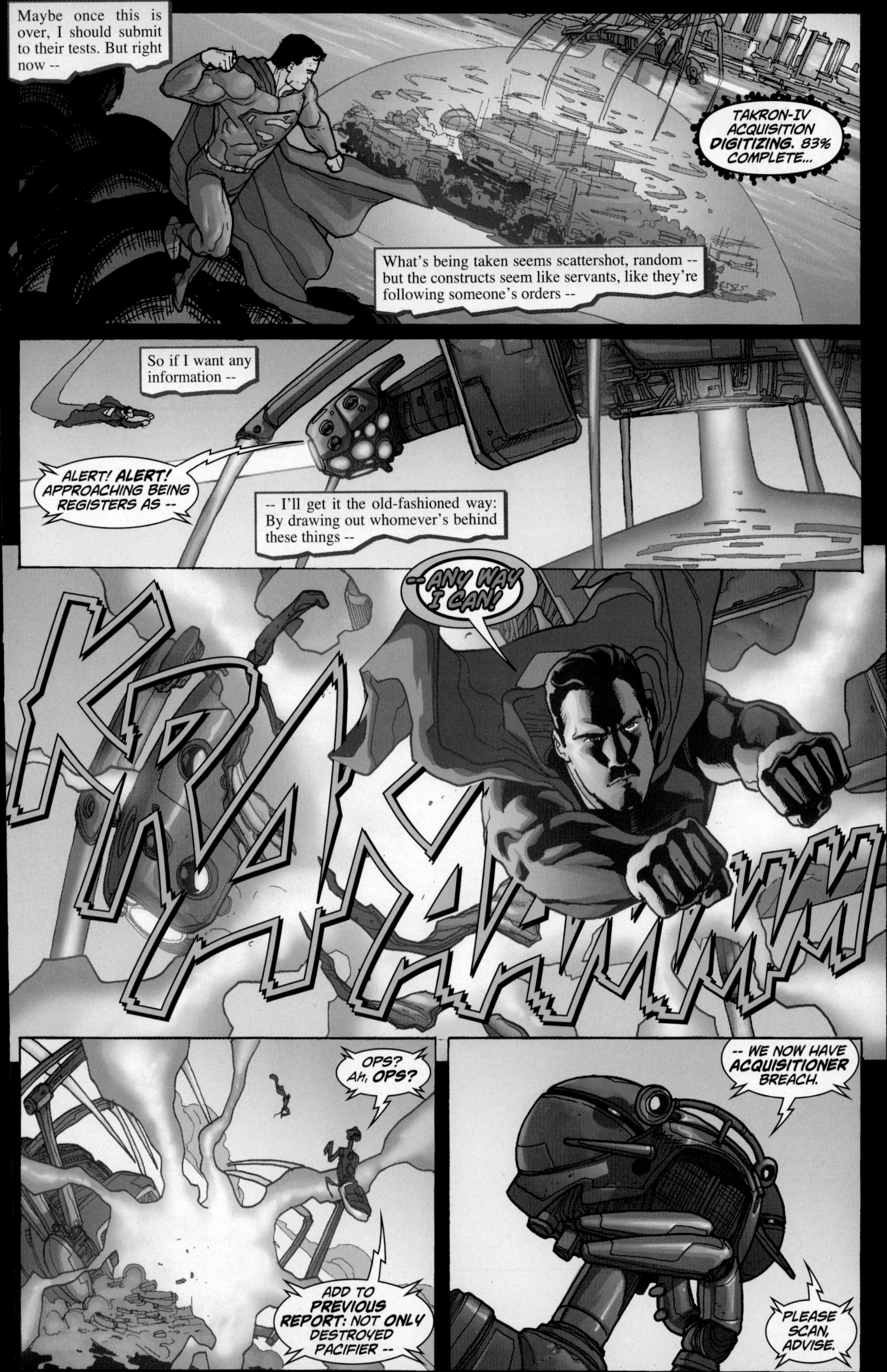
Maybe once this is over, I should submit to their tests. But right now --
TAKRON-IV ACQUISITION DIGITIZING. 83% COMPLETE...
What's being taken seems scattershot, random -- but the constructs seem like servants, like they're following someone's orders --
So if I want any information --
ALERT! ALERT! APPROACHING BEING REGISTERS AS --
-- I'll get it the old-fashioned way: By drawing out whomever's behind these things --
-- ANY WAY I CAN!
KRAKATHHHM
OPS? Ah, OPS?
ADD TO PREVIOUS REPORT: NOT ONLY DESTROYED PACIFIER --
-- WE NOW HAVE ACQUISITIONER BREACH.
PLEASE SCAN, ADVISE.

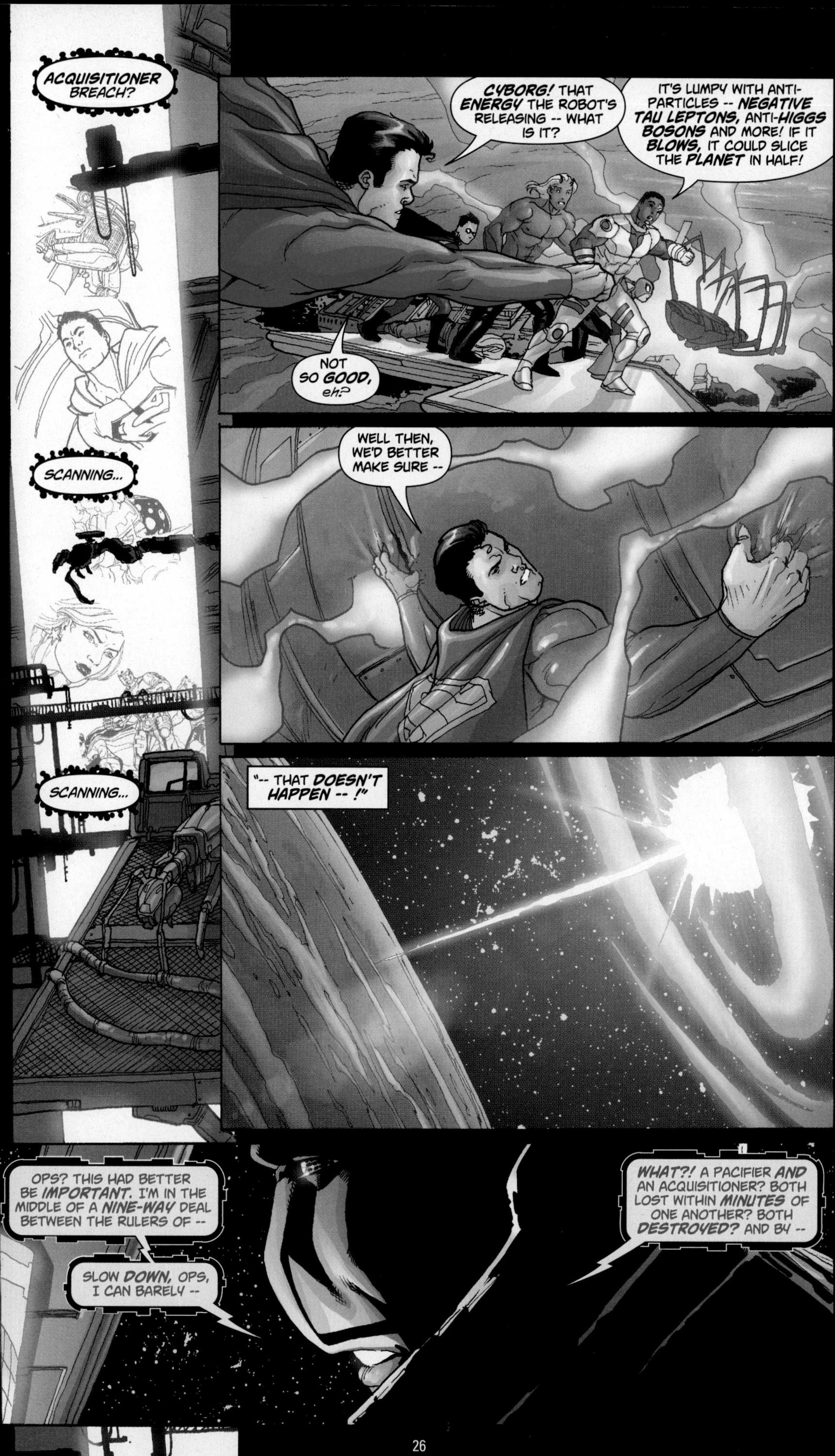
ACQUISITIONER BREACH?
SCANNING...
SCANNING...
CYBORG! THAT ENERGY THE ROBOT'S RELEASING -- WHAT IS IT?
IT'S LUMPY WITH ANTI-PARTICLES -- NEGATIVE TAU LEPTONS, ANTI-HIGGS BOSONS AND MORE! IF IT BLOWS, IT COULD SLICE THE PLANET IN HALF!
NOT SO GOOD, eh?
WELL THEN, WE'D BETTER MAKE SURE --
"-- THAT DOESN'T HAPPEN -- !"
OPS? THIS HAD BETTER BE IMPORTANT. I'M IN THE MIDDLE OF A NINE-WAY DEAL BETWEEN THE RULERS OF --
SLOW DOWN, OPS, I CAN BARELY --
WHAT?! A PACIFIER AND AN ACQUISITIONER? BOTH LOST WITHIN MINUTES OF ONE ANOTHER? BOTH DESTROYED? AND BY --

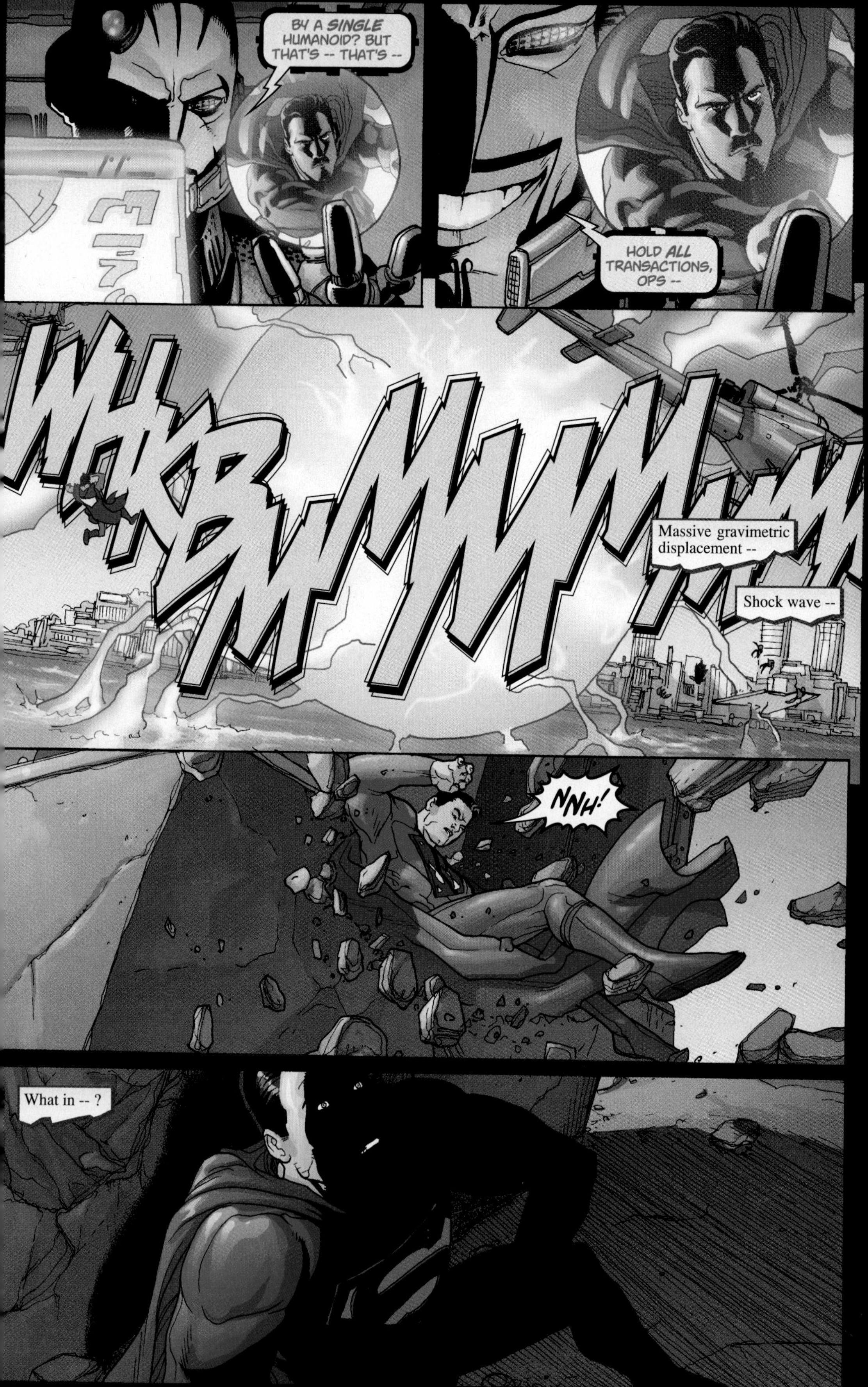
BY A SINGLE HUMANOID? BUT THAT'S -- THAT'S --
HOLD ALL TRANSACTIONS, OPS --
WHBUMMMMMM
Massive gravimetric displacement --
Shock wave --
NNH!
What in -- ?

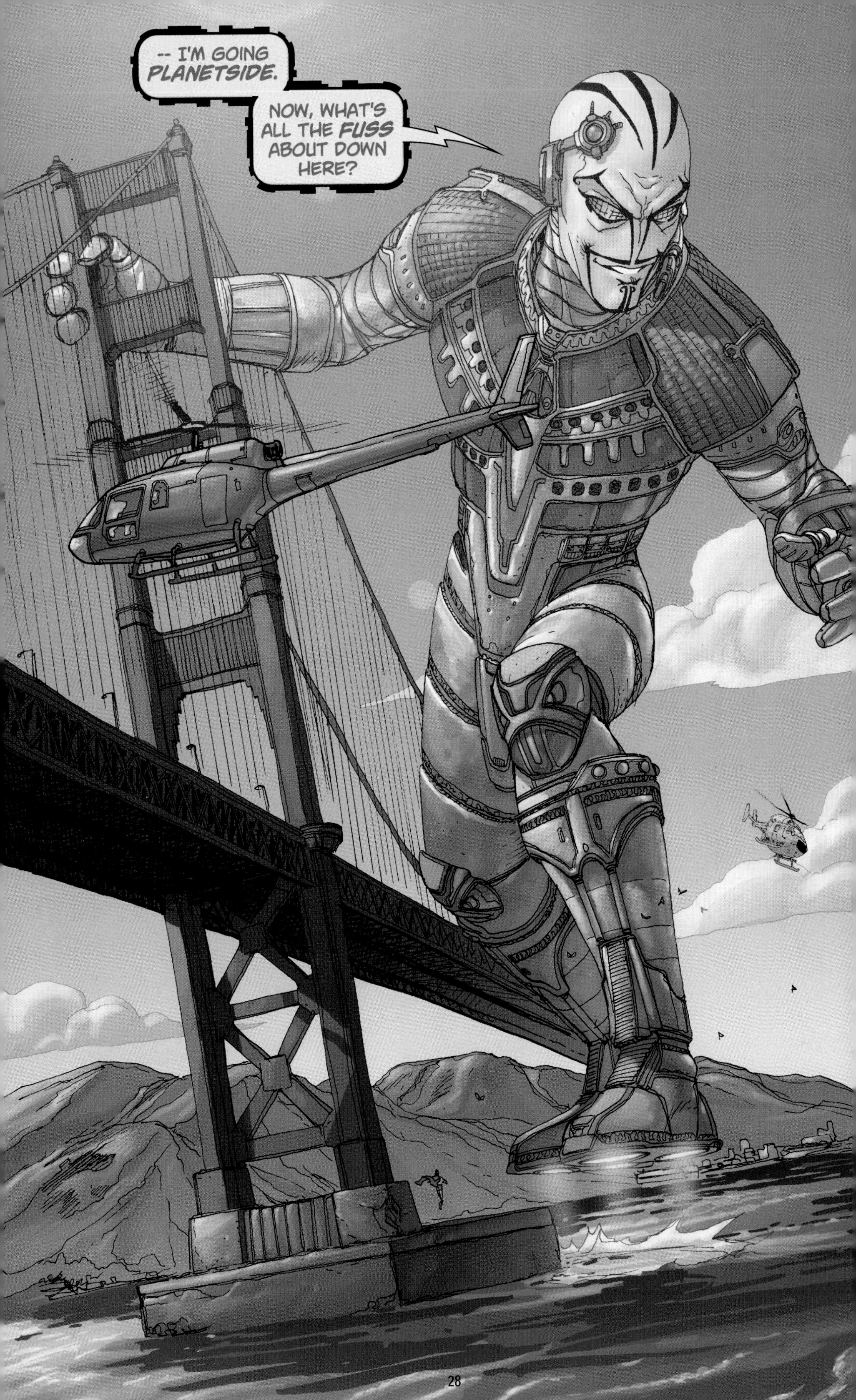
-- I'M GOING PLANETSIDE.
NOW, WHAT'S ALL THE FUSS ABOUT DOWN HERE?

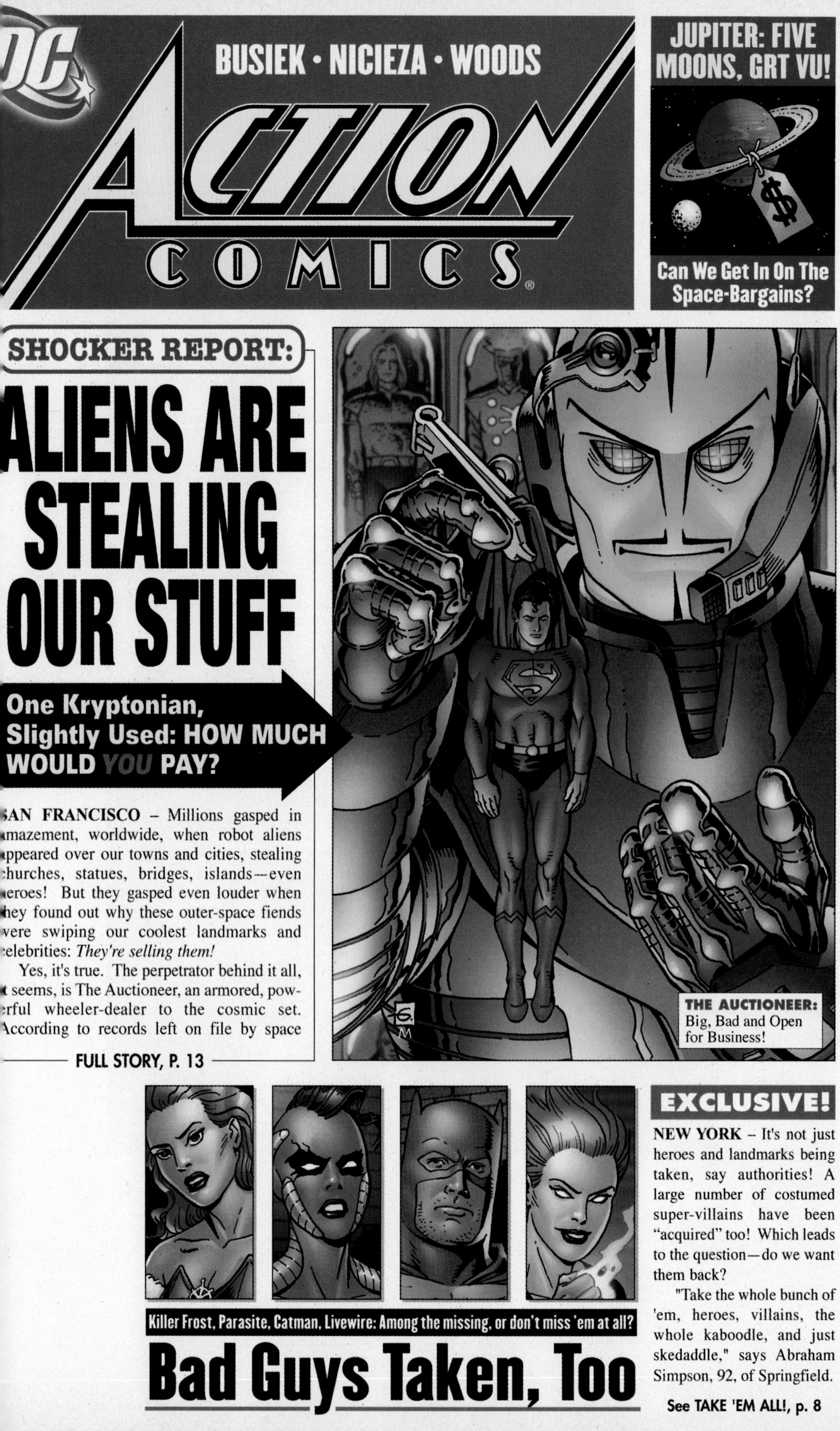
DC
BUSIEK • NICIEZA • WOODS
ACTION COMICS®
JUPITER: FIVE MOONS, GRT VU!
$
Can We Get In On The Space-Bargains?
SHOCKER REPORT:
ALIENS ARE STEALING OUR STUFF
One Kryptonian, Slightly Used: HOW MUCH WOULD *YOU* PAY?
;AN FRANCISCO – Millions gasped in ımazement, worldwide, when robot aliens ıppeared over our towns and cities, stealing :hurches, statues, bridges, islands—even ıeroes! But they gasped even louder when hey found out why these outer-space fiends vere swiping our coolest landmarks and :elebrities: *They're selling them!*
Yes, it's true. The perpetrator behind it all, t seems, is The Auctioneer, an armored, pow-:rful wheeler-dealer to the cosmic set. According to records left on file by space
FULL STORY, P. 13
THE AUCTIONEER: Big, Bad and Open for Business!
EXCLUSIVE!
NEW YORK – It's not just heroes and landmarks being taken, say authorities! A large number of costumed super-villains have been "acquired" too! Which leads to the question—do we want them back?
"Take the whole bunch of 'em, heroes, villains, the whole kaboodle, and just skedaddle," says Abraham Simpson, 92, of Springfield.
See TAKE 'EM ALL!, p. 8
Killer Frost, Parasite, Catman, Livewire: Among the missing, or don't miss 'em at all?
Bad Guys Taken, Too

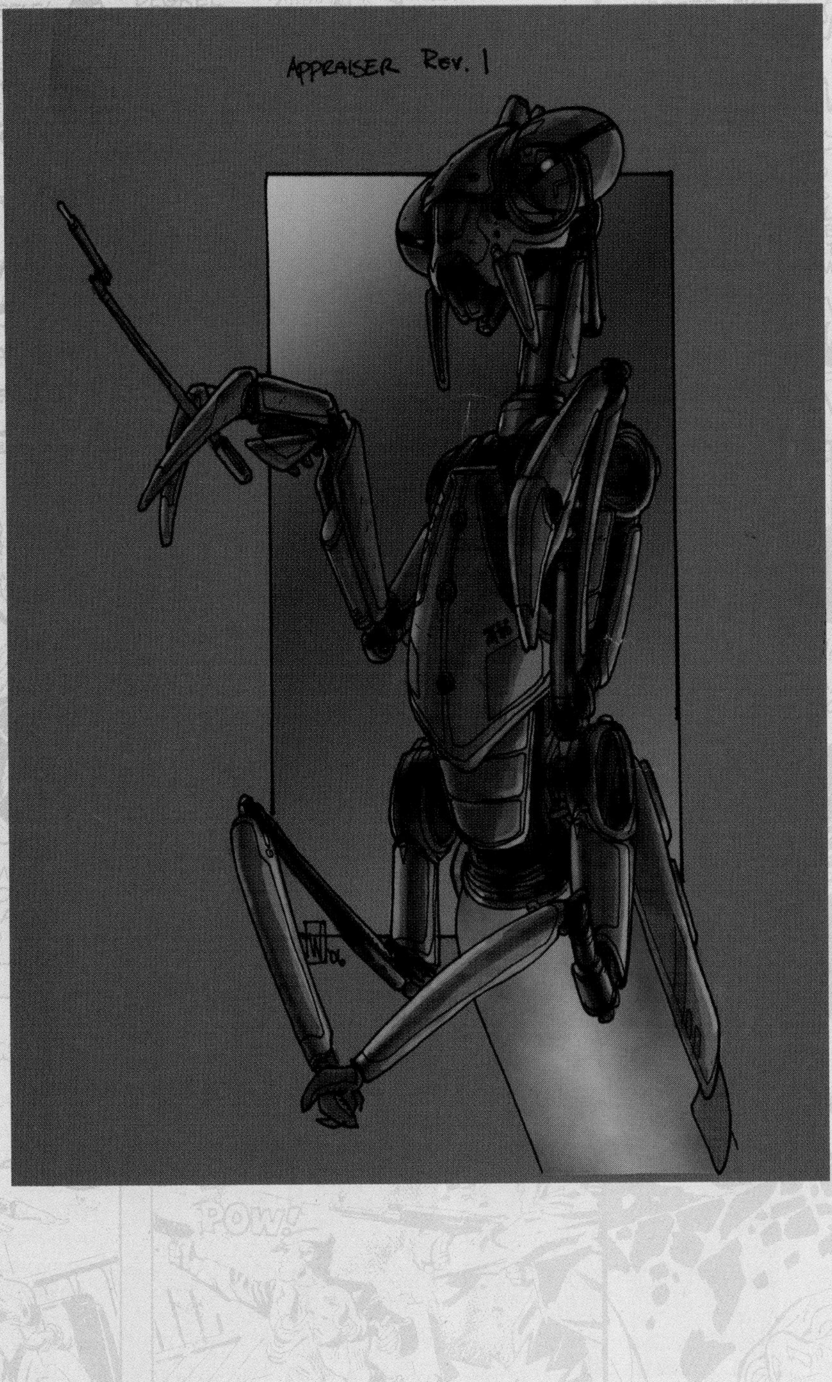
APPRAISER Rev. 1

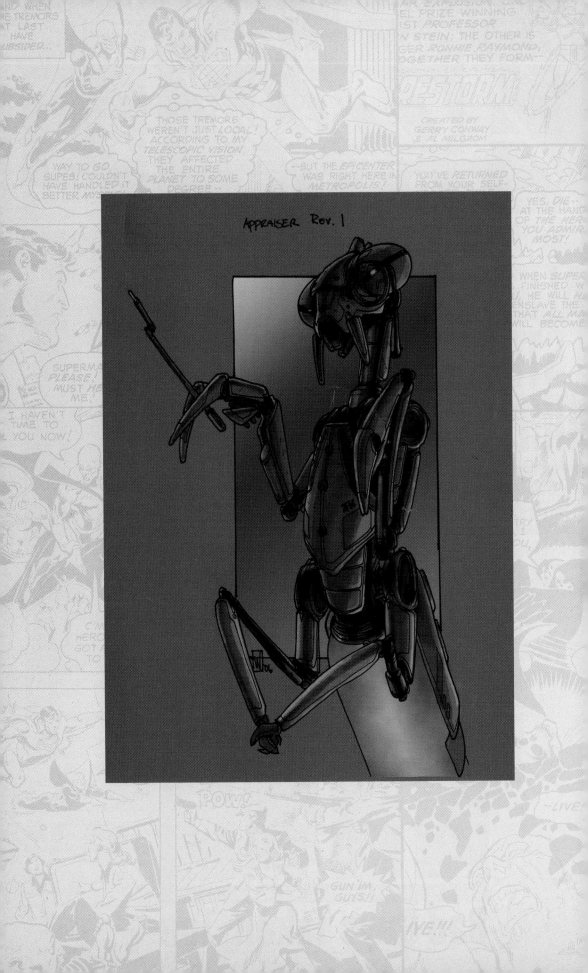

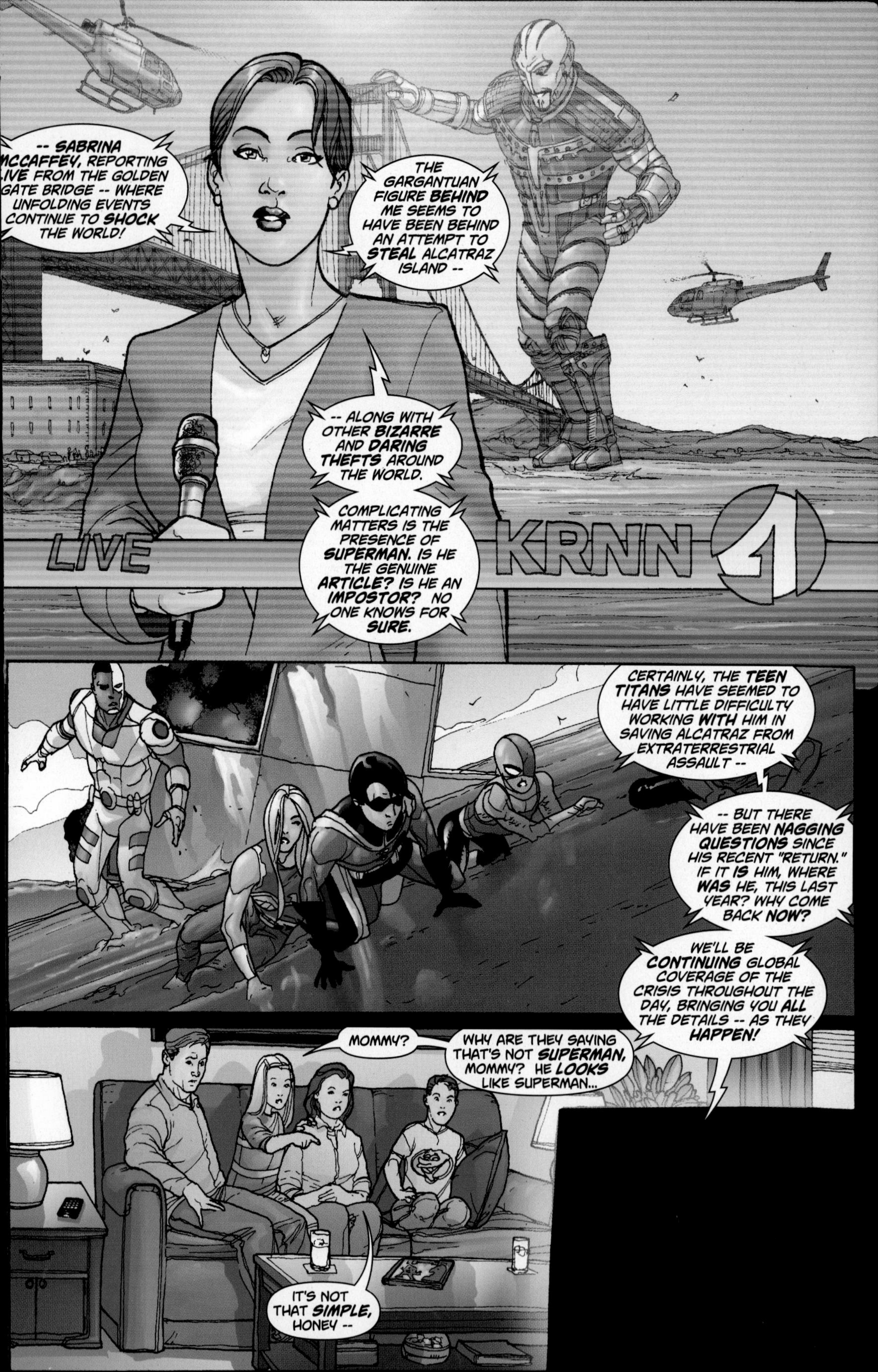
-- SABRINA MCCAFFEY, REPORTING LIVE FROM THE GOLDEN GATE BRIDGE -- WHERE UNFOLDING EVENTS CONTINUE TO SHOCK THE WORLD!
THE GARGANTUAN FIGURE BEHIND ME SEEMS TO HAVE BEEN BEHIND AN ATTEMPT TO STEAL ALCATRAZ ISLAND --
-- ALONG WITH OTHER BIZARRE AND DARING THEFTS AROUND THE WORLD.
LIVE
KRNN 4
COMPLICATING MATTERS IS THE PRESENCE OF SUPERMAN. IS HE THE GENUINE ARTICLE? IS HE AN IMPOSTOR? NO ONE KNOWS FOR SURE.
CERTAINLY, THE TEEN TITANS HAVE SEEMED TO HAVE LITTLE DIFFICULTY WORKING WITH HIM IN SAVING ALCATRAZ FROM EXTRATERRESTRIAL ASSAULT --
-- BUT THERE HAVE BEEN NAGGING QUESTIONS SINCE HIS RECENT "RETURN." IF IT IS HIM, WHERE WAS HE, THIS LAST YEAR? WHY COME BACK NOW?
WE'LL BE CONTINUING GLOBAL COVERAGE OF THE CRISIS THROUGHOUT THE DAY, BRINGING YOU ALL THE DETAILS -- AS THEY HAPPEN!
MOMMY?
WHY ARE THEY SAYING THAT'S NOT SUPERMAN, MOMMY? HE LOOKS LIKE SUPERMAN...
IT'S NOT THAT SIMPLE, HONEY --

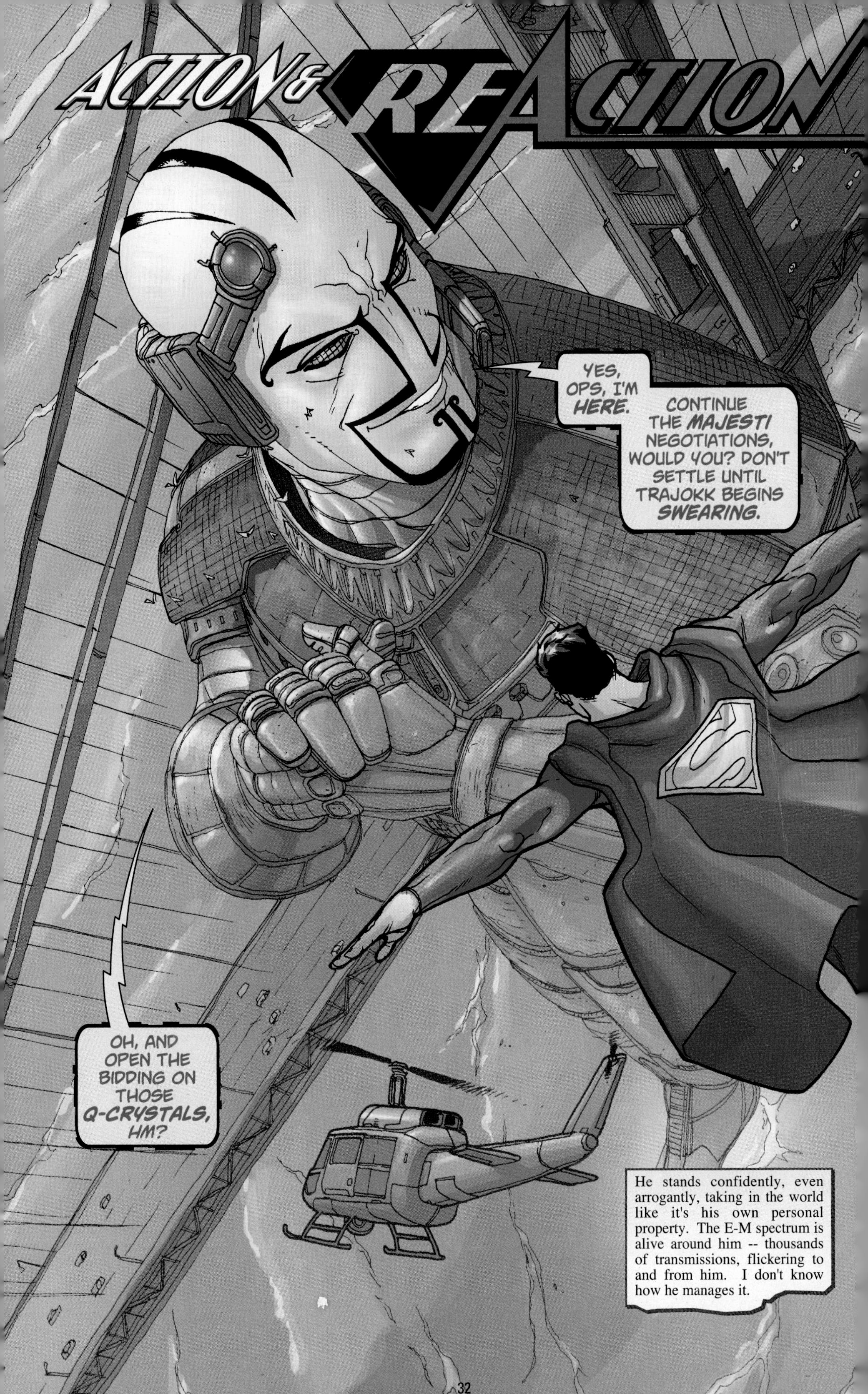
ACTION & REACTION
YES, OPS, I'M HERE. CONTINUE THE MAJESTI NEGOTIATIONS, WOULD YOU? DON'T SETTLE UNTIL TRAJOKK BEGINS SWEARING.
OH, AND OPEN THE BIDDING ON THOSE Q-CRYSTALS, HM?
He stands confidently, even arrogantly, taking in the world like it's his own personal property. The E-M spectrum is alive around him -- thousands of transmissions, flickering to and from him. I don't know how he manages it.

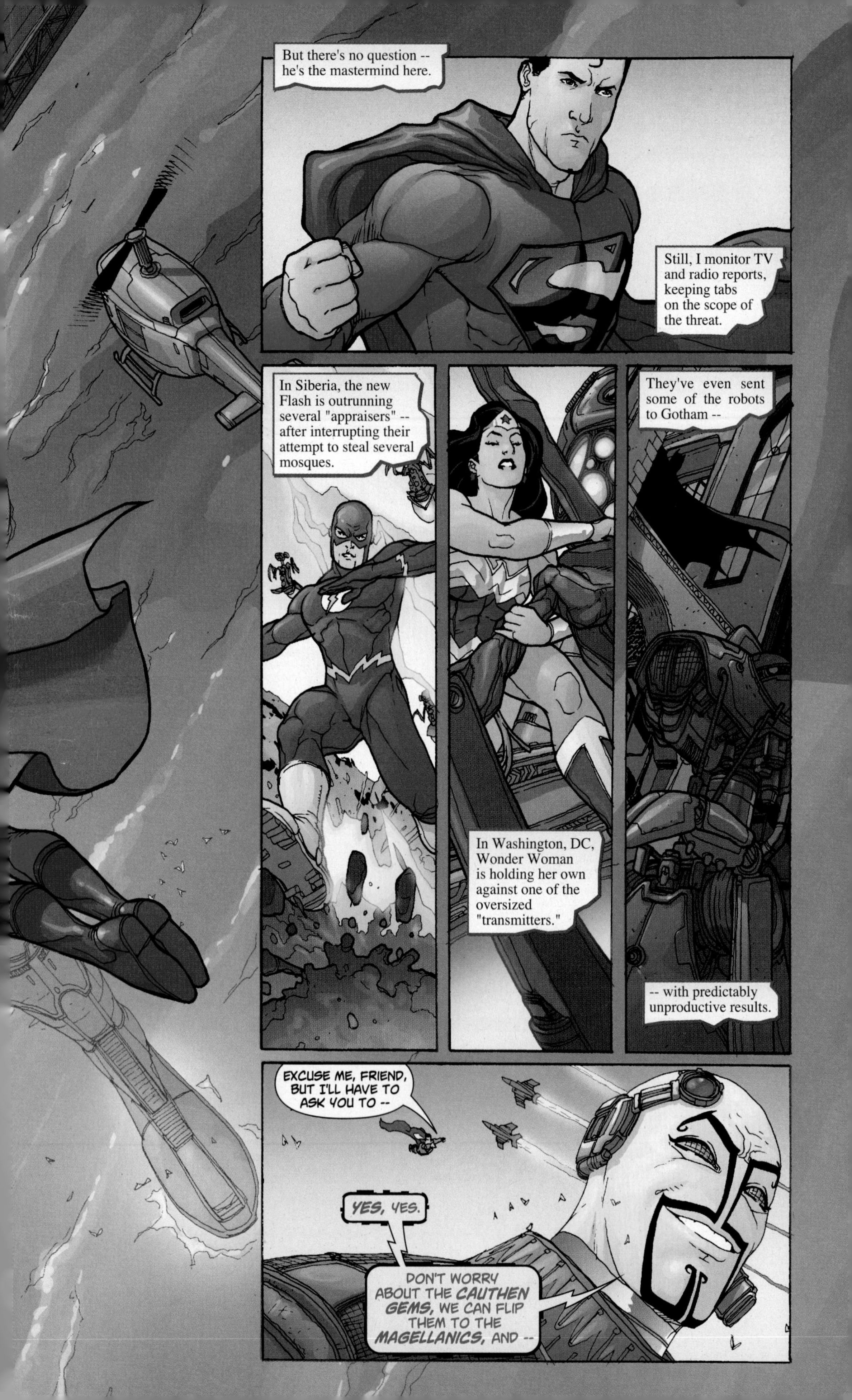
But there's no question -- he's the mastermind here.
Still, I monitor TV and radio reports, keeping tabs on the scope of the threat.
In Siberia, the new Flash is outrunning several "appraisers" -- after interrupting their attempt to steal several mosques.
In Washington, DC, Wonder Woman is holding her own against one of the oversized "transmitters."
They've even sent some of the robots to Gotham --
-- with predictably unproductive results.
EXCUSE ME, FRIEND, BUT I'LL HAVE TO ASK YOU TO --
YES, YES.
DON'T WORRY ABOUT THE CAUTHEN GEMS, WE CAN FLIP THEM TO THE MAGELLANICS, AND --

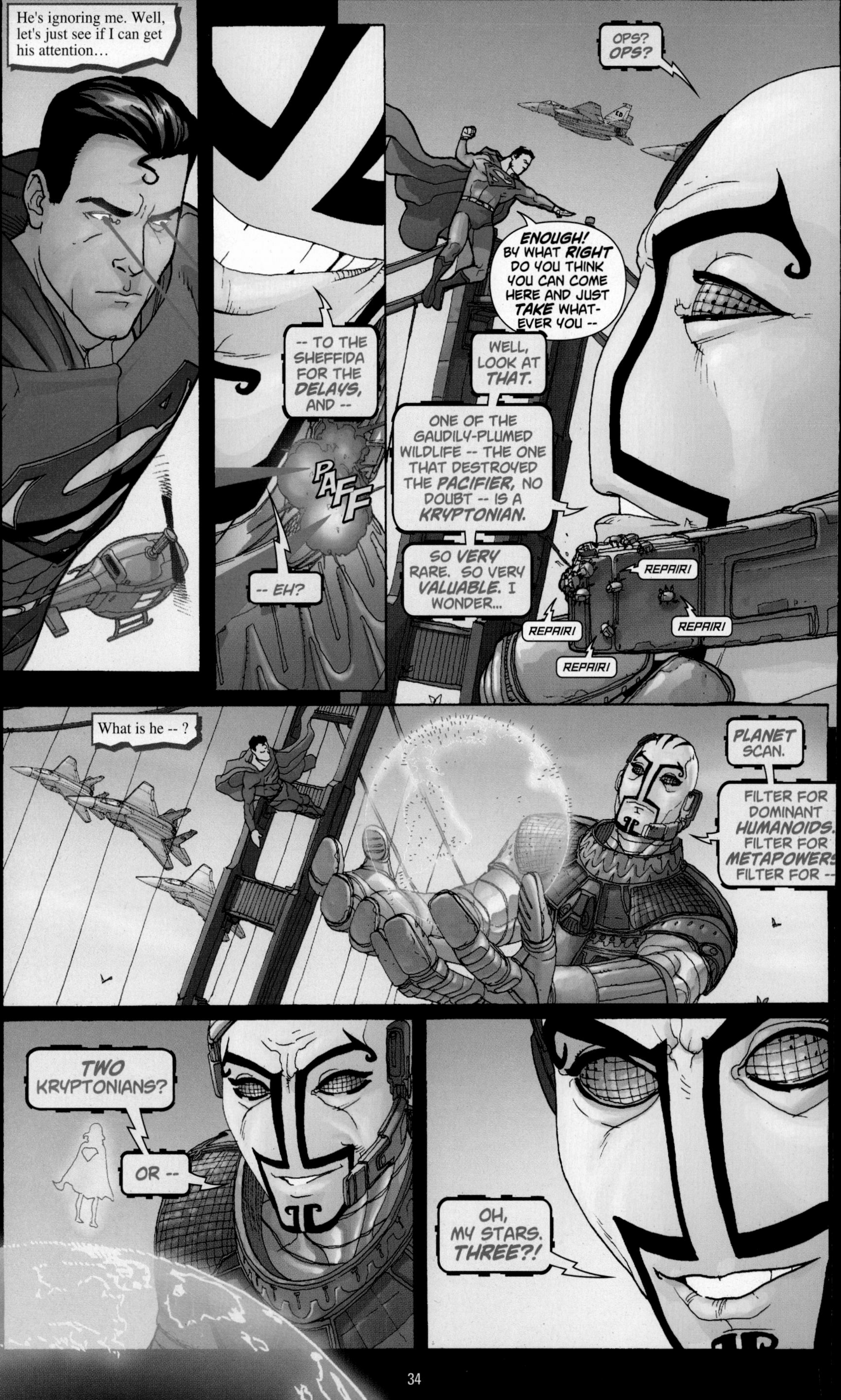

He's ignoring me. Well, let's just see if I can get his attention…
-- TO THE SHEFFIDA FOR THE DELAYS, AND --
PAFF
-- EH?
OPS? OPS?
ENOUGH! BY WHAT RIGHT DO YOU THINK YOU CAN COME HERE AND JUST TAKE WHAT-EVER YOU --
WELL, LOOK AT THAT.
ONE OF THE GAUDILY-PLUMED WILDLIFE -- THE ONE THAT DESTROYED THE PACIFIER, NO DOUBT -- IS A KRYPTONIAN.
SO VERY RARE. SO VERY VALUABLE. I WONDER...
REPAIR!
REPAIR!
REPAIR!
REPAIR!
What is he -- ?
PLANET SCAN.
FILTER FOR DOMINANT HUMANOIDS. FILTER FOR METAPOWERS FILTER FOR --
TWO KRYPTONIANS?
OR --
OH, MY STARS. THREE?!

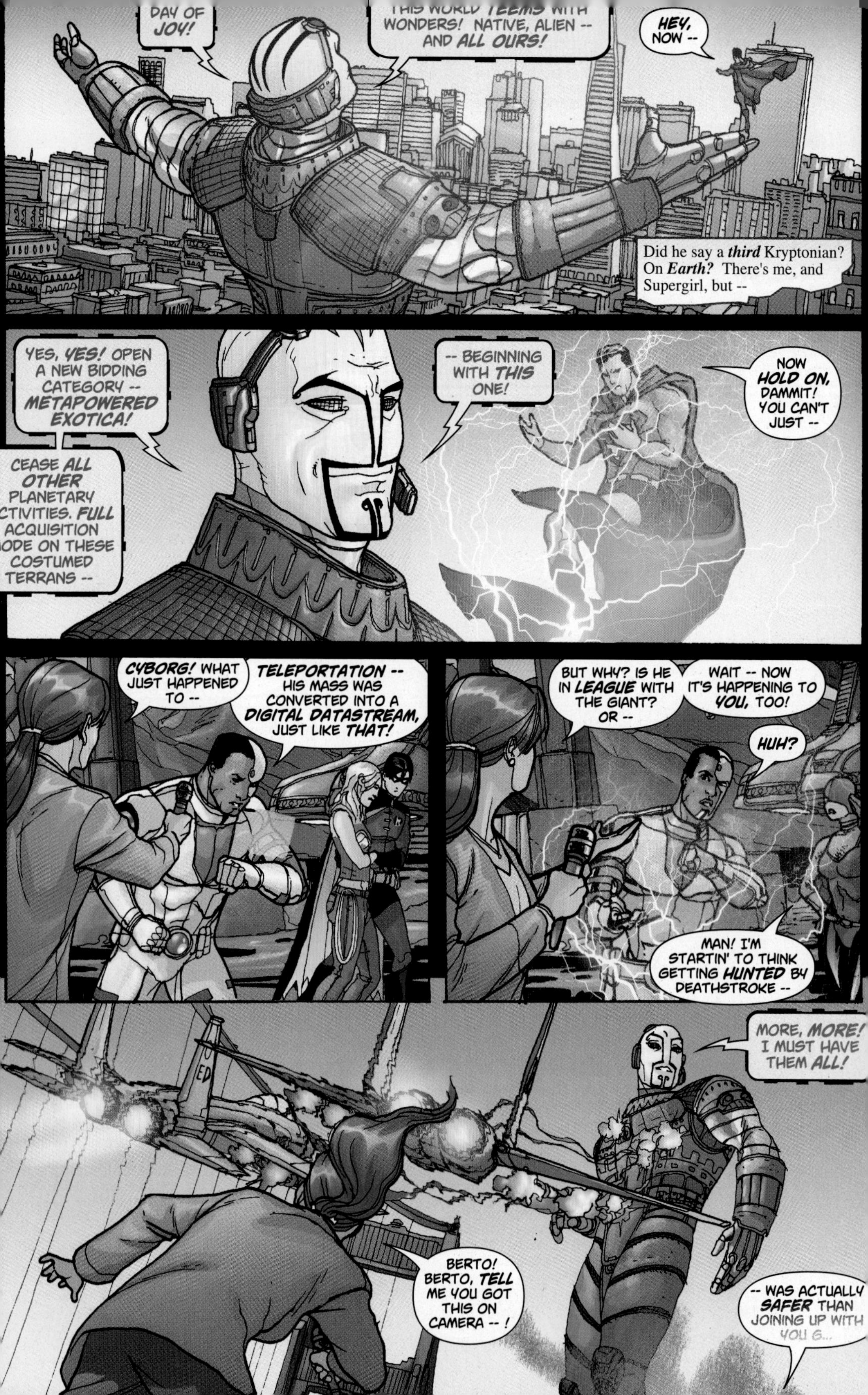
DAY OF JOY!
THIS WORLD TEEMS WITH WONDERS! NATIVE, ALIEN -- AND ALL OURS!
HEY, NOW --
Did he say a *third* Kryptonian? On *Earth?* There's me, and Supergirl, but --
YES, YES! OPEN A NEW BIDDING CATEGORY -- METAPOWERED EXOTICA!
CEASE ALL OTHER PLANETARY CTIVITIES. FULL ACQUISITION ODE ON THESE COSTUMED TERRANS --
-- BEGINNING WITH THIS ONE!
NOW HOLD ON, DAMMIT! YOU CAN'T JUST --
CYBORG! WHAT JUST HAPPENED TO --
TELEPORTATION -- HIS MASS WAS CONVERTED INTO A DIGITAL DATASTREAM, JUST LIKE THAT!
BUT WHY? IS HE IN LEAGUE WITH THE GIANT? OR --
WAIT -- NOW IT'S HAPPENING TO YOU, TOO!
HUH?
MAN! I'M STARTIN' TO THINK GETTING HUNTED BY DEATHSTROKE --
MORE, MORE! I MUST HAVE THEM ALL!
BERTO! BERTO, TELL ME YOU GOT THIS ON CAMERA -- !
-- WAS ACTUALLY SAFER THAN JOINING UP WITH YOU G...

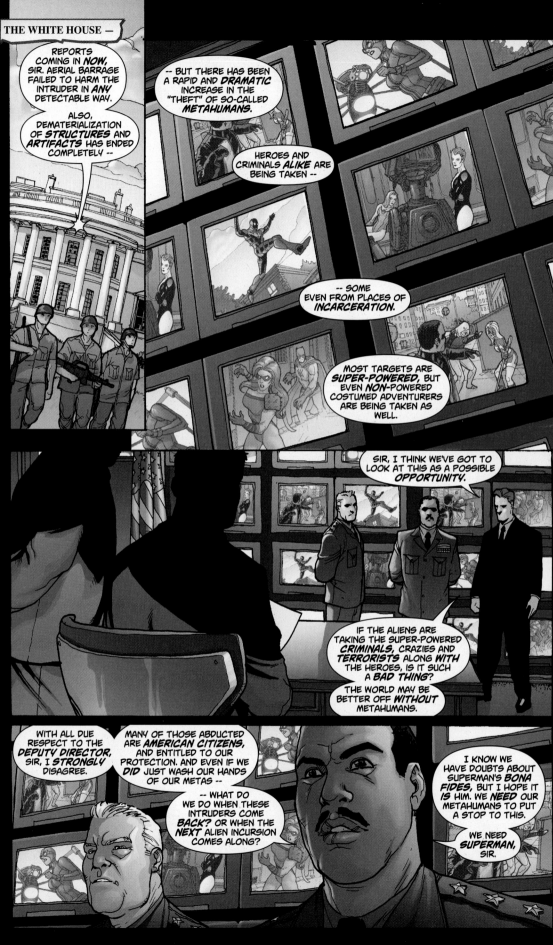

THE WHITE HOUSE —

REPORTS COMING IN *NOW*, SIR. AERIAL BARRAGE FAILED TO HARM THE INTRUDER IN *ANY* DETECTABLE WAY.

ALSO, DEMATERIALIZATION OF *STRUCTURES* AND *ARTIFACTS* HAS ENDED COMPLETELY —

— BUT THERE HAS BEEN A RAPID AND *DRAMATIC* INCREASE IN THE "THEFT" OF SO-CALLED *METAHUMANS*.

HEROES AND CRIMINALS *ALIKE* ARE BEING TAKEN —

— SOME EVEN FROM PLACES OF *INCARCERATION*.

MOST TARGETS ARE *SUPER-POWERED*, BUT EVEN *NON*-POWERED COSTUMED ADVENTURERS ARE BEING TAKEN AS WELL.

SIR, I THINK WE'VE GOT TO LOOK AT THIS AS A POSSIBLE *OPPORTUNITY*.

IF THE ALIENS ARE TAKING THE SUPER-POWERED *CRIMINALS*, CRAZIES AND *TERRORISTS* ALONG *WITH* THE HEROES, IS IT SUCH A *BAD THING*? THE WORLD MAY BE BETTER OFF *WITHOUT* METAHUMANS.

WITH ALL DUE RESPECT TO THE *DEPUTY DIRECTOR*, SIR, I *STRONGLY* DISAGREE.

MANY OF THOSE ABDUCTED ARE *AMERICAN CITIZENS*, AND ENTITLED TO OUR PROTECTION. AND EVEN IF WE *DID* JUST WASH OUR HANDS OF OUR METAS —

— WHAT DO WE DO WHEN THESE INTRUDERS COME *BACK*? OR WHEN THE *NEXT* ALIEN INCURSION COMES ALONG?

I KNOW WE HAVE DOUBTS ABOUT SUPERMAN'S *BONA FIDES*, BUT I HOPE IT *IS* HIM. WE *NEED* OUR METAHUMANS TO PUT A STOP TO THIS.

WE NEED *SUPERMAN*, SIR.

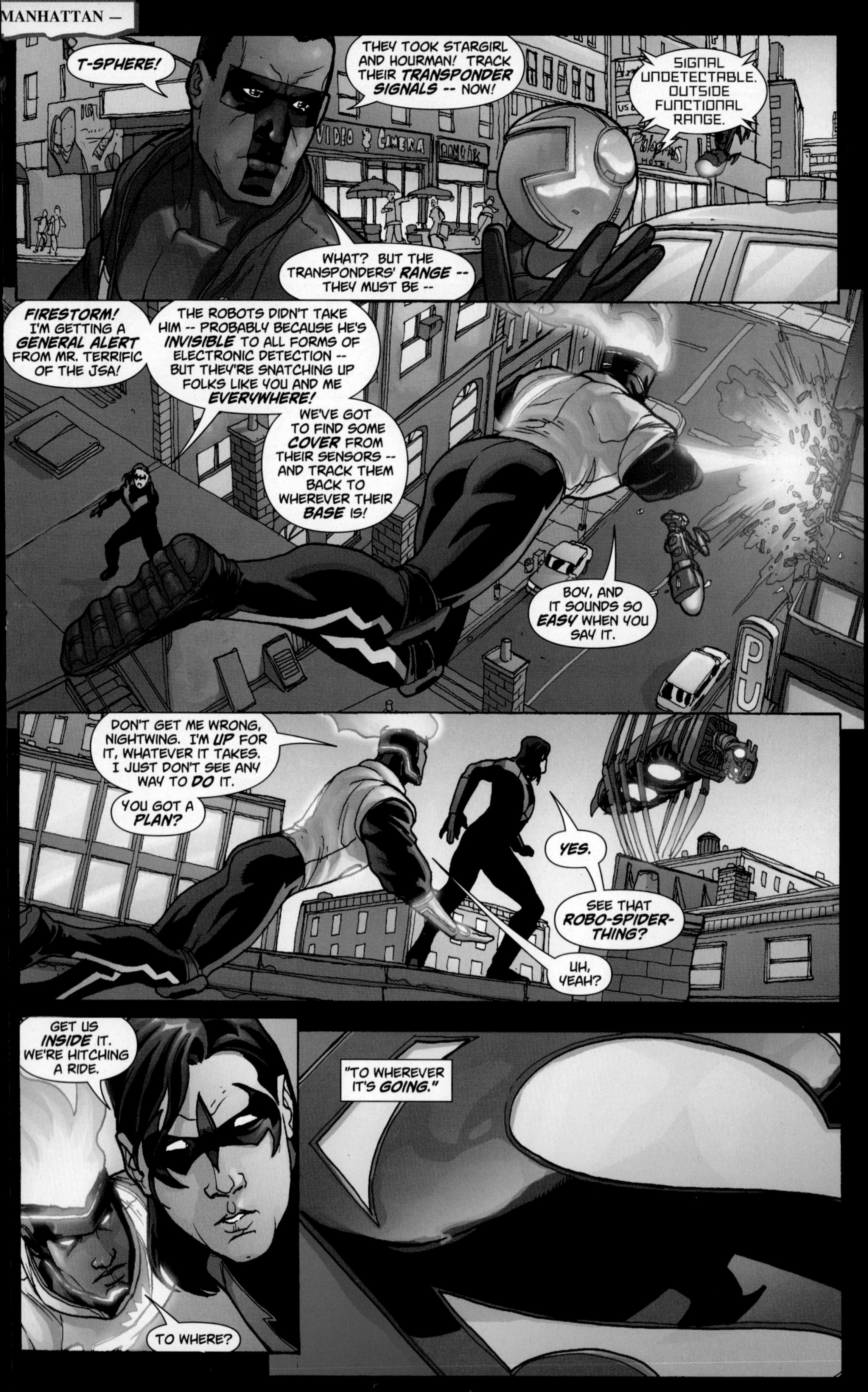

MANHATTAN —
T-SPHERE!
THEY TOOK STARGIRL AND HOURMAN! TRACK THEIR TRANSPONDER SIGNALS -- NOW!
SIGNAL UNDETECTABLE. OUTSIDE FUNCTIONAL RANGE.
WHAT? BUT THE TRANSPONDERS' RANGE -- THEY MUST BE --
FIRESTORM! I'M GETTING A GENERAL ALERT FROM MR. TERRIFIC OF THE JSA!
THE ROBOTS DIDN'T TAKE HIM -- PROBABLY BECAUSE HE'S INVISIBLE TO ALL FORMS OF ELECTRONIC DETECTION -- BUT THEY'RE SNATCHING UP FOLKS LIKE YOU AND ME EVERYWHERE!
WE'VE GOT TO FIND SOME COVER FROM THEIR SENSORS -- AND TRACK THEM BACK TO WHEREVER THEIR BASE IS!
BOY, AND IT SOUNDS SO EASY WHEN YOU SAY IT.
DON'T GET ME WRONG, NIGHTWING. I'M UP FOR IT, WHATEVER IT TAKES. I JUST DON'T SEE ANY WAY TO DO IT.
YOU GOT A PLAN?
YES.
SEE THAT ROBO-SPIDER-THING?
UH, YEAH?
GET US INSIDE IT. WE'RE HITCHING A RIDE.
TO WHERE?
"TO WHEREVER IT'S GOING."

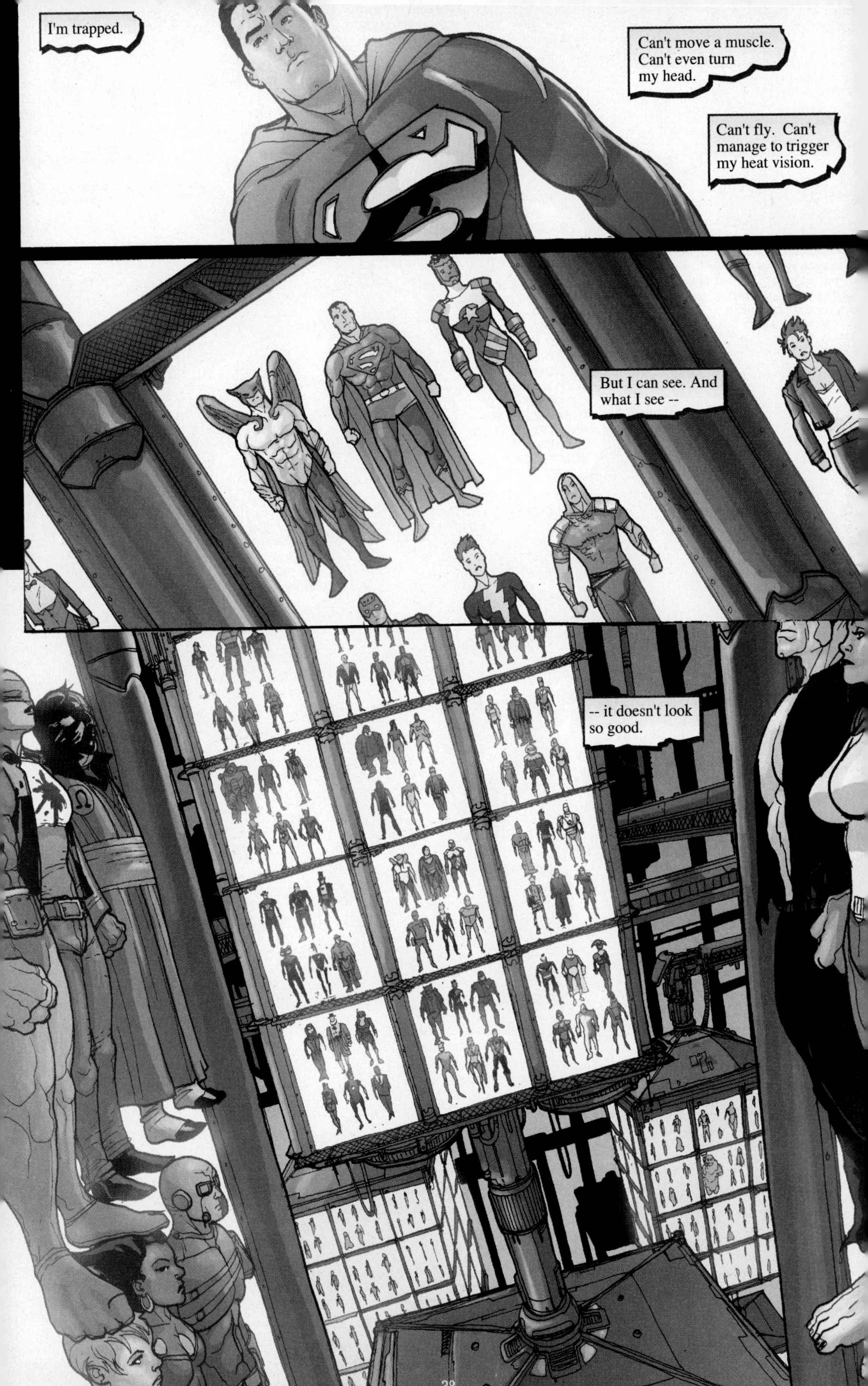
I'm trapped.
Can't move a muscle. Can't even turn my head.
Can't fly. Can't manage to trigger my heat vision.
But I can see. And what I see --
-- it doesn't look so good.

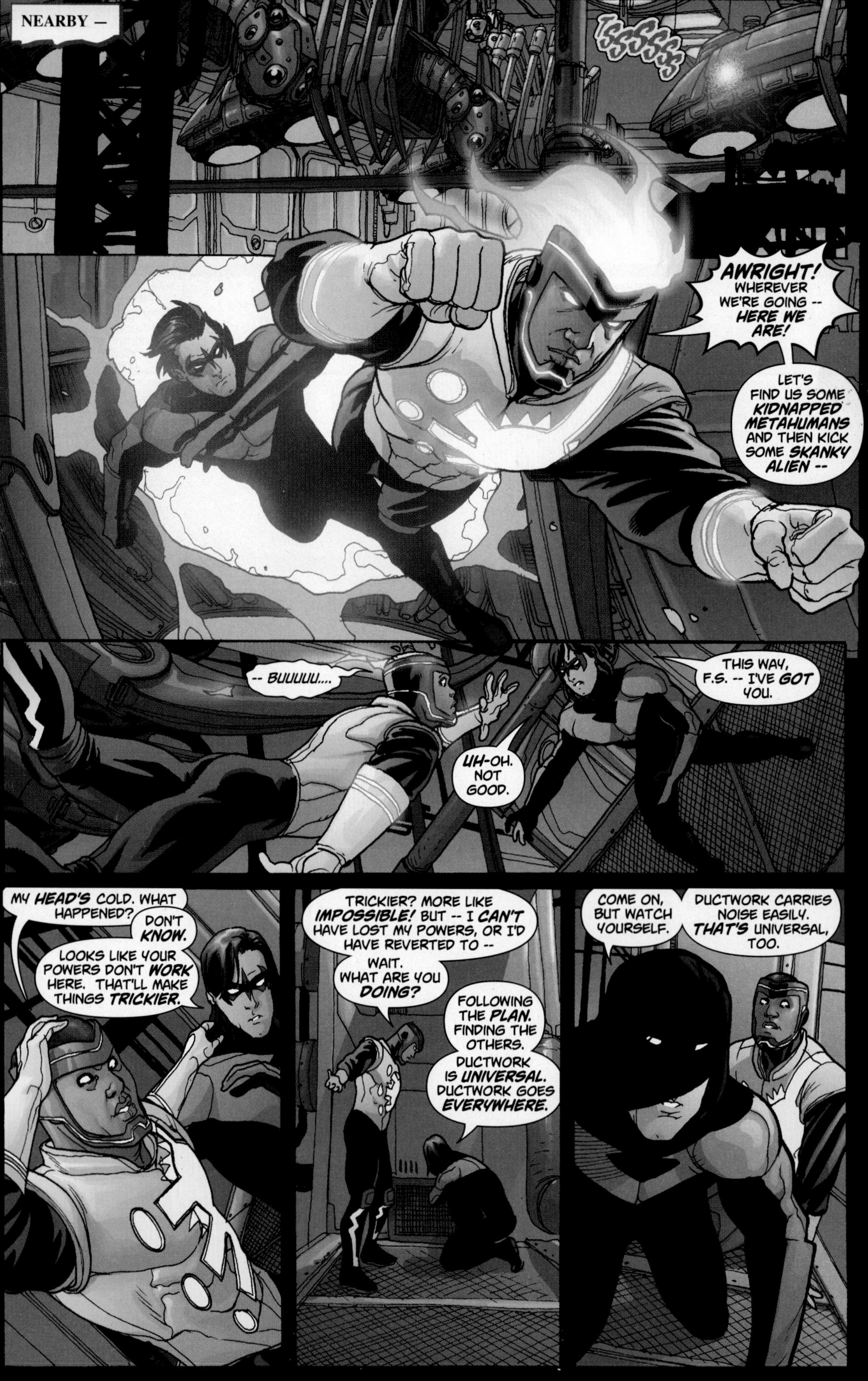
NEARBY —
ISSSSSS
AWRIGHT! WHEREVER WE'RE GOING -- HERE WE ARE!
LET'S FIND US SOME KIDNAPPED METAHUMANS AND THEN KICK SOME SKANKY ALIEN --
-- BUUUUU....
THIS WAY, F.S. -- I'VE GOT YOU.
UH-OH. NOT GOOD.
MY HEAD'S COLD. WHAT HAPPENED?
DON'T KNOW.
LOOKS LIKE YOUR POWERS DON'T WORK HERE. THAT'LL MAKE THINGS TRICKIER.
TRICKIER? MORE LIKE IMPOSSIBLE! BUT -- I CAN'T HAVE LOST MY POWERS, OR I'D HAVE REVERTED TO --
WAIT. WHAT ARE YOU DOING?
FOLLOWING THE PLAN. FINDING THE OTHERS. DUCTWORK IS UNIVERSAL. DUCTWORK GOES EVERYWHERE.
COME ON, BUT WATCH YOURSELF.
DUCTWORK CARRIES NOISE EASILY. THAT'S UNIVERSAL, TOO.

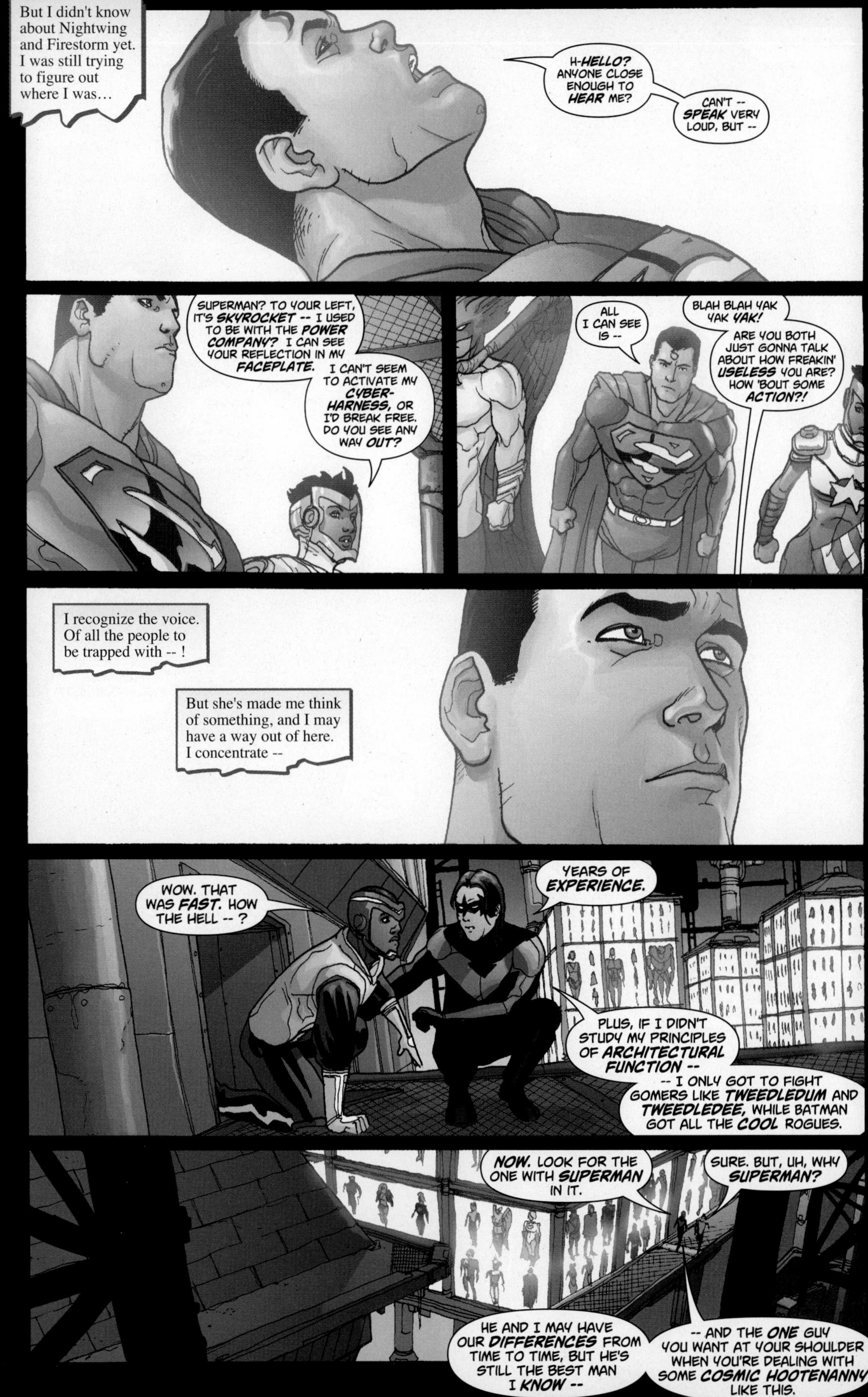
But I didn't know about Nightwing and Firestorm yet. I was still trying to figure out where I was…
H-HELLO? ANYONE CLOSE ENOUGH TO HEAR ME?
CAN'T -- SPEAK VERY LOUD, BUT --
SUPERMAN? TO YOUR LEFT, IT'S SKYROCKET -- I USED TO BE WITH THE POWER COMPANY? I CAN SEE YOUR REFLECTION IN MY FACEPLATE.
I CAN'T SEEM TO ACTIVATE MY CYBER-HARNESS, OR I'D BREAK FREE. DO YOU SEE ANY WAY OUT?
ALL I CAN SEE IS --
BLAH BLAH YAK YAK YAK!
ARE YOU BOTH JUST GONNA TALK ABOUT HOW FREAKIN' USELESS YOU ARE? HOW 'BOUT SOME ACTION?!
I recognize the voice. Of all the people to be trapped with -- !
But she's made me think of something, and I may have a way out of here. I concentrate --
WOW. THAT WAS FAST. HOW THE HELL -- ?
YEARS OF EXPERIENCE.
PLUS, IF I DIDN'T STUDY MY PRINCIPLES OF ARCHITECTURAL FUNCTION --
-- I ONLY GOT TO FIGHT GOMERS LIKE TWEEDLEDUM AND TWEEDLEDEE, WHILE BATMAN GOT ALL THE COOL ROGUES.
NOW. LOOK FOR THE ONE WITH SUPERMAN IN IT.
SURE. BUT, UH, WHY SUPERMAN?
HE AND I MAY HAVE OUR DIFFERENCES FROM TIME TO TIME, BUT HE'S STILL THE BEST MAN I KNOW --
-- AND THE ONE GUY YOU WANT AT YOUR SHOULDER WHEN YOU'RE DEALING WITH SOME COSMIC HOOTENANNY LIKE THIS.

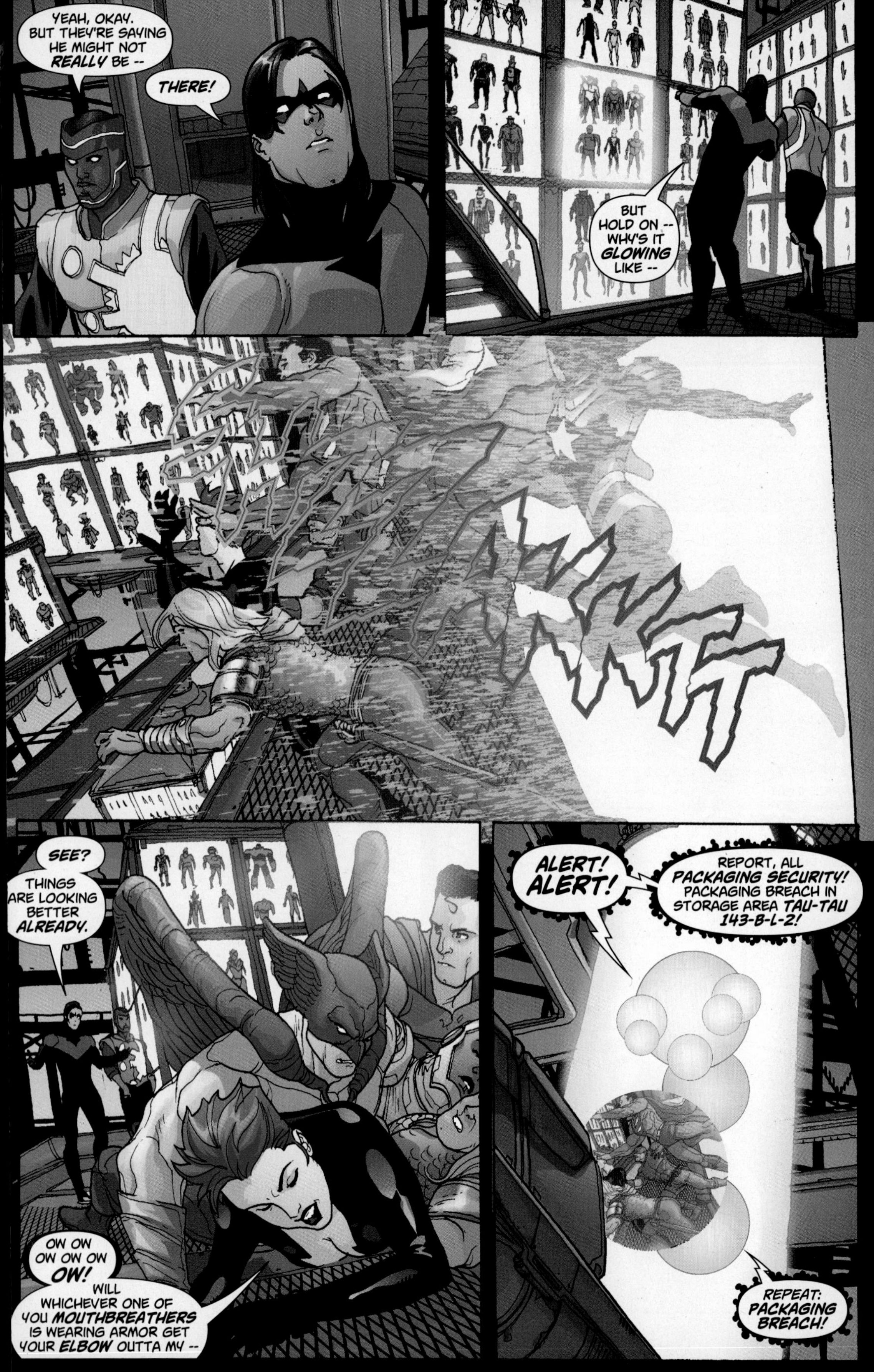
YEAH, OKAY. BUT THEY'RE SAYING HE MIGHT NOT REALLY BE --
THERE!
BUT HOLD ON -- WHY'S IT GLOWING LIKE --
SEE? THINGS ARE LOOKING BETTER ALREADY.
OW OW OW OW OW OW! WILL WHICHEVER ONE OF YOU MOUTHBREATHERS IS WEARING ARMOR GET YOUR ELBOW OUTTA MY --
ALERT! ALERT!
REPORT, ALL PACKAGING SECURITY! PACKAGING BREACH IN STORAGE AREA TAU-TAU 143-B-L-2!
REPEAT: PACKAGING BREACH!

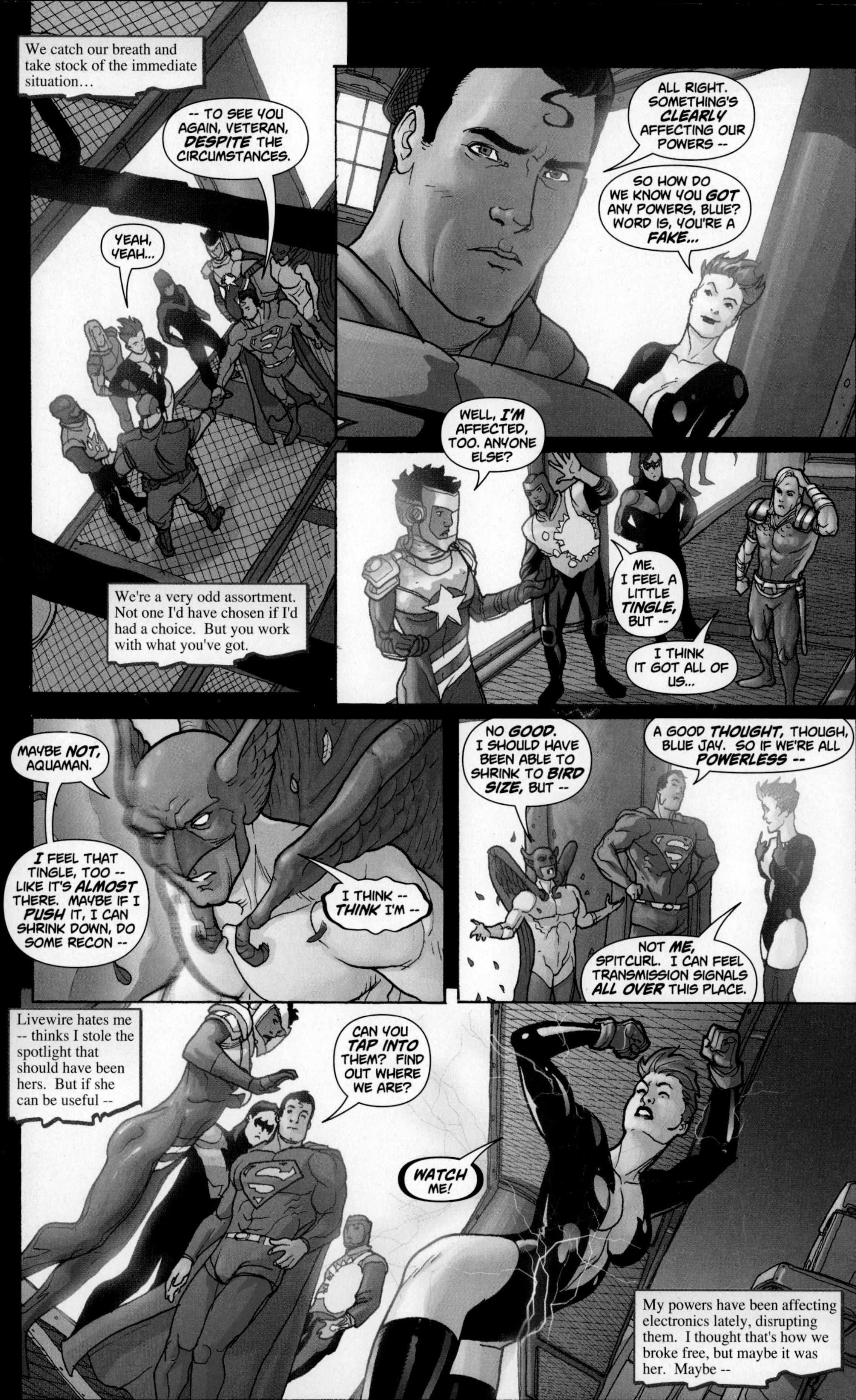

We catch our breath and take stock of the immediate situation…
-- TO SEE YOU AGAIN, VETERAN, DESPITE THE CIRCUMSTANCES.
YEAH, YEAH...
We're a very odd assortment. Not one I'd have chosen if I'd had a choice. But you work with what you've got.
ALL RIGHT. SOMETHING'S CLEARLY AFFECTING OUR POWERS --
SO HOW DO WE KNOW YOU GOT ANY POWERS, BLUE? WORD IS, YOU'RE A FAKE...
WELL, I'M AFFECTED, TOO. ANYONE ELSE?
ME. I FEEL A LITTLE TINGLE, BUT --
I THINK IT GOT ALL OF US...
MAYBE NOT, AQUAMAN.
I FEEL THAT TINGLE, TOO -- LIKE IT'S ALMOST THERE. MAYBE IF I PUSH IT, I CAN SHRINK DOWN, DO SOME RECON --
I THINK -- THINK I'M --
NO GOOD. I SHOULD HAVE BEEN ABLE TO SHRINK TO BIRD SIZE, BUT --
A GOOD THOUGHT, THOUGH, BLUE JAY. SO IF WE'RE ALL POWERLESS --
NOT ME, SPITCURL. I CAN FEEL TRANSMISSION SIGNALS ALL OVER THIS PLACE.
Livewire hates me -- thinks I stole the spotlight that should have been hers. But if she can be useful --
CAN YOU TAP INTO THEM? FIND OUT WHERE WE ARE?
WATCH ME!
My powers have been affecting electronics lately, disrupting them. I thought that's how we broke free, but maybe it was her. Maybe --

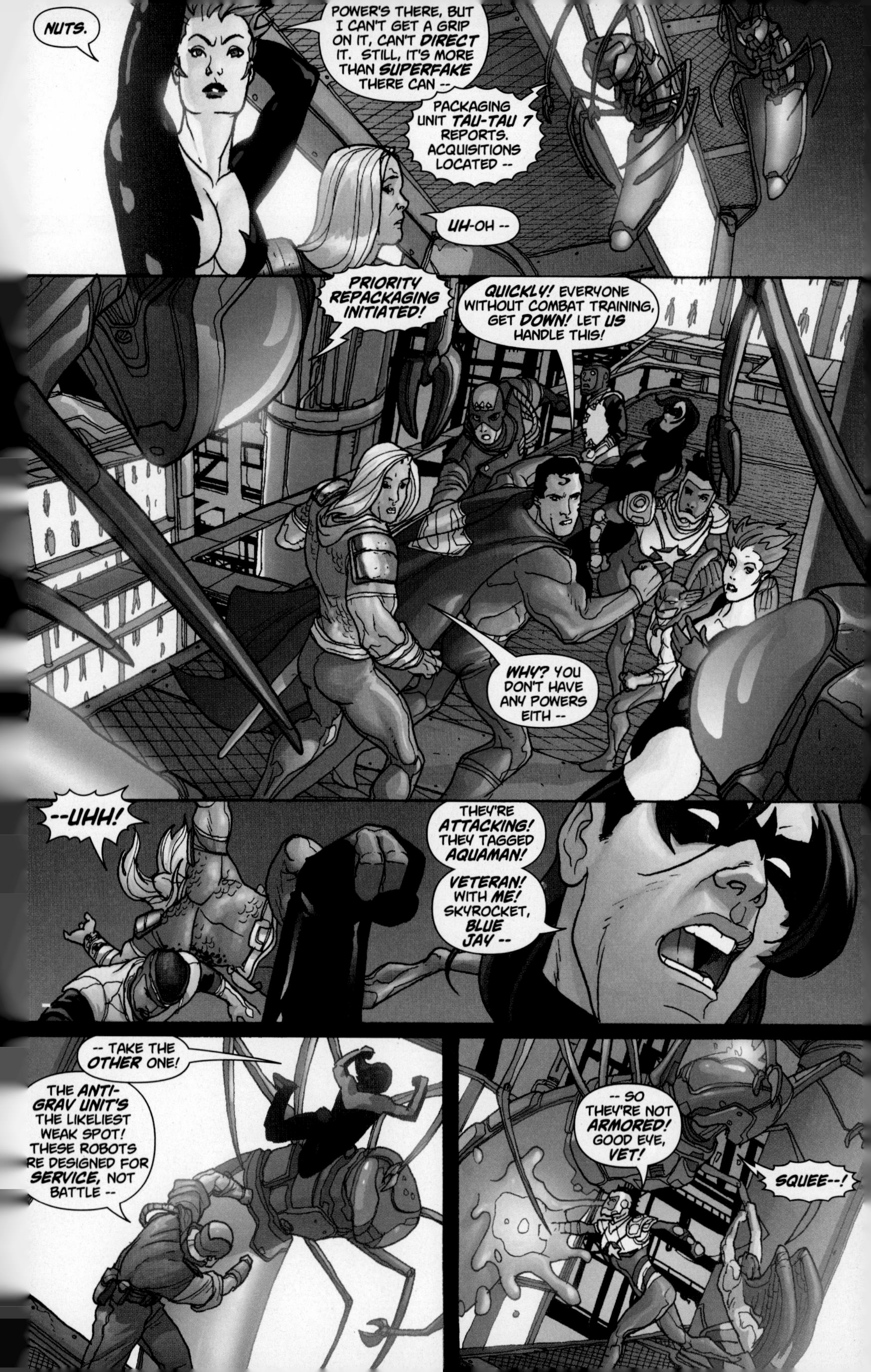
NUTS.
POWER'S THERE, BUT I CAN'T GET A GRIP ON IT, CAN'T DIRECT IT. STILL, IT'S MORE THAN SUPERFAKE THERE CAN --
PACKAGING UNIT TAU-TAU 7 REPORTS. ACQUISITIONS LOCATED --
UH-OH --
PRIORITY REPACKAGING INITIATED!
QUICKLY! EVERYONE WITHOUT COMBAT TRAINING, GET DOWN! LET US HANDLE THIS!
WHY? YOU DON'T HAVE ANY POWERS EITH --
--UHH!
THEY'RE ATTACKING! THEY TAGGED AQUAMAN!
VETERAN! WITH ME! SKYROCKET, BLUE JAY --
-- TAKE THE OTHER ONE!
THE ANTI-GRAV UNIT'S THE LIKELIEST WEAK SPOT! THESE ROBOTS RE DESIGNED FOR SERVICE, NOT BATTLE --
-- SO THEY'RE NOT ARMORED! GOOD EYE, VET!
SQUEE--!

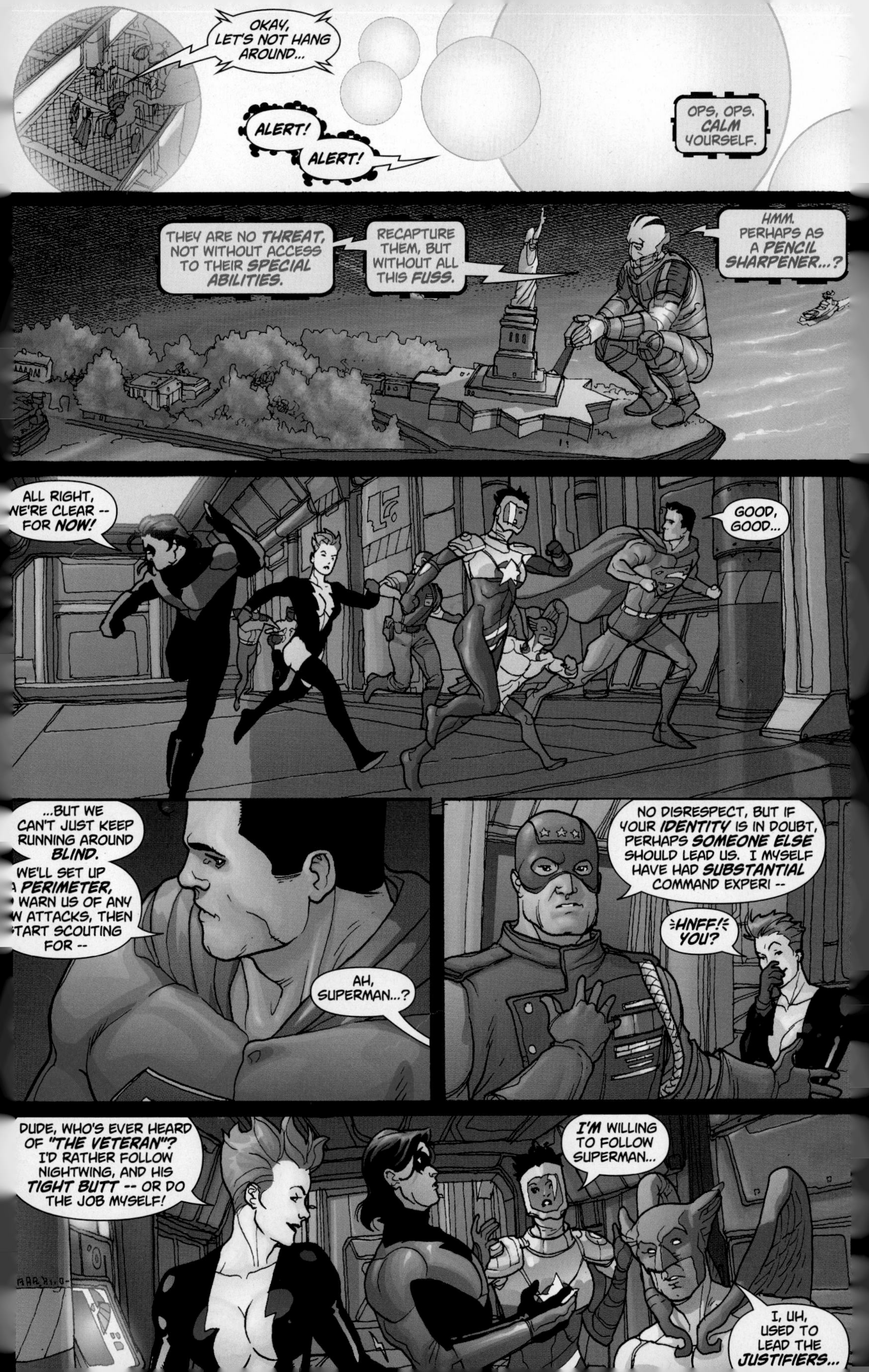

OKAY, LET'S NOT HANG AROUND...
ALERT!
ALERT!
OPS, OPS. CALM YOURSELF.
THEY ARE NO THREAT, NOT WITHOUT ACCESS TO THEIR SPECIAL ABILITIES.
RECAPTURE THEM, BUT WITHOUT ALL THIS FUSS.
HMM. PERHAPS AS A PENCIL SHARPENER...?
ALL RIGHT, WE'RE CLEAR -- FOR NOW!
GOOD, GOOD...
...BUT WE CAN'T JUST KEEP RUNNING AROUND BLIND.
WE'LL SET UP PERIMETER, WARN US OF ANY W ATTACKS, THEN TART SCOUTING FOR --
AH, SUPERMAN...?
NO DISRESPECT, BUT IF YOUR IDENTITY IS IN DOUBT, PERHAPS SOMEONE ELSE SHOULD LEAD US. I MYSELF HAVE HAD SUBSTANTIAL COMMAND EXPERI --
HNFF! YOU?
DUDE, WHO'S EVER HEARD OF "THE VETERAN"? I'D RATHER FOLLOW NIGHTWING, AND HIS TIGHT BUTT -- OR DO THE JOB MYSELF!
I'M WILLING TO FOLLOW SUPERMAN...
I, UH, USED TO LEAD THE JUSTIFIERS...

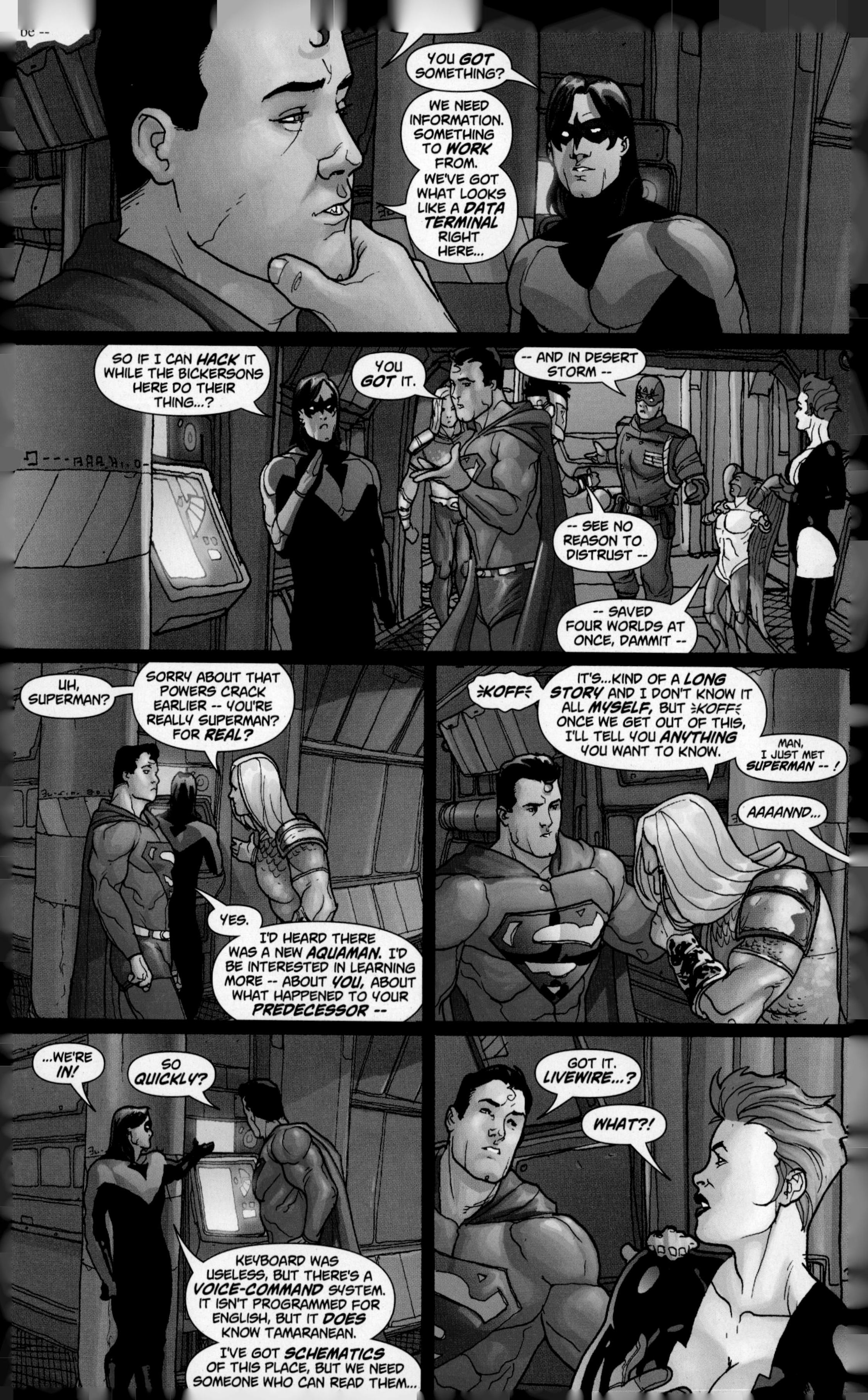
be --
YOU GOT SOMETHING?
WE NEED INFORMATION. SOMETHING TO WORK FROM. WE'VE GOT WHAT LOOKS LIKE A DATA TERMINAL RIGHT HERE...
SO IF I CAN HACK IT WHILE THE BICKERSONS HERE DO THEIR THING...?
YOU GOT IT.
-- AND IN DESERT STORM --
-- SEE NO REASON TO DISTRUST --
-- SAVED FOUR WORLDS AT ONCE, DAMMIT --
UH, SUPERMAN?
SORRY ABOUT THAT POWERS CRACK EARLIER -- YOU'RE REALLY SUPERMAN? FOR REAL?
YES.
I'D HEARD THERE WAS A NEW AQUAMAN. I'D BE INTERESTED IN LEARNING MORE -- ABOUT YOU, ABOUT WHAT HAPPENED TO YOUR PREDECESSOR --
KOFF
IT'S...KIND OF A LONG STORY AND I DON'T KNOW IT ALL MYSELF, BUT KOFF ONCE WE GET OUT OF THIS, I'LL TELL YOU ANYTHING YOU WANT TO KNOW.
MAN, I JUST MET SUPERMAN -- !
AAAANND...
...WE'RE IN!
SO QUICKLY?
KEYBOARD WAS USELESS, BUT THERE'S A VOICE-COMMAND SYSTEM. IT ISN'T PROGRAMMED FOR ENGLISH, BUT IT DOES KNOW TAMARANEAN.
I'VE GOT SCHEMATICS OF THIS PLACE, BUT WE NEED SOMEONE WHO CAN READ THEM...
GOT IT. LIVEWIRE...?
WHAT?!

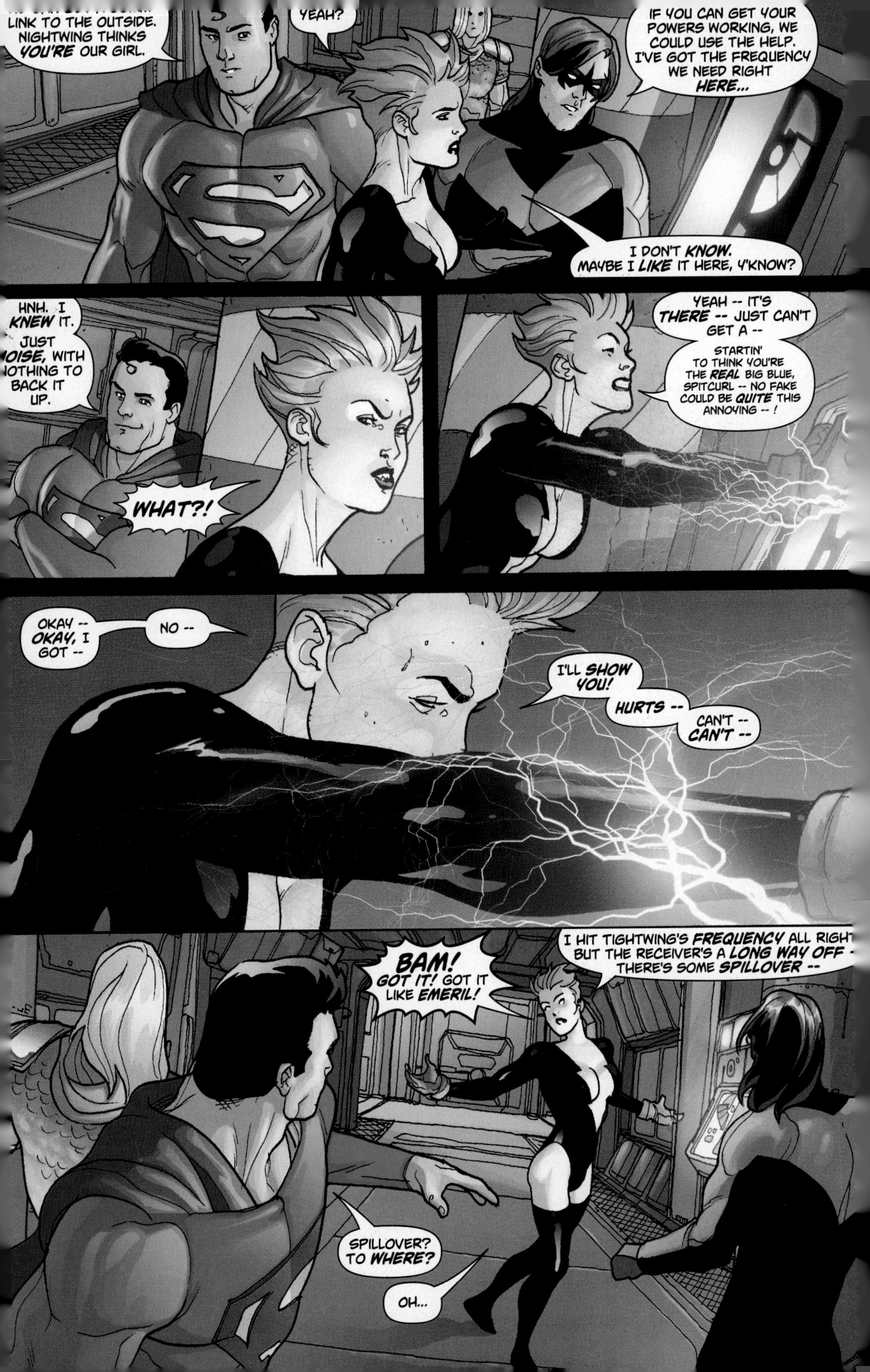
LINK TO THE OUTSIDE. NIGHTWING THINKS YOU'RE OUR GIRL.
YEAH?
IF YOU CAN GET YOUR POWERS WORKING, WE COULD USE THE HELP. I'VE GOT THE FREQUENCY WE NEED RIGHT HERE...
I DON'T KNOW. MAYBE I LIKE IT HERE, Y'KNOW?
HNH. I KNEW IT. JUST OISE, WITH OTHING TO BACK IT UP.
WHAT?!
YEAH -- IT'S THERE -- JUST CAN'T GET A --
STARTIN' TO THINK YOU'RE THE REAL BIG BLUE, SPITCURL -- NO FAKE COULD BE QUITE THIS ANNOYING -- !
OKAY -- OKAY, I GOT --
NO --
I'LL SHOW YOU!
HURTS --
CAN'T -- CAN'T --
BAM! GOT IT! GOT IT LIKE EMERIL!
I HIT TIGHTWING'S FREQUENCY ALL RIGHT BUT THE RECEIVER'S A LONG WAY OFF -- THERE'S SOME SPILLOVER --
SPILLOVER? TO WHERE?
OH...

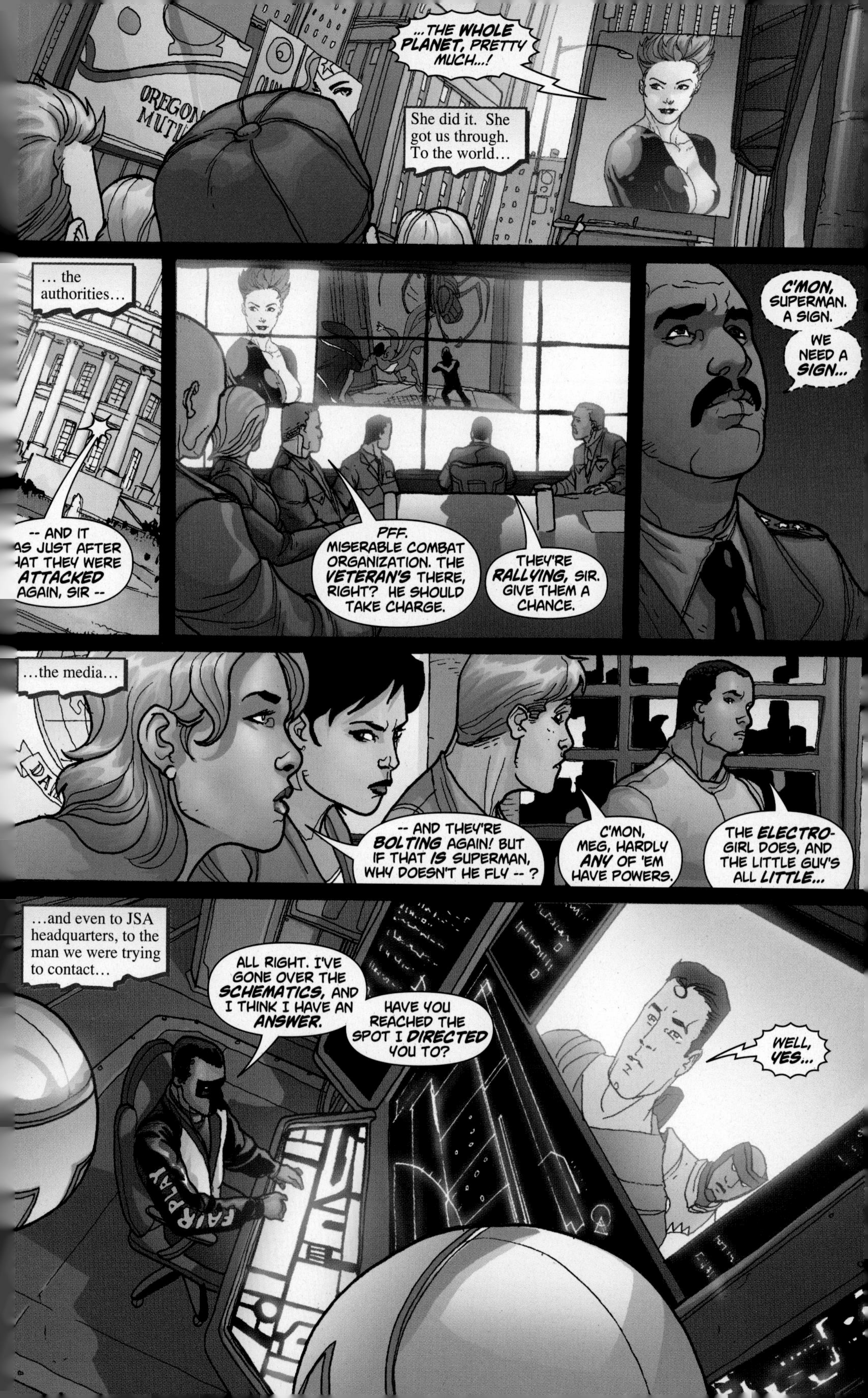
...THE WHOLE PLANET, PRETTY MUCH...!
She did it. She got us through. To the world…
OREGON MUTU
… the authorities…
-- AND IT AS JUST AFTER HAT THEY WERE ATTACKED AGAIN, SIR --
PFF. MISERABLE COMBAT ORGANIZATION. THE VETERAN'S THERE, RIGHT? HE SHOULD TAKE CHARGE.
THEY'RE RALLYING, SIR. GIVE THEM A CHANCE.
C'MON, SUPERMAN. A SIGN.
WE NEED A SIGN...
…the media…
-- AND THEY'RE BOLTING AGAIN! BUT IF THAT IS SUPERMAN, WHY DOESN'T HE FLY -- ?
C'MON, MEG, HARDLY ANY OF 'EM HAVE POWERS.
THE ELECTRO-GIRL DOES, AND THE LITTLE GUY'S ALL LITTLE...
…and even to JSA headquarters, to the man we were trying to contact…
ALL RIGHT. I'VE GONE OVER THE SCHEMATICS, AND I THINK I HAVE AN ANSWER.
HAVE YOU REACHED THE SPOT I DIRECTED YOU TO?
WELL, YES...
FAIR PLAY

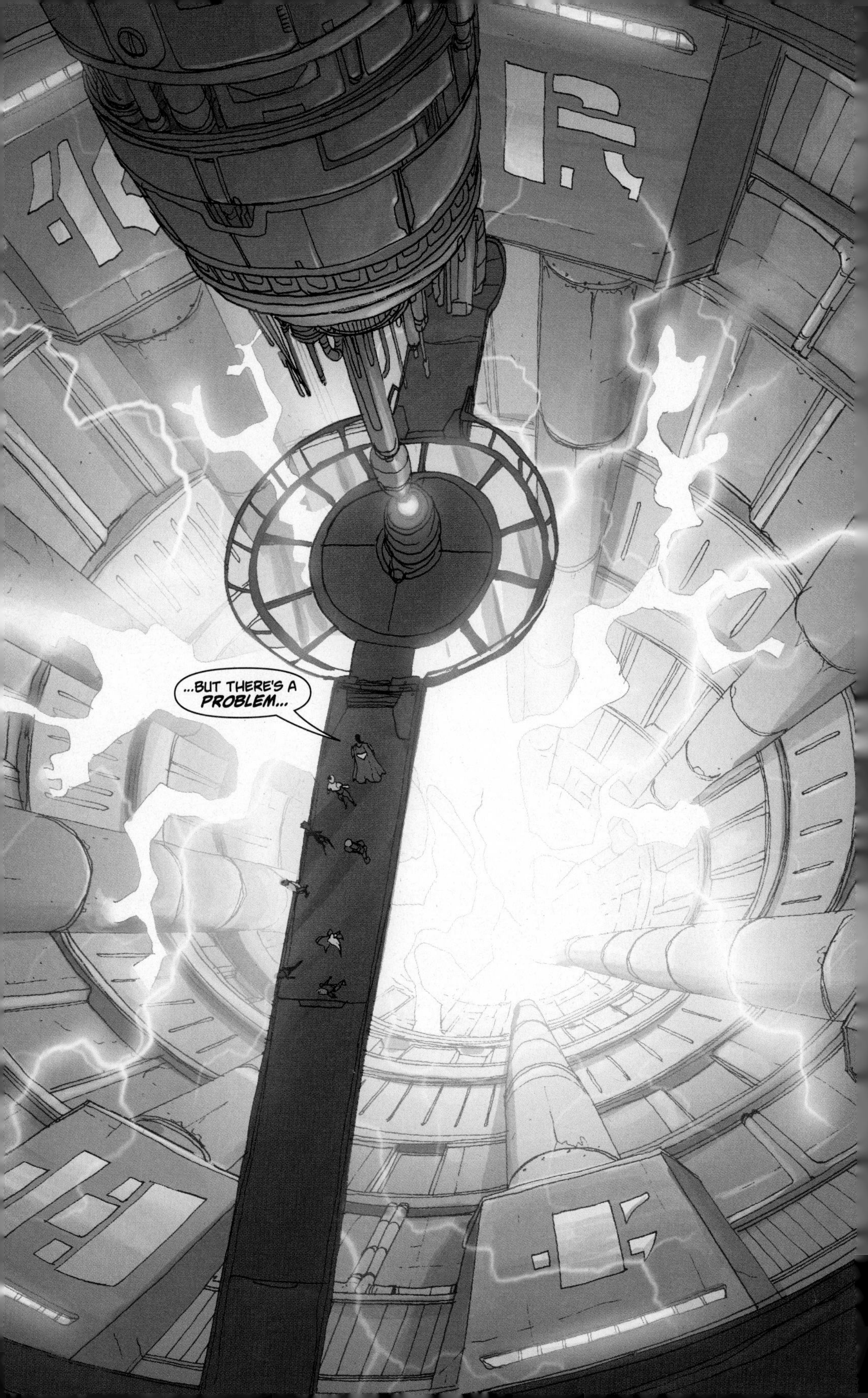
...BUT THERE'S A PROBLEM...

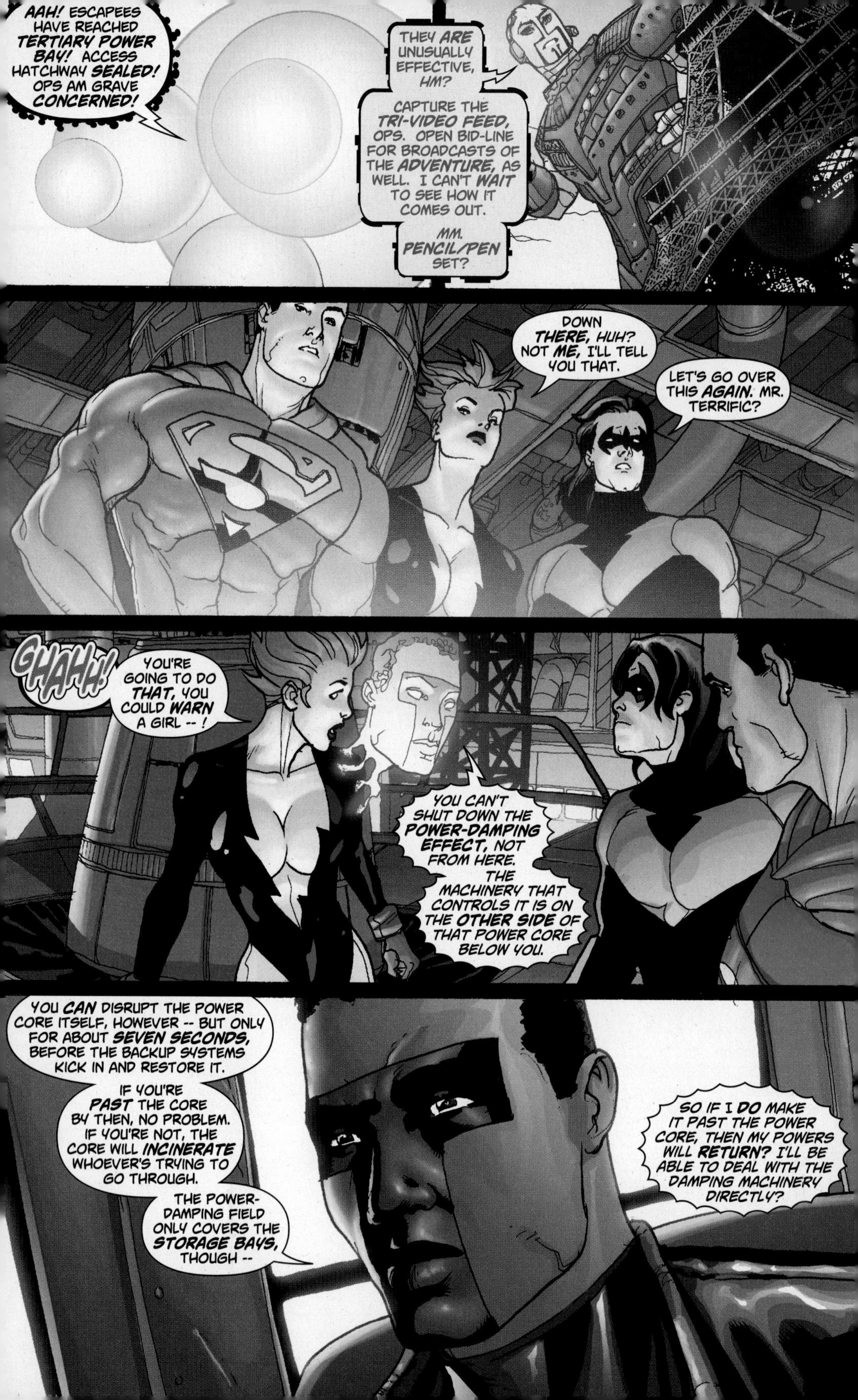
AAH! ESCAPEES HAVE REACHED TERTIARY POWER BAY! ACCESS HATCHWAY SEALED! OPS AM GRAVE CONCERNED!
THEY ARE UNUSUALLY EFFECTIVE, HM?
CAPTURE THE TRI-VIDEO FEED, OPS. OPEN BID-LINE FOR BROADCASTS OF THE ADVENTURE, AS WELL. I CAN'T WAIT TO SEE HOW IT COMES OUT.
MM. PENCIL/PEN SET?
DOWN THERE, HUH? NOT ME, I'LL TELL YOU THAT.
LET'S GO OVER THIS AGAIN. MR. TERRIFIC?
GHAHH!
YOU'RE GOING TO DO THAT, YOU COULD WARN A GIRL -- !
YOU CAN'T SHUT DOWN THE POWER-DAMPING EFFECT, NOT FROM HERE.
THE MACHINERY THAT CONTROLS IT IS ON THE OTHER SIDE OF THAT POWER CORE BELOW YOU.
YOU CAN DISRUPT THE POWER CORE ITSELF, HOWEVER -- BUT ONLY FOR ABOUT SEVEN SECONDS, BEFORE THE BACKUP SYSTEMS KICK IN AND RESTORE IT.
IF YOU'RE PAST THE CORE BY THEN, NO PROBLEM. IF YOU'RE NOT, THE CORE WILL INCINERATE WHOEVER'S TRYING TO GO THROUGH.
THE POWER-DAMPING FIELD ONLY COVERS THE STORAGE BAYS, THOUGH --
SO IF I DO MAKE IT PAST THE POWER CORE, THEN MY POWERS WILL RETURN? I'LL BE ABLE TO DEAL WITH THE DAMPING MACHINERY DIRECTLY?

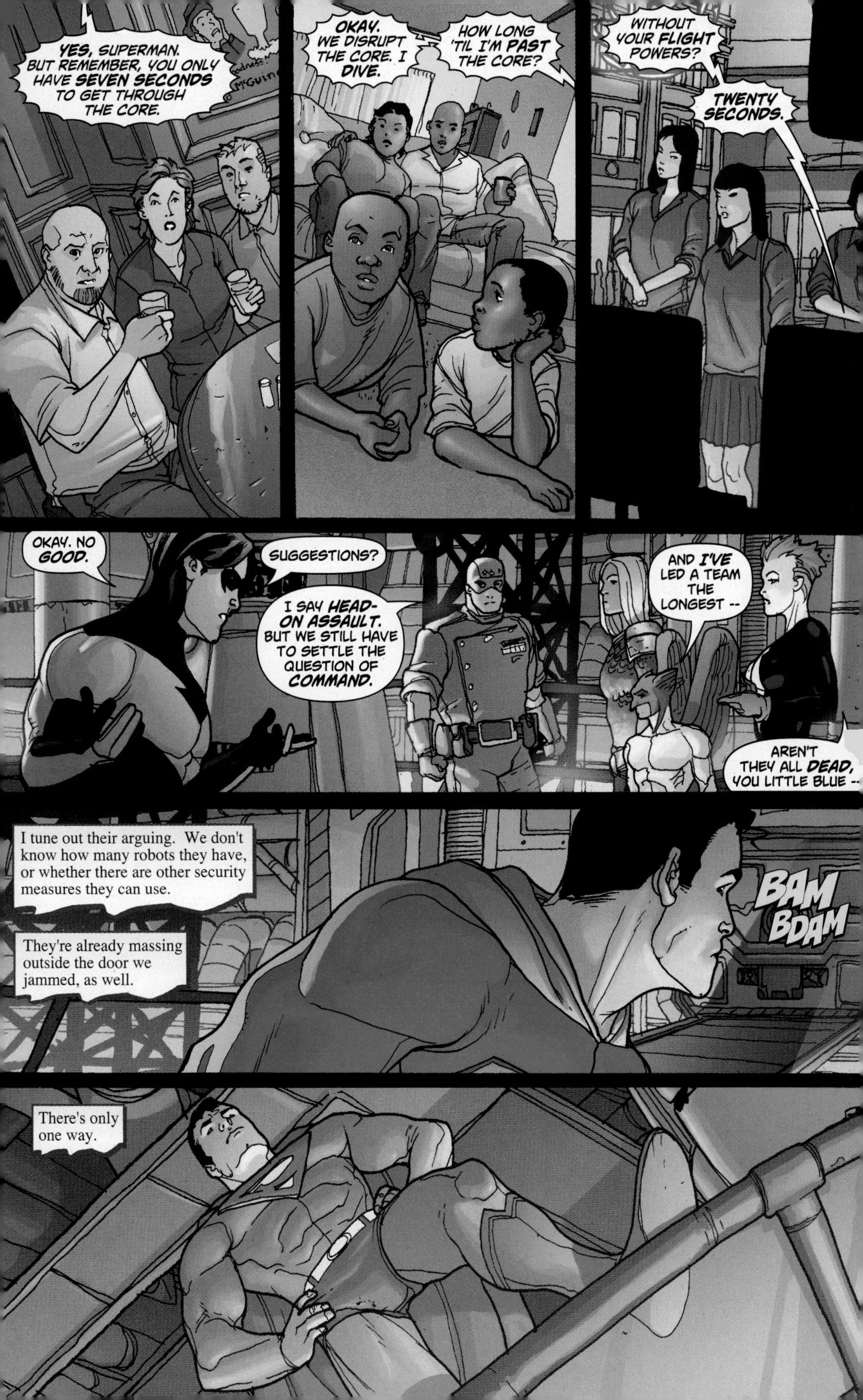
YES, SUPERMAN. BUT REMEMBER, YOU ONLY HAVE SEVEN SECONDS TO GET THROUGH THE CORE.
OKAY. WE DISRUPT THE CORE. I DIVE.
HOW LONG 'TIL I'M PAST THE CORE?
WITHOUT YOUR FLIGHT POWERS?
TWENTY SECONDS.
OKAY. NO GOOD.
SUGGESTIONS?
I SAY HEAD-ON ASSAULT. BUT WE STILL HAVE TO SETTLE THE QUESTION OF COMMAND.
AND I'VE LED A TEAM THE LONGEST --
AREN'T THEY ALL DEAD, YOU LITTLE BLUE --
I tune out their arguing. We don't know how many robots they have, or whether there are other security measures they can use.
They're already massing outside the door we jammed, as well.
BAM BDAM
There's only one way.

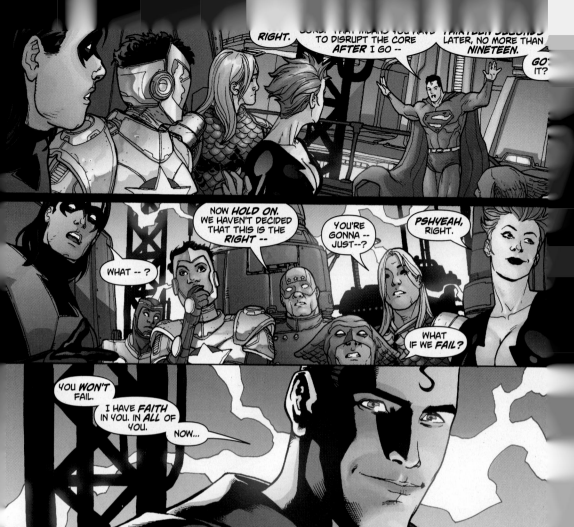

RIGHT.

... THAT MEANS YOU HAVE TO DISRUPT THE CORE *AFTER* I GO --

THIRTEEN SECONDS LATER, NO MORE THAN *NINETEEN.*

GOT IT?

NOW *HOLD ON.* WE HAVEN'T DECIDED THAT THIS IS THE *RIGHT* --

WHAT -- ?

YOU'RE GONNA JUST --?

PSHYEAH, RIGHT.

WHAT IF WE *FAIL?*

YOU *WON'T* FAIL.

I HAVE *FAITH* IN YOU. IN *ALL* OF YOU.

NOW...

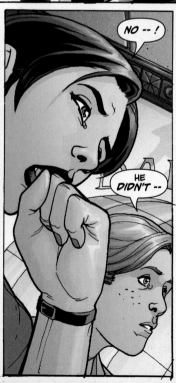

NO -- !

HE *DIDN'T* --

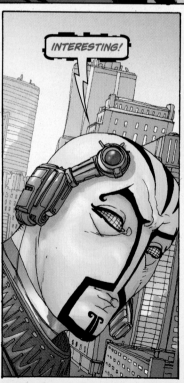

INTERESTING!

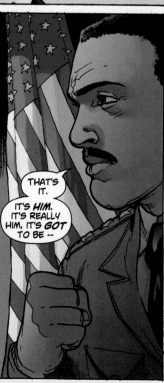

THAT'S IT.

IT'S *HIM.* IT'S REALLY HIM, IT'S *GOT* TO BE --

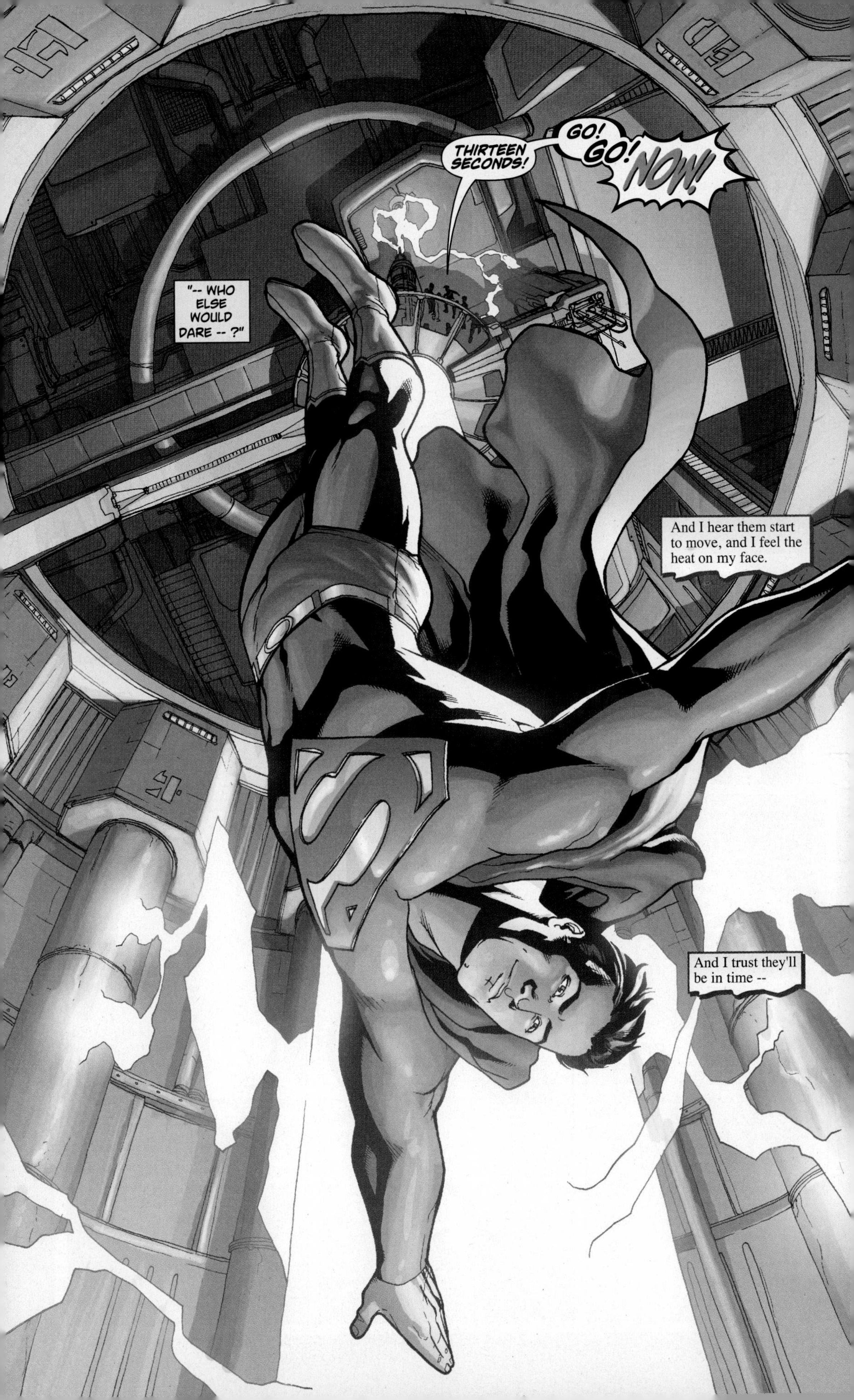
"-- WHO ELSE WOULD DARE -- ?"
THIRTEEN SECONDS!
GO! GO! NOW!
And I hear them start to move, and I feel the heat on my face.
And I trust they'll be in time --

DC

BUSIEK · NICIEZA · WOODS

ACTION COMICS®

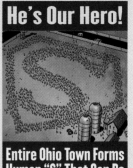

He's Our Hero!

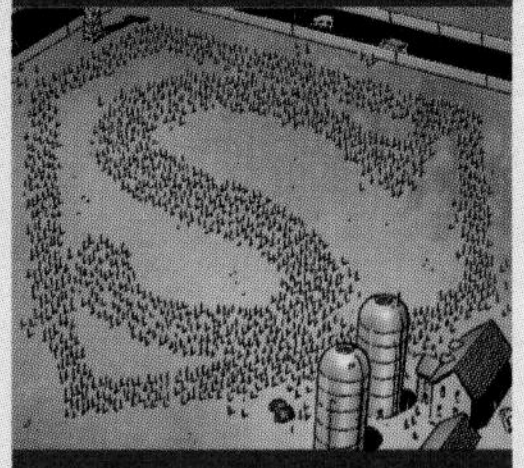

Entire Ohio Town Forms Human "S" That Can Be SEEN FROM SPACE!

SUPERMAN TO ALIENS:

WE'LL SMACK YOU UP!

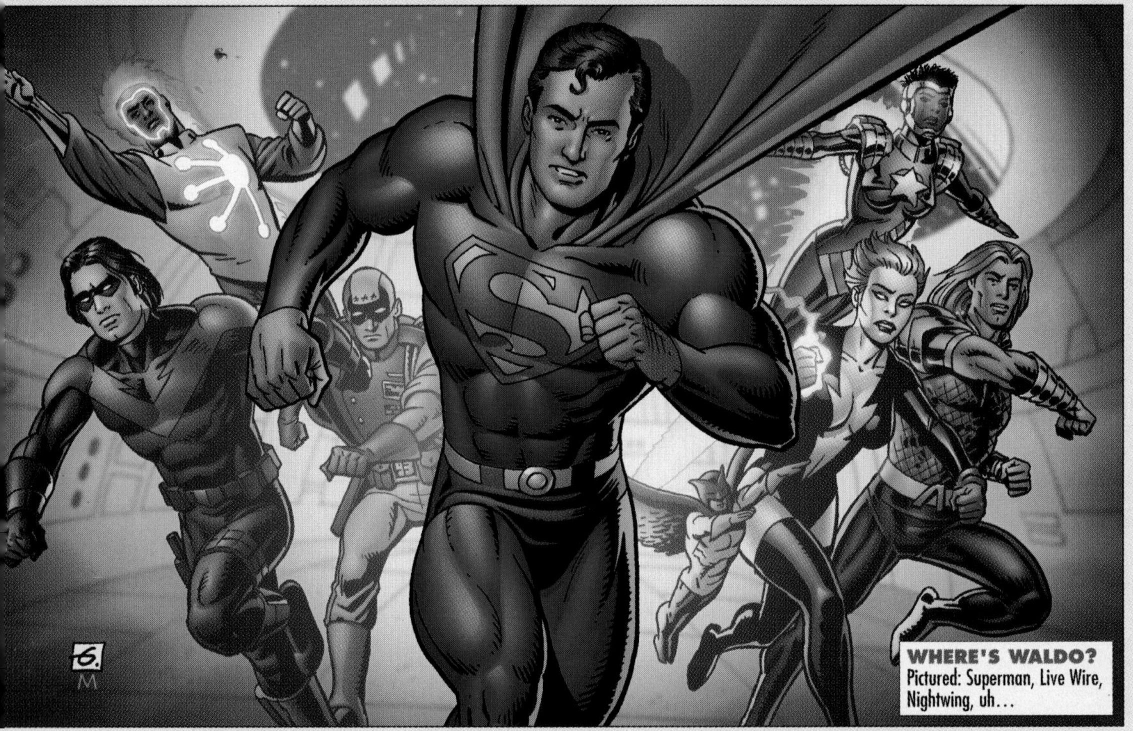

WHERE'S WALDO? Pictured: Superman, Live Wire, Nightwing, uh…

Man of Steel, Other Heroes, Defend Earth

Proves His Bona Fides on Global TV!

HOUSTON – Earth's most powerful telescopes strained to see past the Asteroid Belt, and billions were glued to their television screens, with just one thought: "Go, Superman, go!"

In one corner, wearing chrome-steel and power-blasters, the bad guys: The Auctioneer and his robot (are they even robots?) minions,

[Full Story, p. 3]

Did Gov't Deny Supes Clearance?

SHOCKER EXCLUSIVE!

WASHINGTON – Did authorities in Washington make it easier for the alien threat to overwhelm us? Did they refuse help from the world's greatest superhero? That's what millions are wondering, as reports surface that Superman offered his help immediately, as soon as the alien robots appeared in our skies -- and generals at the Pentagon turned him down!

Pentagon spokesmen stayed mum, refusing to comment on the allegations for what they termed "security reasons," but this paper has learned that communications were indeed initiated between Superman and the U.S. military, after the aliens' abortive attempt to steal the world-renowned St. Patrick's Cathedral -- and Superman was ordered to stand down.

Why? Because they didn't believe it was him. Because his clearance hadn't been fully vetted yet, since his return. We ask you. Frankly, this paper is shocked at such a cavalier

[See THOSE DUMB FEDS, p. 21]

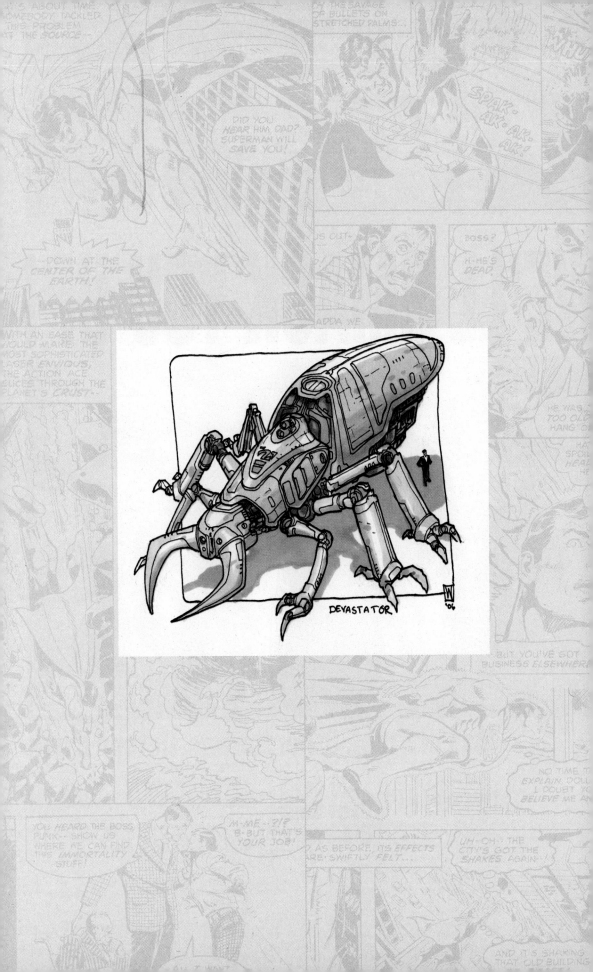

DEVASTATOR

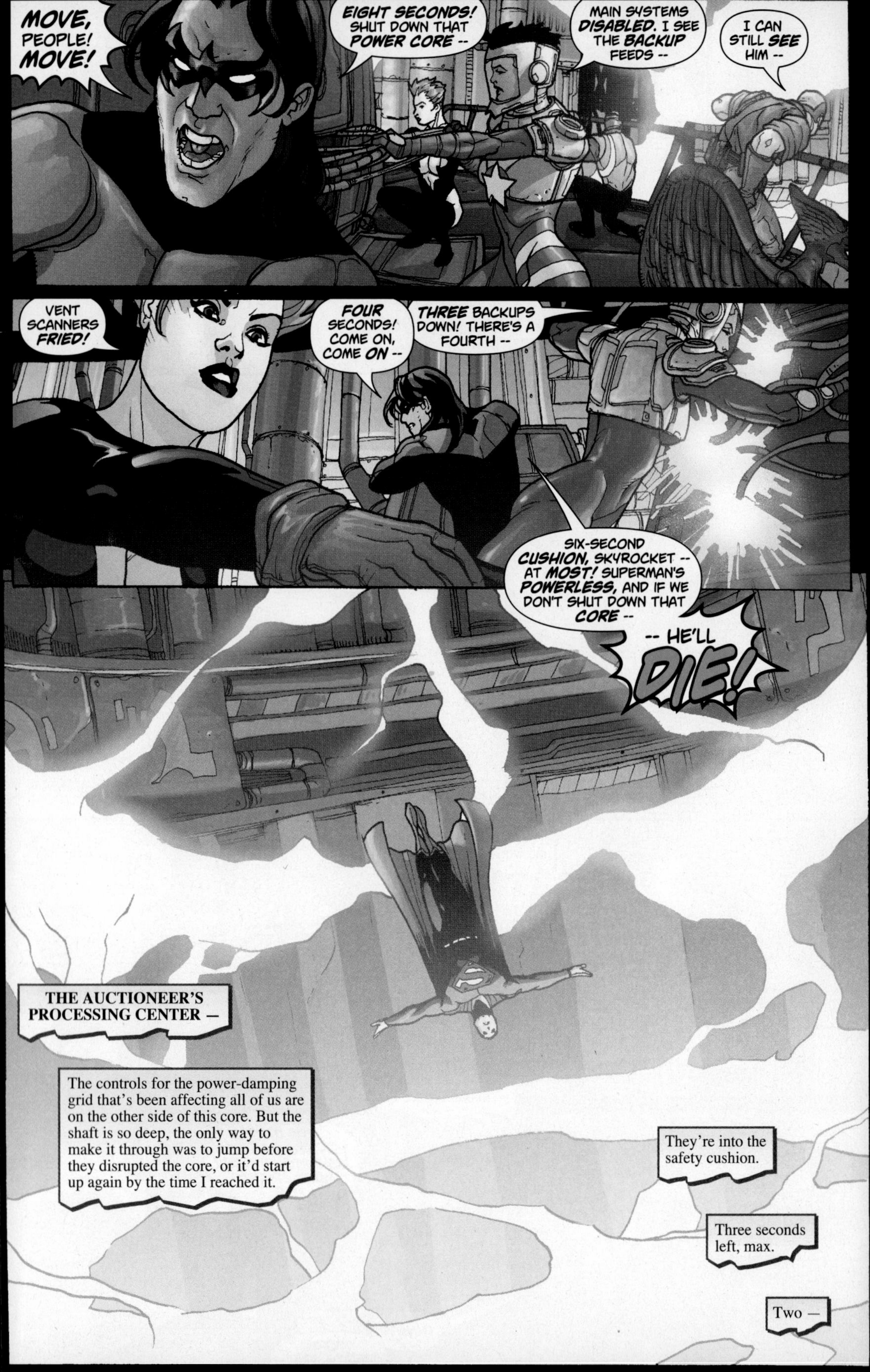

MOVE, PEOPLE! MOVE!
EIGHT SECONDS! SHUT DOWN THAT POWER CORE --
MAIN SYSTEMS DISABLED. I SEE THE BACKUP FEEDS --
I CAN STILL SEE HIM --
VENT SCANNERS FRIED!
FOUR SECONDS! COME ON, COME ON --
THREE BACKUPS DOWN! THERE'S A FOURTH --
SIX-SECOND CUSHION, SKYROCKET -- AT MOST! SUPERMAN'S POWERLESS, AND IF WE DON'T SHUT DOWN THAT CORE --
-- HE'LL DIE!
THE AUCTIONEER'S PROCESSING CENTER —
The controls for the power-damping grid that's been affecting all of us are on the other side of this core. But the shaft is so deep, the only way to make it through was to jump before they disrupted the core, or it'd start up again by the time I reached it.
They're into the safety cushion.
Three seconds left, max.
Two —

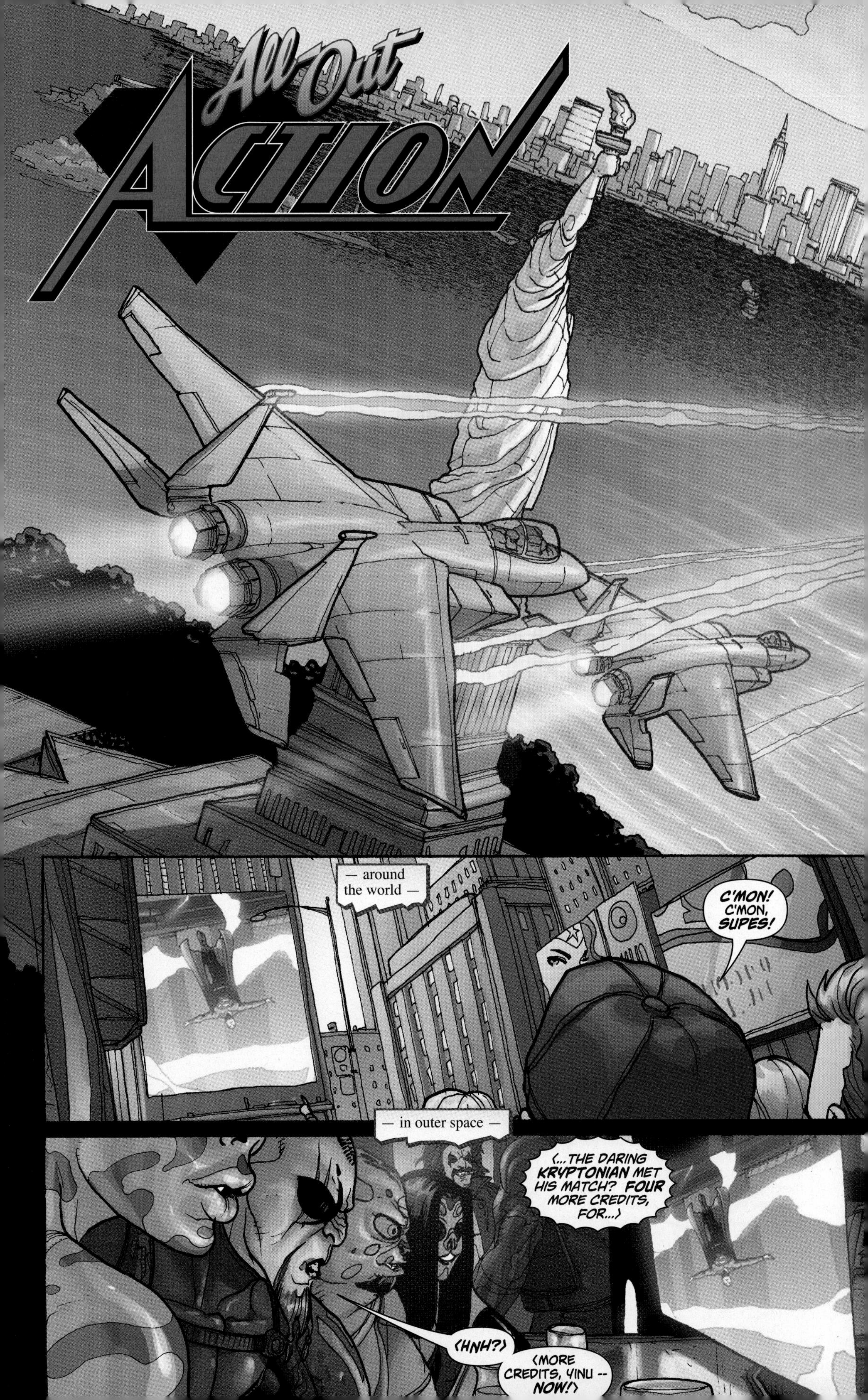
All Out Action
— around the world —
C'MON! C'MON, SUPES!
— in outer space —
‹...THE DARING KRYPTONIAN MET HIS MATCH? FOUR MORE CREDITS, FOR...›
‹HNH?›
‹MORE CREDITS, YINU -- NOW!›

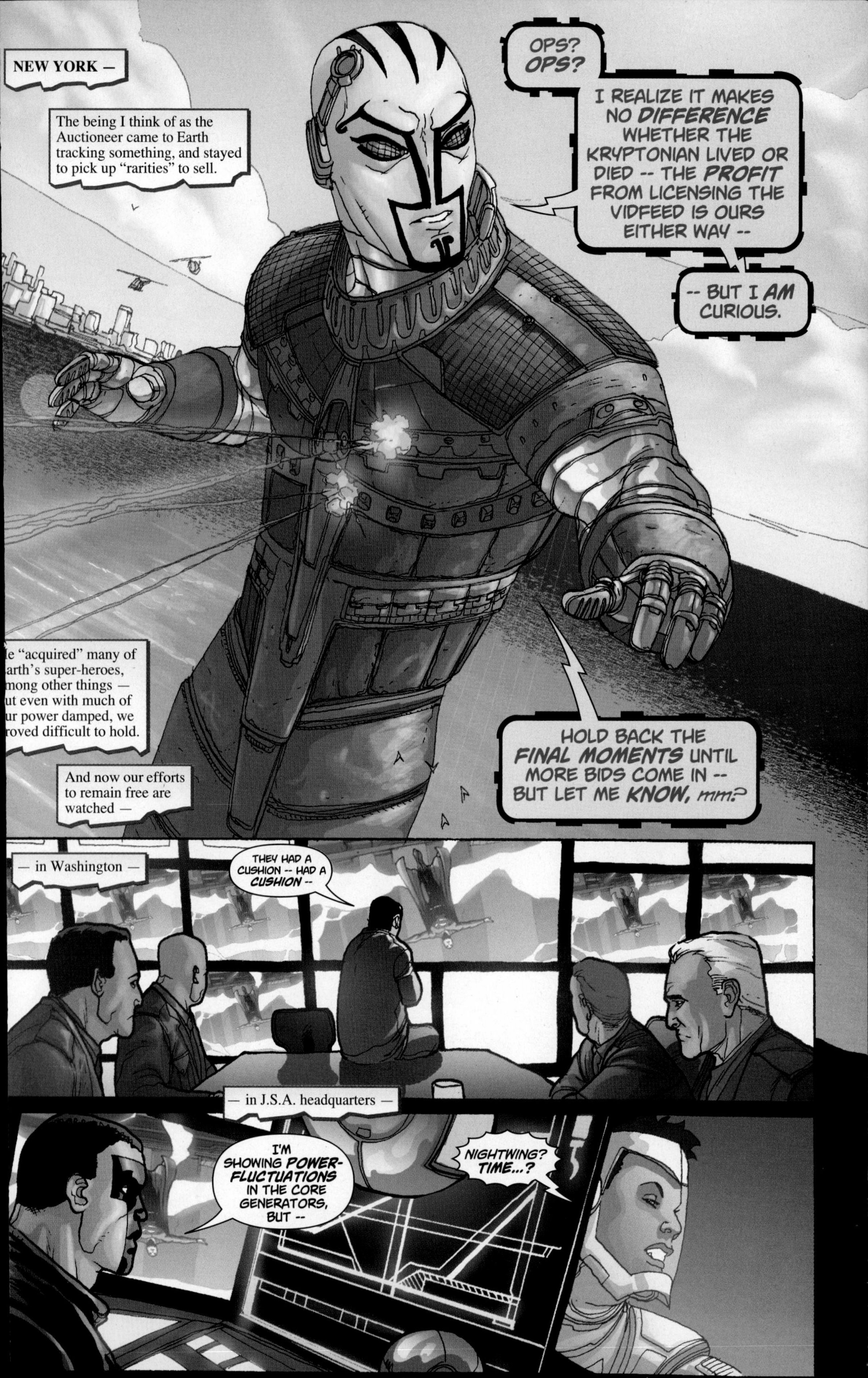
NEW YORK —
The being I think of as the Auctioneer came to Earth tracking something, and stayed to pick up “rarities” to sell.
OPS? OPS?
I REALIZE IT MAKES NO DIFFERENCE WHETHER THE KRYPTONIAN LIVED OR DIED -- THE PROFIT FROM LICENSING THE VIDFEED IS OURS EITHER WAY --
-- BUT I AM CURIOUS.
le “acquired” many of arth’s super-heroes, mong other things — ut even with much of ur power damped, we roved difficult to hold.
HOLD BACK THE FINAL MOMENTS UNTIL MORE BIDS COME IN -- BUT LET ME KNOW, mm?
And now our efforts to remain free are watched —
— in Washington —
THEY HAD A CUSHION -- HAD A CUSHION --
— in J.S.A. headquarters —
I'M SHOWING POWER-FLUCTUATIONS IN THE CORE GENERATORS, BUT --
NIGHTWING? TIME...?

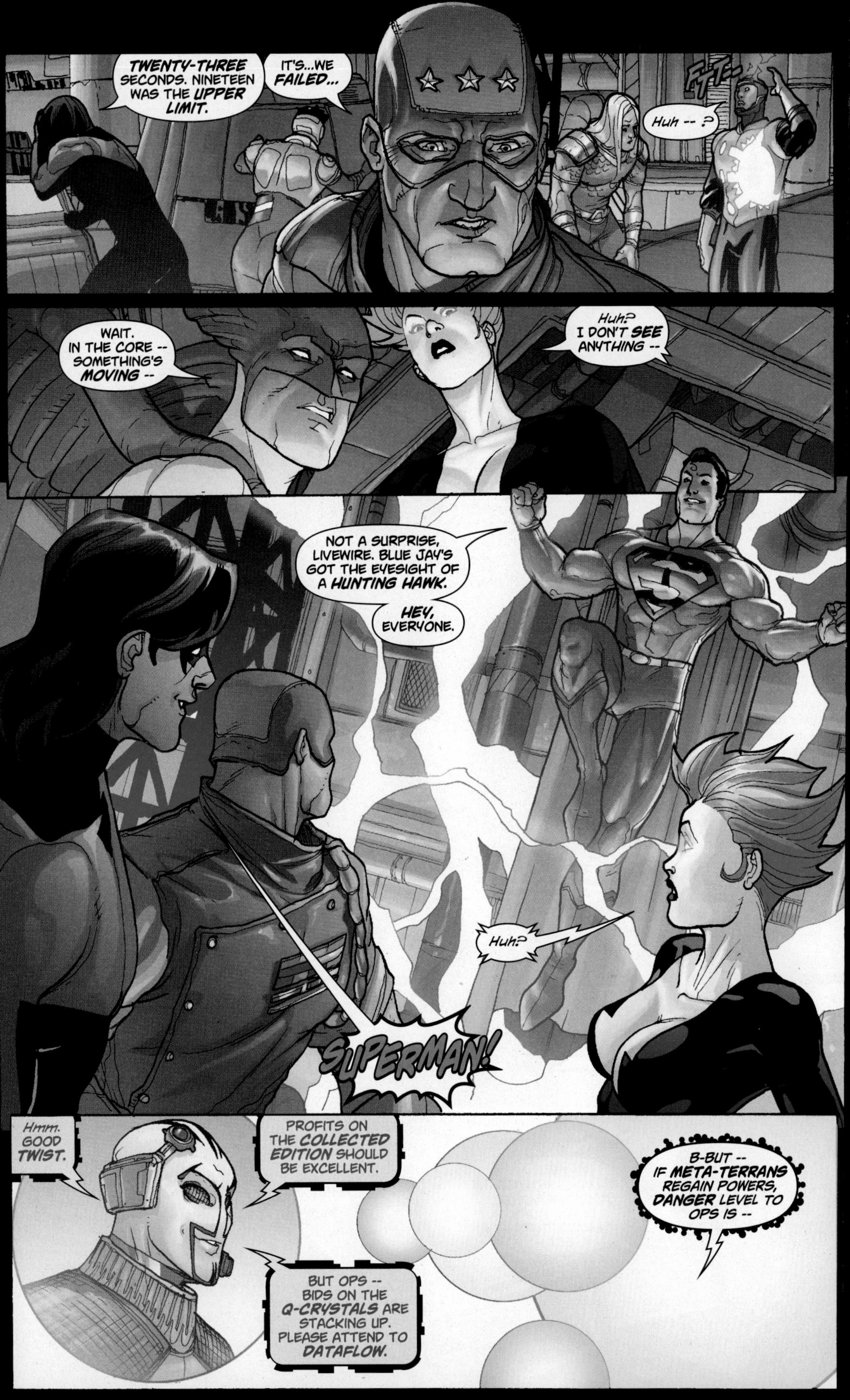
TWENTY-THREE SECONDS. NINETEEN WAS THE UPPER LIMIT.
IT'S...WE FAILED...
FFT--
Huh -- ?
WAIT. IN THE CORE -- SOMETHING'S MOVING --
Huh? I DON'T SEE ANYTHING --
NOT A SURPRISE, LIVEWIRE. BLUE JAY'S GOT THE EYESIGHT OF A HUNTING HAWK.
HEY, EVERYONE.
Huh?
SUPERMAN!
Hmm. GOOD TWIST.
PROFITS ON THE COLLECTED EDITION SHOULD BE EXCELLENT.
BUT OPS -- BIDS ON THE Q-CRYSTALS ARE STACKING UP. PLEASE ATTEND TO DATAFLOW.
B-BUT -- IF META-TERRANS REGAIN POWERS, DANGER LEVEL TO OPS IS --

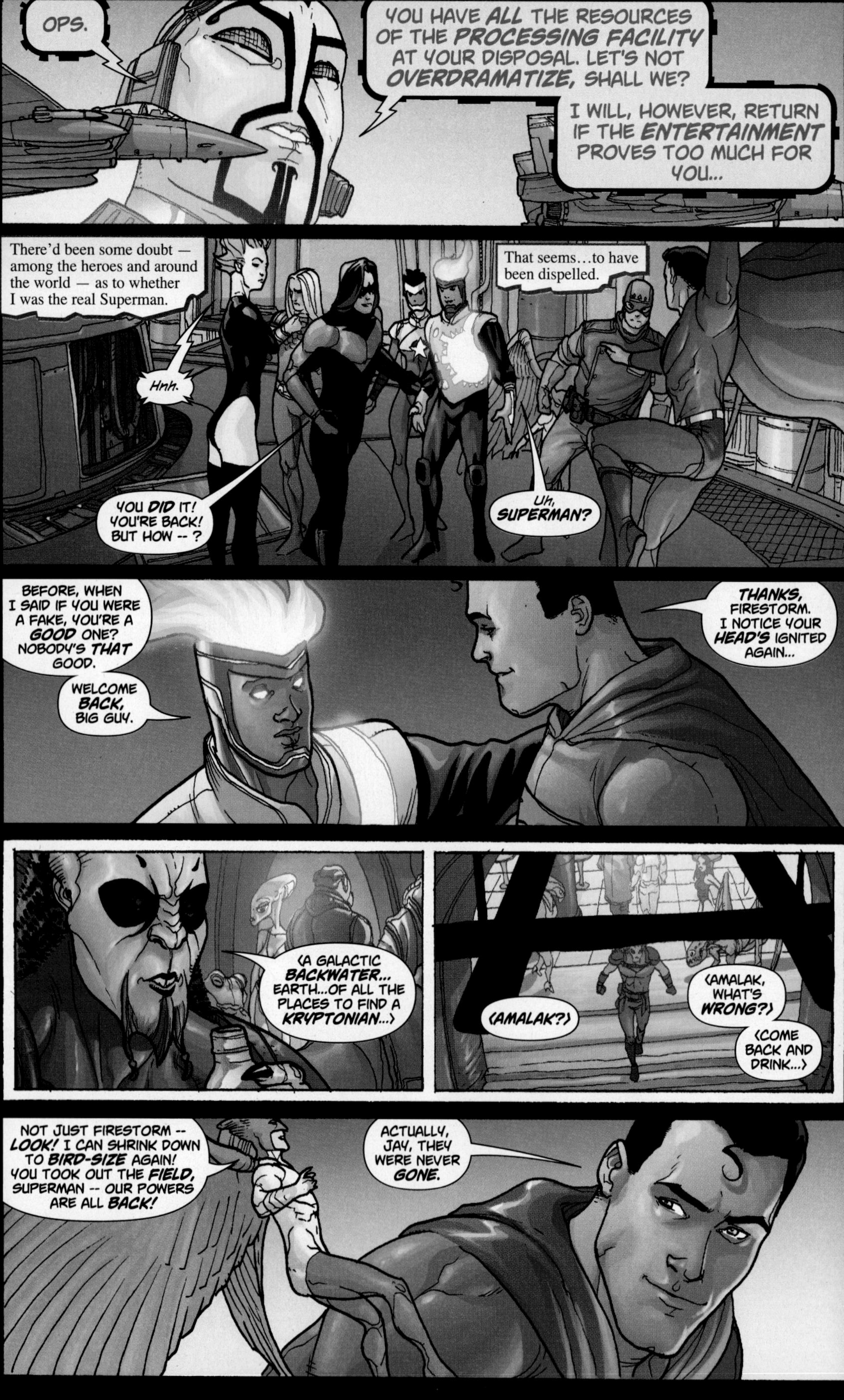
OPS.
YOU HAVE ALL THE RESOURCES OF THE PROCESSING FACILITY AT YOUR DISPOSAL. LET'S NOT OVERDRAMATIZE, SHALL WE?
I WILL, HOWEVER, RETURN IF THE ENTERTAINMENT PROVES TOO MUCH FOR YOU...
There'd been some doubt — among the heroes and around the world — as to whether I was the real Superman.
Hnh.
YOU DID IT! YOU'RE BACK! BUT HOW -- ?
That seems…to have been dispelled.
Uh, SUPERMAN?
BEFORE, WHEN I SAID IF YOU WERE A FAKE, YOU'RE A GOOD ONE? NOBODY'S THAT GOOD.
WELCOME BACK, BIG GUY.
THANKS, FIRESTORM. I NOTICE YOUR HEAD'S IGNITED AGAIN...
(A GALACTIC BACKWATER... EARTH...OF ALL THE PLACES TO FIND A KRYPTONIAN...)
(AMALAK?)
(AMALAK, WHAT'S WRONG?)
(COME BACK AND DRINK...)
NOT JUST FIRESTORM -- LOOK! I CAN SHRINK DOWN TO BIRD-SIZE AGAIN! YOU TOOK OUT THE FIELD, SUPERMAN -- OUR POWERS ARE ALL BACK!
ACTUALLY, JAY, THEY WERE NEVER GONE.

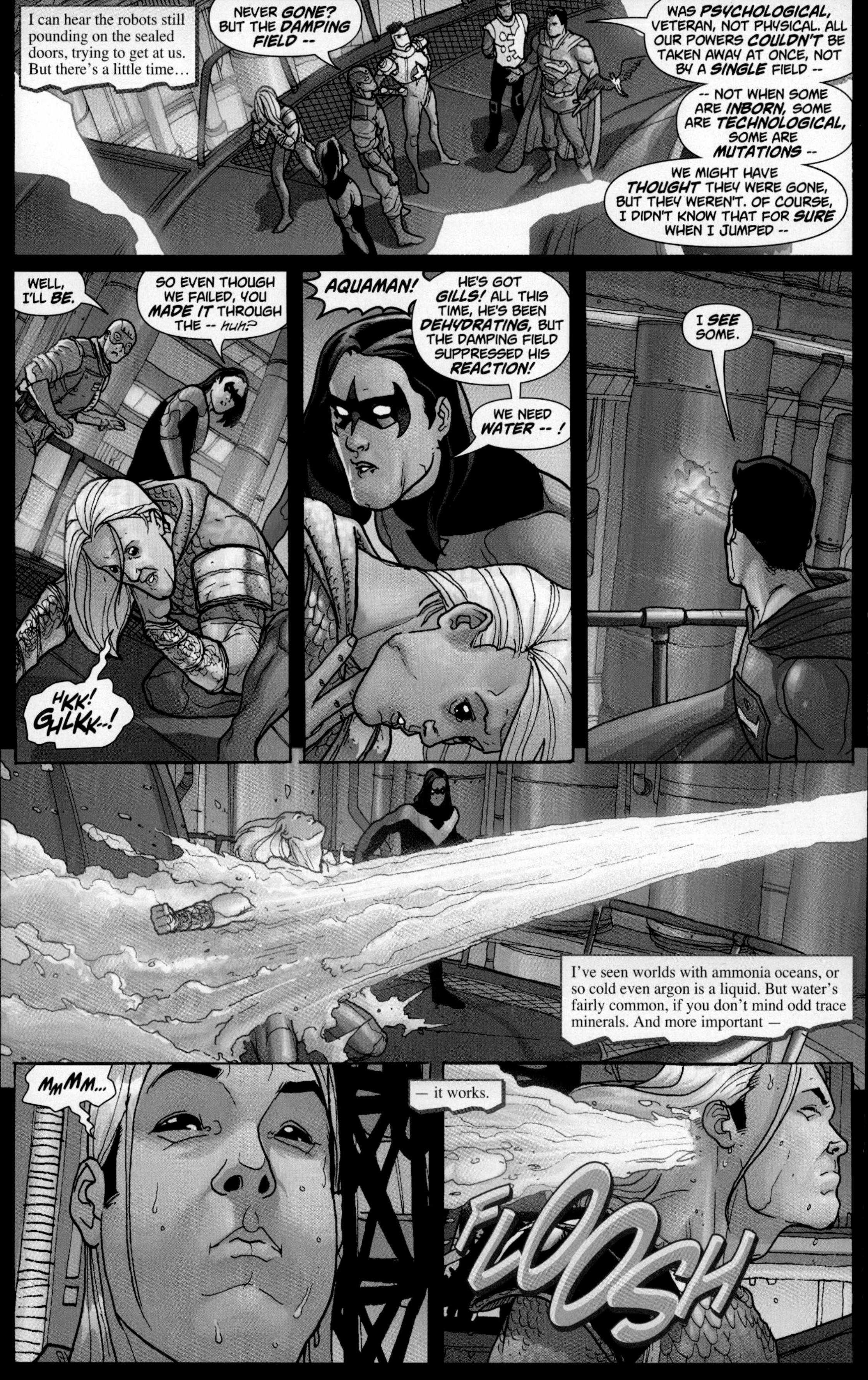
I can hear the robots still pounding on the sealed doors, trying to get at us. But there's a little time…
NEVER GONE? BUT THE DAMPING FIELD --
WAS PSYCHOLOGICAL, VETERAN, NOT PHYSICAL. ALL OUR POWERS COULDN'T BE TAKEN AWAY AT ONCE, NOT BY A SINGLE FIELD --
-- NOT WHEN SOME ARE INBORN, SOME ARE TECHNOLOGICAL, SOME ARE MUTATIONS --
WE MIGHT HAVE THOUGHT THEY WERE GONE, BUT THEY WEREN'T. OF COURSE, I DIDN'T KNOW THAT FOR SURE WHEN I JUMPED --
WELL, I'LL BE.
SO EVEN THOUGH WE FAILED, YOU MADE IT THROUGH THE -- huh?
HKK! GHLKK--!
AQUAMAN!
HE'S GOT GILLS! ALL THIS TIME, HE'S BEEN DEHYDRATING, BUT THE DAMPING FIELD SUPPRESSED HIS REACTION!
WE NEED WATER -- !
I SEE SOME.
I've seen worlds with ammonia oceans, or so cold even argon is a liquid. But water's fairly common, if you don't mind odd trace minerals. And more important —
MMMM...
— it works.
FLOOSH

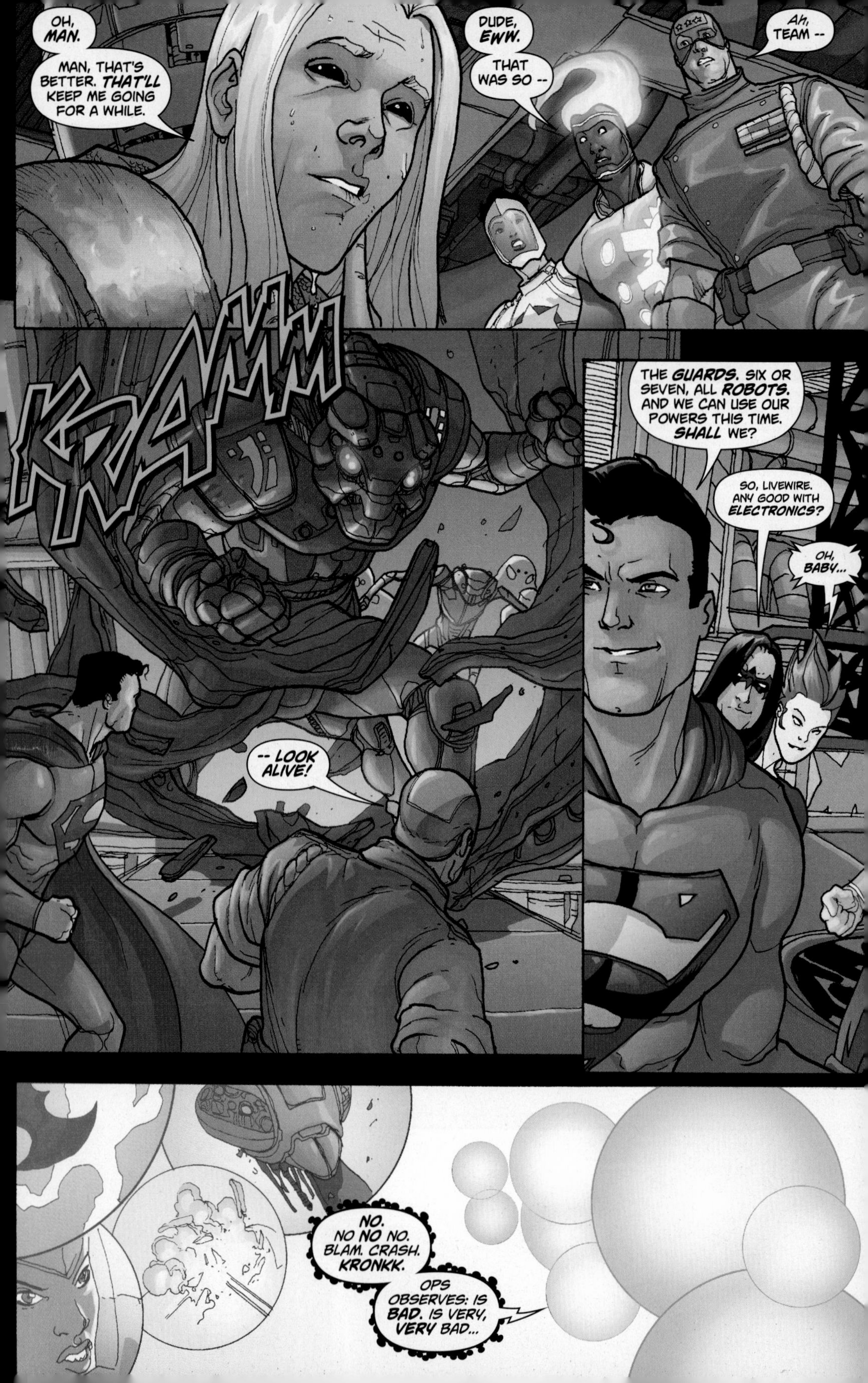

OH, **MAN.**
MAN, THAT'S BETTER. ***THAT'LL*** KEEP ME GOING FOR A WHILE.
DUDE, ***EWW.***
THAT WAS SO --
Ah, TEAM --
KRAMM
-- ***LOOK ALIVE!***
THE ***GUARDS.*** SIX OR SEVEN, ALL ***ROBOTS.*** AND WE CAN USE OUR POWERS THIS TIME. ***SHALL*** WE?
SO, LIVEWIRE. ANY GOOD WITH ***ELECTRONICS?***
OH, ***BABY...***
NO. NO **NO** NO. BLAM. CRASH. **KRONKK.**
OPS OBSERVES: IS ***BAD.*** IS VERY, ***VERY*** BAD...

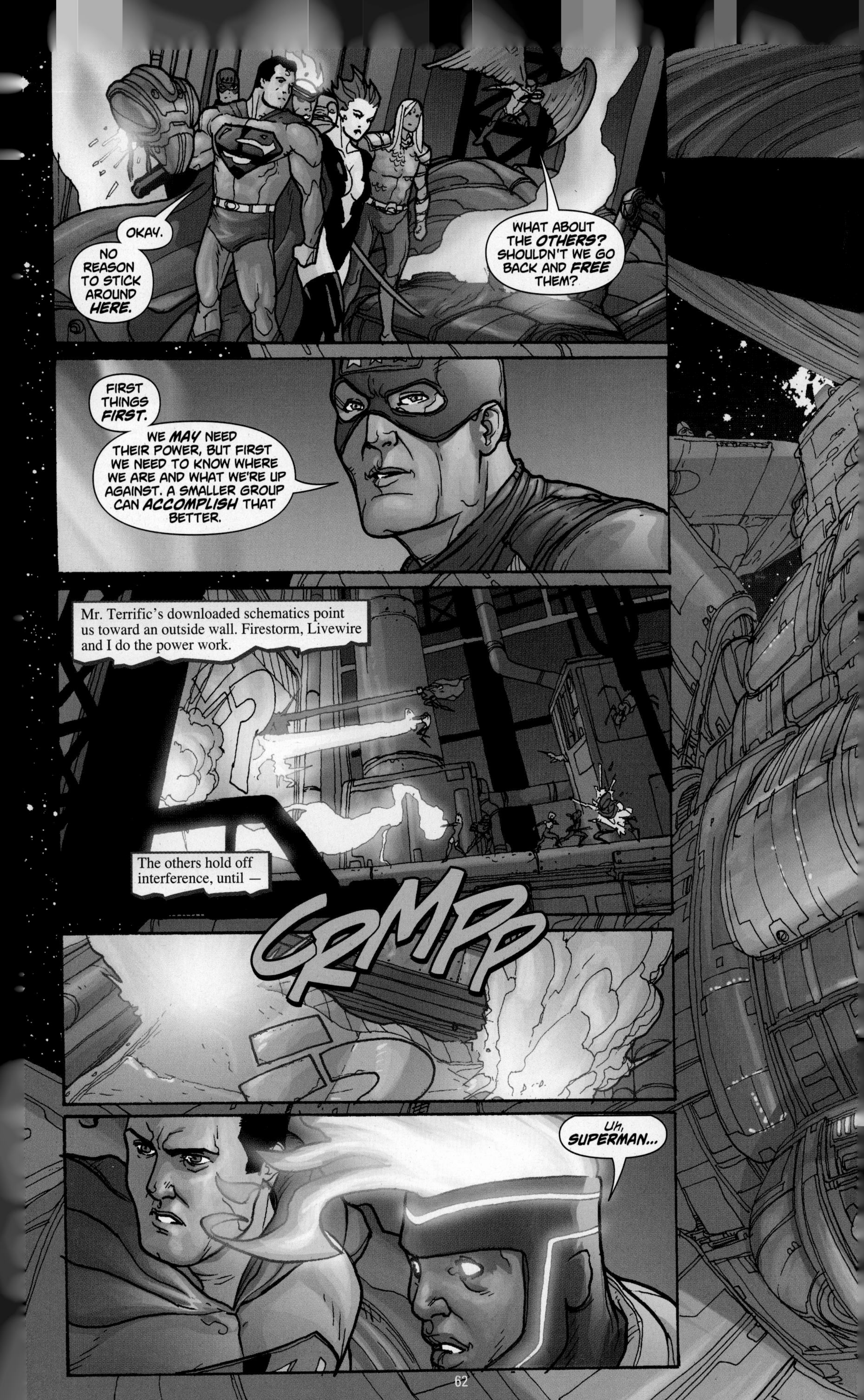

OKAY.
NO REASON TO STICK AROUND HERE.
WHAT ABOUT THE OTHERS? SHOULDN'T WE GO BACK AND FREE THEM?
FIRST THINGS FIRST.
WE MAY NEED THEIR POWER, BUT FIRST WE NEED TO KNOW WHERE WE ARE AND WHAT WE'RE UP AGAINST. A SMALLER GROUP CAN ACCOMPLISH THAT BETTER.
Mr. Terrific's downloaded schematics point us toward an outside wall. Firestorm, Livewire and I do the power work.
The others hold off interference, until —
CRMPP
Uh, SUPERMAN...

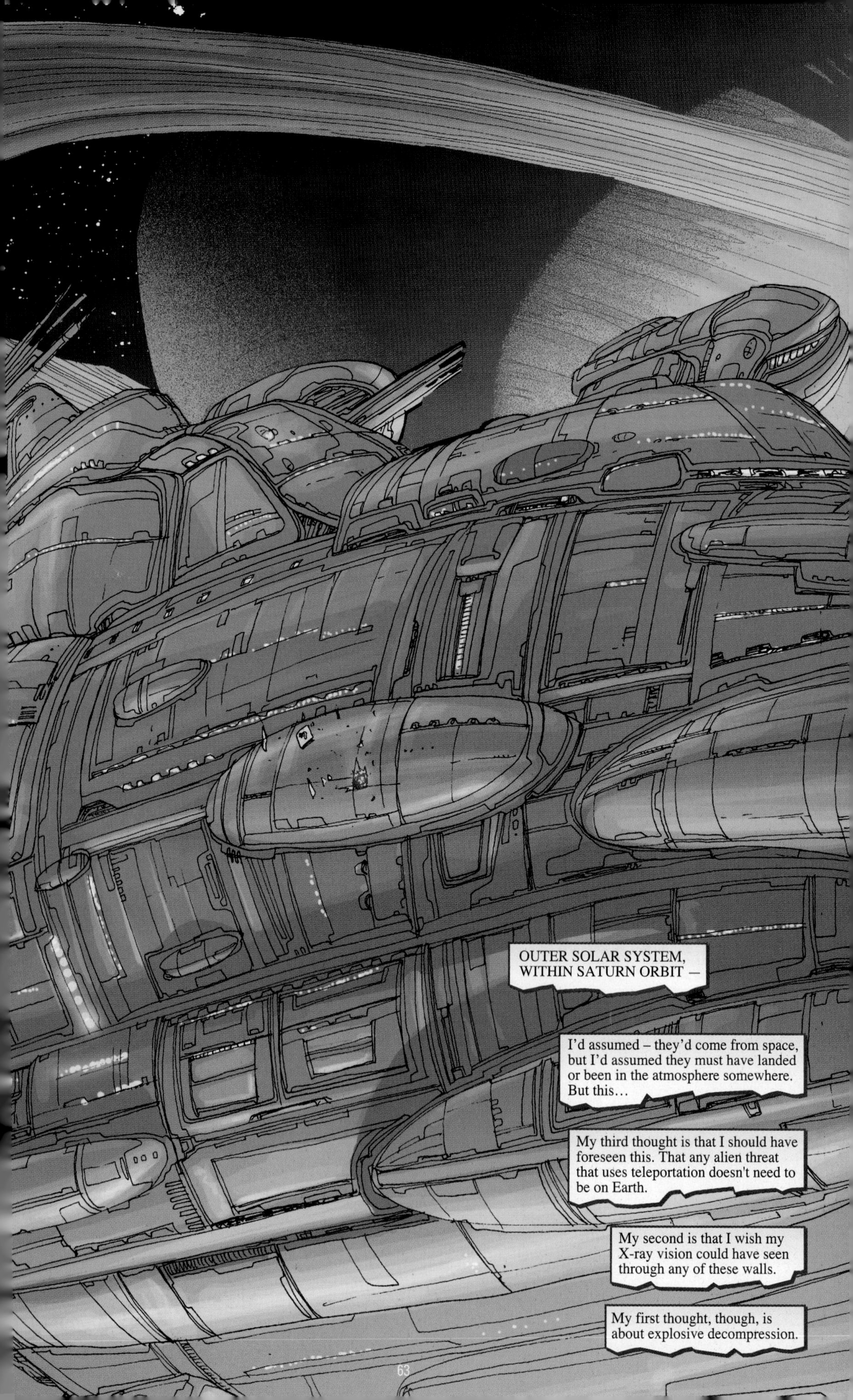
OUTER SOLAR SYSTEM, WITHIN SATURN ORBIT –
I'd assumed – they'd come from space, but I'd assumed they must have landed or been in the atmosphere somewhere. But this…
My third thought is that I should have foreseen this. That any alien threat that uses teleportation doesn't need to be on Earth.
My second is that I wish my X-ray vision could have seen through any of these walls.
My first thought, though, is about explosive decompression.

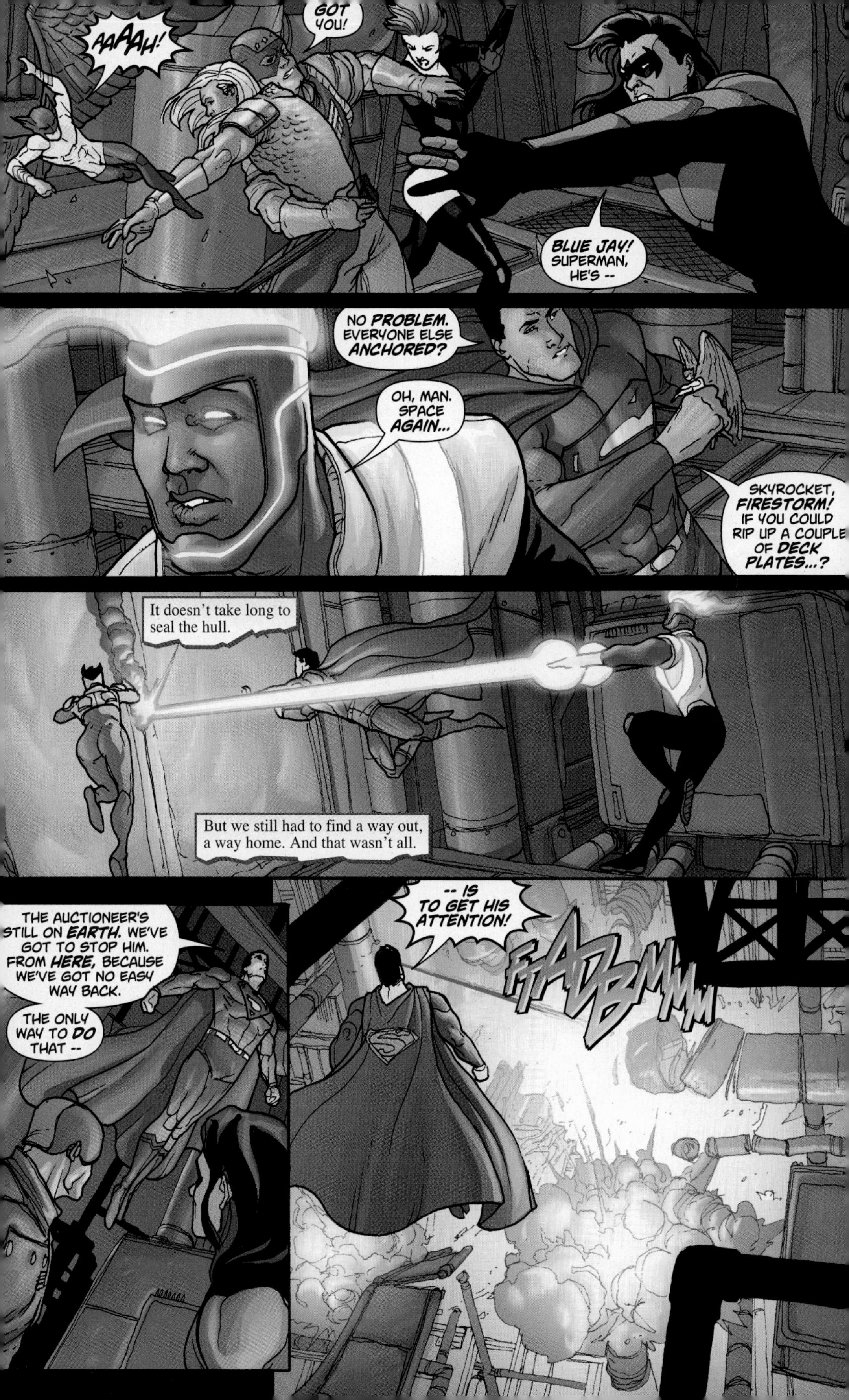
AAAAAH!
GOT YOU!
BLUE JAY! SUPERMAN, HE'S --
NO PROBLEM. EVERYONE ELSE ANCHORED?
OH, MAN. SPACE AGAIN...
SKYROCKET, FIRESTORM! IF YOU COULD RIP UP A COUPLE OF DECK PLATES...?
It doesn't take long to seal the hull.
But we still had to find a way out, a way home. And that wasn't all.
THE AUCTIONEER'S STILL ON EARTH. WE'VE GOT TO STOP HIM. FROM HERE, BECAUSE WE'VE GOT NO EASY WAY BACK.
THE ONLY WAY TO DO THAT --
-- IS TO GET HIS ATTENTION!
FTADBMMM

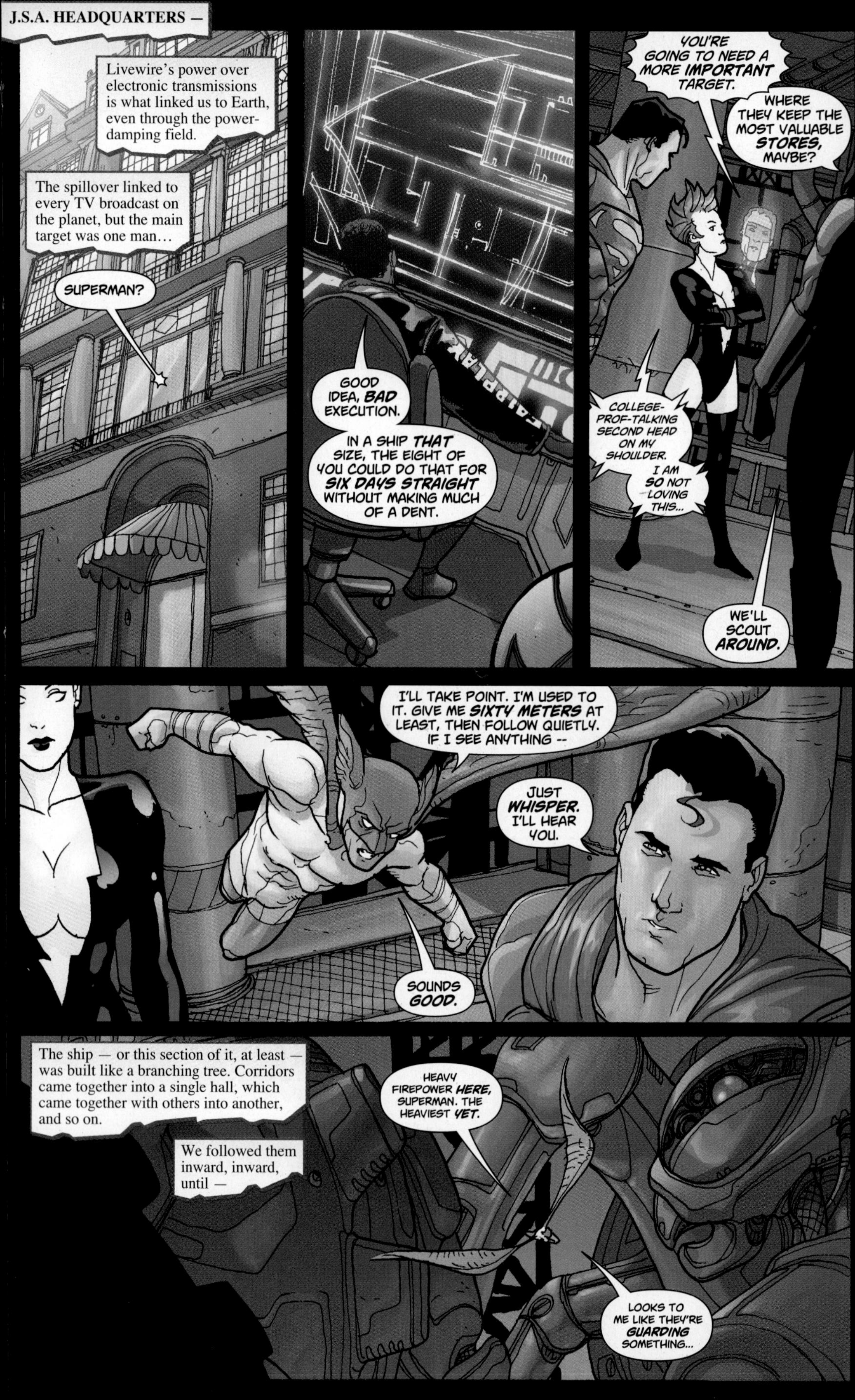
J.S.A. HEADQUARTERS —
Livewire's power over electronic transmissions is what linked us to Earth, even through the power-damping field.
The spillover linked to every TV broadcast on the planet, but the main target was one man…
SUPERMAN?
GOOD IDEA, BAD EXECUTION.
IN A SHIP THAT SIZE, THE EIGHT OF YOU COULD DO THAT FOR SIX DAYS STRAIGHT WITHOUT MAKING MUCH OF A DENT.
YOU'RE GOING TO NEED A MORE IMPORTANT TARGET.
WHERE THEY KEEP THE MOST VALUABLE STORES, MAYBE?
COLLEGE-PROF-TALKING SECOND HEAD ON MY SHOULDER.
I AM SO NOT LOVING THIS...
WE'LL SCOUT AROUND.
I'LL TAKE POINT. I'M USED TO IT. GIVE ME SIXTY METERS AT LEAST, THEN FOLLOW QUIETLY. IF I SEE ANYTHING --
JUST WHISPER. I'LL HEAR YOU.
SOUNDS GOOD.
The ship — or this section of it, at least — was built like a branching tree. Corridors came together into a single hall, which came together with others into another, and so on.
We followed them inward, inward, until —
HEAVY FIREPOWER HERE, SUPERMAN. THE HEAVIEST YET.
LOOKS TO ME LIKE THEY'RE GUARDING SOMETHING...

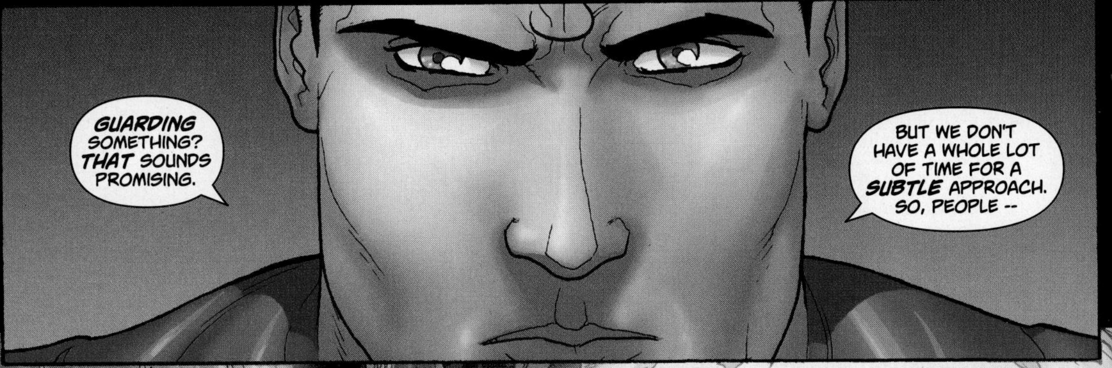
GUARDING SOMETHING? THAT SOUNDS PROMISING.
BUT WE DON'T HAVE A WHOLE LOT OF TIME FOR A SUBTLE APPROACH. SO, PEOPLE --
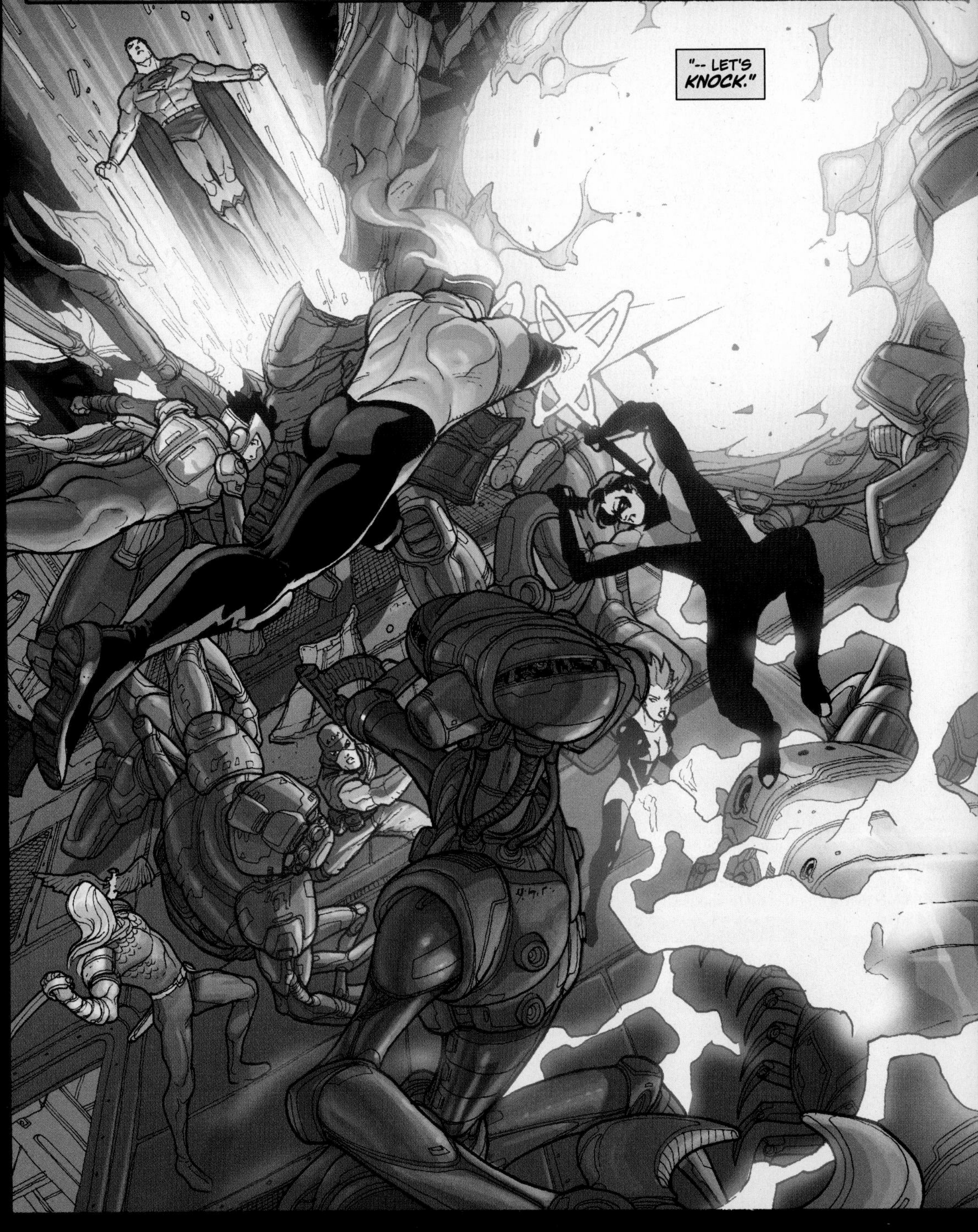
"-- LET'S KNOCK."

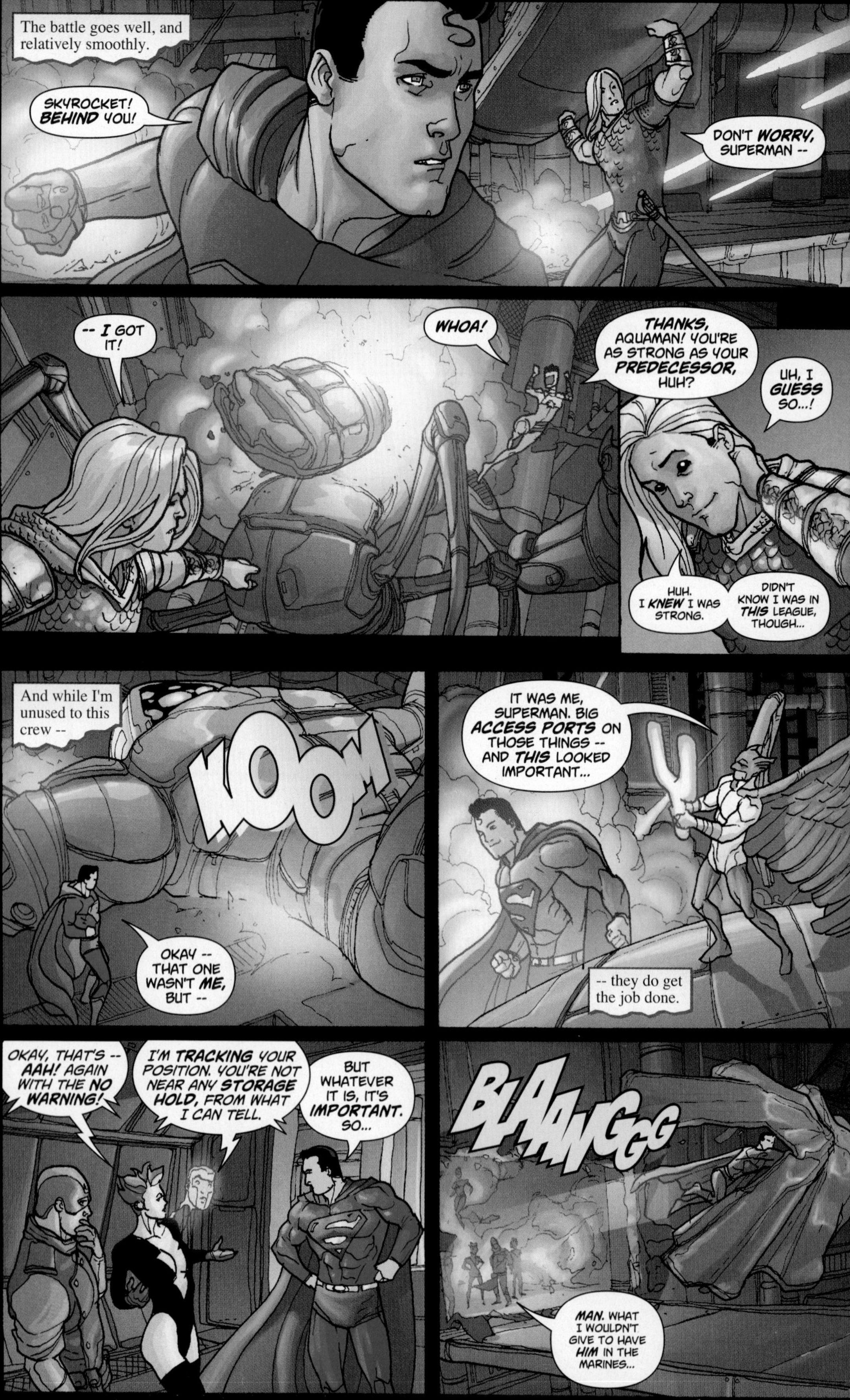

The battle goes well, and relatively smoothly.
SKYROCKET! BEHIND YOU!
DON'T WORRY, SUPERMAN --
-- I GOT IT!
WHOA!
THANKS, AQUAMAN! YOU'RE AS STRONG AS YOUR PREDECESSOR, HUH?
UH, I GUESS SO...!
HUH. I KNEW I WAS STRONG.
DIDN'T KNOW I WAS IN THIS LEAGUE, THOUGH...
And while I'm unused to this crew --
KOOM
OKAY -- THAT ONE WASN'T ME, BUT --
IT WAS ME, SUPERMAN. BIG ACCESS PORTS ON THOSE THINGS -- AND THIS LOOKED IMPORTANT...
-- they do get the job done.
OKAY, THAT'S -- AAH! AGAIN WITH THE NO WARNING!
I'M TRACKING YOUR POSITION. YOU'RE NOT NEAR ANY STORAGE HOLD, FROM WHAT I CAN TELL.
BUT WHATEVER IT IS, IT'S IMPORTANT. SO...
BLAANGGG
MAN. WHAT I WOULDN'T GIVE TO HAVE HIM IN THE MARINES...

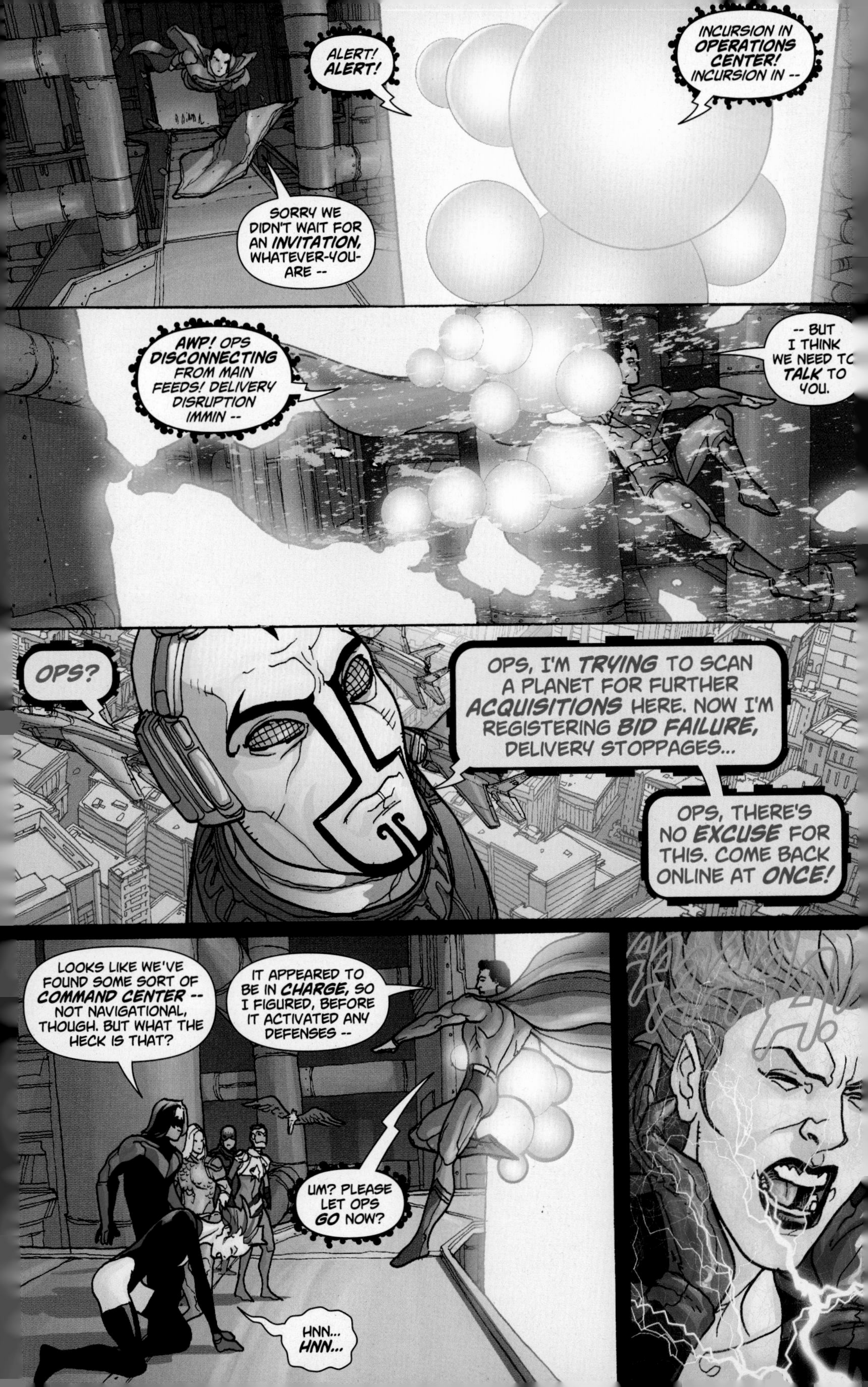
ALERT! ALERT!
INCURSION IN OPERATIONS CENTER! INCURSION IN --
SORRY WE DIDN'T WAIT FOR AN INVITATION, WHATEVER-YOU-ARE --
AWP! OPS DISCONNECTING FROM MAIN FEEDS! DELIVERY DISRUPTION IMMIN --
-- BUT I THINK WE NEED TO TALK TO YOU.
OPS?
OPS, I'M TRYING TO SCAN A PLANET FOR FURTHER ACQUISITIONS HERE. NOW I'M REGISTERING BID FAILURE, DELIVERY STOPPAGES...
OPS, THERE'S NO EXCUSE FOR THIS. COME BACK ONLINE AT ONCE!
LOOKS LIKE WE'VE FOUND SOME SORT OF COMMAND CENTER -- NOT NAVIGATIONAL, THOUGH. BUT WHAT THE HECK IS THAT?
IT APPEARED TO BE IN CHARGE, SO I FIGURED, BEFORE IT ACTIVATED ANY DEFENSES --
UM? PLEASE LET OPS GO NOW?
HNN... HNN...

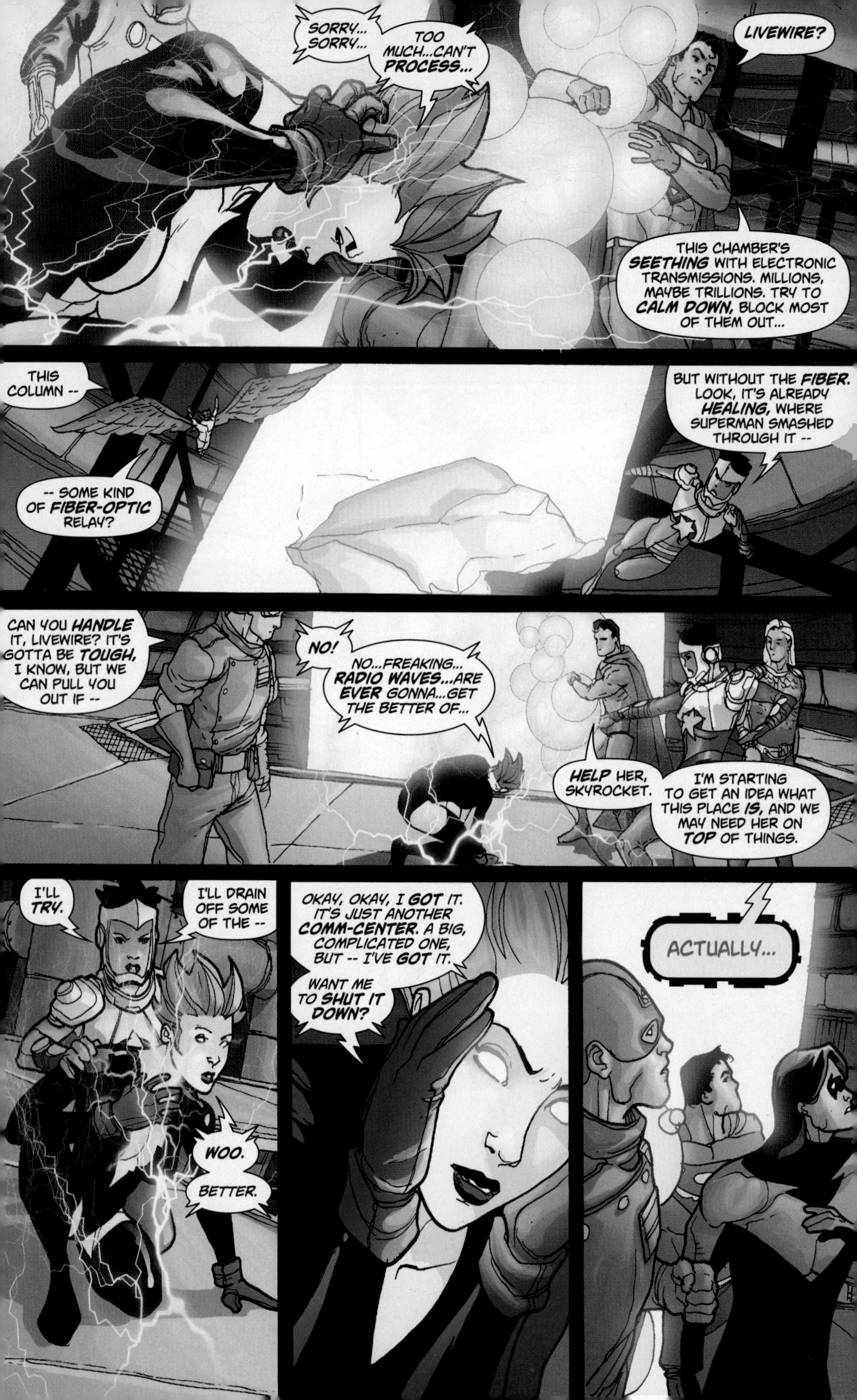
SORRY... SORRY...
TOO MUCH...CAN'T PROCESS...
LIVEWIRE?
THIS CHAMBER'S SEETHING WITH ELECTRONIC TRANSMISSIONS. MILLIONS, MAYBE TRILLIONS. TRY TO CALM DOWN, BLOCK MOST OF THEM OUT...
THIS COLUMN --
-- SOME KIND OF FIBER-OPTIC RELAY?
BUT WITHOUT THE FIBER. LOOK, IT'S ALREADY HEALING, WHERE SUPERMAN SMASHED THROUGH IT --
CAN YOU HANDLE IT, LIVEWIRE? IT'S GOTTA BE TOUGH, I KNOW, BUT WE CAN PULL YOU OUT IF --
NO!
NO...FREAKING... RADIO WAVES...ARE EVER GONNA...GET THE BETTER OF...
HELP HER, SKYROCKET.
I'M STARTING TO GET AN IDEA WHAT THIS PLACE IS, AND WE MAY NEED HER ON TOP OF THINGS.
I'LL TRY.
I'LL DRAIN OFF SOME OF THE --
WOO.
BETTER.
OKAY, OKAY, I GOT IT. IT'S JUST ANOTHER COMM-CENTER. A BIG, COMPLICATED ONE, BUT -- I'VE GOT IT.
WANT ME TO SHUT IT DOWN?
ACTUALLY...

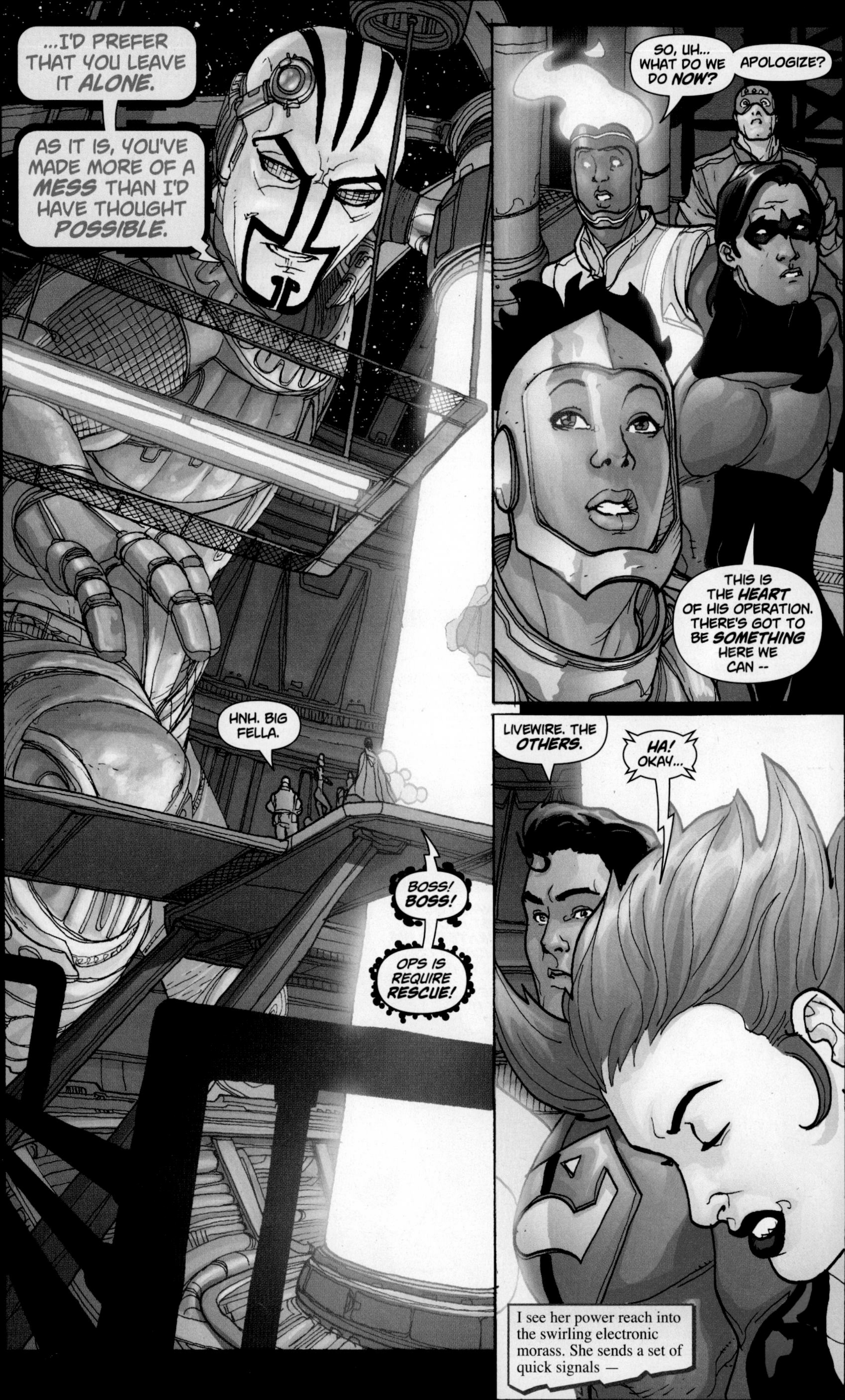
...I'D PREFER THAT YOU LEAVE IT ALONE.
AS IT IS, YOU'VE MADE MORE OF A MESS THAN I'D HAVE THOUGHT POSSIBLE.
HNH. BIG FELLA.
BOSS! BOSS!
OPS IS REQUIRE RESCUE!
SO, UH... WHAT DO WE DO NOW?
APOLOGIZE?
THIS IS THE HEART OF HIS OPERATION. THERE'S GOT TO BE SOMETHING HERE WE CAN --
LIVEWIRE. THE OTHERS.
HA! OKAY...
I see her power reach into the swirling electronic morass. She sends a set of quick signals —

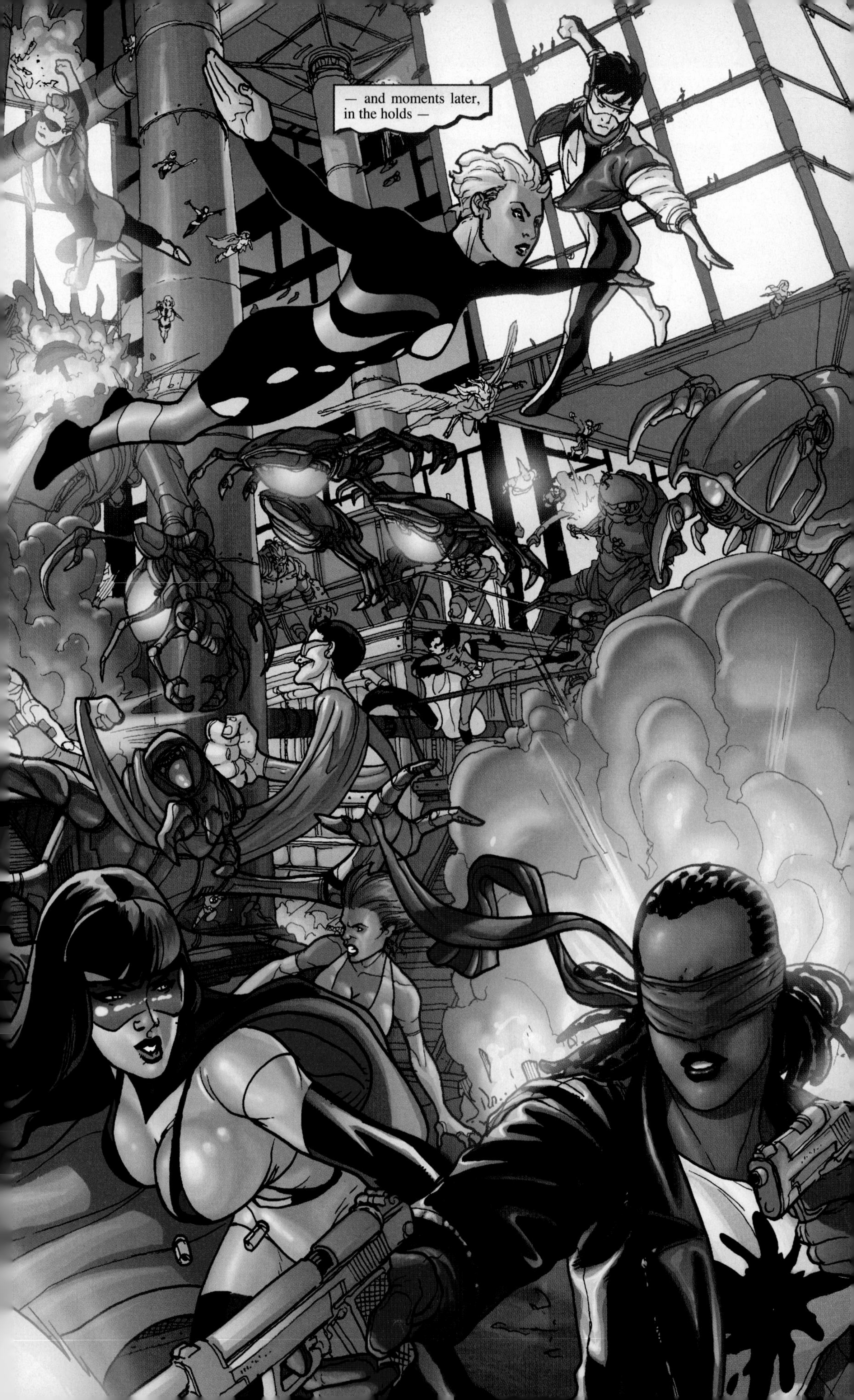
— and moments later, in the holds —

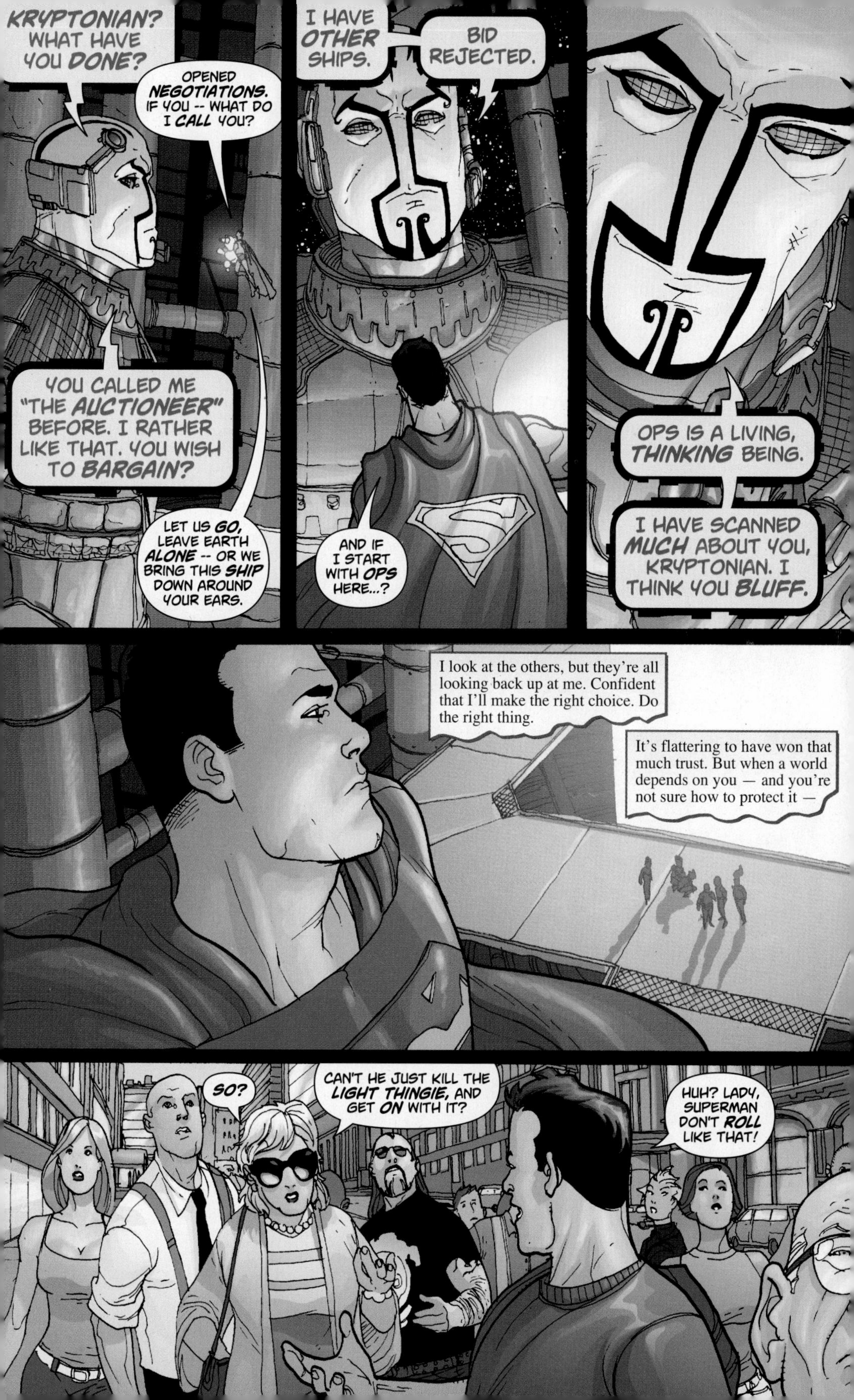
KRYPTONIAN? WHAT HAVE YOU DONE?
OPENED NEGOTIATIONS. IF YOU -- WHAT DO I CALL YOU?
YOU CALLED ME "THE AUCTIONEER" BEFORE. I RATHER LIKE THAT. YOU WISH TO BARGAIN?
LET US GO, LEAVE EARTH ALONE -- OR WE BRING THIS SHIP DOWN AROUND YOUR EARS.
I HAVE OTHER SHIPS.
BID REJECTED.
AND IF I START WITH OPS HERE...?
OPS IS A LIVING, THINKING BEING.
I HAVE SCANNED MUCH ABOUT YOU, KRYPTONIAN. I THINK YOU BLUFF.
I look at the others, but they're all looking back up at me. Confident that I'll make the right choice. Do the right thing.
It's flattering to have won that much trust. But when a world depends on you — and you're not sure how to protect it —
SO?
CAN'T HE JUST KILL THE LIGHT THINGIE, AND GET ON WITH IT?
HUH? LADY, SUPERMAN DON'T ROLL LIKE THAT!

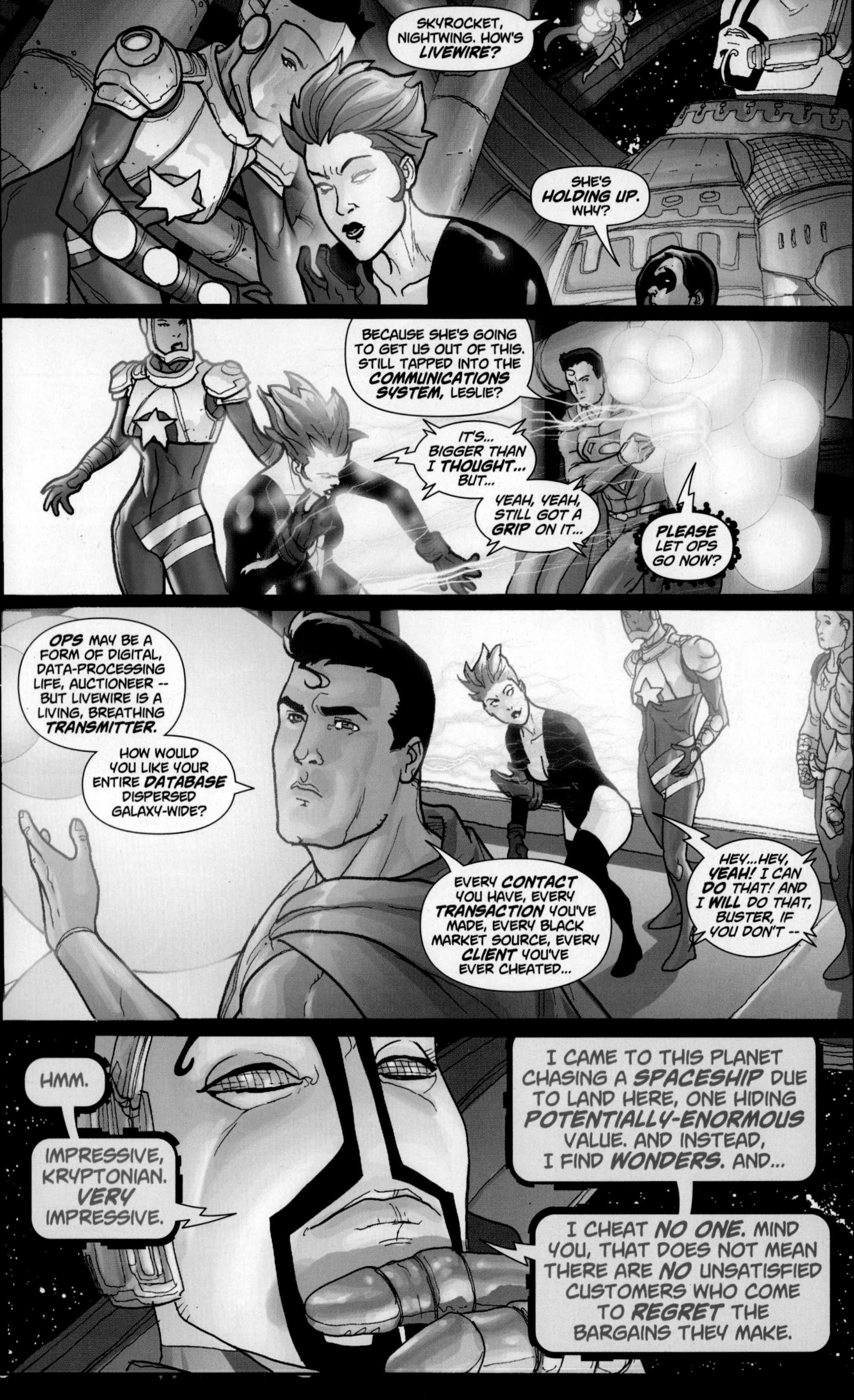
SKYROCKET, NIGHTWING. HOW'S LIVEWIRE?
SHE'S HOLDING UP. WHY?
BECAUSE SHE'S GOING TO GET US OUT OF THIS. STILL TAPPED INTO THE COMMUNICATIONS SYSTEM, LESLIE?
IT'S... BIGGER THAN I THOUGHT... BUT...
YEAH, YEAH, STILL GOT A GRIP ON IT...
PLEASE LET OPS GO NOW?
OPS MAY BE A FORM OF DIGITAL, DATA-PROCESSING LIFE, AUCTIONEER -- BUT LIVEWIRE IS A LIVING, BREATHING TRANSMITTER.
HOW WOULD YOU LIKE YOUR ENTIRE DATABASE DISPERSED GALAXY-WIDE?
EVERY CONTACT YOU HAVE, EVERY TRANSACTION YOU'VE MADE, EVERY BLACK MARKET SOURCE, EVERY CLIENT YOU'VE EVER CHEATED...
HEY...HEY, YEAH! I CAN DO THAT! AND I WILL DO THAT, BUSTER, IF YOU DON'T --
HMM.
IMPRESSIVE, KRYPTONIAN. VERY IMPRESSIVE.
I CAME TO THIS PLANET CHASING A SPACESHIP DUE TO LAND HERE, ONE HIDING POTENTIALLY-ENORMOUS VALUE. AND INSTEAD, I FIND WONDERS. AND...
I CHEAT NO ONE. MIND YOU, THAT DOES NOT MEAN THERE ARE NO UNSATISFIED CUSTOMERS WHO COME TO REGRET THE BARGAINS THEY MAKE.

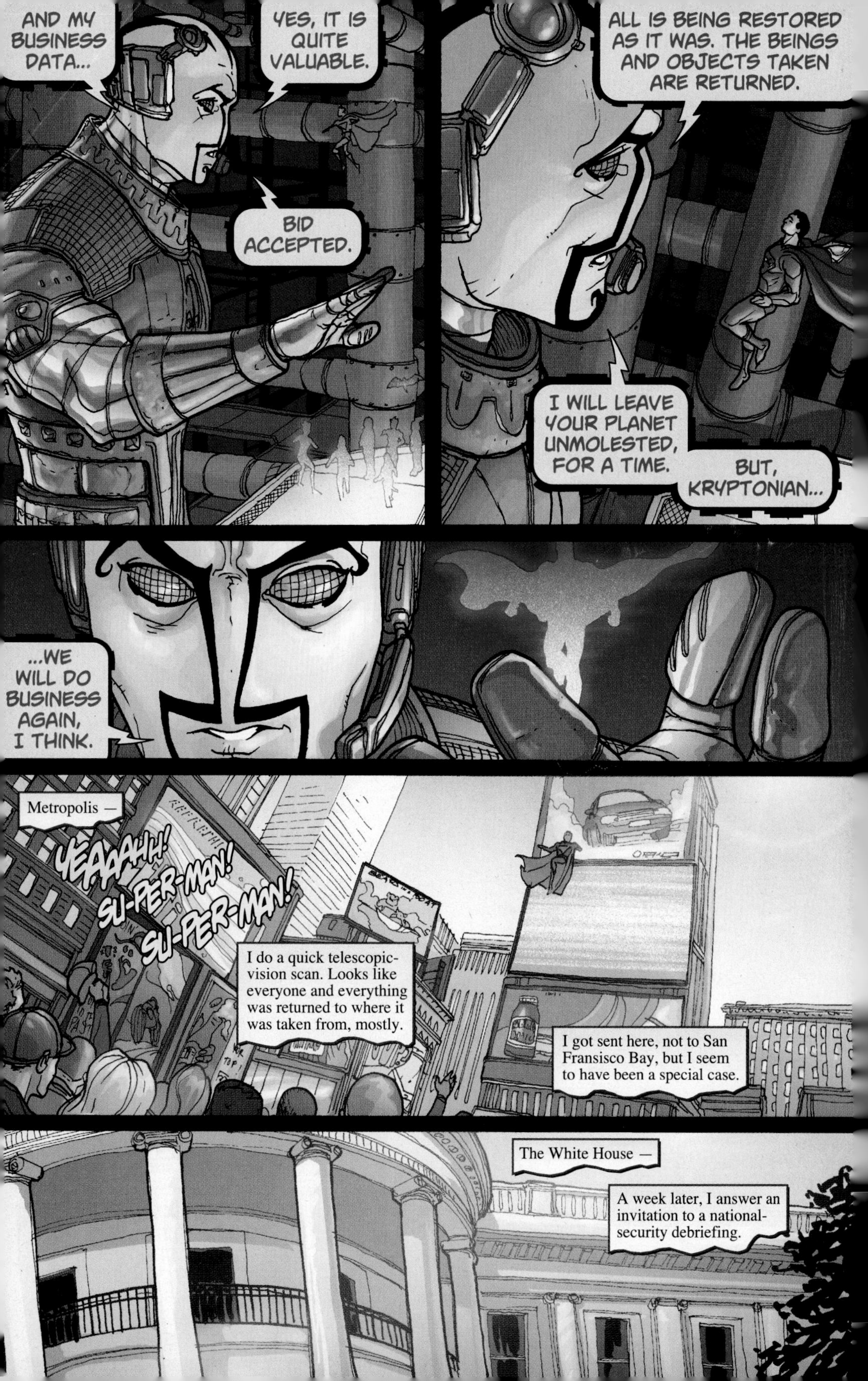
AND MY BUSINESS DATA...
YES, IT IS QUITE VALUABLE.
BID ACCEPTED.
ALL IS BEING RESTORED AS IT WAS. THE BEINGS AND OBJECTS TAKEN ARE RETURNED.
I WILL LEAVE YOUR PLANET UNMOLESTED, FOR A TIME.
BUT, KRYPTONIAN...
...WE WILL DO BUSINESS AGAIN, I THINK.
Metropolis —
YEAAAHH! SU-PER-MAN! SU-PER-MAN!
I do a quick telescopic-vision scan. Looks like everyone and everything was returned to where it was taken from, mostly.
I got sent here, not to San Fransisco Bay, but I seem to have been a special case.
The White House —
A week later, I answer an invitation to a national-security debriefing.

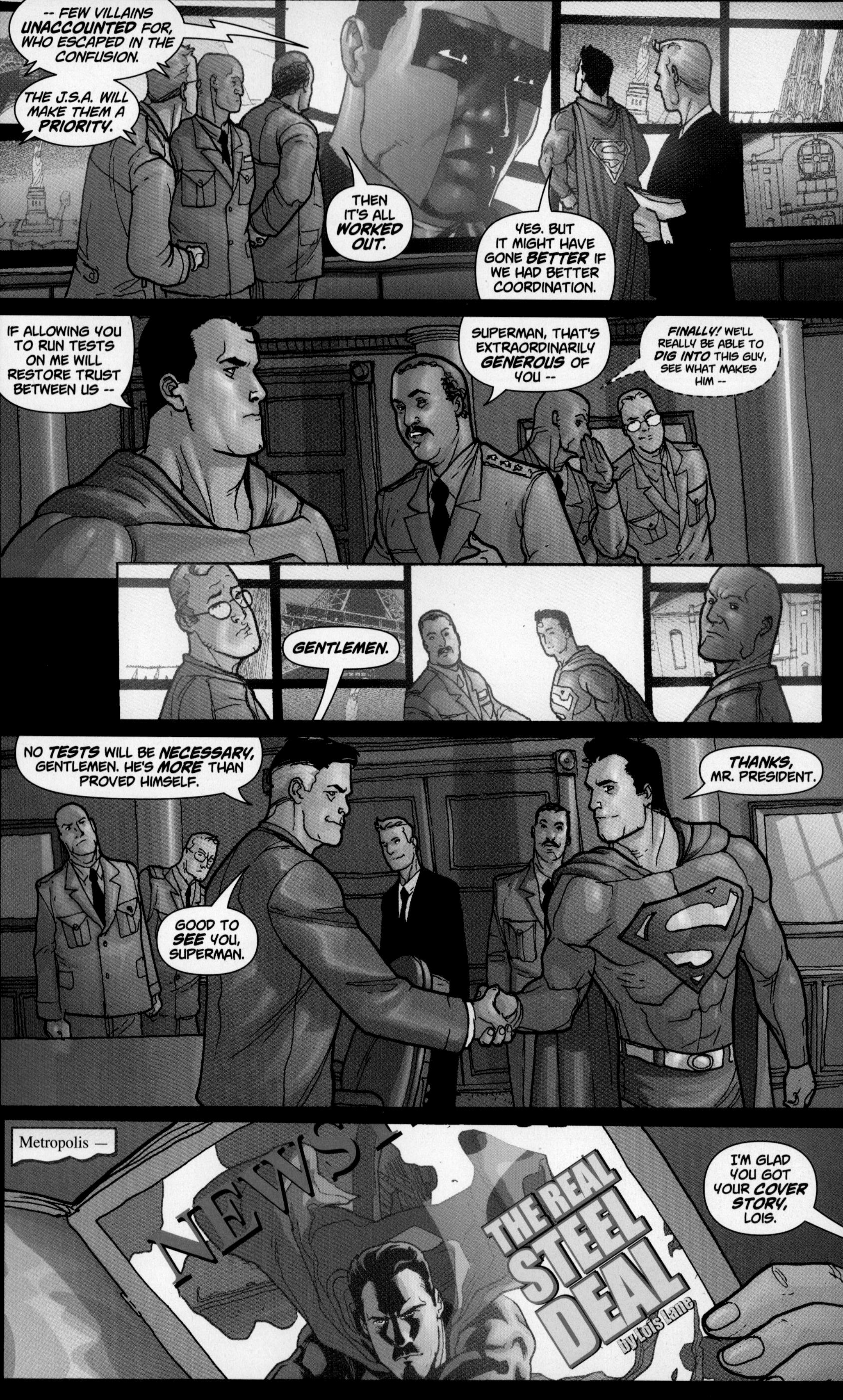
-- FEW VILLAINS UNACCOUNTED FOR, WHO ESCAPED IN THE CONFUSION.
THE J.S.A. WILL MAKE THEM A PRIORITY.
THEN IT'S ALL WORKED OUT.
YES. BUT IT MIGHT HAVE GONE BETTER IF WE HAD BETTER COORDINATION.
IF ALLOWING YOU TO RUN TESTS ON ME WILL RESTORE TRUST BETWEEN US --
SUPERMAN, THAT'S EXTRAORDINARILY GENEROUS OF YOU --
FINALLY! WE'LL REALLY BE ABLE TO DIG INTO THIS GUY, SEE WHAT MAKES HIM --
GENTLEMEN.
NO TESTS WILL BE NECESSARY, GENTLEMEN. HE'S MORE THAN PROVED HIMSELF.
GOOD TO SEE YOU, SUPERMAN.
THANKS, MR. PRESIDENT.
Metropolis —
NEWS
THE REAL STEEL DEAL
by Lois Lane
I'M GLAD YOU GOT YOUR COVER STORY, LOIS.

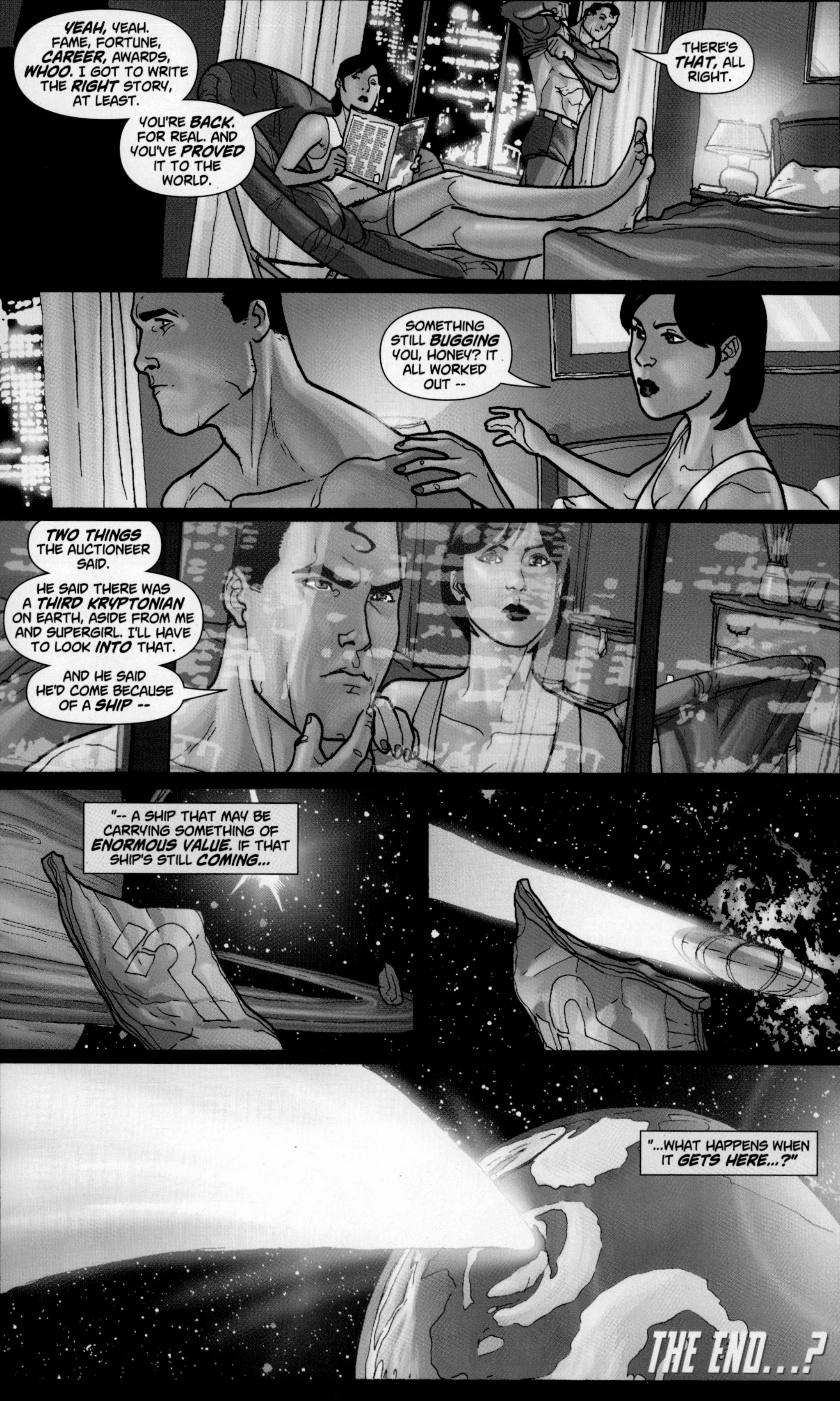
YEAH, YEAH. FAME, FORTUNE, CAREER, AWARDS, WHOO. I GOT TO WRITE THE RIGHT STORY, AT LEAST.
YOU'RE BACK. FOR REAL. AND YOU'VE PROVED IT TO THE WORLD.
THERE'S THAT, ALL RIGHT.
SOMETHING STILL BUGGING YOU, HONEY? IT ALL WORKED OUT --
TWO THINGS THE AUCTIONEER SAID.
HE SAID THERE WAS A THIRD KRYPTONIAN ON EARTH, ASIDE FROM ME AND SUPERGIRL. I'LL HAVE TO LOOK INTO THAT.
AND HE SAID HE'D COME BECAUSE OF A SHIP --
"-- A SHIP THAT MAY BE CARRYING SOMETHING OF ENORMOUS VALUE. IF THAT SHIP'S STILL COMING...
"...WHAT HAPPENS WHEN IT GETS HERE...?"
THE END...?

ACTION-PLUS
Or, "What Is All This Stuff in the Back of the Book, Anyway?"

When it came time to plan this collection you hold in your hands, we faced one simple problem. The "Back in Action" story was three issues long — and while that's what it needed to be, for monthly-magazine purposes, it's a bit short for book-collection purposes. So we needed to include something else, to pull together a satisfying and entertaining package.

What to do, what to do…?

It didn't take long to figure it out. "Back in Action," with all its offbeat guest stars, was inspired in large part by Superman team-ups of the past — so why not pick some of those stories? Tales where Superman battled alongside other DCU heroes, but not the familiar allies from the ranks of the JLA?

The end result was what you're about to read — a trio of adventures from *DC Comics Presents*, Superman's team-up series of the late 1970s and early 1980s, where Superman tended to interact with the rest of the DC Universe, beyond his own regular cast and the JLA. As an a bonus, they're all drawn by the legendary José Luis García-López, so they're a visual treat as well.

So turn the page, and take a walk with me through DC's storied past…

—**Kurt Busiek**

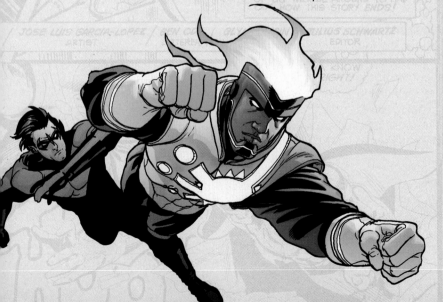

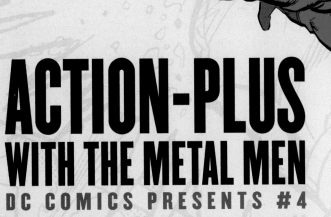

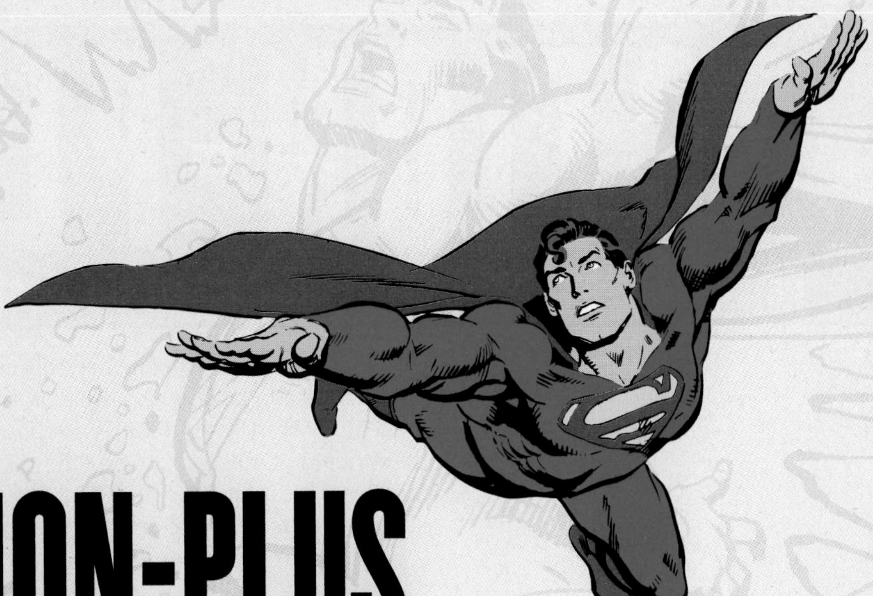

ACTION-PLUS
WITH THE METAL MEN
DC COMICS PRESENTS #4

This was the comic where I fell in love with the Metal Men. Also with Chemo, Dr. Jenet Klyburn, the villainous Mr. I.Q. and over and above all that, the artwork of José Luis García-López.

I'd seen and admired García-López's work before, of course — notably on lots of DC covers and on the first few issues of *DCCP* — but this issue just hit me like a sledgehammer. From that gorgeous and complex scene-setting panel on the beach on page two, to the charmingly drawn Metal Men tennis match to that panel of Chemo, all hunched-up and listening to I.Q.monologue…wow!

Len Wein did a nice job, too, with a tight, well-constructed story that captured the Metal Men's personalities perfectly — but it was José who made me want to write just about everyone in this book someday. I've managed it with Jenet Klyburn, in *Power Company*, but every time I'm actually on the verge of using Chemo, they drop him on Blüdhaven or something. But I.Q., the Metal Men…I'll get to 'em!

— **kdb**

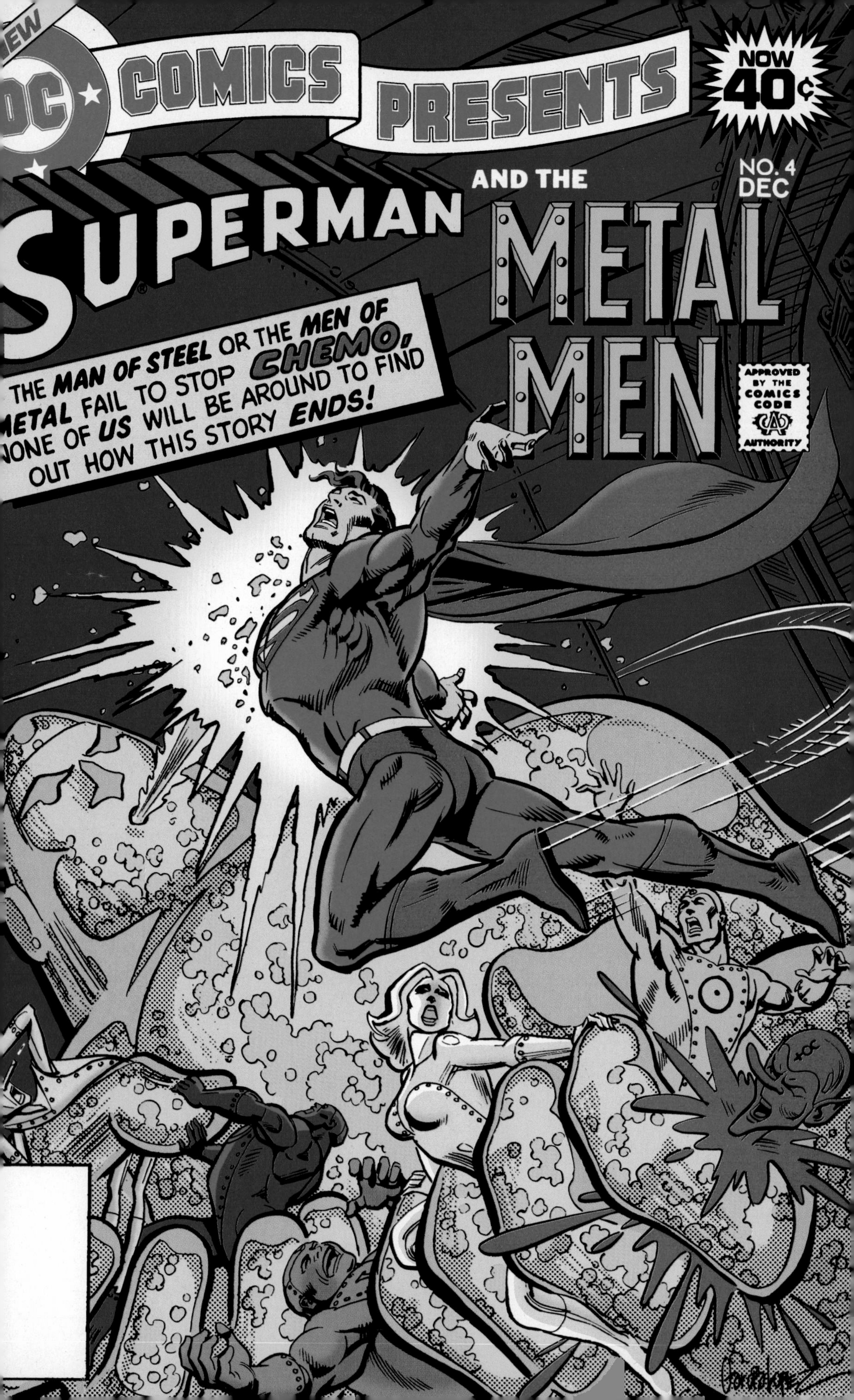
NEW
DC COMICS PRESENTS
NOW 40¢
SUPERMAN
AND THE
NO. 4
DEC
METAL MEN
IF THE MAN OF STEEL OR THE MEN OF METAL FAIL TO STOP CHEMO, NONE OF US WILL BE AROUND TO FIND OUT HOW THIS STORY ENDS!
APPROVED BY THE COMICS CODE AUTHORITY

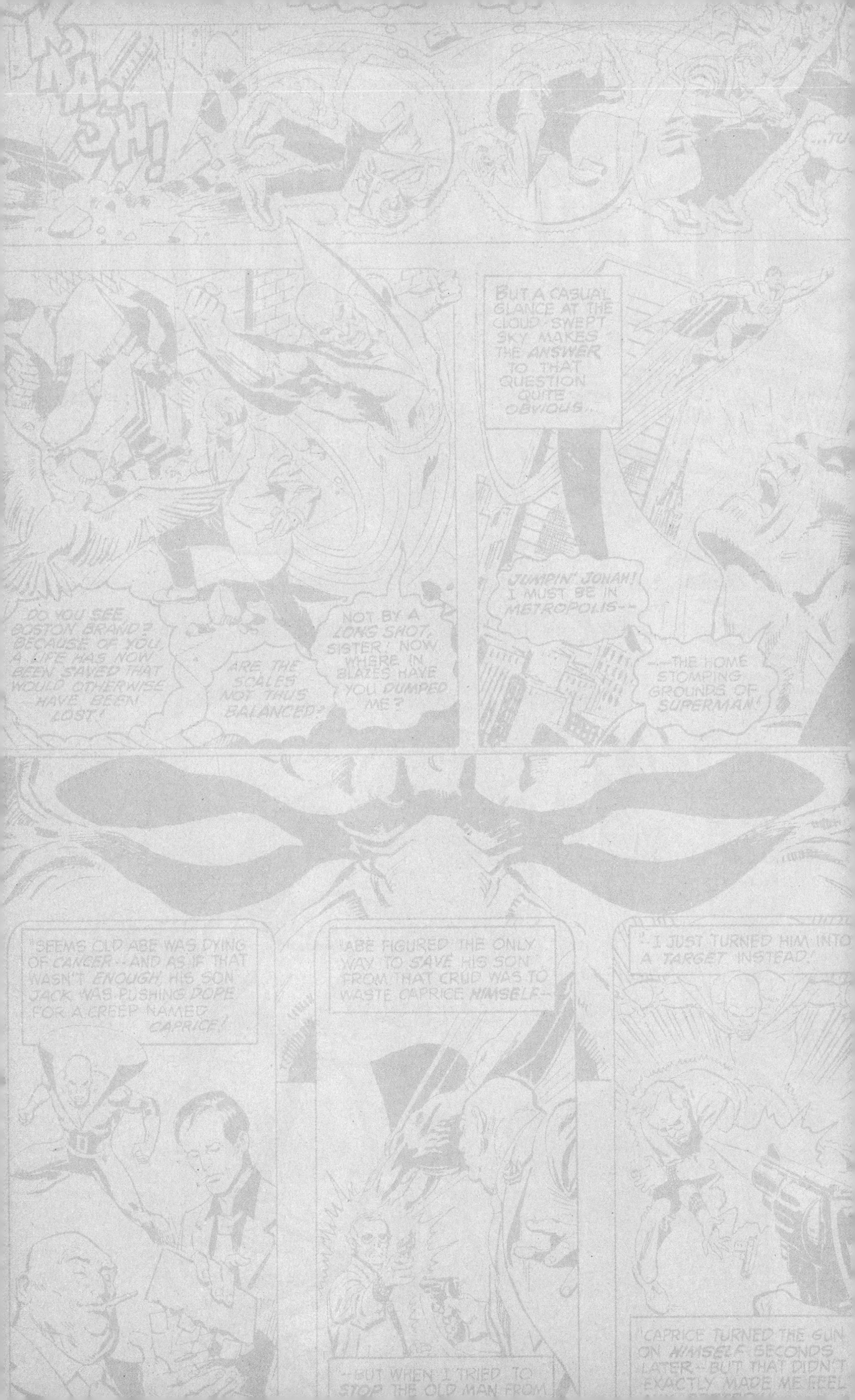
DO YOU SEE, BOSTON BRAND? BECAUSE OF YOU, A LIFE HAS NOW BEEN SAVED THAT WOULD OTHERWISE HAVE BEEN LOST!
ARE THE SCALES NOT THUS BALANCED?
NOT BY A LONG SHOT, SISTER! NOW WHERE IN BLAZES HAVE YOU DUMPED ME?
BUT A CASUAL GLANCE AT THE CLOUD-SWEPT SKY MAKES THE ANSWER TO THAT QUESTION QUITE OBVIOUS...
JUMPIN' JONAH! I MUST BE IN METROPOLIS--
--THE HOME STOMPING GROUNDS OF SUPERMAN!
"SEEMS OLD ABE WAS DYING OF CANCER--AND AS IF THAT WASN'T ENOUGH, HIS SON JACK WAS PUSHING DOPE FOR A CREEP NAMED CAPRICE!
"ABE FIGURED THE ONLY WAY TO SAVE HIS SON FROM THAT CRUD WAS TO WASTE CAPRICE HIMSELF--
"--BUT WHEN I TRIED TO STOP THE OLD MAN FROM
"...I JUST TURNED HIM INTO A TARGET INSTEAD!
"CAPRICE TURNED THE GUN ON HIMSELF SECONDS LATER--BUT THAT DIDN'T EXACTLY MADE ME FEEL

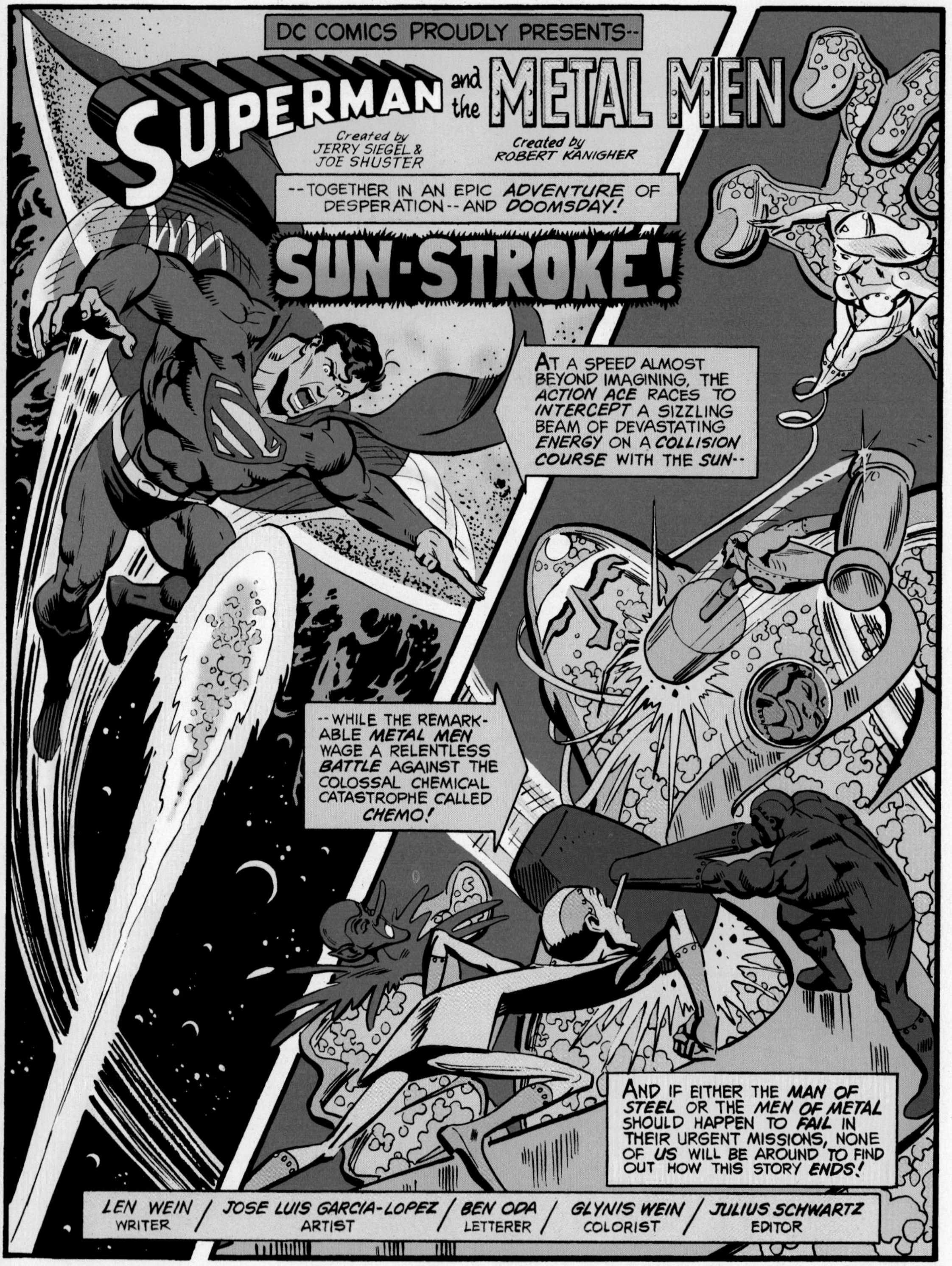
DC COMICS PROUDLY PRESENTS--
SUPERMAN and the METAL MEN
Created by JERRY SIEGEL & JOE SHUSTER
Created by ROBERT KANIGHER
--TOGETHER IN AN EPIC ADVENTURE OF DESPERATION--AND DOOMSDAY!
SUN-STROKE!
AT A SPEED ALMOST BEYOND IMAGINING, THE ACTION ACE RACES TO INTERCEPT A SIZZLING BEAM OF DEVASTATING ENERGY ON A COLLISION COURSE WITH THE SUN--
--WHILE THE REMARKABLE METAL MEN WAGE A RELENTLESS BATTLE AGAINST THE COLOSSAL CHEMICAL CATASTROPHE CALLED CHEMO!
AND IF EITHER THE MAN OF STEEL OR THE MEN OF METAL SHOULD HAPPEN TO FAIL IN THEIR URGENT MISSIONS, NONE OF US WILL BE AROUND TO FIND OUT HOW THIS STORY ENDS!
LEN WEIN WRITER / JOSE LUIS GARCIA-LOPEZ ARTIST / BEN ODA LETTERER / GLYNIS WEIN COLORIST / JULIUS SCHWARTZ EDITOR

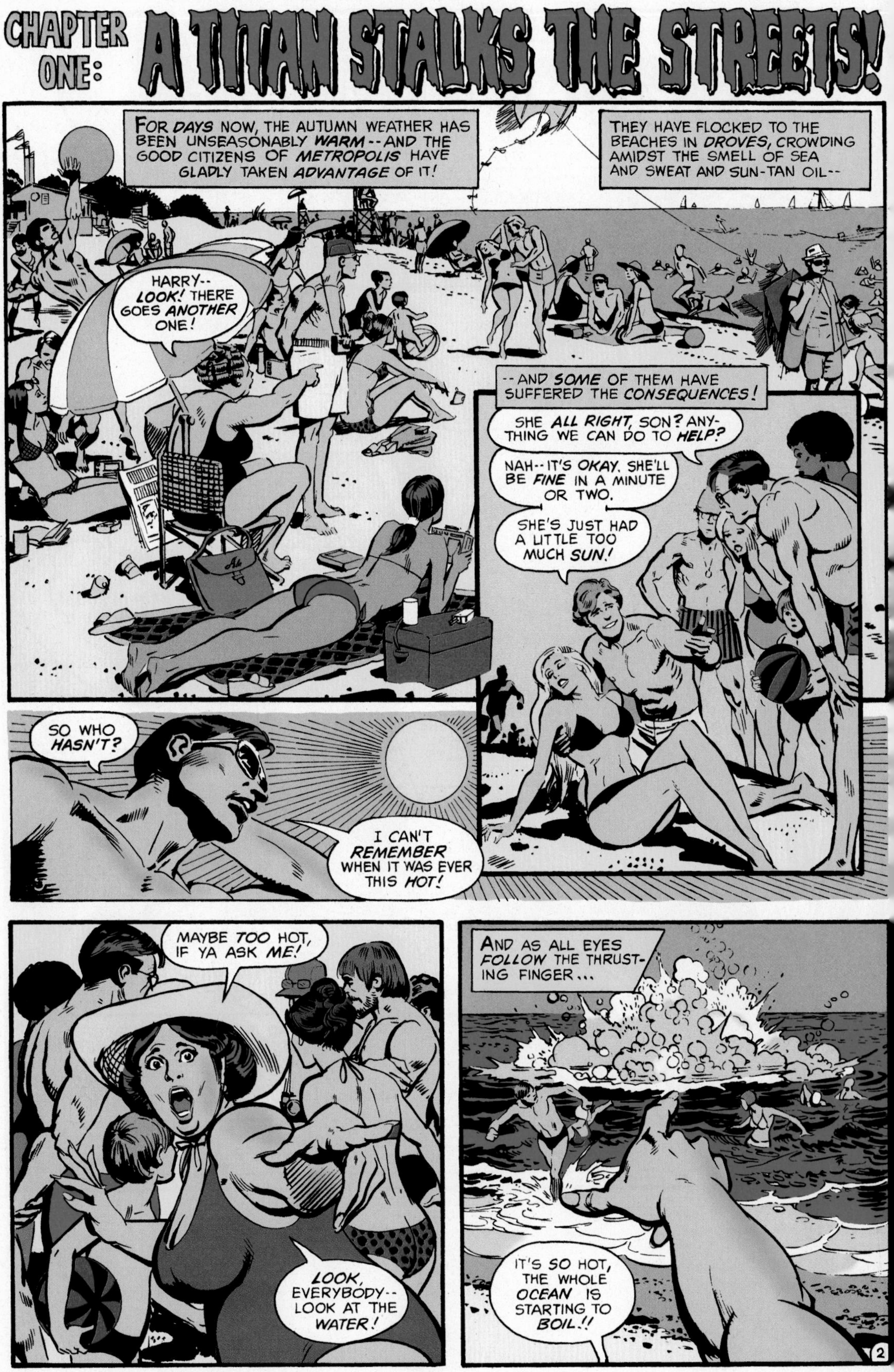
CHAPTER ONE: A TITAN STALKS THE STREETS!
FOR DAYS NOW, THE AUTUMN WEATHER HAS BEEN UNSEASONABLY WARM -- AND THE GOOD CITIZENS OF METROPOLIS HAVE GLADLY TAKEN ADVANTAGE OF IT!
THEY HAVE FLOCKED TO THE BEACHES IN DROVES, CROWDING AMIDST THE SMELL OF SEA AND SWEAT AND SUN-TAN OIL--
HARRY-- LOOK! THERE GOES ANOTHER ONE!
--AND SOME OF THEM HAVE SUFFERED THE CONSEQUENCES!
SHE ALL RIGHT, SON? ANY-THING WE CAN DO TO HELP?
NAH-- IT'S OKAY. SHE'LL BE FINE IN A MINUTE OR TWO.
SHE'S JUST HAD A LITTLE TOO MUCH SUN!
SO WHO HASN'T?
I CAN'T REMEMBER WHEN IT WAS EVER THIS HOT!
MAYBE TOO HOT, IF YA ASK ME!
LOOK, EVERYBODY-- LOOK AT THE WATER!
AND AS ALL EYES FOLLOW THE THRUST-ING FINGER...
IT'S SO HOT, THE WHOLE OCEAN IS STARTING TO BOIL!!
2

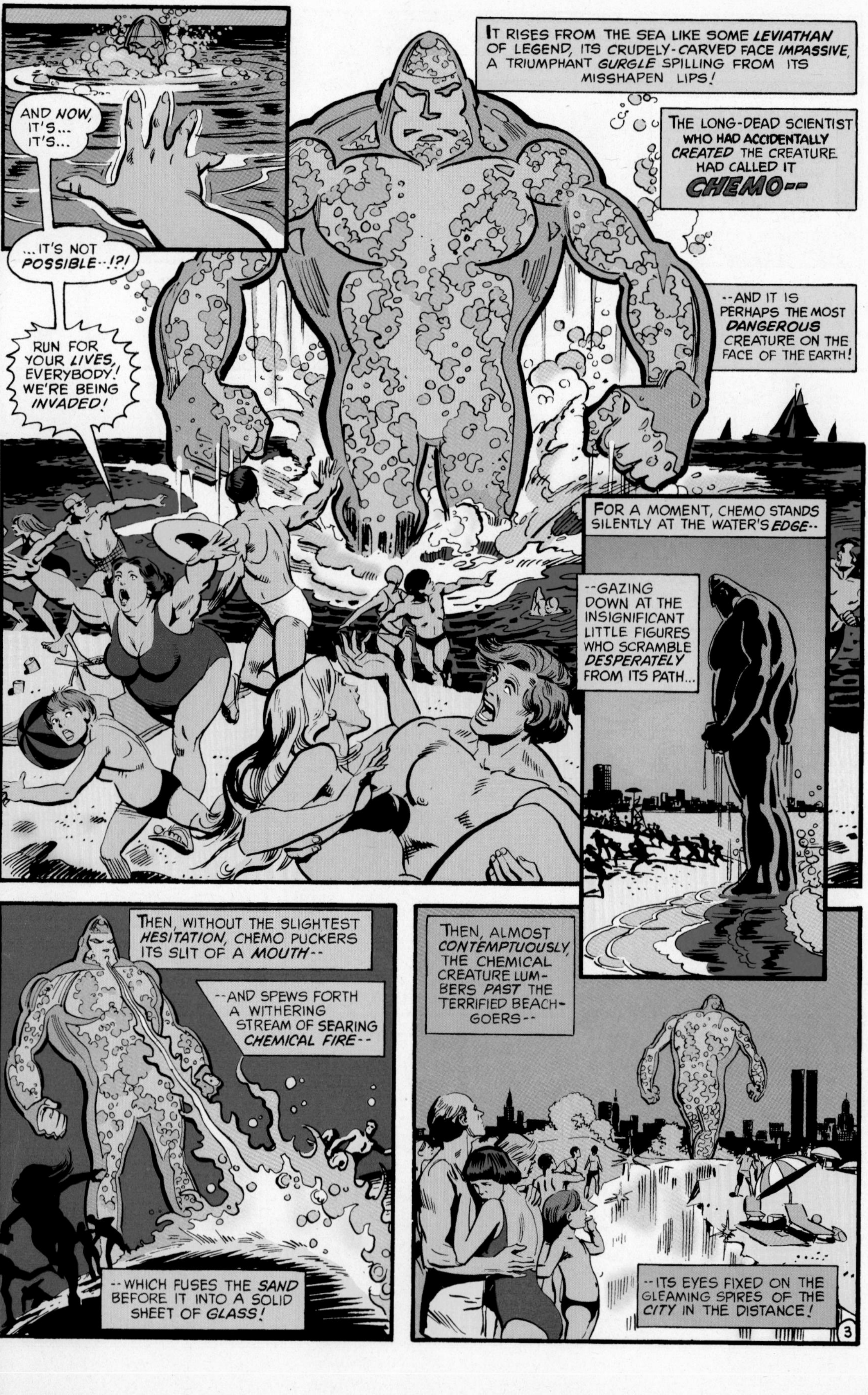
AND NOW, IT'S... IT'S...
...IT'S NOT POSSIBLE..!?!
IT RISES FROM THE SEA LIKE SOME LEVIATHAN OF LEGEND, ITS CRUDELY-CARVED FACE IMPASSIVE, A TRIUMPHANT GURGLE SPILLING FROM ITS MISSHAPEN LIPS!
THE LONG-DEAD SCIENTIST WHO HAD ACCIDENTALLY CREATED THE CREATURE HAD CALLED IT
CHEMO--
--AND IT IS PERHAPS THE MOST DANGEROUS CREATURE ON THE FACE OF THE EARTH!
RUN FOR YOUR LIVES, EVERYBODY! WE'RE BEING INVADED!
FOR A MOMENT, CHEMO STANDS SILENTLY AT THE WATER'S EDGE--
--GAZING DOWN AT THE INSIGNIFICANT LITTLE FIGURES WHO SCRAMBLE DESPERATELY FROM ITS PATH...
THEN, WITHOUT THE SLIGHTEST HESITATION, CHEMO PUCKERS ITS SLIT OF A MOUTH--
--AND SPEWS FORTH A WITHERING STREAM OF SEARING CHEMICAL FIRE--
--WHICH FUSES THE SAND BEFORE IT INTO A SOLID SHEET OF GLASS!
THEN, ALMOST CONTEMPTUOUSLY, THE CHEMICAL CREATURE LUMBERS PAST THE TERRIFIED BEACH-GOERS--
--ITS EYES FIXED ON THE GLEAMING SPIRES OF THE CITY IN THE DISTANCE!
3

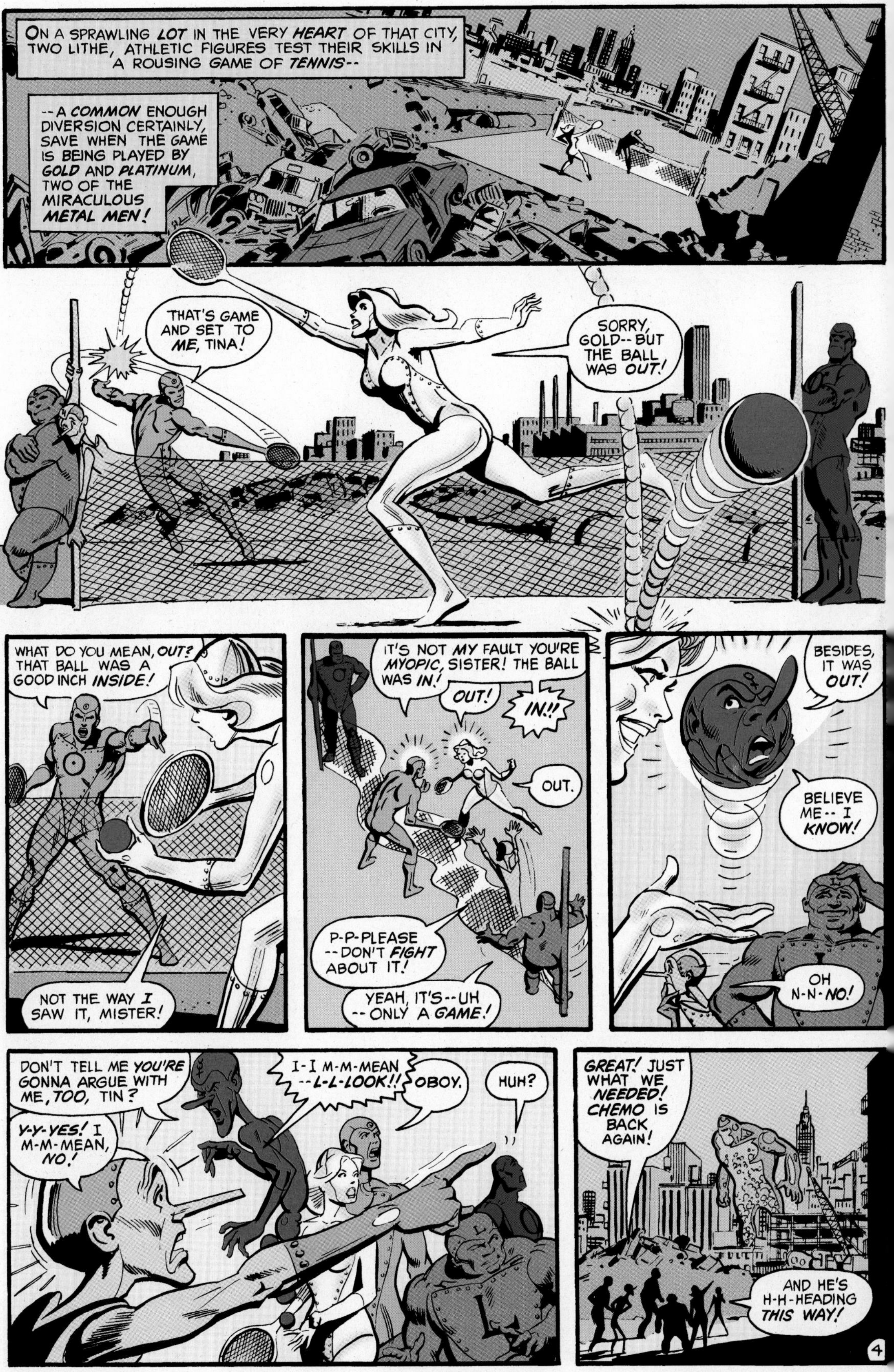
ON A SPRAWLING LOT IN THE VERY HEART OF THAT CITY, TWO LITHE, ATHLETIC FIGURES TEST THEIR SKILLS IN A ROUSING GAME OF TENNIS--
--A COMMON ENOUGH DIVERSION CERTAINLY, SAVE WHEN THE GAME IS BEING PLAYED BY GOLD AND PLATINUM, TWO OF THE MIRACULOUS METAL MEN!
THAT'S GAME AND SET TO ME, TINA!
SORRY, GOLD-- BUT THE BALL WAS OUT!
WHAT DO YOU MEAN, OUT? THAT BALL WAS A GOOD INCH INSIDE!
NOT THE WAY I SAW IT, MISTER!
IT'S NOT MY FAULT YOU'RE MYOPIC, SISTER! THE BALL WAS IN!
OUT!
IN!!
OUT.
P-P-PLEASE --DON'T FIGHT ABOUT IT!
YEAH, IT'S--UH --ONLY A GAME!
BESIDES, IT WAS OUT!
BELIEVE ME-- I KNOW!
OH N-N-NO!
DON'T TELL ME YOU'RE GONNA ARGUE WITH ME, TOO, TIN?
Y-Y-YES! I M-M-MEAN, NO!
I-I M-M-MEAN --L-L-LOOK!!
OBOY.
HUH?
GREAT! JUST WHAT WE NEEDED! CHEMO IS BACK AGAIN!
AND HE'S H-H-HEADING THIS WAY!
4

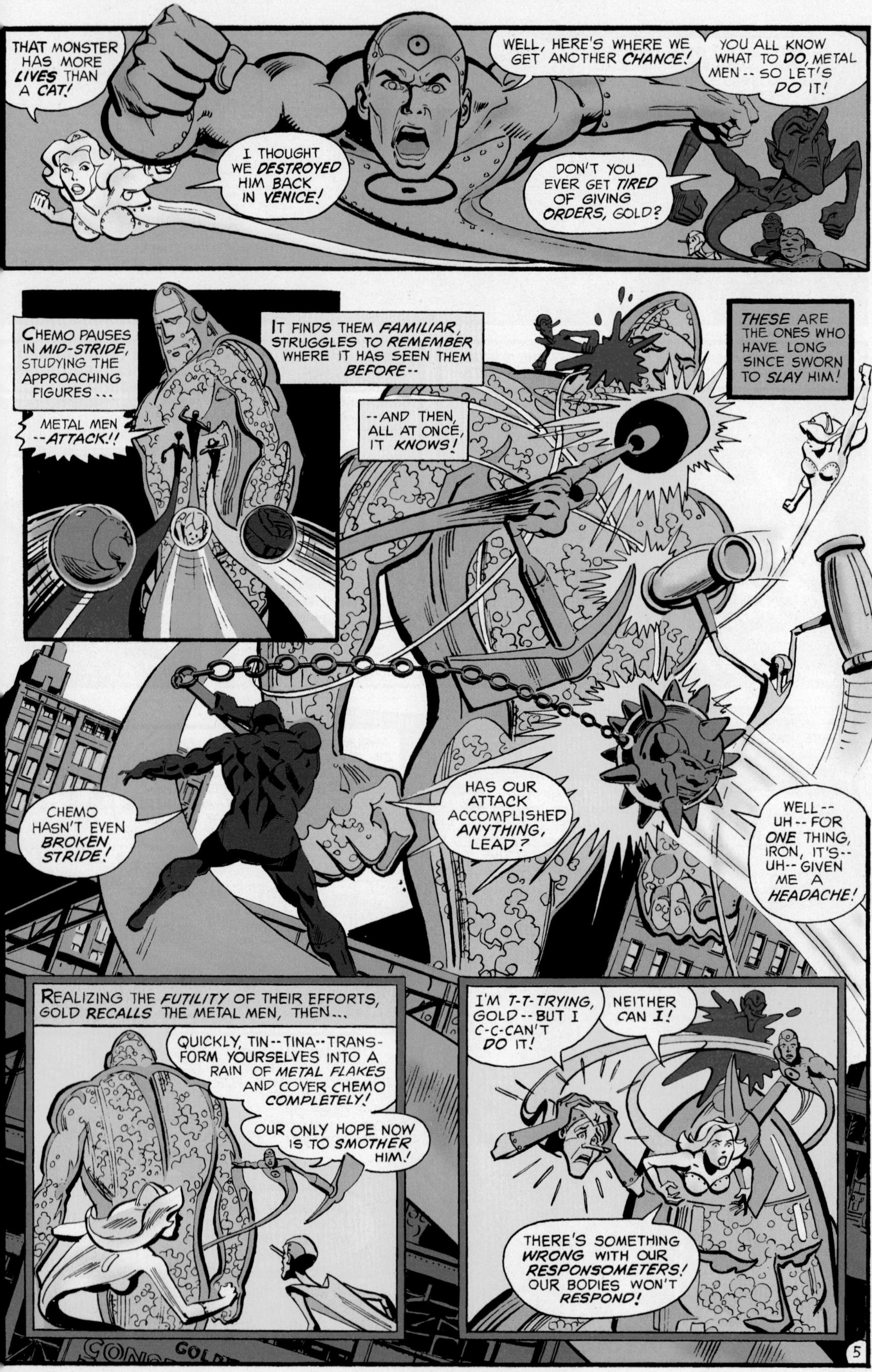
THAT MONSTER HAS MORE LIVES THAN A CAT!
I THOUGHT WE DESTROYED HIM BACK IN VENICE!
WELL, HERE'S WHERE WE GET ANOTHER CHANCE!
YOU ALL KNOW WHAT TO DO, METAL MEN -- SO LET'S DO IT!
DON'T YOU EVER GET TIRED OF GIVING ORDERS, GOLD?
CHEMO PAUSES IN MID-STRIDE, STUDYING THE APPROACHING FIGURES...
METAL MEN --ATTACK!!
IT FINDS THEM FAMILIAR, STRUGGLES TO REMEMBER WHERE IT HAS SEEN THEM BEFORE--
--AND THEN, ALL AT ONCE, IT KNOWS!
THESE ARE THE ONES WHO HAVE LONG SINCE SWORN TO SLAY HIM!
CHEMO HASN'T EVEN BROKEN STRIDE!
HAS OUR ATTACK ACCOMPLISHED ANYTHING, LEAD?
WELL -- UH -- FOR ONE THING, IRON, IT'S -- UH -- GIVEN ME A HEADACHE!
REALIZING THE FUTILITY OF THEIR EFFORTS, GOLD RECALLS THE METAL MEN, THEN...
QUICKLY, TIN -- TINA -- TRANSFORM YOURSELVES INTO A RAIN OF METAL FLAKES AND COVER CHEMO COMPLETELY!
OUR ONLY HOPE NOW IS TO SMOTHER HIM!
I'M T-T-TRYING, GOLD -- BUT I C-C-CAN'T DO IT!
NEITHER CAN I!
THERE'S SOMETHING WRONG WITH OUR RESPONSOMETERS! OUR BODIES WON'T RESPOND!
5

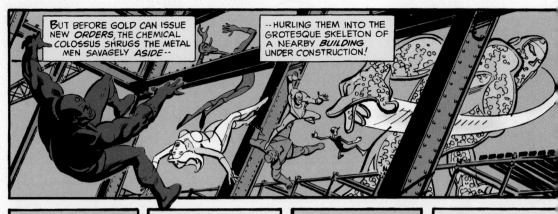

BUT BEFORE GOLD CAN ISSUE NEW *ORDERS*, THE CHEMICAL COLOSSUS SHRUGS THE METAL MEN SAVAGELY *ASIDE*--

--HURLING THEM INTO THE GROTESQUE SKELETON OF A NEARBY *BUILDING* UNDER CONSTRUCTION!

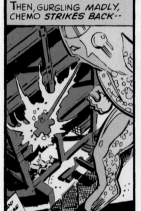

THEN, GURGLING *MADLY*, CHEMO *STRIKES BACK*--

--*SHEARING* THE STRUCTURE'S *MAIN SUPPORTS*--

--THUS *BURYING* THE HAPLESS METAL MEN UNDER *TONS* OF TWISTED *STEEL*!

FOR SEVERAL MINUTES, NOTHING *STIRS* WITHIN THE RUBBLE, SAVE FOR BILLOWING SPUMES OF *DUST*--

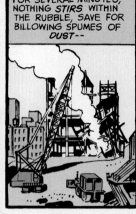

--BUT, AT LAST, A RUINED *GIRDER* SUDDENLY SHIFTS *ASIDE*--

--FOLLOWED BY *ANOTHER*--

--AND ANOTHER AFTER *THAT*--

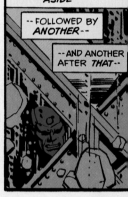

--UNTIL THE METAL MEN ARE *FREE* ONCE MORE!!

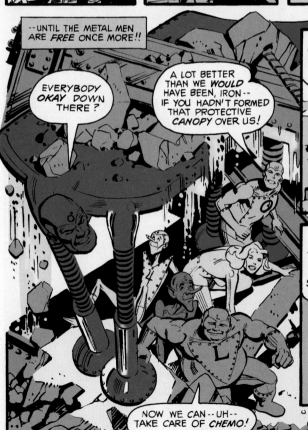

EVERYBODY *OKAY* DOWN THERE?

A LOT BETTER THAN WE *WOULD* HAVE BEEN, IRON-- IF YOU HADN'T FORMED THAT PROTECTIVE *CANOPY* OVER US!

NOW WE CAN--UH-- TAKE CARE OF *CHEMO*!

ASSUMING, OF COURSE, WE MANAGE TO *FIND* HIM AGAIN!

CHEMO WENT *UNDERGROUND* WHILE WE WERE TRAPPED IN THE *RUINS*--AND THERE'S NO WAY WE CAN *TRACK* HIM!

THEN WE'LL JUST HAVE TO PUT CHEMO ON THE *BACK BURNER* FOR NOW-- WHILE WE TAKE CARE OF SOMETHING MORE *IMPORTANT*!

SOMETHING IS *HAPPENING* TO OUR *POWERS*-- AND WE'D BETTER FIND OUT *WHY*!

AND IF YOU THINK THE *METAL MEN* HAVE TROUBLES, WAIT'LL YOU SEE WHAT *SUPERMAN* MUST FACE IN *CHAPTER TWO*--WHICH BEGINS ON THE NEXT PAGE FOLLOWING!

6

CHAPTER TWO: WATER, WATER, EVERYWHERE...!

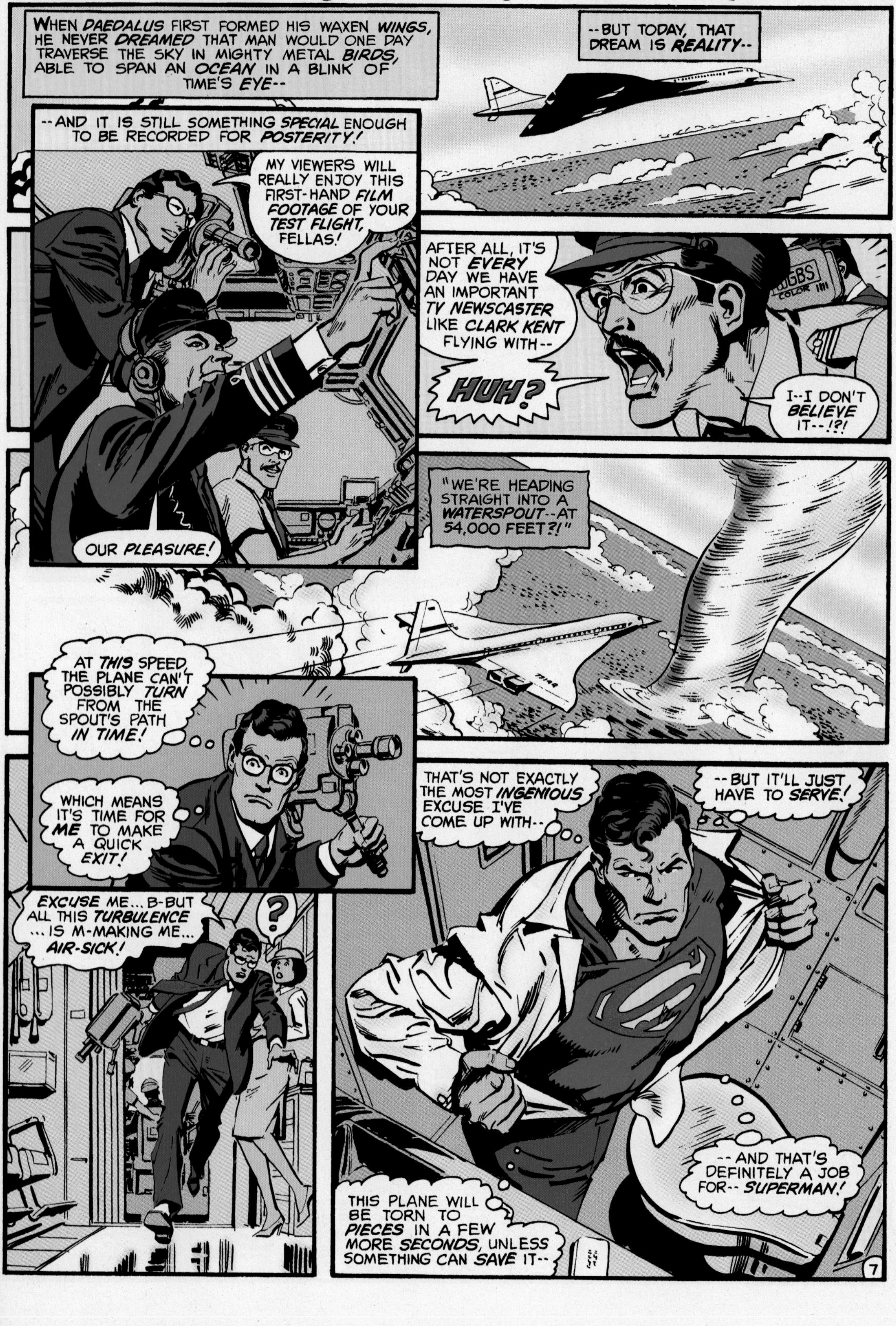

WHEN DAEDALUS FIRST FORMED HIS WAXEN WINGS, HE NEVER DREAMED THAT MAN WOULD ONE DAY TRAVERSE THE SKY IN MIGHTY METAL BIRDS, ABLE TO SPAN AN OCEAN IN A BLINK OF TIME'S EYE--
--BUT TODAY, THAT DREAM IS REALITY--
--AND IT IS STILL SOMETHING SPECIAL ENOUGH TO BE RECORDED FOR POSTERITY!
MY VIEWERS WILL REALLY ENJOY THIS FIRST-HAND FILM FOOTAGE OF YOUR TEST FLIGHT, FELLAS!
OUR PLEASURE!
AFTER ALL, IT'S NOT EVERY DAY WE HAVE AN IMPORTANT TV NEWSCASTER LIKE CLARK KENT FLYING WITH--
HUH?
I--I DON'T BELIEVE IT--!?!
WGBS COLOR
"WE'RE HEADING STRAIGHT INTO A WATERSPOUT--AT 54,000 FEET?!"
AT THIS SPEED, THE PLANE CAN'T POSSIBLY TURN FROM THE SPOUT'S PATH IN TIME!
WHICH MEANS IT'S TIME FOR ME TO MAKE A QUICK EXIT!
EXCUSE ME... B-BUT ALL THIS TURBULENCE ...IS M-MAKING ME... AIR-SICK!
?
THAT'S NOT EXACTLY THE MOST INGENIOUS EXCUSE I'VE COME UP WITH--
--BUT IT'LL JUST HAVE TO SERVE!
THIS PLANE WILL BE TORN TO PIECES IN A FEW MORE SECONDS, UNLESS SOMETHING CAN SAVE IT--
--AND THAT'S DEFINITELY A JOB FOR-- SUPERMAN!
7

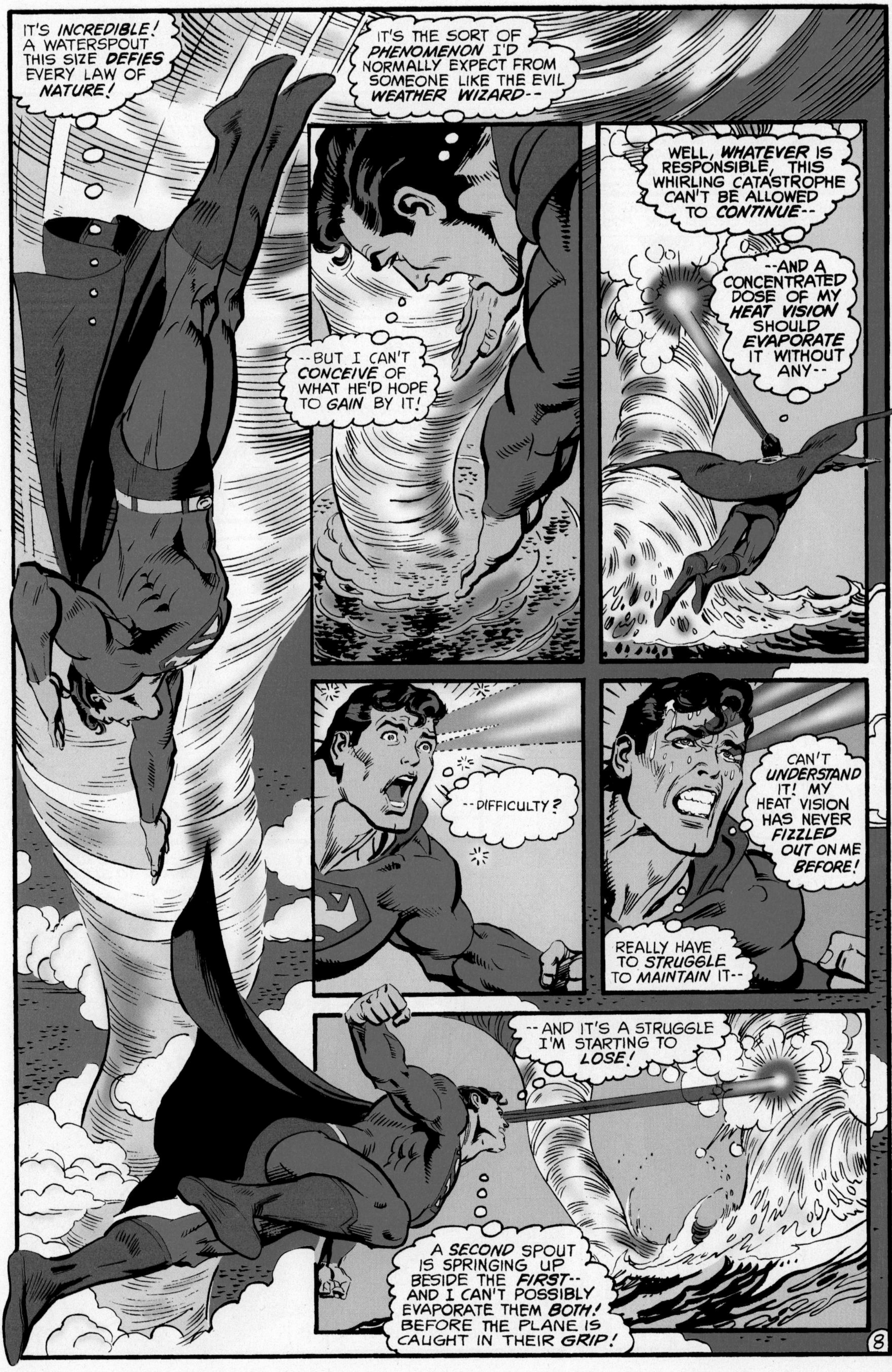
IT'S INCREDIBLE! A WATERSPOUT THIS SIZE DEFIES EVERY LAW OF NATURE!
IT'S THE SORT OF PHENOMENON I'D NORMALLY EXPECT FROM SOMEONE LIKE THE EVIL WEATHER WIZARD--
--BUT I CAN'T CONCEIVE OF WHAT HE'D HOPE TO GAIN BY IT!
WELL, WHATEVER IS RESPONSIBLE, THIS WHIRLING CATASTROPHE CAN'T BE ALLOWED TO CONTINUE--
--AND A CONCENTRATED DOSE OF MY HEAT VISION SHOULD EVAPORATE IT WITHOUT ANY--
--DIFFICULTY?
CAN'T UNDERSTAND IT! MY HEAT VISION HAS NEVER FIZZLED OUT ON ME BEFORE!
REALLY HAVE TO STRUGGLE TO MAINTAIN IT--
--AND IT'S A STRUGGLE I'M STARTING TO LOSE!
A SECOND SPOUT IS SPRINGING UP BESIDE THE FIRST-- AND I CAN'T POSSIBLY EVAPORATE THEM BOTH! BEFORE THE PLANE IS CAUGHT IN THEIR GRIP!
8

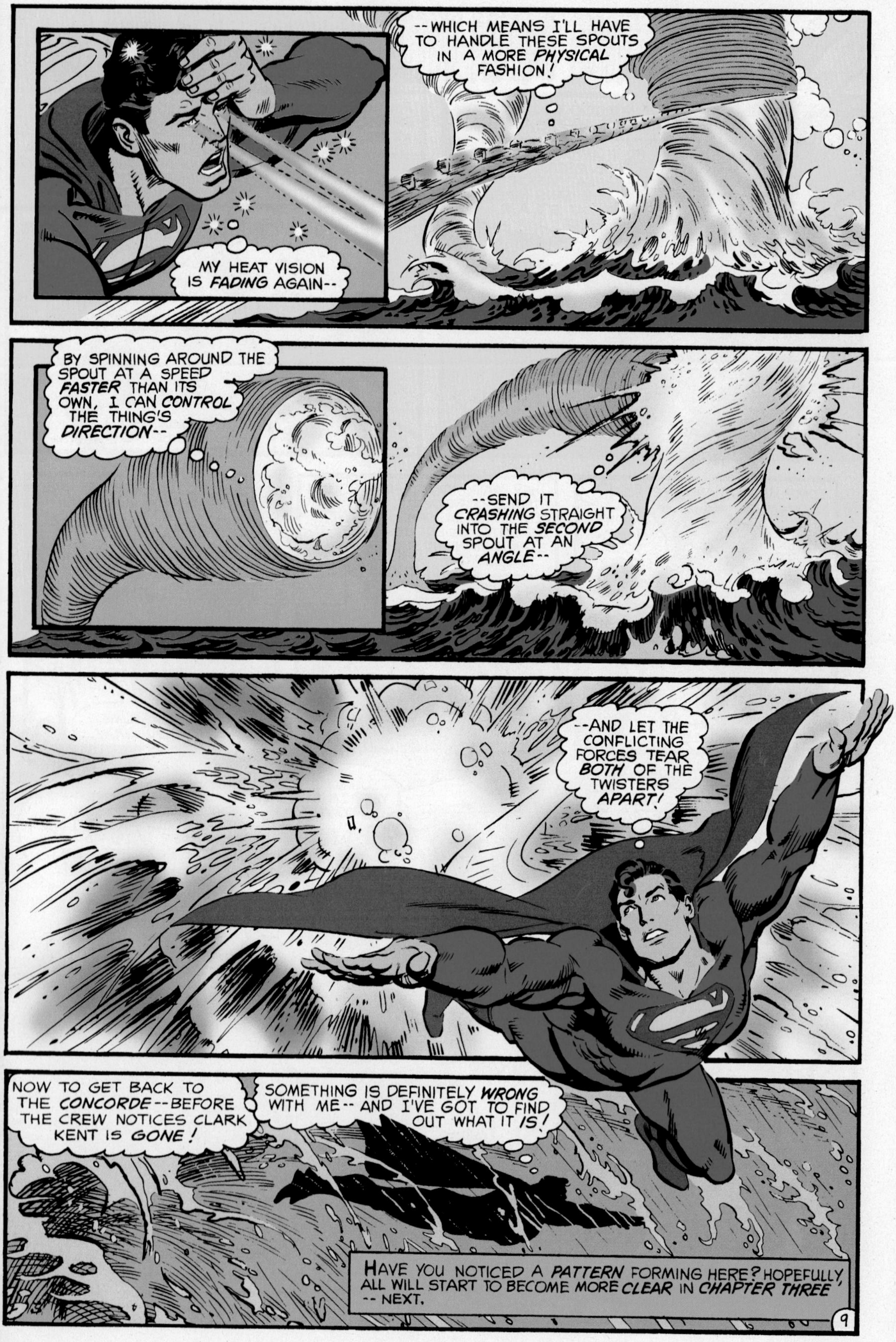
MY HEAT VISION IS FADING AGAIN--
--WHICH MEANS I'LL HAVE TO HANDLE THESE SPOUTS IN A MORE PHYSICAL FASHION!
BY SPINNING AROUND THE SPOUT AT A SPEED FASTER THAN ITS OWN, I CAN CONTROL THE THING'S DIRECTION--
--SEND IT CRASHING STRAIGHT INTO THE SECOND SPOUT AT AN ANGLE--
--AND LET THE CONFLICTING FORCES TEAR BOTH OF THE TWISTERS APART!
NOW TO GET BACK TO THE CONCORDE--BEFORE THE CREW NOTICES CLARK KENT IS GONE!
SOMETHING IS DEFINITELY WRONG WITH ME-- AND I'VE GOT TO FIND OUT WHAT IT IS!
HAVE YOU NOTICED A PATTERN FORMING HERE? HOPEFULLY, ALL WILL START TO BECOME MORE CLEAR IN CHAPTER THREE -- NEXT.
9

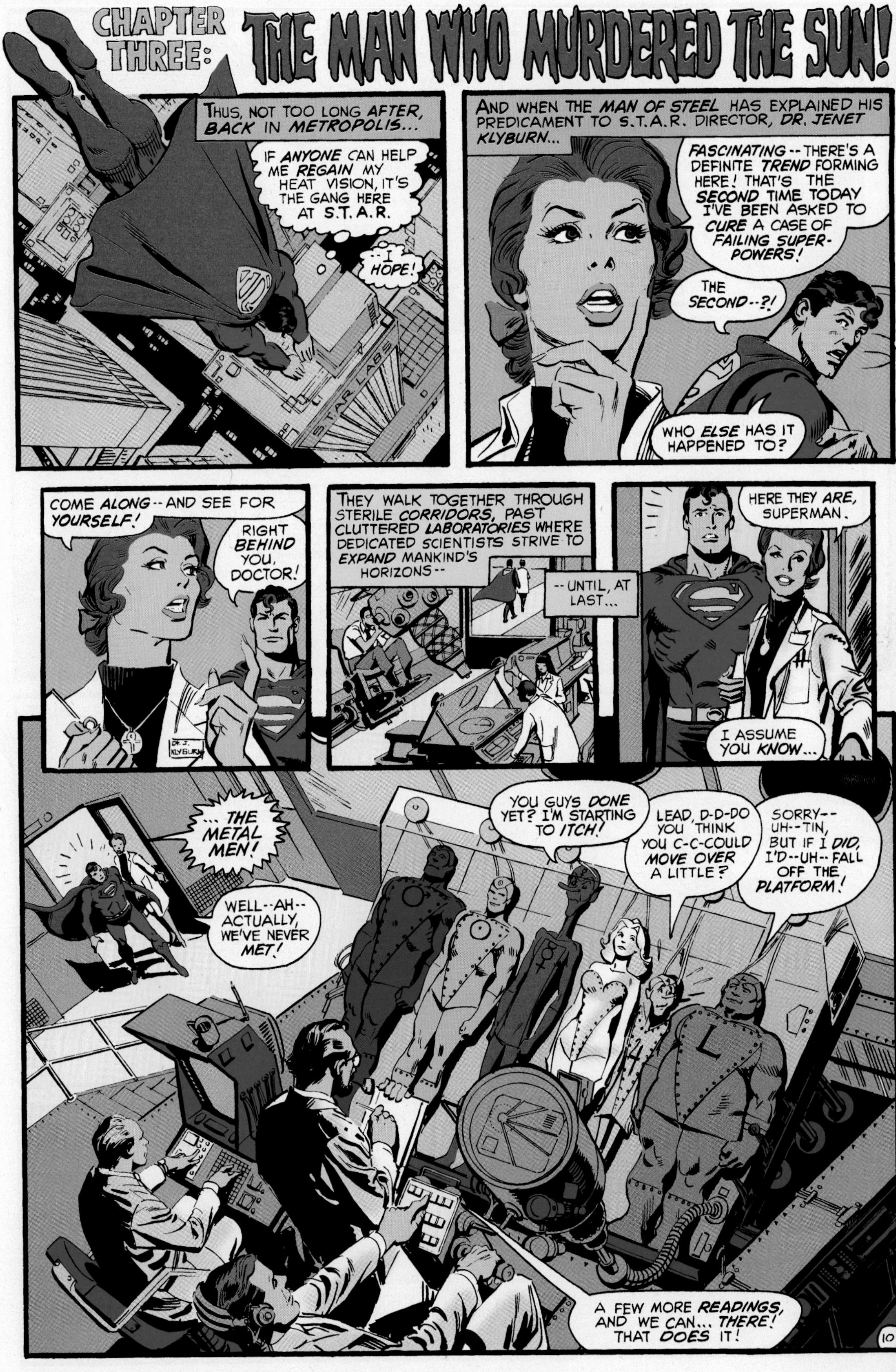
CHAPTER THREE: THE MAN WHO MURDERED THE SUN!
THUS, NOT TOO LONG AFTER, BACK IN METROPOLIS...
IF ANYONE CAN HELP ME REGAIN MY HEAT VISION, IT'S THE GANG HERE AT S.T.A.R.
--I HOPE!
S.T.A.R. LABS
AND WHEN THE MAN OF STEEL HAS EXPLAINED HIS PREDICAMENT TO S.T.A.R. DIRECTOR, DR. JENET KLYBURN...
FASCINATING--THERE'S A DEFINITE TREND FORMING HERE! THAT'S THE SECOND TIME TODAY I'VE BEEN ASKED TO CURE A CASE OF FAILING SUPER-POWERS!
THE SECOND--?!
WHO ELSE HAS IT HAPPENED TO?
COME ALONG--AND SEE FOR YOURSELF!
RIGHT BEHIND YOU, DOCTOR!
DR. J. KLYBURN
THEY WALK TOGETHER THROUGH STERILE CORRIDORS, PAST CLUTTERED LABORATORIES WHERE DEDICATED SCIENTISTS STRIVE TO EXPAND MANKIND'S HORIZONS--
--UNTIL, AT LAST...
HERE THEY ARE, SUPERMAN.
I ASSUME YOU KNOW...
...THE METAL MEN!
WELL--AH--ACTUALLY, WE'VE NEVER MET!
YOU GUYS DONE YET? I'M STARTING TO ITCH!
LEAD, D-D-DO YOU THINK YOU C-C-COULD MOVE OVER A LITTLE?
SORRY--UH--TIN, BUT IF I DID, I'D--UH--FALL OFF THE PLATFORM!
A FEW MORE READINGS, AND WE CAN... THERE! THAT DOES IT!
10

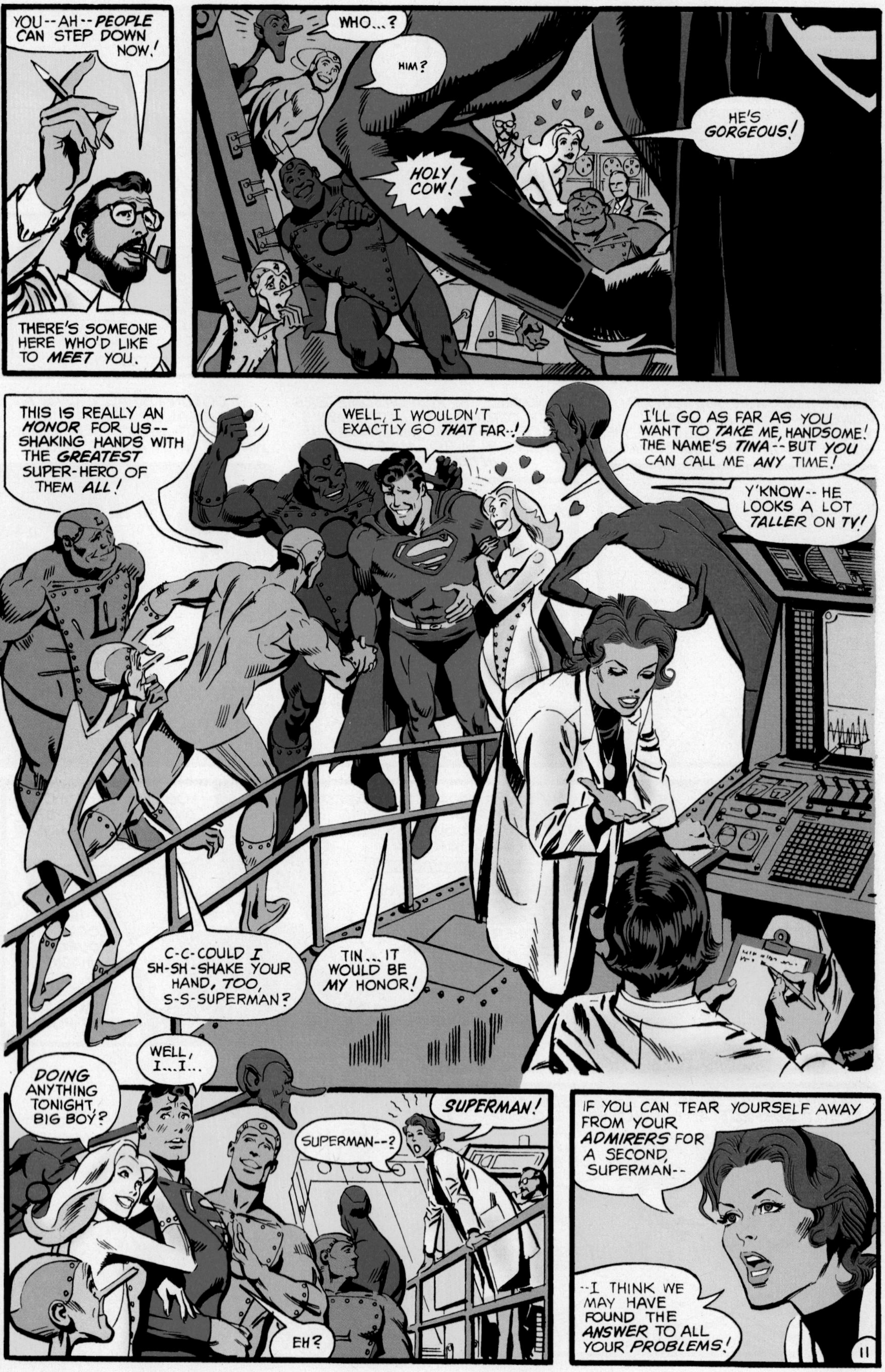
YOU--AH--PEOPLE CAN STEP DOWN NOW!
THERE'S SOMEONE HERE WHO'D LIKE TO MEET YOU.
WHO...?
HIM?
HOLY COW!
HE'S GORGEOUS!
THIS IS REALLY AN HONOR FOR US--SHAKING HANDS WITH THE GREATEST SUPER-HERO OF THEM ALL!
WELL, I WOULDN'T EXACTLY GO THAT FAR..!
I'LL GO AS FAR AS YOU WANT TO TAKE ME, HANDSOME! THE NAME'S TINA--BUT YOU CAN CALL ME ANY TIME!
Y'KNOW--HE LOOKS A LOT TALLER ON TV!
C-C-COULD I SH-SH-SHAKE YOUR HAND, TOO, S-S-SUPERMAN?
TIN... IT WOULD BE MY HONOR!
DOING ANYTHING TONIGHT, BIG BOY?
WELL, I...I...
SUPERMAN--?
SUPERMAN!
EH?
IF YOU CAN TEAR YOURSELF AWAY FROM YOUR ADMIRERS FOR A SECOND, SUPERMAN--
--I THINK WE MAY HAVE FOUND THE ANSWER TO ALL YOUR PROBLEMS!
11

AND MOMENTS LATER, IN AN ADJOINING *LAB*...

SEVERAL DAYS AGO, OUR *SENSORS* DETECTED AN INCREDIBLY POWERFUL BEAM OF *MAGNETIC ENERGY* BEING BROADCAST FROM SOMEWHERE HERE ON *EARTH*--

--DIRECTLY INTO THE *HEART* OF THE *SUN!*

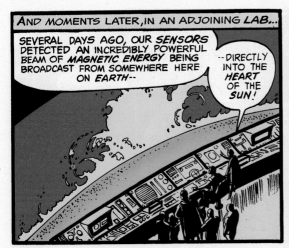

"THE *RESULT* OF THIS AWESOME MAGNETIC BOMBARDMENT APPEARS TO BE DRASTICALLY-INCREASED *SUNSPOT* ACTIVITY--

"--AND A SERIES OF *SOLAR PROMINENCES* THAT HAVE BLOWN THE *MEASURING NEEDLE* CLEAN OFF THE *SCALE!*

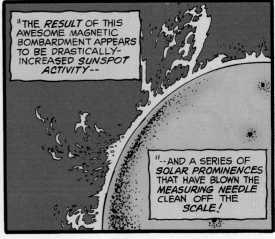

"SINCE YOUR *NON-MUSCULAR* POWERS--SUCH AS *HEAT VISION*--ARE A PRODUCT OF THE SUN'S *YELLOW RAYS*, SUPERMAN...

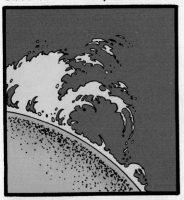

"...AND SINCE THE *RESPONSOMETERS* WHICH CONTROL THE METAL MEN'S *SHAPE-CHANGING ABILITIES* ARE SUSCEPTIBLE TO *MAGNETIC INTERFERENCE*...

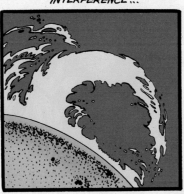

"...IT DOESN'T REALLY TAKE A GREAT DEAL OF *EFFORT* TO FIGURE OUT WHAT'S BEEN GOING *WRONG* WITH ALL OF YOU!"

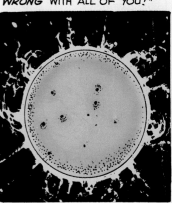

AND *NOW* IT SEEMS THE INCREASED *ULTRA-VIOLET RADIATION* BEING GIVEN OFF BY THE SUN HAS BEGUN TO AFFECT *EVERYONE!*

PEOPLE RUSHING TO THE *BEACHES* DUE TO THE *UNSEASONABLY WARM* WEATHER ARE TAKING *ILL* AT AN ALARMING *RATE!*

LOGICALLY, THE MOST *DIRECT* METHOD OF *REVERSING* THE SOLAR DISTURBANCES--

--IS TO *LOCATE* THE *SOURCE* OF THE MAGNETIC RAY THAT *CAUSED* THEM IN THE *FIRST* PLACE!

AND SINCE MOST OF MY *SUPER-SENSES* ARE PRETTY *SUSPECT* AT THE MOMENT, I COULD USE A LITTLE *HELP* IN THAT DEPARTMENT...

...IF YOU *METAL MEN* ARE WILLING TO *PROVIDE* IT!

WE'RE *WITH* YOU, SUPERMAN--*ALL THE WAY!!*

WHOOPEE!

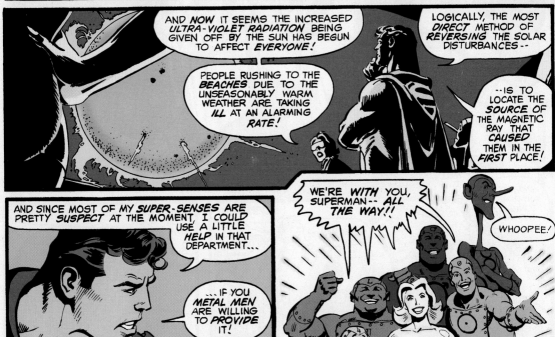

12

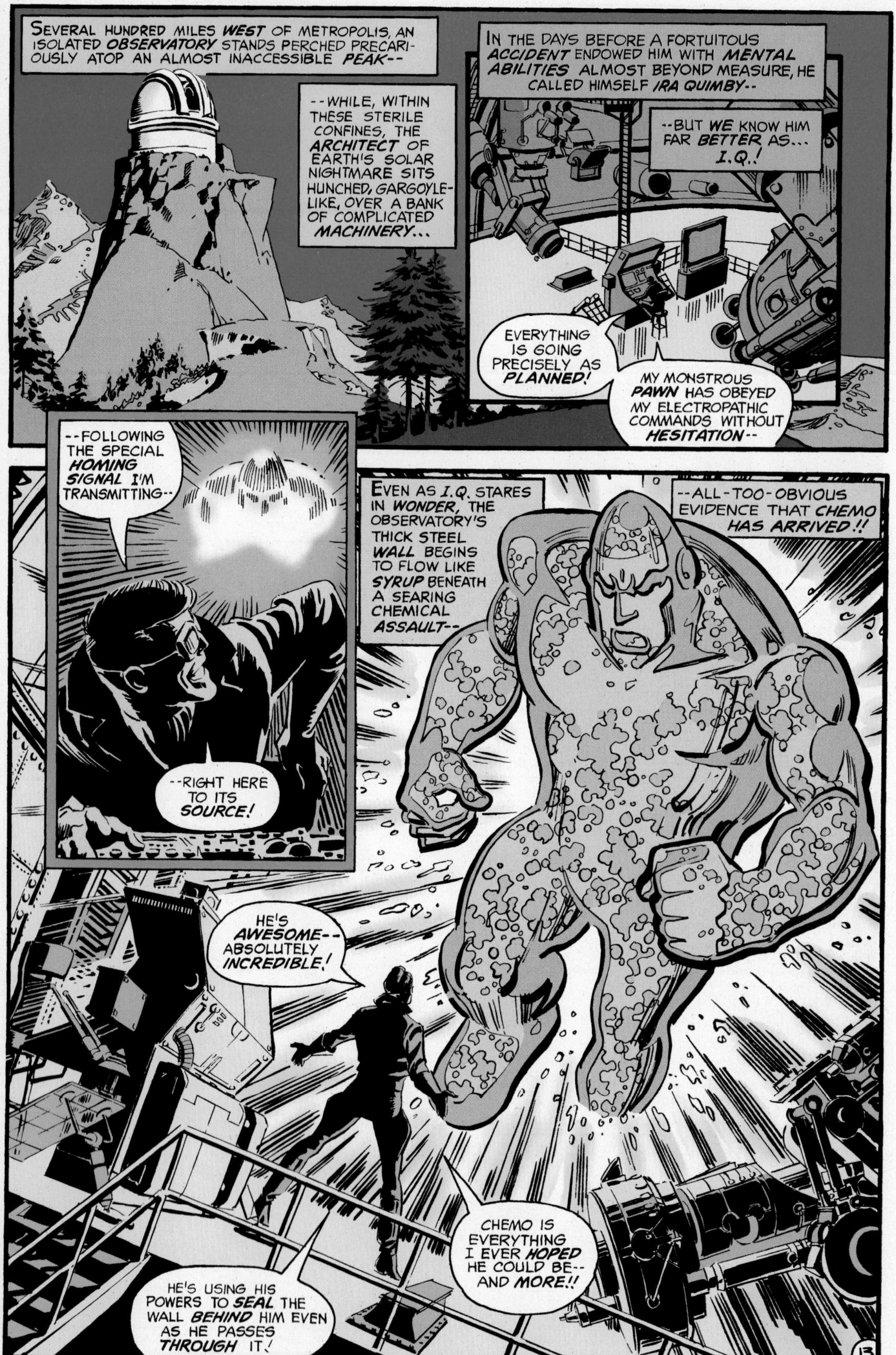
SEVERAL HUNDRED MILES WEST OF METROPOLIS, AN ISOLATED OBSERVATORY STANDS PERCHED PRECARIOUSLY ATOP AN ALMOST INACCESSIBLE PEAK--
--WHILE, WITHIN THESE STERILE CONFINES, THE ARCHITECT OF EARTH'S SOLAR NIGHTMARE SITS HUNCHED, GARGOYLE-LIKE, OVER A BANK OF COMPLICATED MACHINERY...
IN THE DAYS BEFORE A FORTUITOUS ACCIDENT ENDOWED HIM WITH MENTAL ABILITIES ALMOST BEYOND MEASURE, HE CALLED HIMSELF IRA QUIMBY--
--BUT WE KNOW HIM FAR BETTER AS... I.Q.!
EVERYTHING IS GOING PRECISELY AS PLANNED!
MY MONSTROUS PAWN HAS OBEYED MY ELECTROPATHIC COMMANDS WITHOUT HESITATION--
--FOLLOWING THE SPECIAL HOMING SIGNAL I'M TRANSMITTING--
--RIGHT HERE TO ITS SOURCE!
EVEN AS I.Q. STARES IN WONDER, THE OBSERVATORY'S THICK STEEL WALL BEGINS TO FLOW LIKE SYRUP BENEATH A SEARING CHEMICAL ASSAULT--
--ALL-TOO-OBVIOUS EVIDENCE THAT CHEMO HAS ARRIVED!!
HE'S AWESOME--ABSOLUTELY INCREDIBLE!
HE'S USING HIS POWERS TO SEAL THE WALL BEHIND HIM EVEN AS HE PASSES THROUGH IT!
CHEMO IS EVERYTHING I EVER HOPED HE COULD BE--AND MORE!!
13

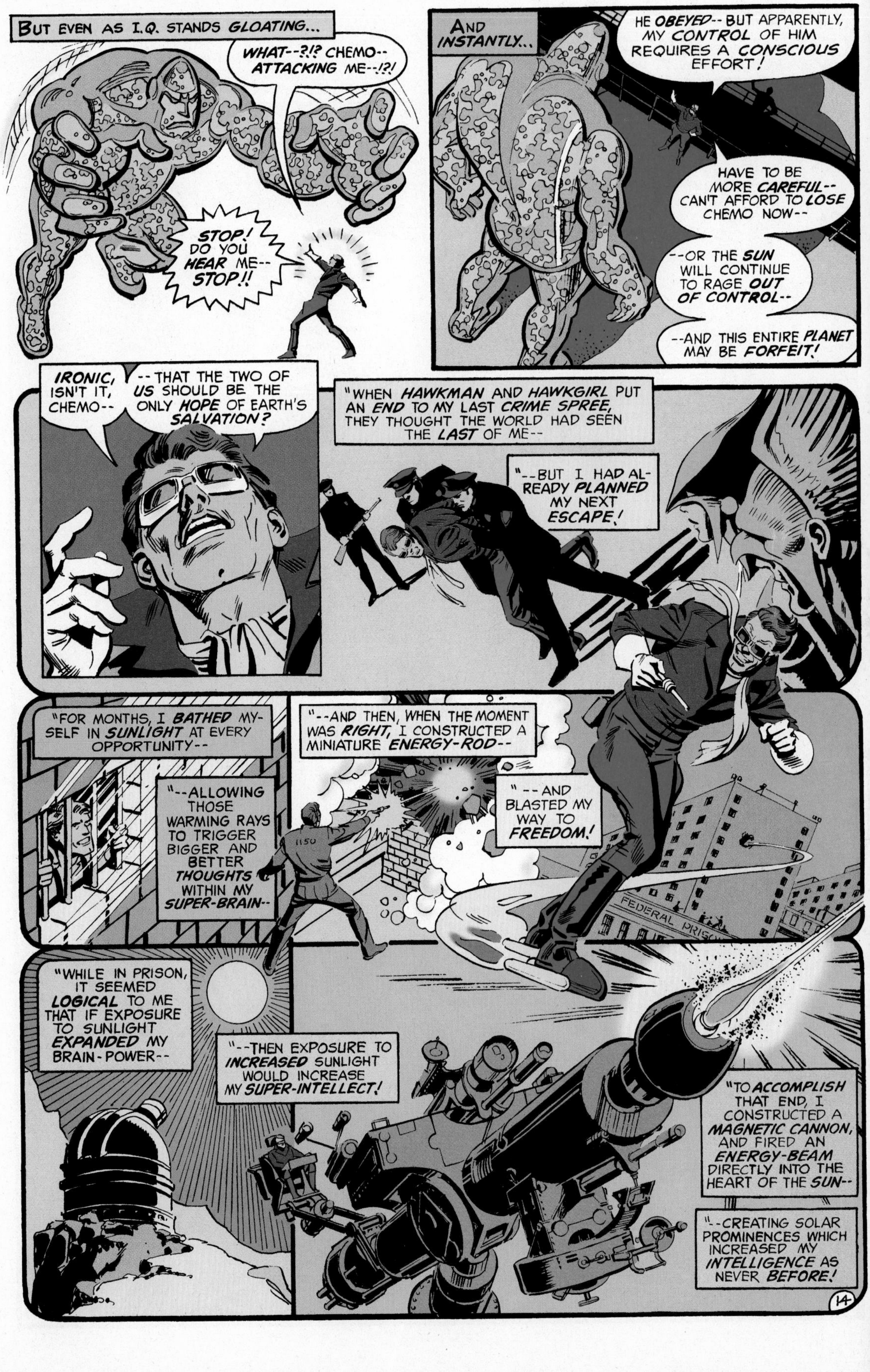
BUT EVEN AS I.Q. STANDS GLOATING...
WHAT--?!? CHEMO-- ATTACKING ME--!?!
STOP! DO YOU HEAR ME-- STOP!!
AND INSTANTLY...
HE OBEYED-- BUT APPARENTLY, MY CONTROL OF HIM REQUIRES A CONSCIOUS EFFORT!
HAVE TO BE MORE CAREFUL-- CAN'T AFFORD TO LOSE CHEMO NOW--
--OR THE SUN WILL CONTINUE TO RAGE OUT OF CONTROL--
--AND THIS ENTIRE PLANET MAY BE FORFEIT!
IRONIC, ISN'T IT, CHEMO--
--THAT THE TWO OF US SHOULD BE THE ONLY HOPE OF EARTH'S SALVATION?
"WHEN HAWKMAN AND HAWKGIRL PUT AN END TO MY LAST CRIME SPREE, THEY THOUGHT THE WORLD HAD SEEN THE LAST OF ME--
"--BUT I HAD ALREADY PLANNED MY NEXT ESCAPE!
"FOR MONTHS, I BATHED MYSELF IN SUNLIGHT AT EVERY OPPORTUNITY--
"--ALLOWING THOSE WARMING RAYS TO TRIGGER BIGGER AND BETTER THOUGHTS WITHIN MY SUPER-BRAIN--
"--AND THEN, WHEN THE MOMENT WAS RIGHT, I CONSTRUCTED A MINIATURE ENERGY-ROD--
1150
"--AND BLASTED MY WAY TO FREEDOM!
FEDERAL PRISON
"WHILE IN PRISON, IT SEEMED LOGICAL TO ME THAT IF EXPOSURE TO SUNLIGHT EXPANDED MY BRAIN-POWER--
"--THEN EXPOSURE TO INCREASED SUNLIGHT WOULD INCREASE MY SUPER-INTELLECT!
"TO ACCOMPLISH THAT END, I CONSTRUCTED A MAGNETIC CANNON, AND FIRED AN ENERGY-BEAM DIRECTLY INTO THE HEART OF THE SUN--
"--CREATING SOLAR PROMINENCES WHICH INCREASED MY INTELLIGENCE AS NEVER BEFORE!
14

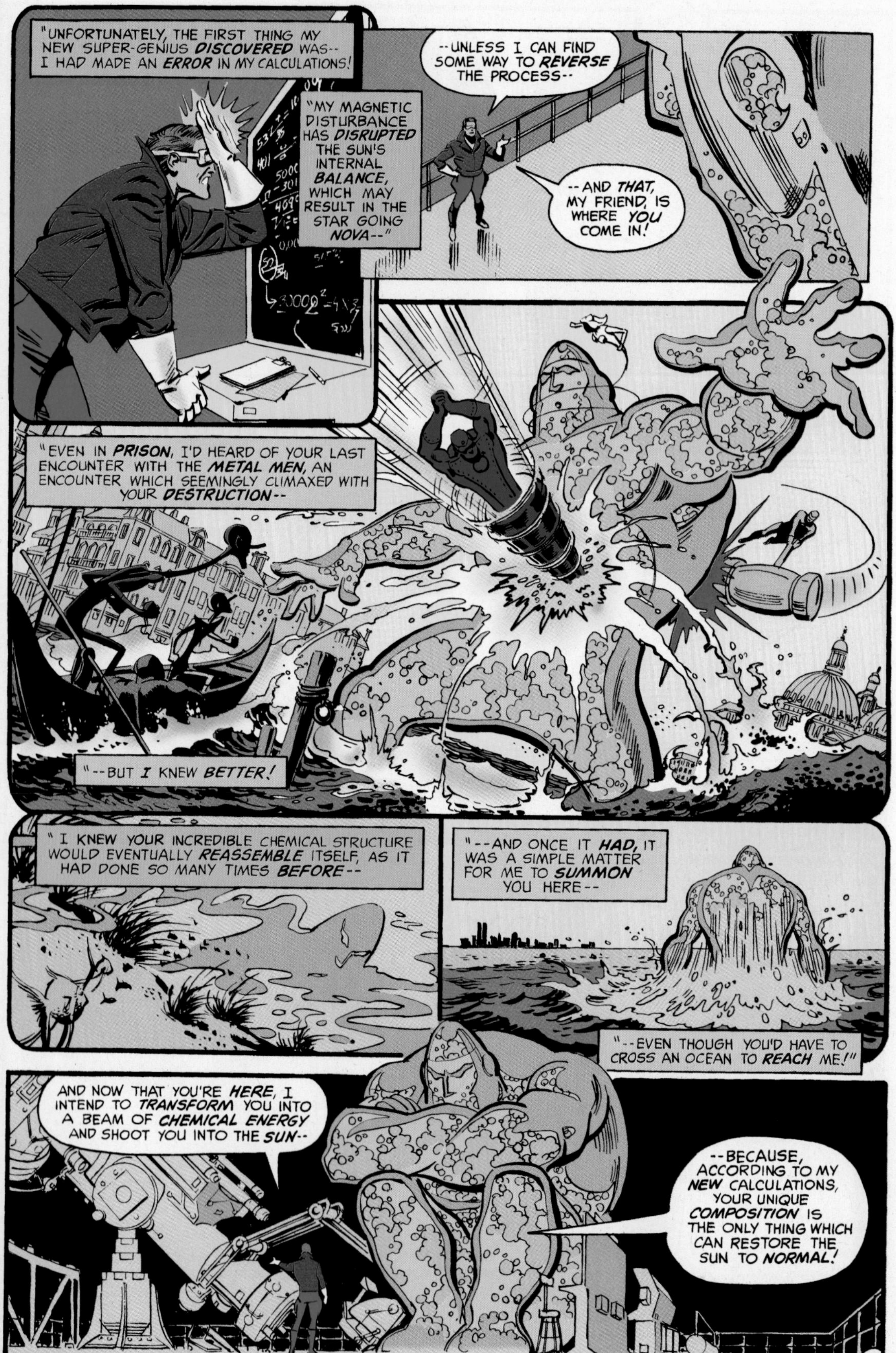
"UNFORTUNATELY, THE FIRST THING MY NEW SUPER-GENIUS DISCOVERED WAS-- I HAD MADE AN ERROR IN MY CALCULATIONS!
"MY MAGNETIC DISTURBANCE HAS DISRUPTED THE SUN'S INTERNAL BALANCE, WHICH MAY RESULT IN THE STAR GOING NOVA--"
--UNLESS I CAN FIND SOME WAY TO REVERSE THE PROCESS--
--AND THAT, MY FRIEND, IS WHERE YOU COME IN!
"EVEN IN PRISON, I'D HEARD OF YOUR LAST ENCOUNTER WITH THE METAL MEN, AN ENCOUNTER WHICH SEEMINGLY CLIMAXED WITH YOUR DESTRUCTION--
"--BUT I KNEW BETTER!
"I KNEW YOUR INCREDIBLE CHEMICAL STRUCTURE WOULD EVENTUALLY REASSEMBLE ITSELF, AS IT HAD DONE SO MANY TIMES BEFORE--
"--AND ONCE IT HAD, IT WAS A SIMPLE MATTER FOR ME TO SUMMON YOU HERE--
"--EVEN THOUGH YOU'D HAVE TO CROSS AN OCEAN TO REACH ME!"
AND NOW THAT YOU'RE HERE, I INTEND TO TRANSFORM YOU INTO A BEAM OF CHEMICAL ENERGY AND SHOOT YOU INTO THE SUN--
--BECAUSE, ACCORDING TO MY NEW CALCULATIONS, YOUR UNIQUE COMPOSITION IS THE ONLY THING WHICH CAN RESTORE THE SUN TO NORMAL!
15

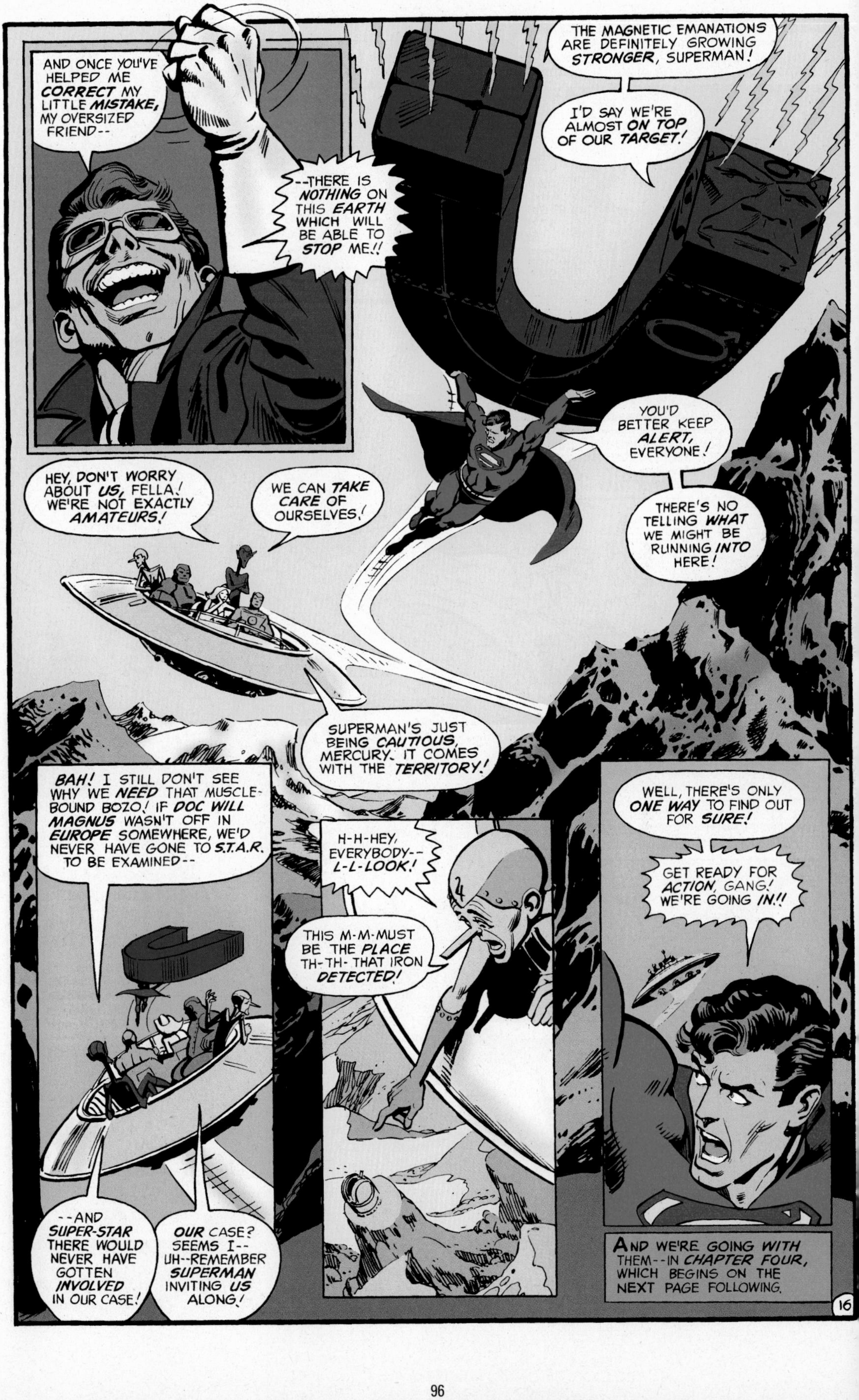
AND ONCE YOU'VE HELPED ME CORRECT MY LITTLE MISTAKE, MY OVERSIZED FRIEND--
--THERE IS NOTHING ON THIS EARTH WHICH WILL BE ABLE TO STOP ME!!
THE MAGNETIC EMANATIONS ARE DEFINITELY GROWING STRONGER, SUPERMAN!
I'D SAY WE'RE ALMOST ON TOP OF OUR TARGET!
YOU'D BETTER KEEP ALERT, EVERYONE!
THERE'S NO TELLING WHAT WE MIGHT BE RUNNING INTO HERE!
HEY, DON'T WORRY ABOUT US, FELLA! WE'RE NOT EXACTLY AMATEURS!
WE CAN TAKE CARE OF OURSELVES!
SUPERMAN'S JUST BEING CAUTIOUS, MERCURY. IT COMES WITH THE TERRITORY!
BAH! I STILL DON'T SEE WHY WE NEED THAT MUSCLE-BOUND BOZO! IF DOC WILL MAGNUS WASN'T OFF IN EUROPE SOMEWHERE, WE'D NEVER HAVE GONE TO S.T.A.R. TO BE EXAMINED--
--AND SUPER-STAR THERE WOULD NEVER HAVE GOTTEN INVOLVED IN OUR CASE!
OUR CASE? SEEMS I--UH--REMEMBER SUPERMAN INVITING US ALONG!
H-H-HEY, EVERYBODY-- L-L-LOOK!
THIS M-M-MUST BE THE PLACE TH-TH- THAT IRON DETECTED!
WELL, THERE'S ONLY ONE WAY TO FIND OUT FOR SURE!
GET READY FOR ACTION, GANG! WE'RE GOING IN!!
AND WE'RE GOING WITH THEM--IN CHAPTER FOUR, WHICH BEGINS ON THE NEXT PAGE FOLLOWING.
16

CHAPTER FOUR: IS THIS THE WAY THE WORLD ENDS?

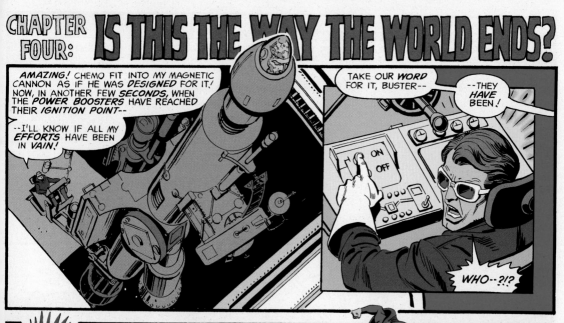

AMAZING! CHEMO FIT INTO MY MAGNETIC CANNON AS IF HE WAS *DESIGNED* FOR IT! NOW, IN ANOTHER FEW *SECONDS*, WHEN THE *POWER BOOSTERS* HAVE REACHED THEIR *IGNITION POINT*--

--I'LL KNOW IF ALL MY *EFFORTS* HAVE BEEN IN *VAIN!*

TAKE OUR *WORD* FOR IT, BUSTER--

--THEY *HAVE* BEEN!

WHO--?!?

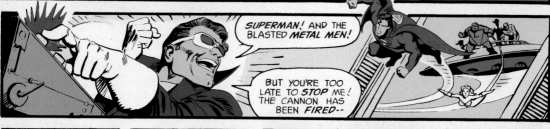

SUPERMAN! AND THE BLASTED *METAL MEN!*

BUT YOU'RE TOO LATE TO *STOP* ME! THE CANNON HAS BEEN *FIRED*--

"--AND IN *8.3* MINUTES, MY *CHEMO-BEAM* WILL PIERCE THE VERY *HEART* OF THE *SUN!*"

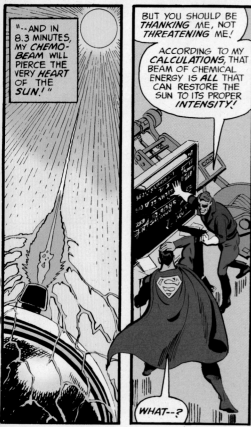

BUT YOU SHOULD BE *THANKING* ME, NOT *THREATENING* ME!

ACCORDING TO MY *CALCULATIONS*, THAT BEAM OF CHEMICAL ENERGY IS *ALL* THAT CAN RESTORE THE SUN TO ITS PROPER *INTENSITY!*

WHAT--?

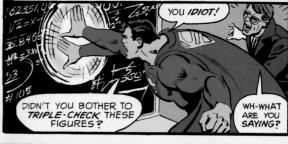

YOU *IDIOT!*

DIDN'T YOU BOTHER TO *TRIPLE-CHECK* THESE FIGURES?

WH-WHAT ARE YOU SAYING?

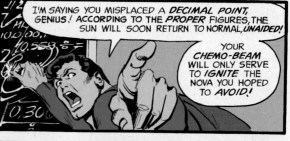

I'M SAYING YOU MISPLACED A *DECIMAL POINT*, GENIUS! ACCORDING TO THE *PROPER* FIGURES, THE SUN WILL SOON RETURN TO NORMAL, *UNAIDED!*

YOUR *CHEMO-BEAM* WILL ONLY SERVE TO *IGNITE* THE NOVA YOU HOPED TO *AVOID!*

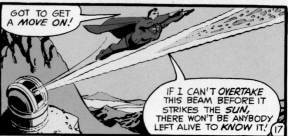

GOT TO GET A *MOVE ON!*

IF I CAN'T *OVERTAKE* THIS BEAM BEFORE IT STRIKES THE *SUN*, THERE WON'T BE ANYBODY LEFT ALIVE TO *KNOW* IT!

17

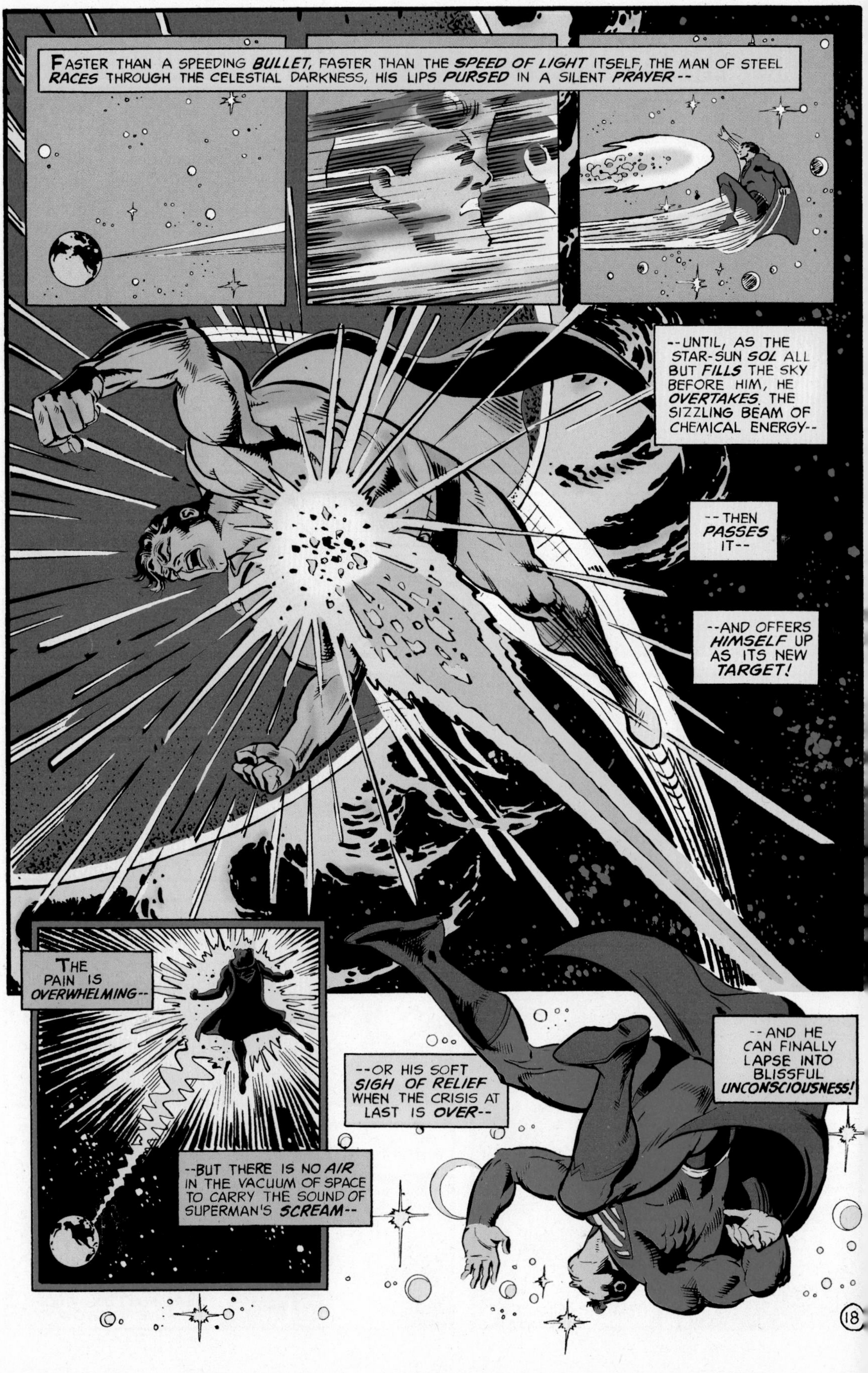
FASTER THAN A SPEEDING BULLET, FASTER THAN THE SPEED OF LIGHT ITSELF, THE MAN OF STEEL RACES THROUGH THE CELESTIAL DARKNESS, HIS LIPS PURSED IN A SILENT PRAYER--
--UNTIL, AS THE STAR-SUN SOL ALL BUT FILLS THE SKY BEFORE HIM, HE OVERTAKES THE SIZZLING BEAM OF CHEMICAL ENERGY--
--THEN PASSES IT--
--AND OFFERS HIMSELF UP AS ITS NEW TARGET!
THE PAIN IS OVERWHELMING--
--BUT THERE IS NO AIR IN THE VACUUM OF SPACE TO CARRY THE SOUND OF SUPERMAN'S SCREAM--
--OR HIS SOFT SIGH OF RELIEF WHEN THE CRISIS AT LAST IS OVER--
--AND HE CAN FINALLY LAPSE INTO BLISSFUL UNCONSCIOUSNESS!
18

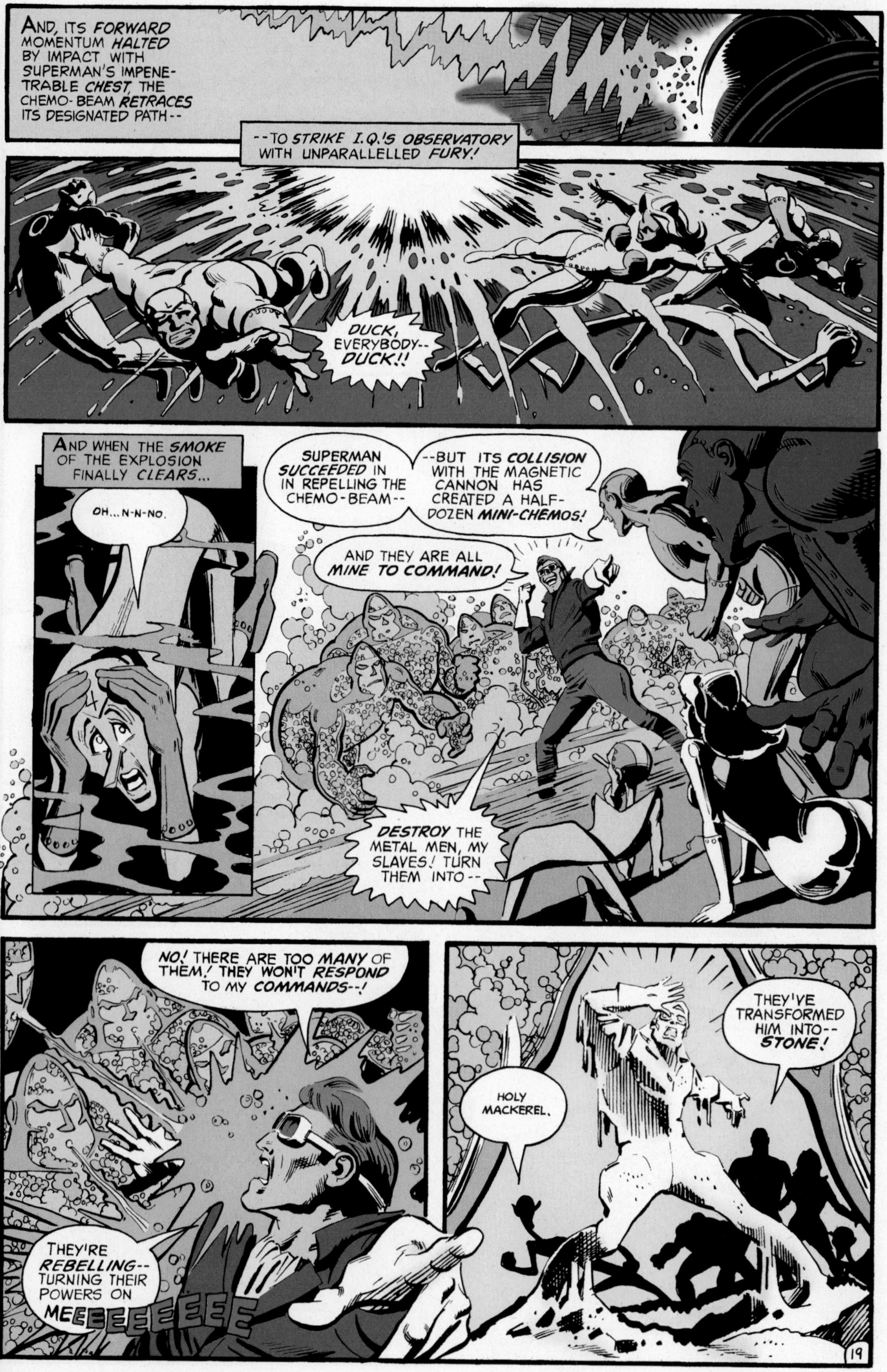
AND, ITS FORWARD MOMENTUM HALTED BY IMPACT WITH SUPERMAN'S IMPENETRABLE CHEST, THE CHEMO-BEAM RETRACES ITS DESIGNATED PATH--
--TO STRIKE I.Q.'S OBSERVATORY WITH UNPARALLELLED FURY!
DUCK, EVERYBODY--DUCK!!
AND WHEN THE SMOKE OF THE EXPLOSION FINALLY CLEARS...
OH... N-N-NO.
SUPERMAN SUCCEEDED IN IN REPELLING THE CHEMO-BEAM--
--BUT ITS COLLISION WITH THE MAGNETIC CANNON HAS CREATED A HALF-DOZEN MINI-CHEMOS!
AND THEY ARE ALL MINE TO COMMAND!
DESTROY THE METAL MEN, MY SLAVES! TURN THEM INTO--
NO! THERE ARE TOO MANY OF THEM! THEY WON'T RESPOND TO MY COMMANDS--!
THEY'RE REBELLING--TURNING THEIR POWERS ON MEEEEEEEEE
THEY'VE TRANSFORMED HIM INTO--STONE!
HOLY MACKEREL.
19

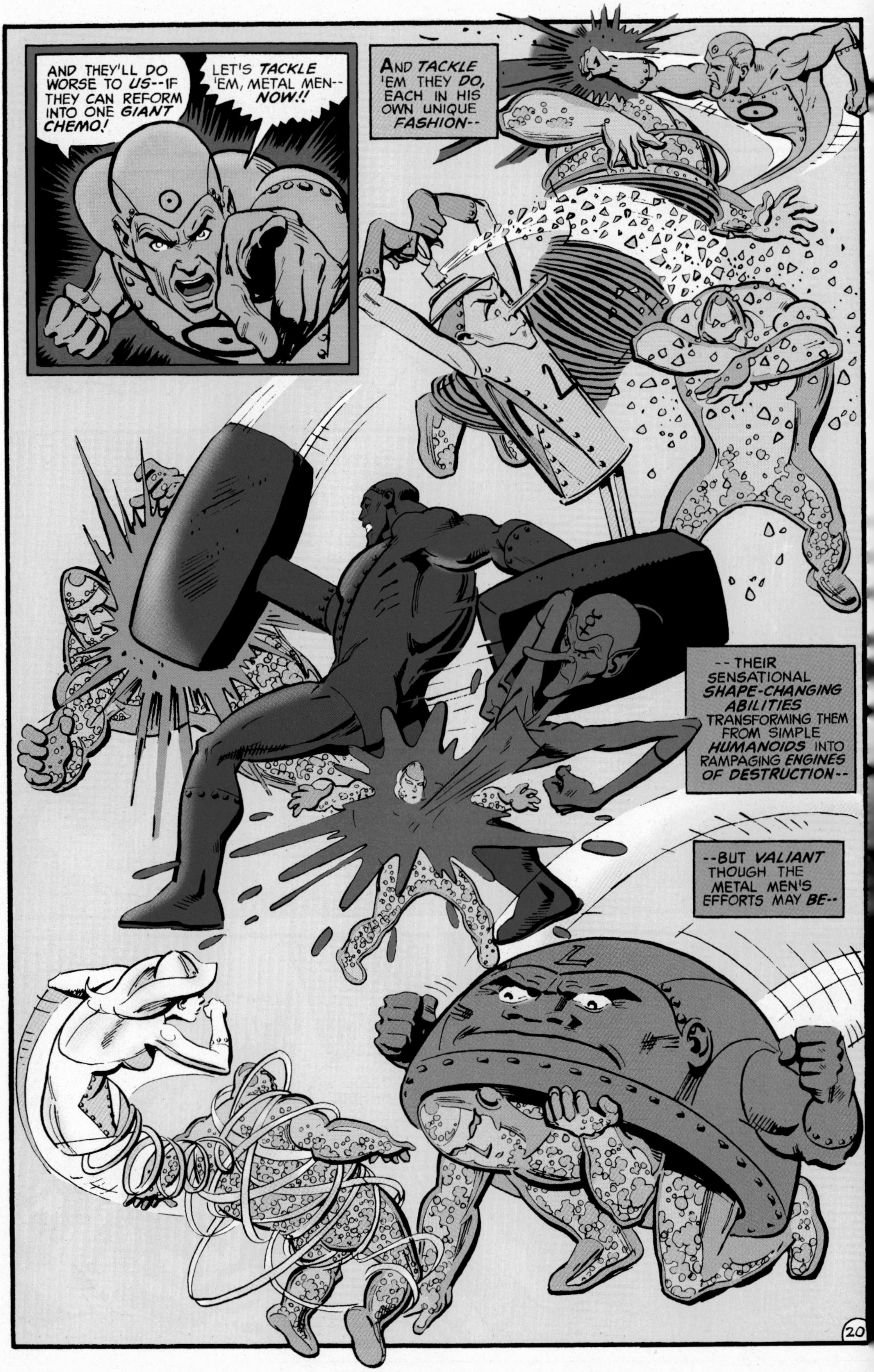
AND THEY'LL DO WORSE TO US--IF THEY CAN REFORM INTO ONE GIANT CHEMO!
LET'S TACKLE 'EM, METAL MEN-- NOW!!
AND TACKLE 'EM THEY DO, EACH IN HIS OWN UNIQUE FASHION--
--THEIR SENSATIONAL SHAPE-CHANGING ABILITIES TRANSFORMING THEM FROM SIMPLE HUMANOIDS INTO RAMPAGING ENGINES OF DESTRUCTION--
--BUT VALIANT THOUGH THE METAL MEN'S EFFORTS MAY BE--
20

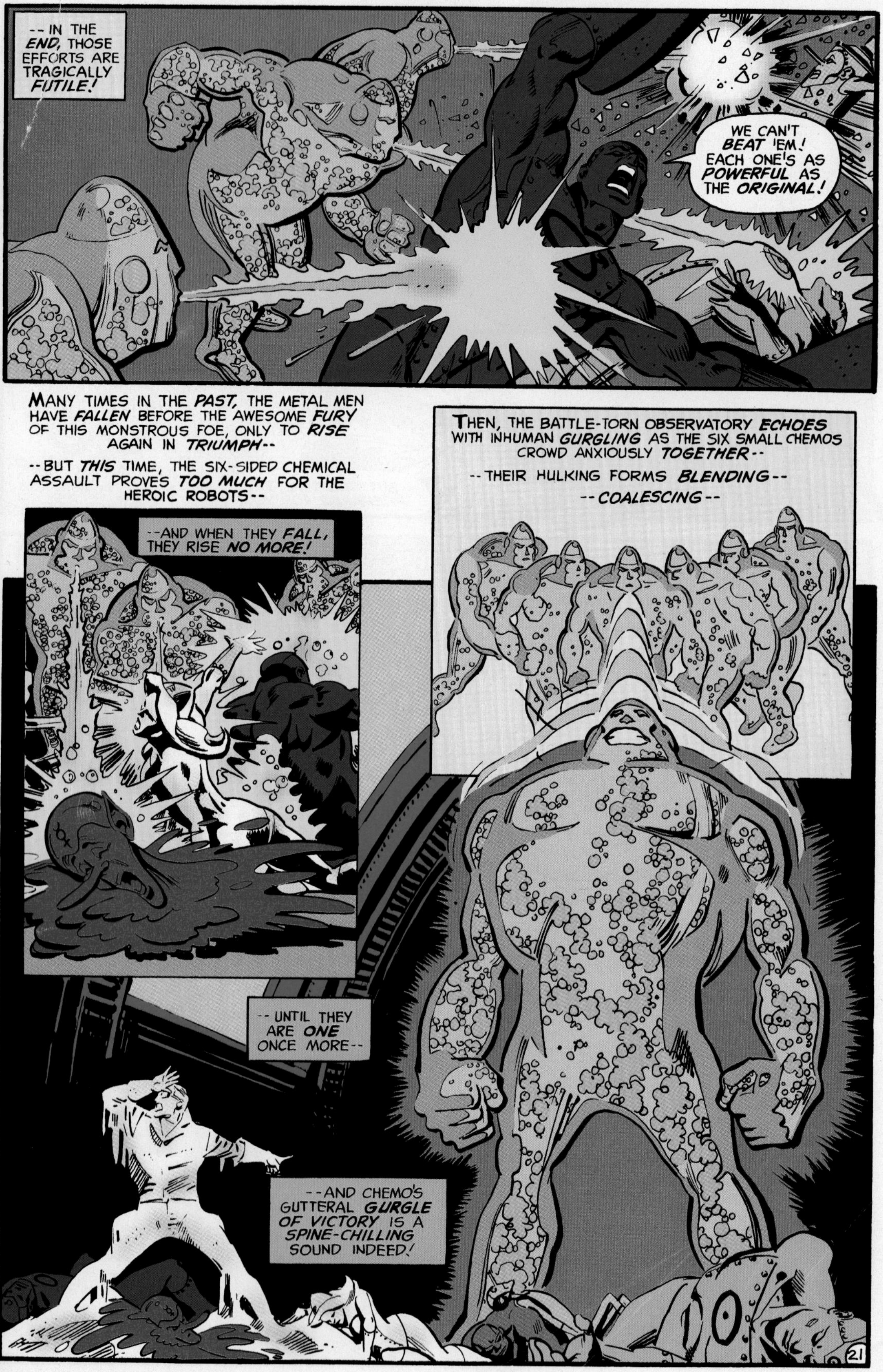
-- IN THE END, THOSE EFFORTS ARE TRAGICALLY FUTILE!
WE CAN'T BEAT 'EM! EACH ONE'S AS POWERFUL AS THE ORIGINAL!
MANY TIMES IN THE PAST, THE METAL MEN HAVE FALLEN BEFORE THE AWESOME FURY OF THIS MONSTROUS FOE, ONLY TO RISE AGAIN IN TRIUMPH--
-- BUT THIS TIME, THE SIX-SIDED CHEMICAL ASSAULT PROVES TOO MUCH FOR THE HEROIC ROBOTS--
--AND WHEN THEY FALL, THEY RISE NO MORE!
THEN, THE BATTLE-TORN OBSERVATORY ECHOES WITH INHUMAN GURGLING AS THE SIX SMALL CHEMOS CROWD ANXIOUSLY TOGETHER--
-- THEIR HULKING FORMS BLENDING--
-- COALESCING--
-- UNTIL THEY ARE ONE ONCE MORE--
--AND CHEMO'S GUTTERAL GURGLE OF VICTORY IS A SPINE-CHILLING SOUND INDEED!
21

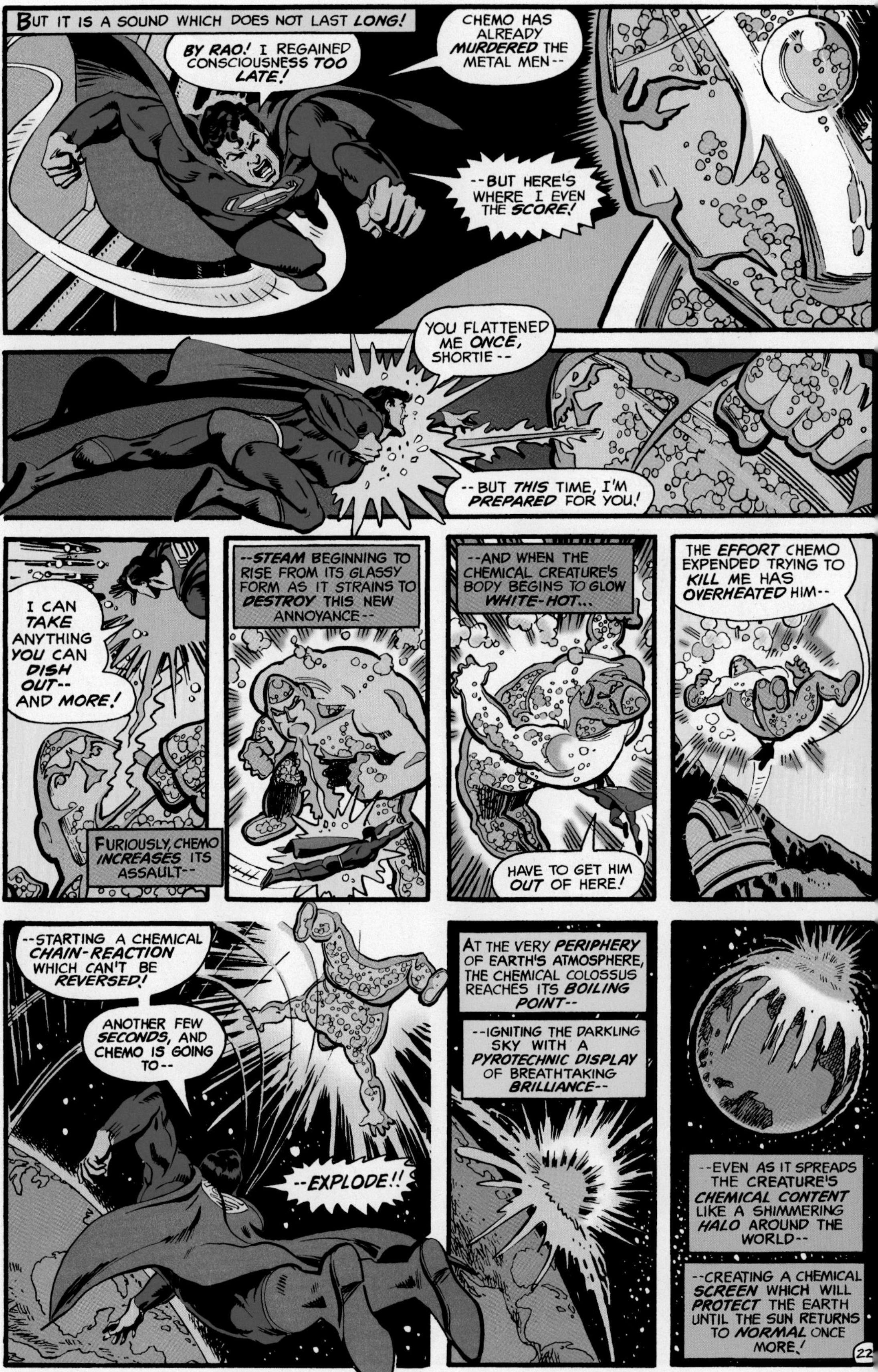
BUT IT IS A SOUND WHICH DOES NOT LAST LONG!
BY RAO! I REGAINED CONSCIOUSNESS TOO LATE!
CHEMO HAS ALREADY MURDERED THE METAL MEN--
--BUT HERE'S WHERE I EVEN THE SCORE!
YOU FLATTENED ME ONCE, SHORTIE--
--BUT THIS TIME, I'M PREPARED FOR YOU!
I CAN TAKE ANYTHING YOU CAN DISH OUT-- AND MORE!
FURIOUSLY, CHEMO INCREASES ITS ASSAULT--
--STEAM BEGINNING TO RISE FROM ITS GLASSY FORM AS IT STRAINS TO DESTROY THIS NEW ANNOYANCE--
--AND WHEN THE CHEMICAL CREATURE'S BODY BEGINS TO GLOW WHITE-HOT...
HAVE TO GET HIM OUT OF HERE!
THE EFFORT CHEMO EXPENDED TRYING TO KILL ME HAS OVERHEATED HIM--
--STARTING A CHEMICAL CHAIN-REACTION WHICH CAN'T BE REVERSED!
ANOTHER FEW SECONDS, AND CHEMO IS GOING TO--
--EXPLODE!!
AT THE VERY PERIPHERY OF EARTH'S ATMOSPHERE, THE CHEMICAL COLOSSUS REACHES ITS BOILING POINT--
--IGNITING THE DARKLING SKY WITH A PYROTECHNIC DISPLAY OF BREATHTAKING BRILLIANCE--
--EVEN AS IT SPREADS THE CREATURE'S CHEMICAL CONTENT LIKE A SHIMMERING HALO AROUND THE WORLD--
--CREATING A CHEMICAL SCREEN WHICH WILL PROTECT THE EARTH UNTIL THE SUN RETURNS TO NORMAL ONCE MORE!
22

EPILOGUE: AFTER THE BRAWL IS OVER...!

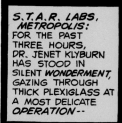

S.T.A.R. LABS, METROPOLIS: FOR THE PAST THREE HOURS, DR. JENET KLYBURN HAS STOOD IN SILENT *WONDERMENT*, GAZING THROUGH THICK PLEXIGLASS AT A MOST DELICATE *OPERATION*--

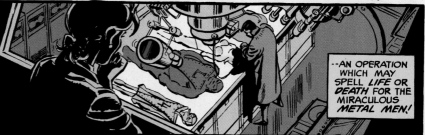

--AN OPERATION WHICH MAY SPELL *LIFE* OR *DEATH* FOR THE MIRACULOUS *METAL MEN!*

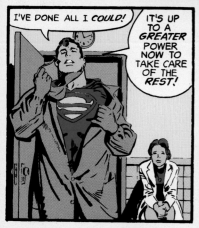

I'VE DONE ALL I *COULD!*

IT'S UP TO A *GREATER* POWER NOW TO TAKE CARE OF THE *REST!*

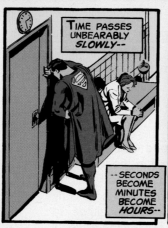

TIME PASSES UNBEARABLY *SLOWLY*--

--SECONDS BECOME MINUTES BECOME *HOURS*--

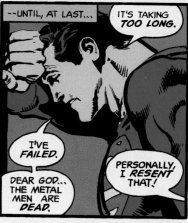

--UNTIL, AT LAST...

IT'S TAKING *TOO LONG.*

I'VE *FAILED.*

DEAR GOD... THE METAL MEN ARE *DEAD.*

PERSONALLY, I *RESENT* THAT!

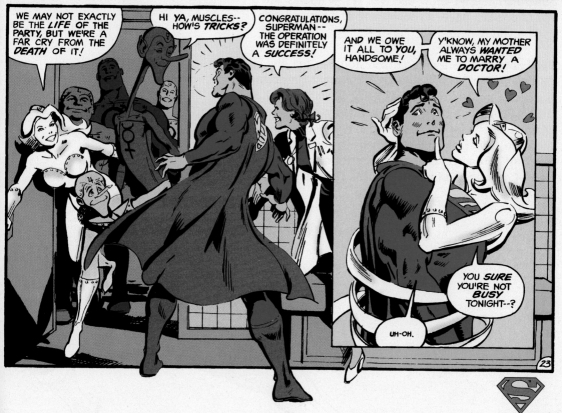

WE MAY NOT EXACTLY BE THE *LIFE* OF THE PARTY, BUT WE'RE A FAR CRY FROM THE *DEATH* OF IT!

HI YA, MUSCLES-- HOW'S *TRICKS?*

CONGRATULATIONS, SUPERMAN -- THE OPERATION WAS DEFINITELY A *SUCCESS!*

AND WE OWE IT ALL TO *YOU*, HANDSOME!

Y'KNOW, MY MOTHER ALWAYS *WANTED* ME TO MARRY A *DOCTOR!*

YOU *SURE* YOU'RE NOT *BUSY* TONIGHT--?

UH-OH.

23

103

ACTION-PLUS
WITH FIRESTORM

DC COMICS PRESENTS #17

"Wait a minute," I hear you say. You thought this was supposed to be offbeat team-ups. Firestorm's a main-line superhero, and one of Superman's Justice League buddies, isn't he?

Well, yes. And no.

First off, we did think it was a good idea to have at least one of the characters featured in the lead story represented here in the back of the book, so Firestorm fits the bill pretty well there. Second, this is an early Firestorm story, back before he joined the League, so Superman doesn't know him well yet — and as you'll see on the last page, it's something of a turning point for the young hero.

I will note that it's a *different* Firestorm — the guy in "Back in Action" is Jason Rusch, the current Firestorm, bonded with Senator Lorraine Reilly, while this guy is the original, Ronnie Raymond, bonded with Professor Martin Stein. A lot has happened in the DCU between then and now, but none of it needs to keep you from enjoying an energetic story by Firestorm's co-creator, Gerry Conway, and the ineffable Mr. García-López…

— kdb

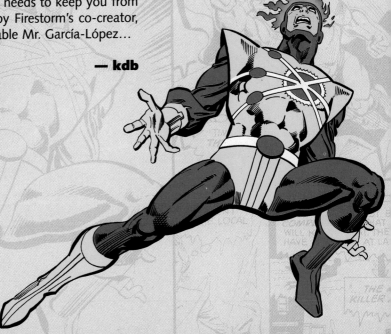

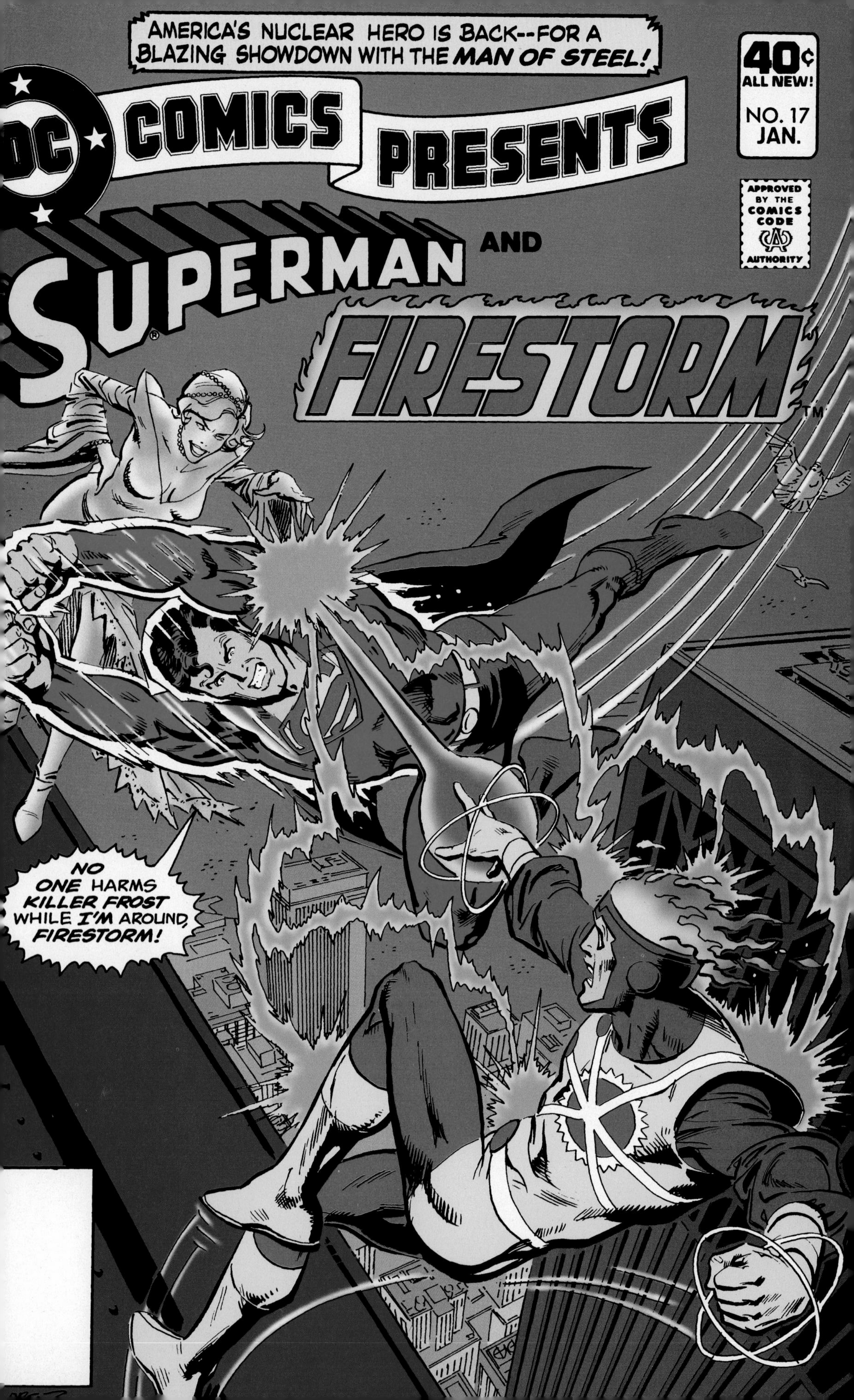
AMERICA'S NUCLEAR HERO IS BACK--FOR A BLAZING SHOWDOWN WITH THE MAN OF STEEL!
40¢ ALL NEW!
NO. 17 JAN.
DC COMICS PRESENTS
APPROVED BY THE COMICS CODE AUTHORITY
SUPERMAN AND FIRESTORM
NO ONE HARMS KILLER FROST WHILE I'M AROUND, FIRESTORM!

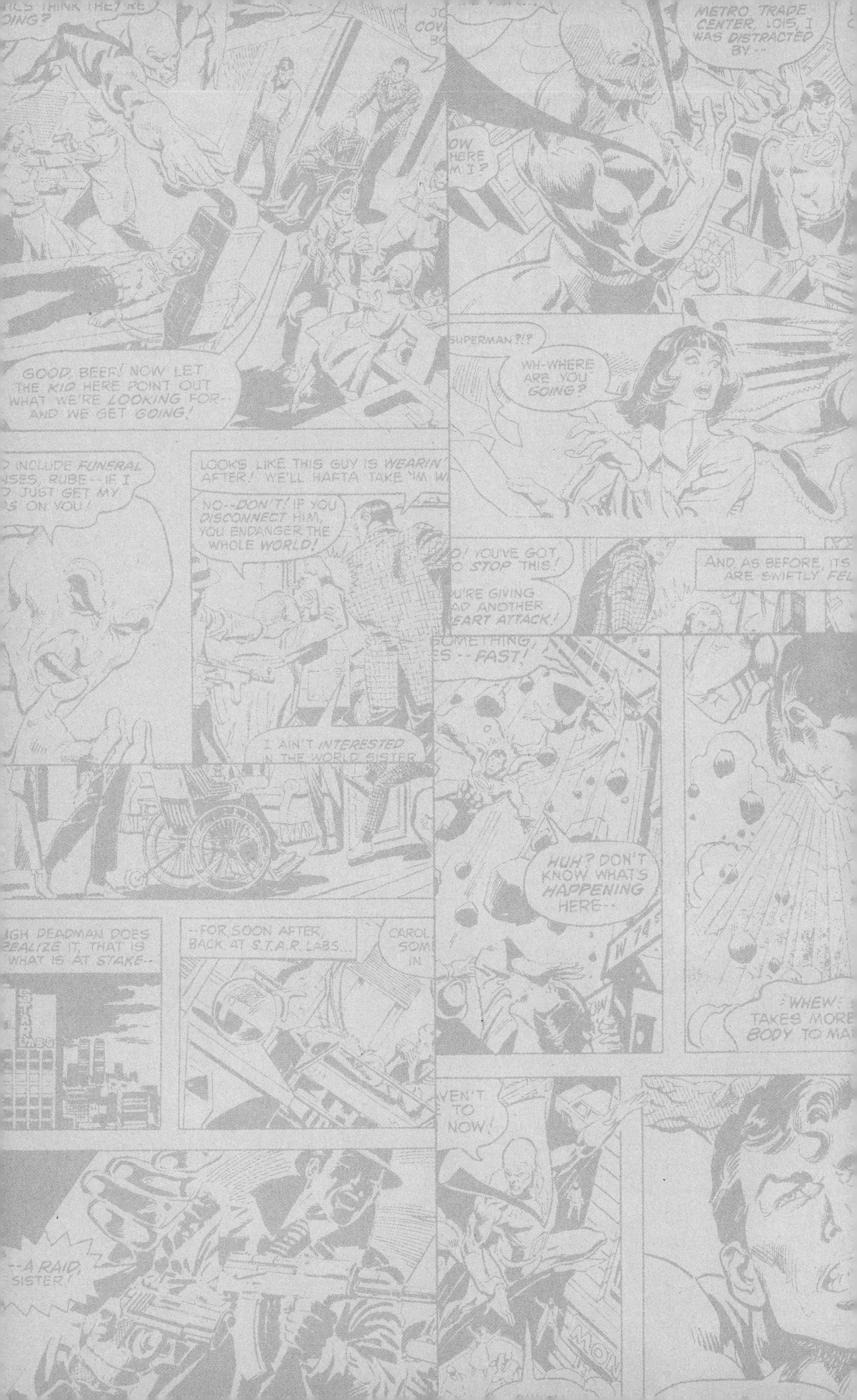

METRO TRADE CENTER, LOIS, I WAS DISTRACTED BY--
GOOD, BEEF! NOW LET THE KID HERE POINT OUT WHAT WE'RE LOOKING FOR-- AND WE GET GOING!
SUPERMAN?!?
WH-WHERE ARE YOU GOING?
LOOKS LIKE THIS GUY IS WEARIN'
NO--DON'T! IF YOU DISCONNECT HIM, YOU ENDANGER THE WHOLE WORLD!
AND AS BEFORE, ITS
ARE SWIFTLY
I AIN'T INTERESTED
HUH? DON'T KNOW WHAT'S HAPPENING HERE--
--FOR, SOON AFTER, BACK AT S.T.A.R. LABS...
WHEW
TAKES MORE
--A RAID, SISTER!

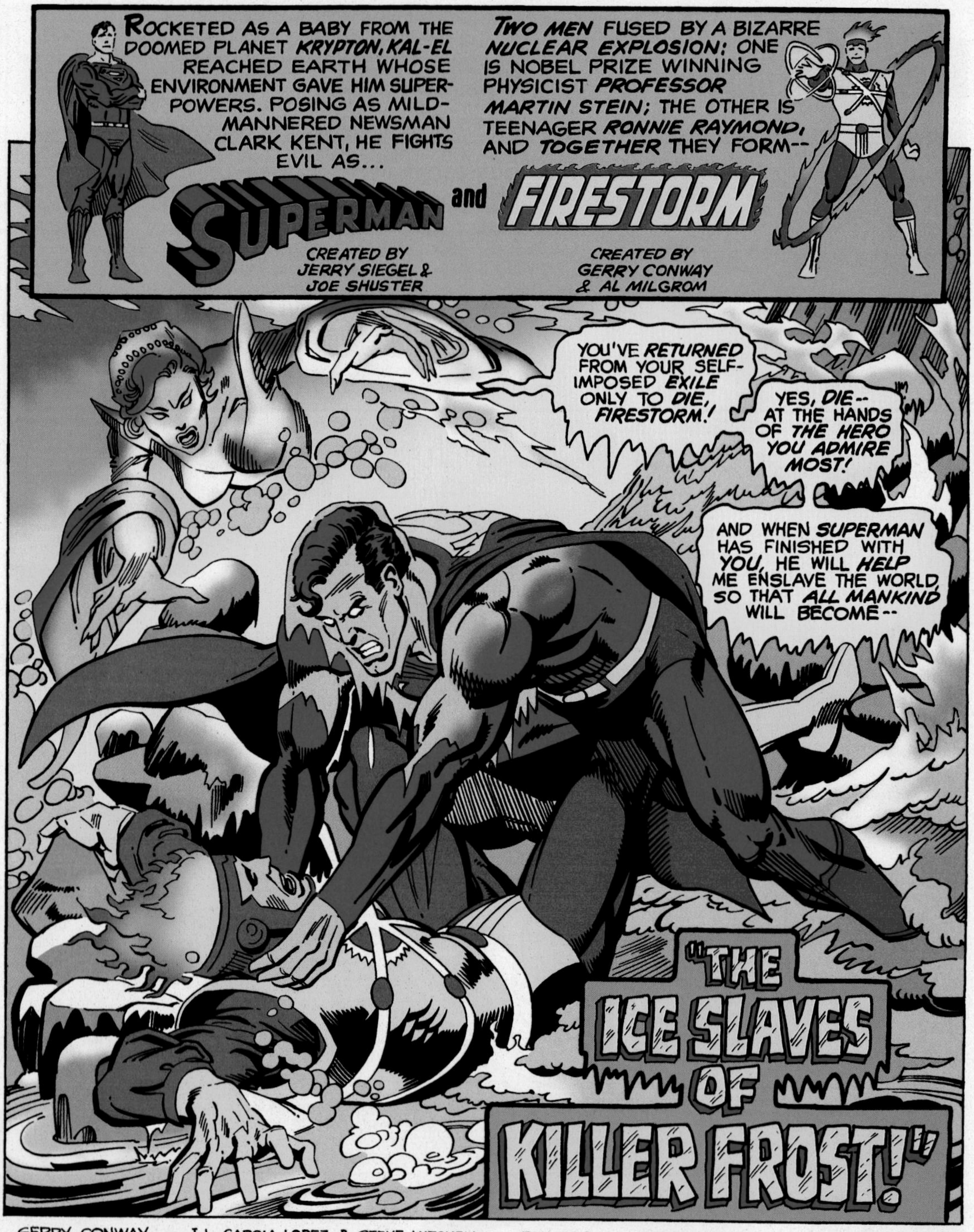
ROCKETED AS A BABY FROM THE DOOMED PLANET KRYPTON, KAL-EL REACHED EARTH WHOSE ENVIRONMENT GAVE HIM SUPER-POWERS. POSING AS MILD-MANNERED NEWSMAN CLARK KENT, HE FIGHTS EVIL AS...
TWO MEN FUSED BY A BIZARRE NUCLEAR EXPLOSION: ONE IS NOBEL PRIZE WINNING PHYSICIST PROFESSOR MARTIN STEIN; THE OTHER IS TEENAGER RONNIE RAYMOND, AND TOGETHER THEY FORM--
SUPERMAN and FIRESTORM
CREATED BY JERRY SIEGEL & JOE SHUSTER
CREATED BY GERRY CONWAY & AL MILGROM
YOU'VE RETURNED FROM YOUR SELF-IMPOSED EXILE ONLY TO DIE, FIRESTORM!
YES, DIE-- AT THE HANDS OF THE HERO YOU ADMIRE MOST!
AND WHEN SUPERMAN HAS FINISHED WITH YOU, HE WILL HELP ME ENSLAVE THE WORLD, SO THAT ALL MANKIND WILL BECOME--
"THE ICE SLAVES OF KILLER FROST!"

GERRY CONWAY WRITER * J.L. GARCIA LOPEZ & STEVE MITCHELL ARTISTS * BEN ODA LETTERER * JERRY SERPE COLORIST * JULIUS SCHWARTZ EDITOR

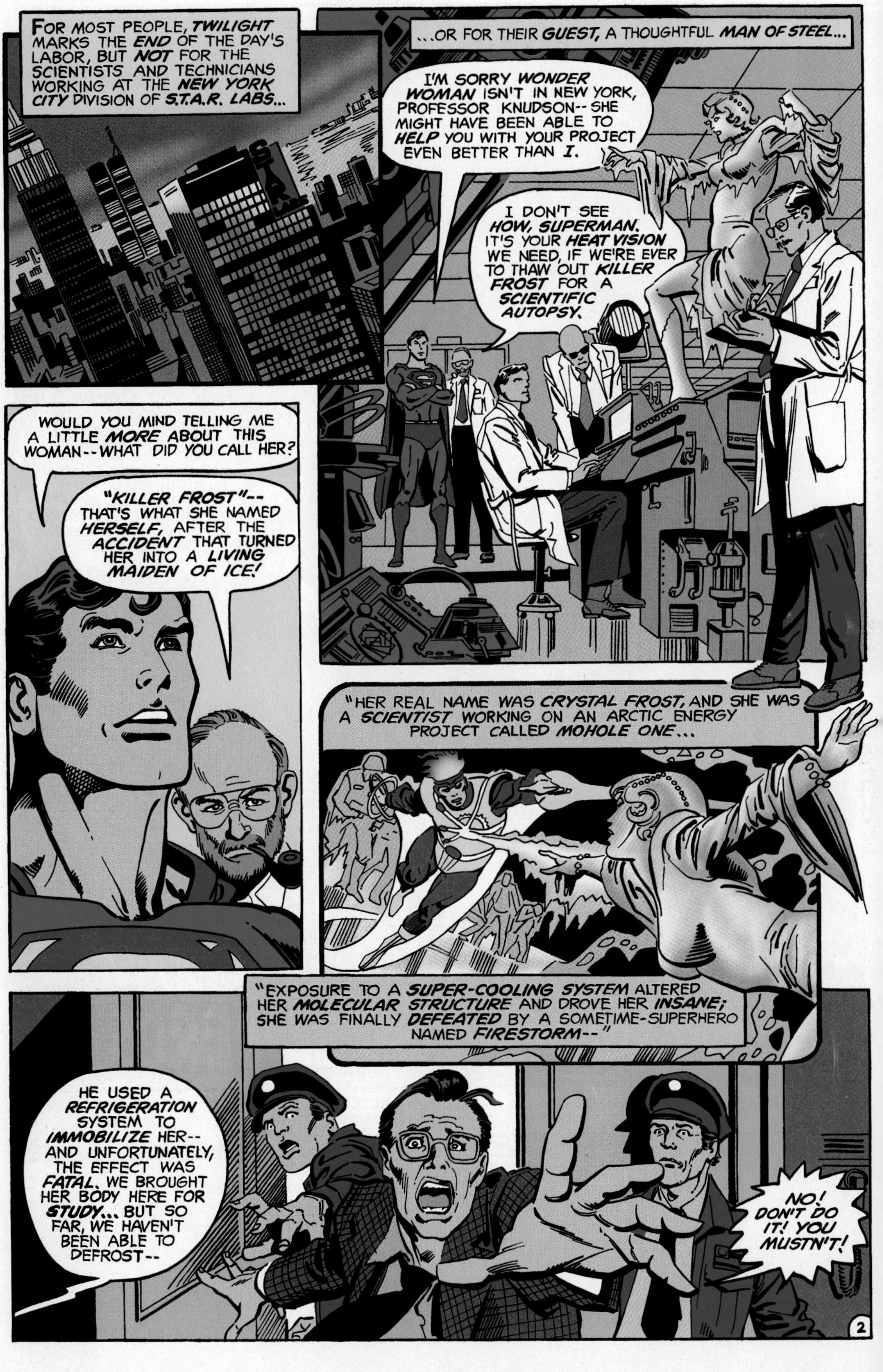
FOR MOST PEOPLE, TWILIGHT MARKS THE END OF THE DAY'S LABOR, BUT NOT FOR THE SCIENTISTS AND TECHNICIANS WORKING AT THE NEW YORK CITY DIVISION OF S.T.A.R. LABS...
...OR FOR THEIR GUEST, A THOUGHTFUL MAN OF STEEL...
I'M SORRY WONDER WOMAN ISN'T IN NEW YORK, PROFESSOR KNUDSON-- SHE MIGHT HAVE BEEN ABLE TO HELP YOU WITH YOUR PROJECT EVEN BETTER THAN I.
I DON'T SEE HOW, SUPERMAN. IT'S YOUR HEAT VISION WE NEED, IF WE'RE EVER TO THAW OUT KILLER FROST FOR A SCIENTIFIC AUTOPSY.
WOULD YOU MIND TELLING ME A LITTLE MORE ABOUT THIS WOMAN--WHAT DID YOU CALL HER?
"KILLER FROST"-- THAT'S WHAT SHE NAMED HERSELF, AFTER THE ACCIDENT THAT TURNED HER INTO A LIVING MAIDEN OF ICE!
"HER REAL NAME WAS CRYSTAL FROST, AND SHE WAS A SCIENTIST WORKING ON AN ARCTIC ENERGY PROJECT CALLED MOHOLE ONE...
"EXPOSURE TO A SUPER-COOLING SYSTEM ALTERED HER MOLECULAR STRUCTURE AND DROVE HER INSANE; SHE WAS FINALLY DEFEATED BY A SOMETIME-SUPERHERO NAMED FIRESTORM--"
HE USED A REFRIGERATION SYSTEM TO IMMOBILIZE HER-- AND UNFORTUNATELY, THE EFFECT WAS FATAL. WE BROUGHT HER BODY HERE FOR STUDY... BUT SO FAR, WE HAVEN'T BEEN ABLE TO DEFROST--
NO! DON'T DO IT! YOU MUSTN'T!
2

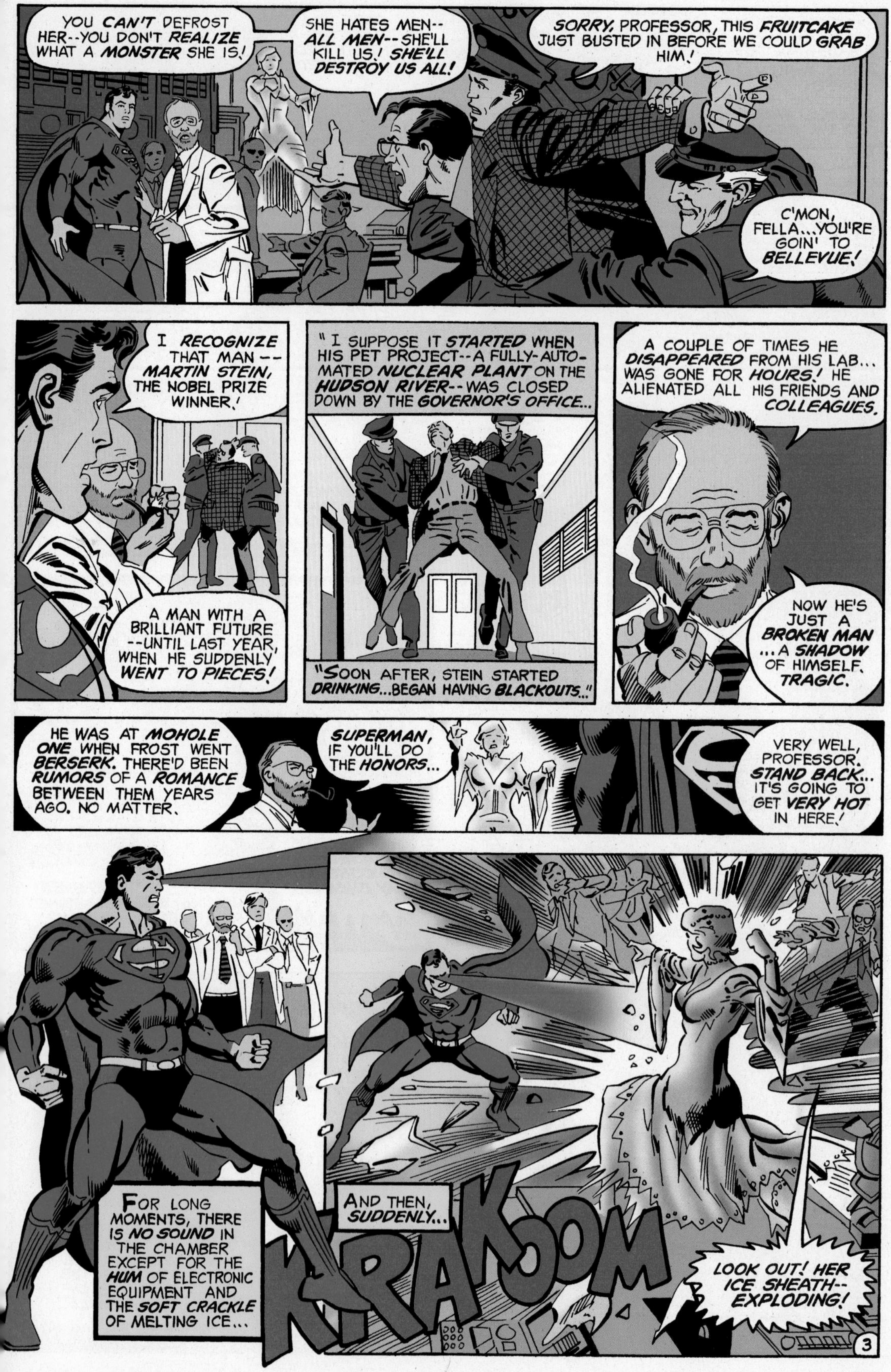

YOU CAN'T DEFROST HER--YOU DON'T REALIZE WHAT A MONSTER SHE IS!
SHE HATES MEN--ALL MEN--SHE'LL KILL US! SHE'LL DESTROY US ALL!
SORRY, PROFESSOR, THIS FRUITCAKE JUST BUSTED IN BEFORE WE COULD GRAB HIM!
C'MON, FELLA...YOU'RE GOIN' TO BELLEVUE!
I RECOGNIZE THAT MAN--MARTIN STEIN, THE NOBEL PRIZE WINNER!
A MAN WITH A BRILLIANT FUTURE--UNTIL LAST YEAR, WHEN HE SUDDENLY WENT TO PIECES!
"I SUPPOSE IT STARTED WHEN HIS PET PROJECT--A FULLY-AUTOMATED NUCLEAR PLANT ON THE HUDSON RIVER--WAS CLOSED DOWN BY THE GOVERNOR'S OFFICE...
"SOON AFTER, STEIN STARTED DRINKING...BEGAN HAVING BLACKOUTS..."
A COUPLE OF TIMES HE DISAPPEARED FROM HIS LAB... WAS GONE FOR HOURS! HE ALIENATED ALL HIS FRIENDS AND COLLEAGUES.
NOW HE'S JUST A BROKEN MAN...A SHADOW OF HIMSELF. TRAGIC.
HE WAS AT MOHOLE ONE WHEN FROST WENT BERSERK. THERE'D BEEN RUMORS OF A ROMANCE BETWEEN THEM YEARS AGO. NO MATTER.
SUPERMAN, IF YOU'LL DO THE HONORS...
VERY WELL, PROFESSOR. STAND BACK... IT'S GOING TO GET VERY HOT IN HERE!
FOR LONG MOMENTS, THERE IS NO SOUND IN THE CHAMBER EXCEPT FOR THE HUM OF ELECTRONIC EQUIPMENT AND THE SOFT CRACKLE OF MELTING ICE...
AND THEN, SUDDENLY...
KRAKOOM
LOOK OUT! HER ICE SHEATH--EXPLODING!
3

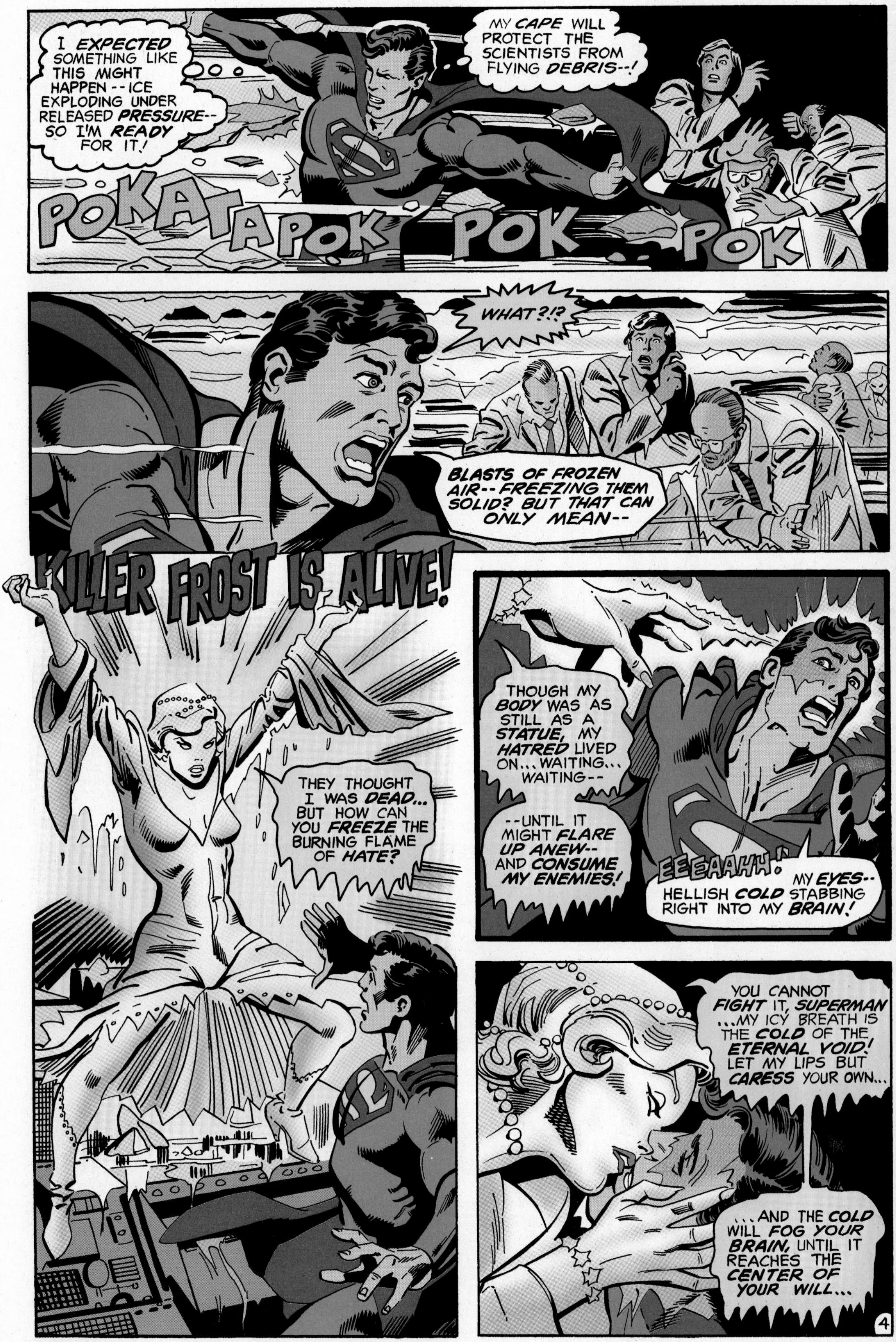
I EXPECTED SOMETHING LIKE THIS MIGHT HAPPEN--ICE EXPLODING UNDER RELEASED PRESSURE--SO I'M READY FOR IT!
MY CAPE WILL PROTECT THE SCIENTISTS FROM FLYING DEBRIS--!
POKATAPOK POK POK
WHAT?!?
BLASTS OF FROZEN AIR--FREEZING THEM SOLID? BUT THAT CAN ONLY MEAN--
KILLER FROST IS ALIVE!
THEY THOUGHT I WAS DEAD... BUT HOW CAN YOU FREEZE THE BURNING FLAME OF HATE?
THOUGH MY BODY WAS AS STILL AS A STATUE, MY HATRED LIVED ON... WAITING... WAITING--
--UNTIL IT MIGHT FLARE UP ANEW--AND CONSUME MY ENEMIES!
EEEAAHH!
MY EYES--HELLISH COLD STABBING RIGHT INTO MY BRAIN!
YOU CANNOT FIGHT IT, SUPERMAN ...MY ICY BREATH IS THE COLD OF THE ETERNAL VOID! LET MY LIPS BUT CARESS YOUR OWN...
...AND THE COLD WILL FOG YOUR BRAIN, UNTIL IT REACHES THE CENTER OF YOUR WILL...
4

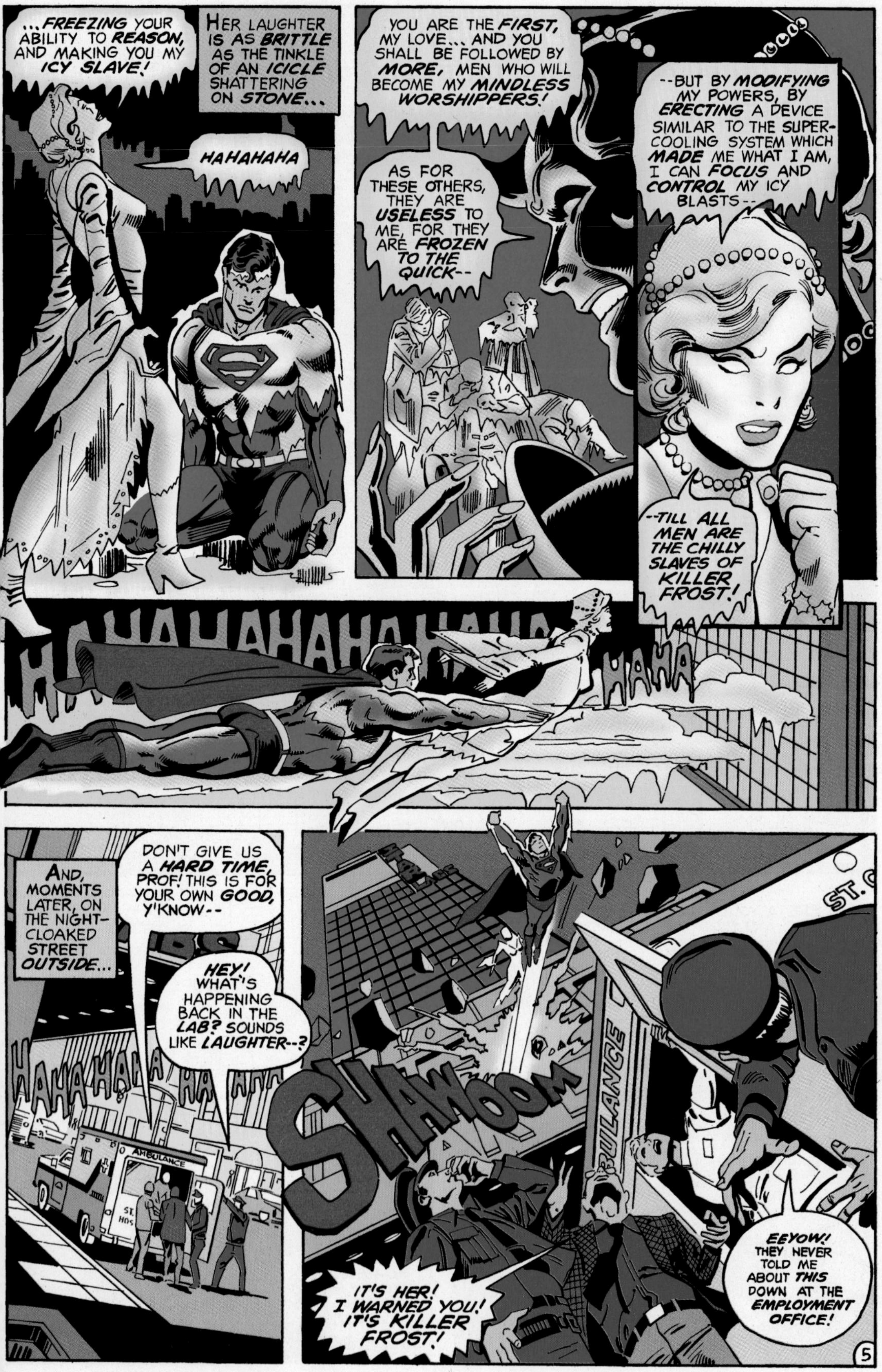
...FREEZING YOUR ABILITY TO REASON, AND MAKING YOU MY ICY SLAVE!
HER LAUGHTER IS AS BRITTLE AS THE TINKLE OF AN ICICLE SHATTERING ON STONE...
HAHAHAHA
YOU ARE THE FIRST, MY LOVE... AND YOU SHALL BE FOLLOWED BY MORE, MEN WHO WILL BECOME MY MINDLESS WORSHIPPERS!
AS FOR THESE OTHERS, THEY ARE USELESS TO ME, FOR THEY ARE FROZEN TO THE QUICK--
--BUT BY MODIFYING MY POWERS, BY ERECTING A DEVICE SIMILAR TO THE SUPER-COOLING SYSTEM WHICH MADE ME WHAT I AM, I CAN FOCUS AND CONTROL MY ICY BLASTS--
--TILL ALL MEN ARE THE CHILLY SLAVES OF KILLER FROST!
HAHA
AND, MOMENTS LATER, ON THE NIGHT-CLOAKED STREET OUTSIDE...
DON'T GIVE US A HARD TIME, PROF! THIS IS FOR YOUR OWN GOOD, Y'KNOW--
HEY! WHAT'S HAPPENING BACK IN THE LAB? SOUNDS LIKE LAUGHTER--?
AMBULANCE
SHAWOOM
IT'S HER! I WARNED YOU! IT'S KILLER FROST!
EEYOW! THEY NEVER TOLD ME ABOUT THIS DOWN AT THE EMPLOYMENT OFFICE!
5

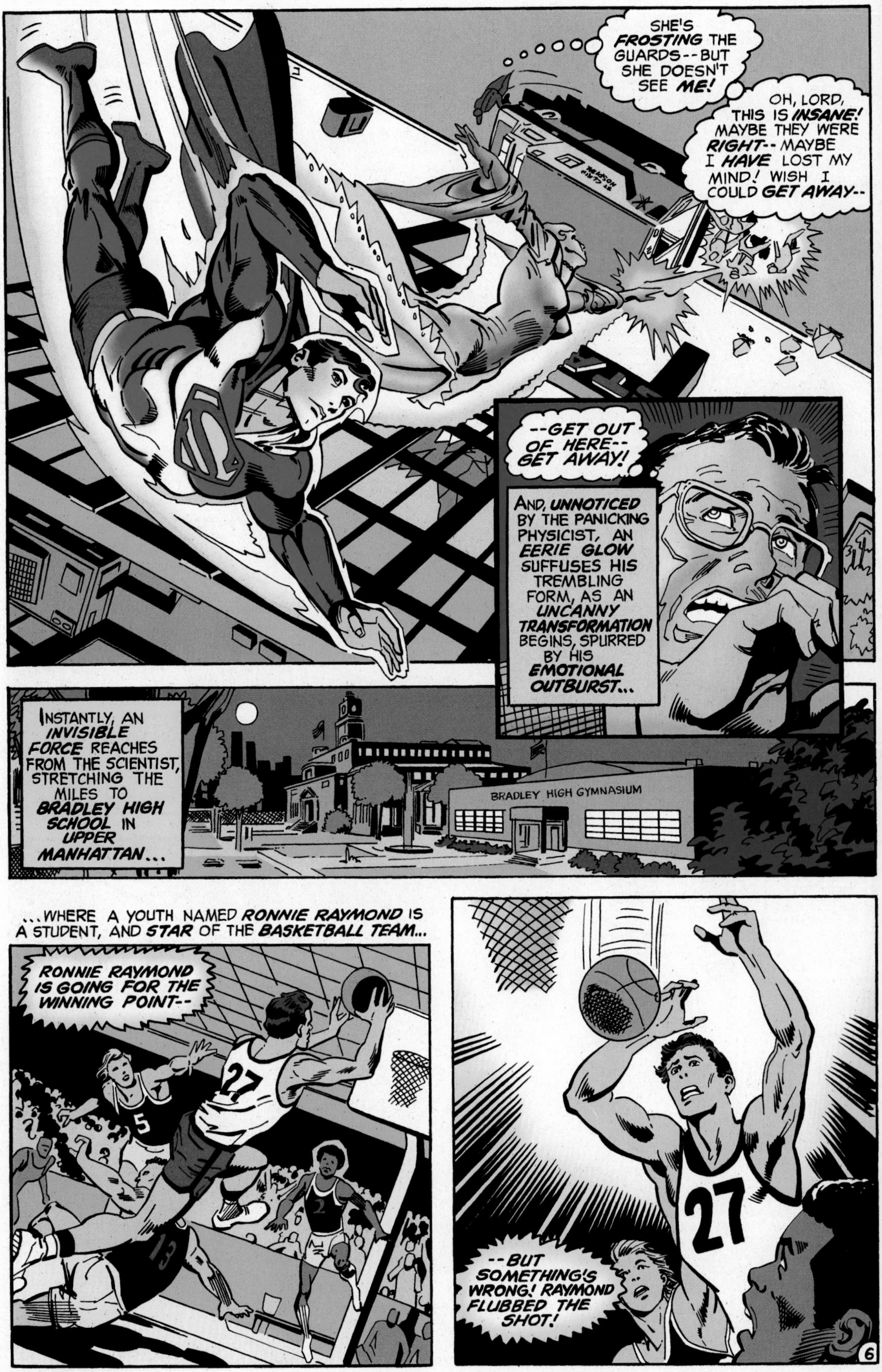
SHE'S FROSTING THE GUARDS--BUT SHE DOESN'T SEE ME!
OH, LORD, THIS IS INSANE! MAYBE THEY WERE RIGHT--MAYBE I HAVE LOST MY MIND! WISH I COULD GET AWAY--
--GET OUT OF HERE--GET AWAY!
AND, UNNOTICED BY THE PANICKING PHYSICIST, AN EERIE GLOW SUFFUSES HIS TREMBLING FORM, AS AN UNCANNY TRANSFORMATION BEGINS, SPURRED BY HIS EMOTIONAL OUTBURST...
INSTANTLY, AN INVISIBLE FORCE REACHES FROM THE SCIENTIST, STRETCHING THE MILES TO BRADLEY HIGH SCHOOL IN UPPER MANHATTAN...
BRADLEY HIGH GYMNASIUM
...WHERE A YOUTH NAMED RONNIE RAYMOND IS A STUDENT, AND STAR OF THE BASKETBALL TEAM...
RONNIE RAYMOND IS GOING FOR THE WINNING POINT--
--BUT SOMETHING'S WRONG! RAYMOND FLUBBED THE SHOT!
6

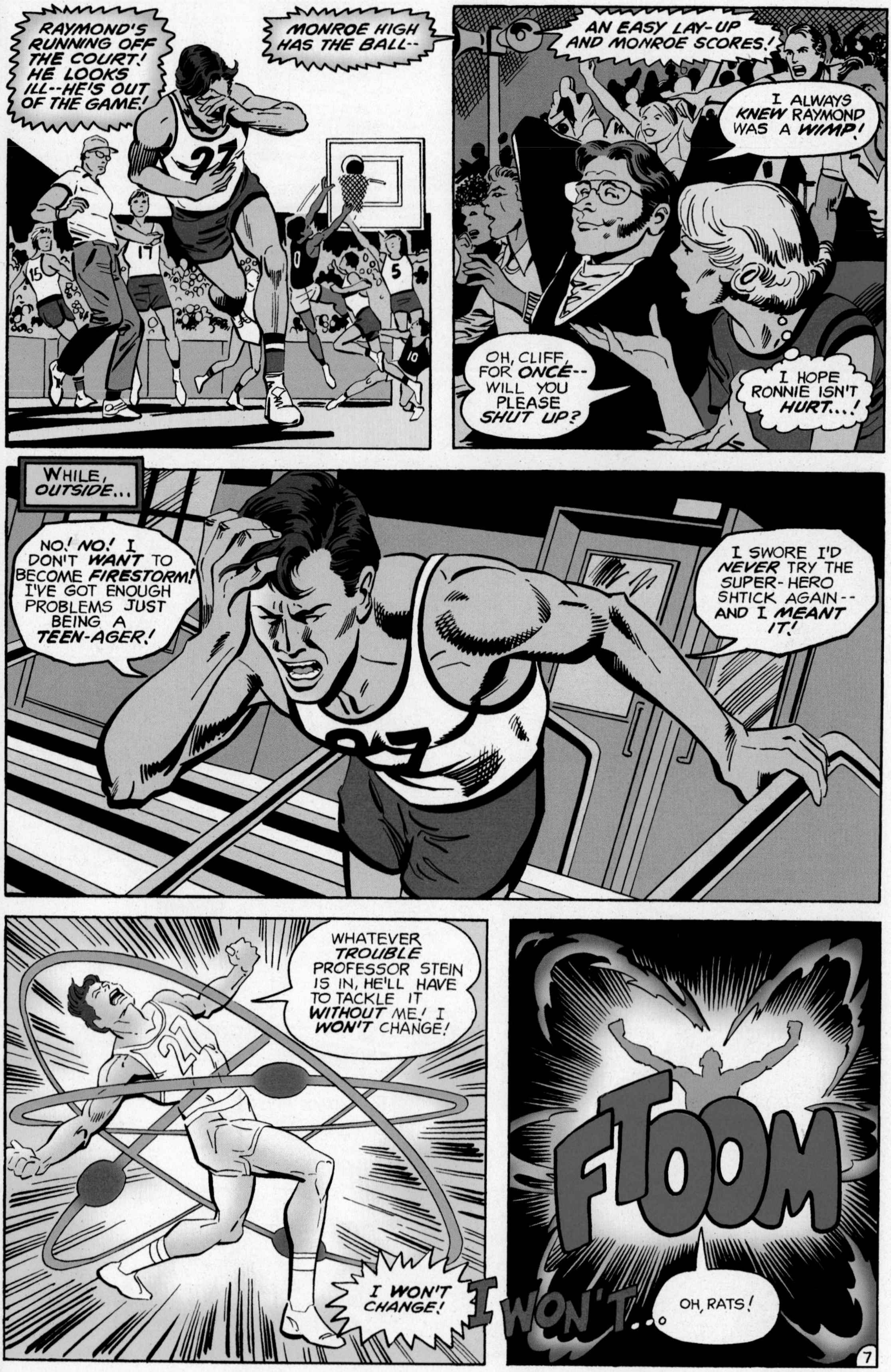
RAYMOND'S RUNNING OFF THE COURT! HE LOOKS ILL--HE'S OUT OF THE GAME!
MONROE HIGH HAS THE BALL--
AN EASY LAY-UP AND MONROE SCORES!
I ALWAYS KNEW RAYMOND WAS A WIMP!
OH, CLIFF, FOR ONCE-- WILL YOU PLEASE SHUT UP?
I HOPE RONNIE ISN'T HURT...!
WHILE, OUTSIDE...
NO! NO! I DON'T WANT TO BECOME FIRESTORM! I'VE GOT ENOUGH PROBLEMS JUST BEING A TEEN-AGER!
I SWORE I'D NEVER TRY THE SUPER-HERO SHTICK AGAIN-- AND I MEANT IT!
WHATEVER TROUBLE PROFESSOR STEIN IS IN, HE'LL HAVE TO TACKLE IT WITHOUT ME! I WON'T CHANGE!
I WON'T CHANGE!
I WON'T...
FTOOM
OH, RATS!
7

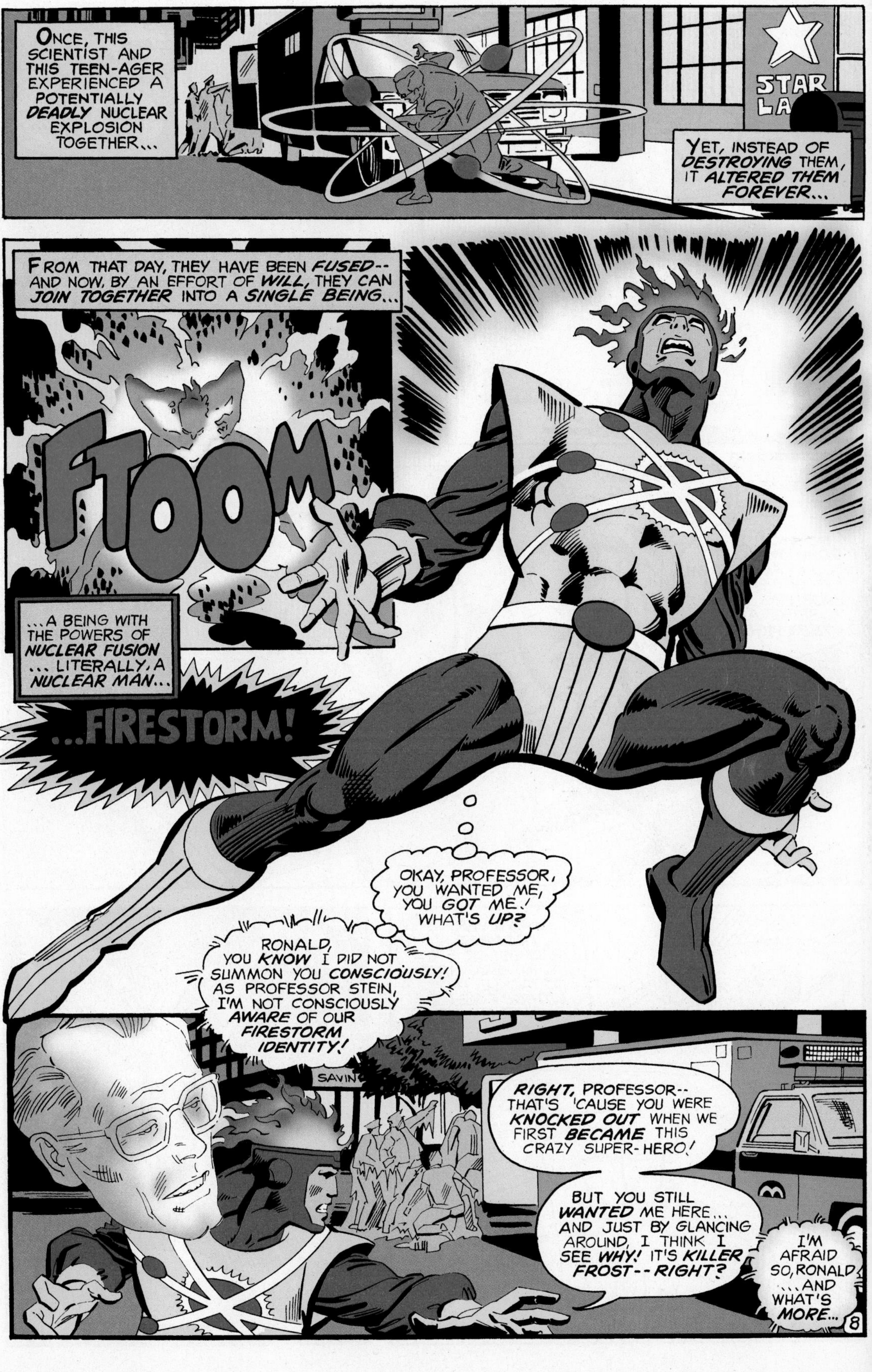

ONCE, THIS SCIENTIST AND THIS TEEN-AGER EXPERIENCED A POTENTIALLY DEADLY NUCLEAR EXPLOSION TOGETHER...
STAR LA
YET, INSTEAD OF DESTROYING THEM, IT ALTERED THEM FOREVER...
FROM THAT DAY, THEY HAVE BEEN FUSED-- AND NOW, BY AN EFFORT OF WILL, THEY CAN JOIN TOGETHER INTO A SINGLE BEING...
FTOOM
...A BEING WITH THE POWERS OF NUCLEAR FUSION ... LITERALLY, A NUCLEAR MAN...
...FIRESTORM!
OKAY, PROFESSOR, YOU WANTED ME, YOU GOT ME! WHAT'S UP?
RONALD, YOU KNOW I DID NOT SUMMON YOU CONSCIOUSLY! AS PROFESSOR STEIN, I'M NOT CONSCIOUSLY AWARE OF OUR FIRESTORM IDENTITY!
SAVIN
RIGHT, PROFESSOR-- THAT'S 'CAUSE YOU WERE KNOCKED OUT WHEN WE FIRST BECAME THIS CRAZY SUPER-HERO!
BUT YOU STILL WANTED ME HERE... AND JUST BY GLANCING AROUND, I THINK I SEE WHY! IT'S KILLER FROST--RIGHT?
I'M AFRAID SO, RONALD ... AND WHAT'S MORE...
8

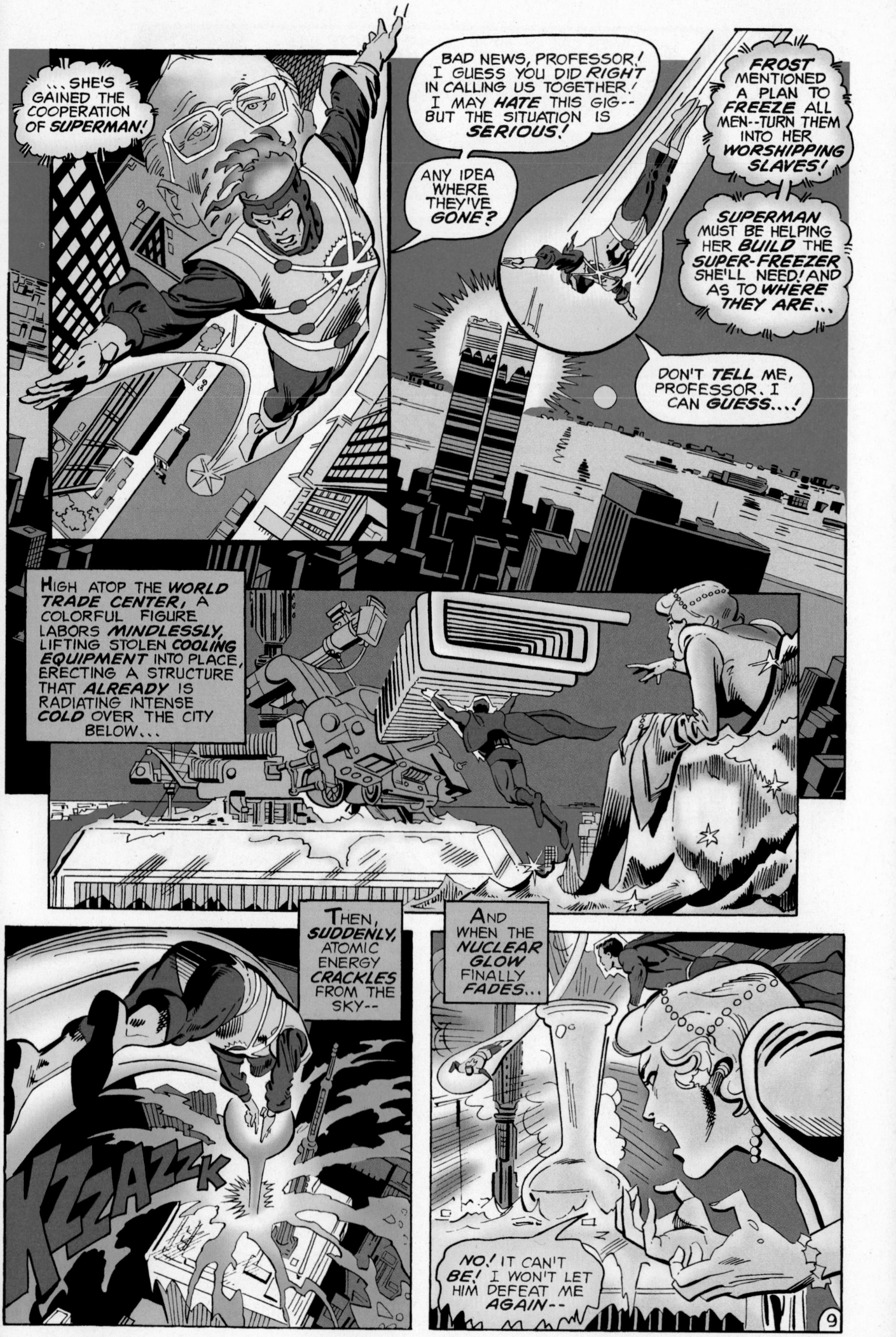

...SHE'S GAINED THE COOPERATION OF SUPERMAN!
BAD NEWS, PROFESSOR! I GUESS YOU DID RIGHT IN CALLING US TOGETHER! I MAY HATE THIS GIG--BUT THE SITUATION IS SERIOUS!
ANY IDEA WHERE THEY'VE GONE?
FROST MENTIONED A PLAN TO FREEZE ALL MEN--TURN THEM INTO HER WORSHIPPING SLAVES!
SUPERMAN MUST BE HELPING HER BUILD THE SUPER-FREEZER SHE'LL NEED! AND AS TO WHERE THEY ARE...
DON'T TELL ME, PROFESSOR. I CAN GUESS...!
HIGH ATOP THE WORLD TRADE CENTER, A COLORFUL FIGURE LABORS MINDLESSLY, LIFTING STOLEN COOLING EQUIPMENT INTO PLACE, ERECTING A STRUCTURE THAT ALREADY IS RADIATING INTENSE COLD OVER THE CITY BELOW...
THEN, SUDDENLY, ATOMIC ENERGY CRACKLES FROM THE SKY--
KZZAZZK
AND WHEN THE NUCLEAR GLOW FINALLY FADES...
NO! IT CAN'T BE! I WON'T LET HIM DEFEAT ME AGAIN--
9

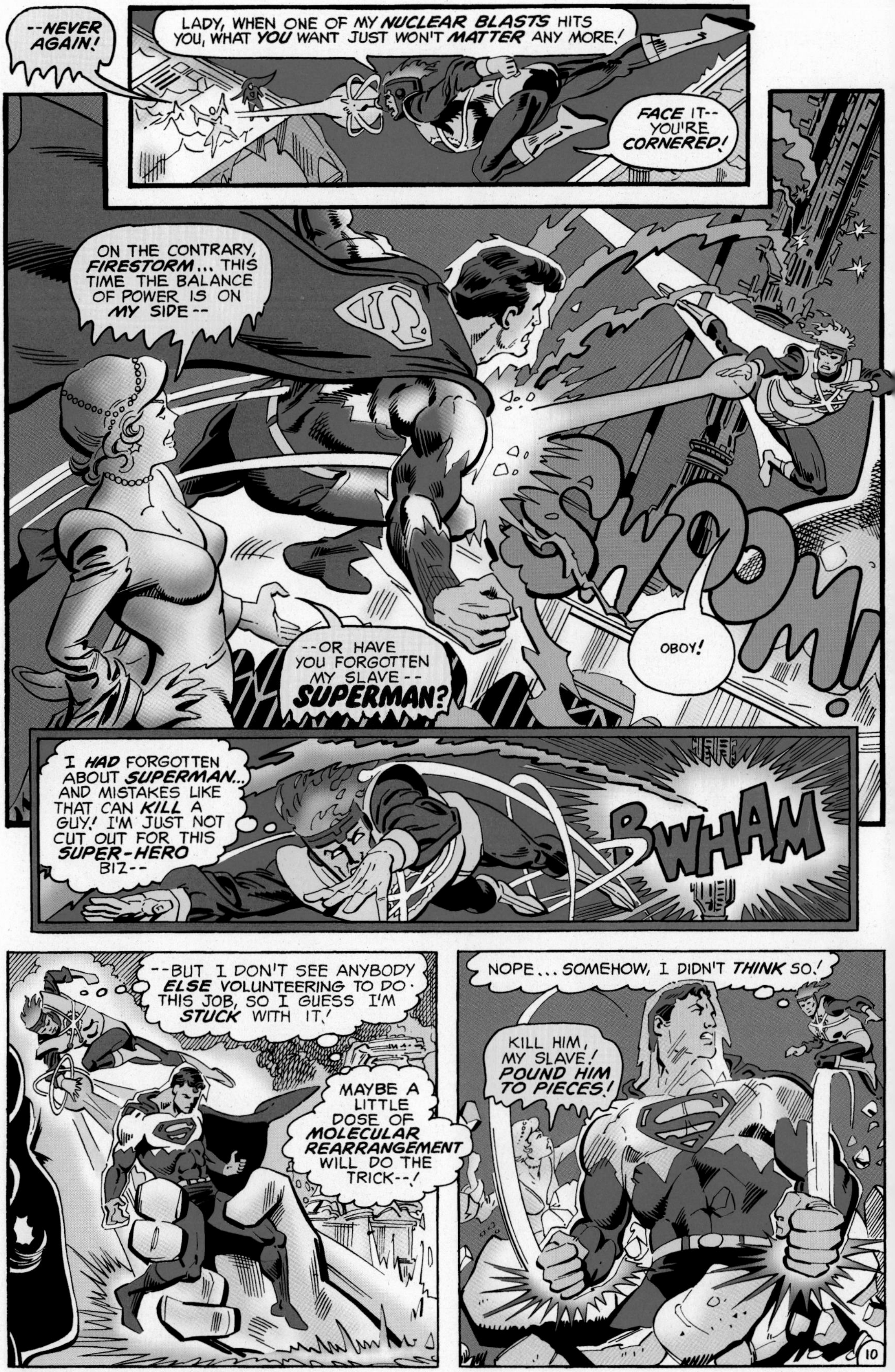
--NEVER AGAIN!
LADY, WHEN ONE OF MY NUCLEAR BLASTS HITS YOU, WHAT YOU WANT JUST WON'T MATTER ANY MORE!
FACE IT-- YOU'RE CORNERED!
ON THE CONTRARY, FIRESTORM... THIS TIME THE BALANCE OF POWER IS ON MY SIDE--
--OR HAVE YOU FORGOTTEN MY SLAVE-- SUPERMAN?
SWOOM!
OBOY!
I HAD FORGOTTEN ABOUT SUPERMAN... AND MISTAKES LIKE THAT CAN KILL A GUY! I'M JUST NOT CUT OUT FOR THIS SUPER-HERO BIZ--
BWHAM
--BUT I DON'T SEE ANYBODY ELSE VOLUNTEERING TO DO THIS JOB, SO I GUESS I'M STUCK WITH IT!
MAYBE A LITTLE DOSE OF MOLECULAR REARRANGEMENT WILL DO THE TRICK--!
NOPE... SOMEHOW, I DIDN'T THINK SO!
KILL HIM, MY SLAVE! POUND HIM TO PIECES!
10

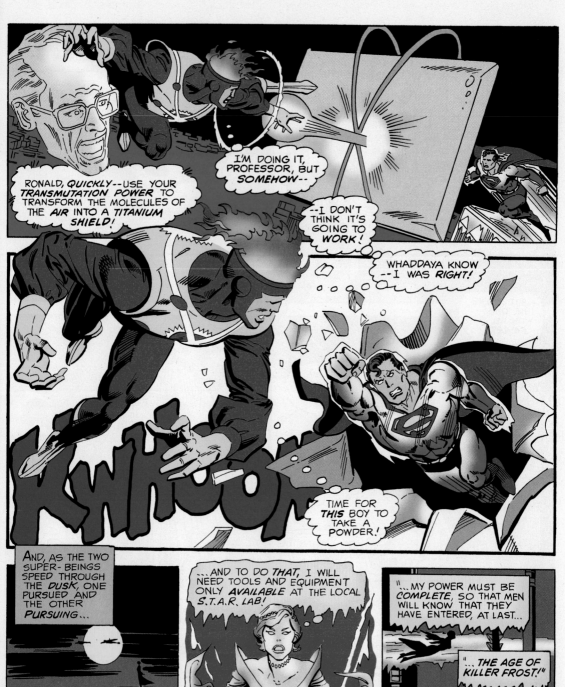

RONALD, *QUICKLY* -- USE YOUR *TRANSMUTATION POWER* TO TRANSFORM THE MOLECULES OF THE *AIR* INTO A *TITANIUM SHIELD!*

I'M DOING IT, PROFESSOR, BUT *SOMEHOW* --

-- I DON'T THINK IT'S GOING TO *WORK!*

WHADDAYA KNOW -- I WAS *RIGHT!*

KWHOOM

TIME FOR *THIS* BOY TO TAKE A *POWDER!*

AND, AS THE TWO SUPER-BEINGS SPEED THROUGH THE *DUSK,* ONE PURSUED AND THE OTHER *PURSUING...*

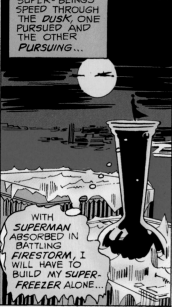

WITH *SUPERMAN* ABSORBED IN BATTLING *FIRESTORM,* I WILL HAVE TO BUILD MY *SUPER-FREEZER* ALONE...

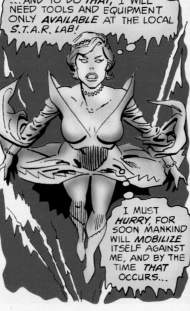

...AND TO DO *THAT,* I WILL NEED TOOLS AND EQUIPMENT ONLY *AVAILABLE* AT THE LOCAL *S.T.A.R. LAB!*

I MUST *HURRY,* FOR SOON MANKIND WILL *MOBILIZE* ITSELF AGAINST ME, AND BY THE TIME *THAT* OCCURS...

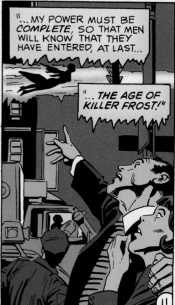

"...MY POWER MUST BE *COMPLETE,* SO THAT MEN WILL KNOW THAT THEY HAVE ENTERED, AT LAST...

"...*THE AGE OF KILLER FROST!*"

11

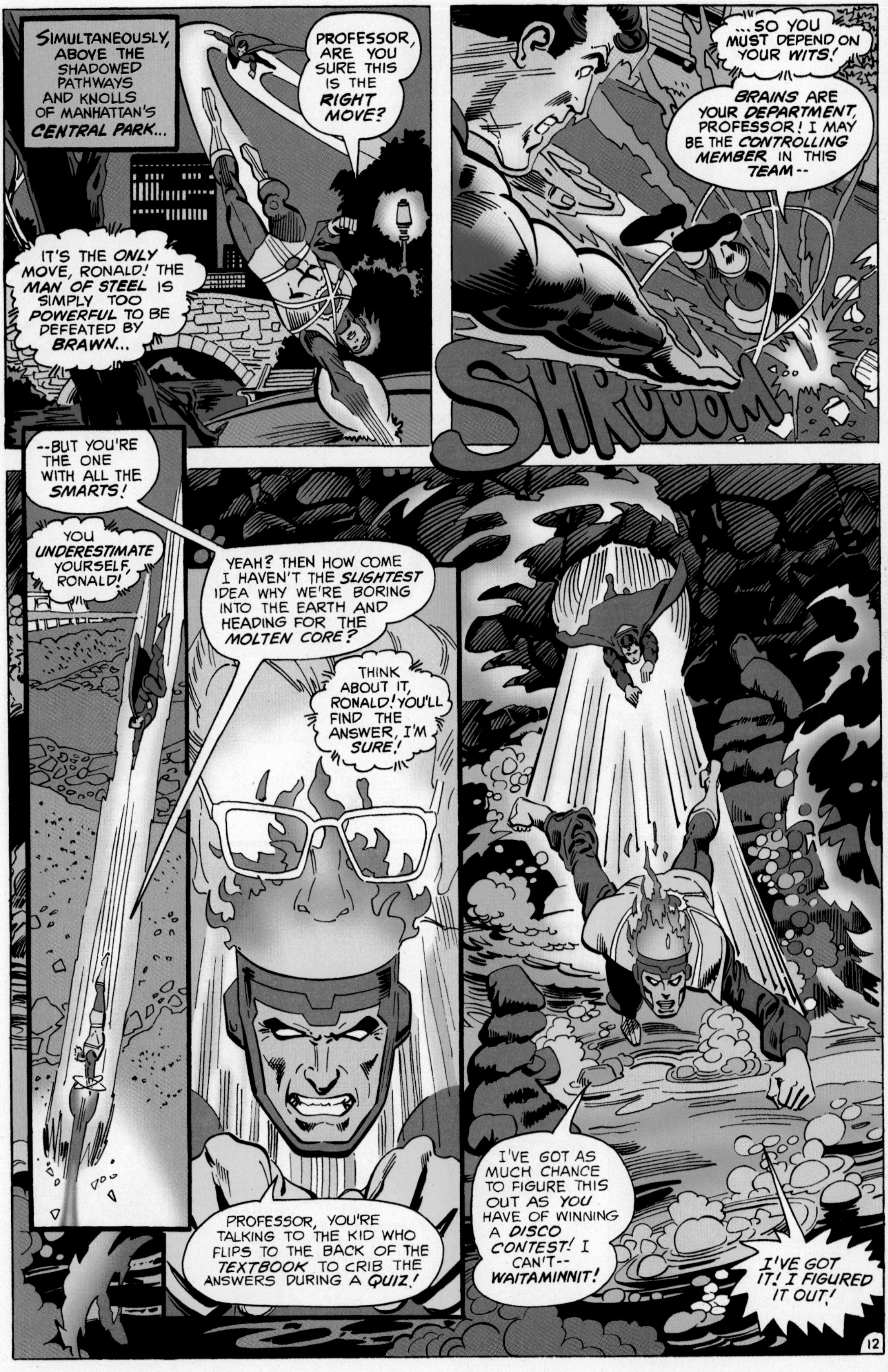
SIMULTANEOUSLY, ABOVE THE SHADOWED PATHWAYS AND KNOLLS OF MANHATTAN'S CENTRAL PARK...
PROFESSOR, ARE YOU SURE THIS IS THE RIGHT MOVE?
IT'S THE ONLY MOVE, RONALD! THE MAN OF STEEL IS SIMPLY TOO POWERFUL TO BE DEFEATED BY BRAWN...
...SO YOU MUST DEPEND ON YOUR WITS!
BRAINS ARE YOUR DEPARTMENT, PROFESSOR! I MAY BE THE CONTROLLING MEMBER IN THIS TEAM --
SHROOOOM
--BUT YOU'RE THE ONE WITH ALL THE SMARTS!
YOU UNDERESTIMATE YOURSELF, RONALD!
YEAH? THEN HOW COME I HAVEN'T THE SLIGHTEST IDEA WHY WE'RE BORING INTO THE EARTH AND HEADING FOR THE MOLTEN CORE?
THINK ABOUT IT, RONALD! YOU'LL FIND THE ANSWER, I'M SURE!
PROFESSOR, YOU'RE TALKING TO THE KID WHO FLIPS TO THE BACK OF THE TEXTBOOK TO CRIB THE ANSWERS DURING A QUIZ!
I'VE GOT AS MUCH CHANCE TO FIGURE THIS OUT AS YOU HAVE OF WINNING A DISCO CONTEST! I CAN'T-- WAITAMINNIT!
I'VE GOT IT! I FIGURED IT OUT!
12

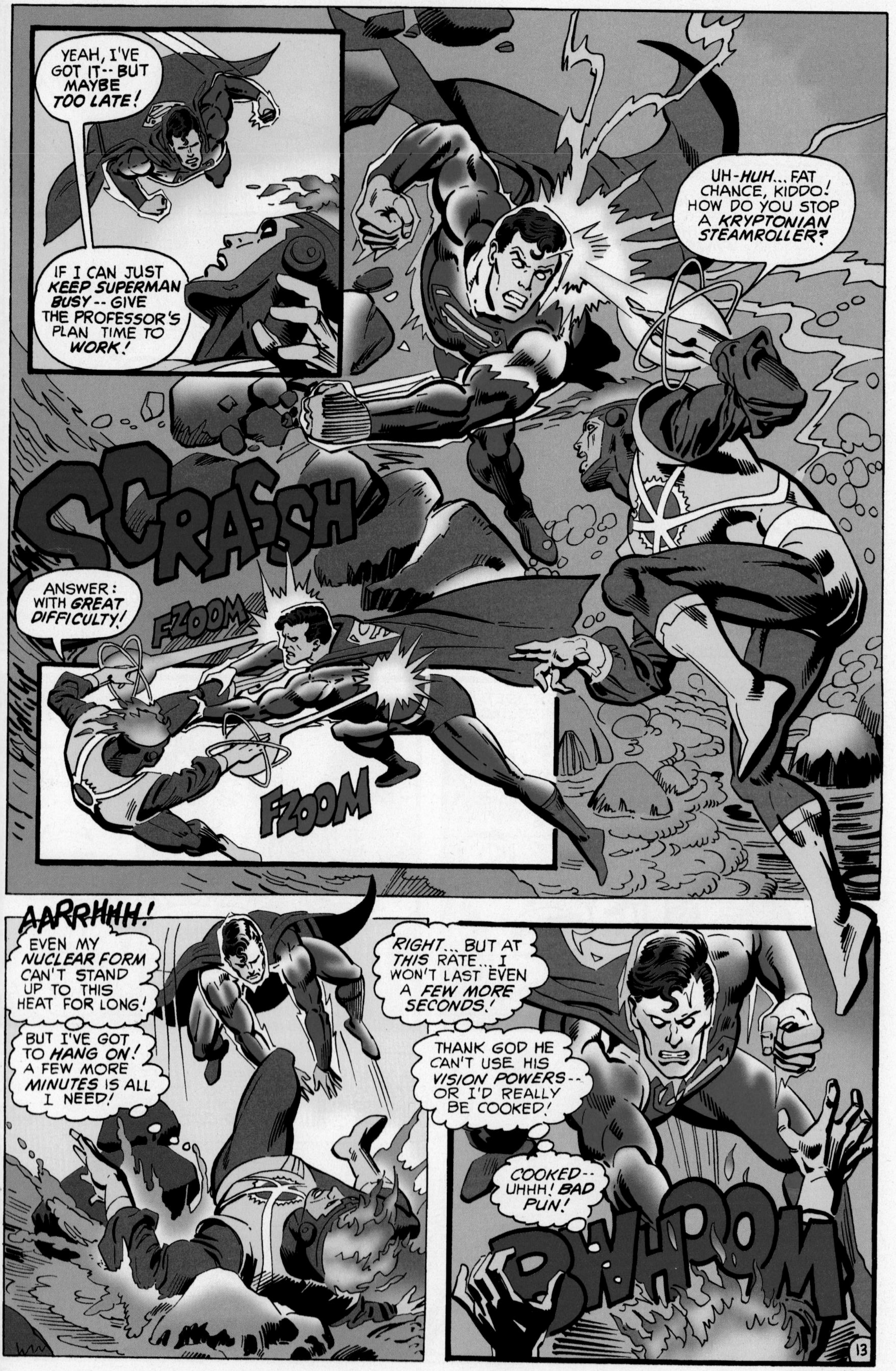
YEAH, I'VE GOT IT-- BUT MAYBE TOO LATE!
IF I CAN JUST KEEP SUPERMAN BUSY -- GIVE THE PROFESSOR'S PLAN TIME TO WORK!
UH-HUH... FAT CHANCE, KIDDO! HOW DO YOU STOP A KRYPTONIAN STEAMROLLER?
SCRASSH
ANSWER: WITH GREAT DIFFICULTY!
FZOOM
FZOOM
AARRHHH!
EVEN MY NUCLEAR FORM CAN'T STAND UP TO THIS HEAT FOR LONG!
BUT I'VE GOT TO HANG ON! A FEW MORE MINUTES IS ALL I NEED!
RIGHT... BUT AT THIS RATE... I WON'T LAST EVEN A FEW MORE SECONDS!
THANK GOD HE CAN'T USE HIS VISION POWERS-- OR I'D REALLY BE COOKED!
COOKED-- UHHH! BAD PUN!
BWHOOM
13

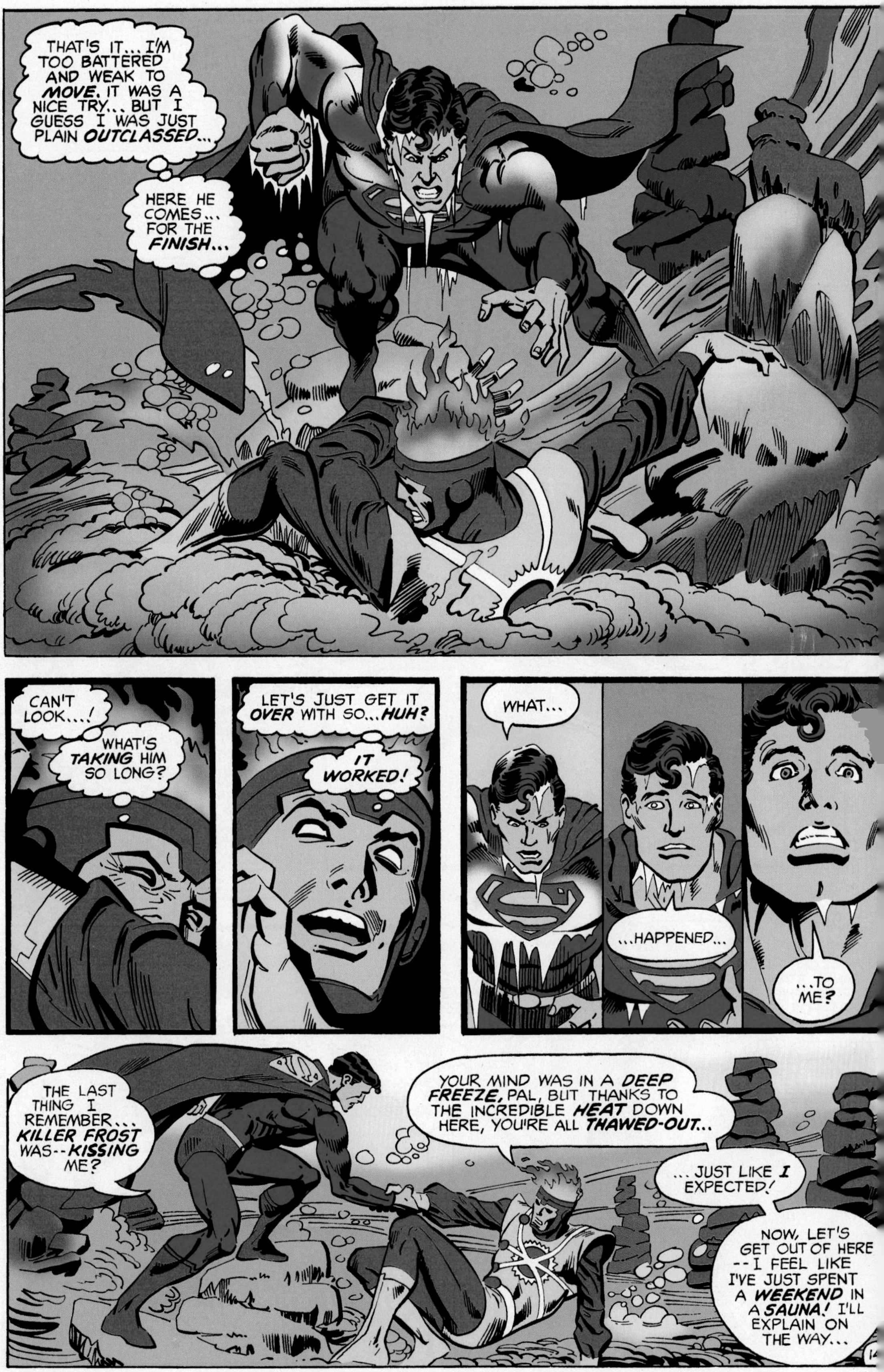
THAT'S IT... I'M TOO BATTERED AND WEAK TO MOVE. IT WAS A NICE TRY... BUT I GUESS I WAS JUST PLAIN OUTCLASSED...
HERE HE COMES... FOR THE FINISH...
CAN'T LOOK...!
WHAT'S TAKING HIM SO LONG?
LET'S JUST GET IT OVER WITH SO... HUH?
IT WORKED!
WHAT...
...HAPPENED...
...TO ME?
THE LAST THING I REMEMBER... KILLER FROST WAS--KISSING ME?
YOUR MIND WAS IN A DEEP FREEZE, PAL, BUT THANKS TO THE INCREDIBLE HEAT DOWN HERE, YOU'RE ALL THAWED-OUT...
... JUST LIKE I EXPECTED!
NOW, LET'S GET OUT OF HERE --I FEEL LIKE I'VE JUST SPENT A WEEKEND IN A SAUNA! I'LL EXPLAIN ON THE WAY...

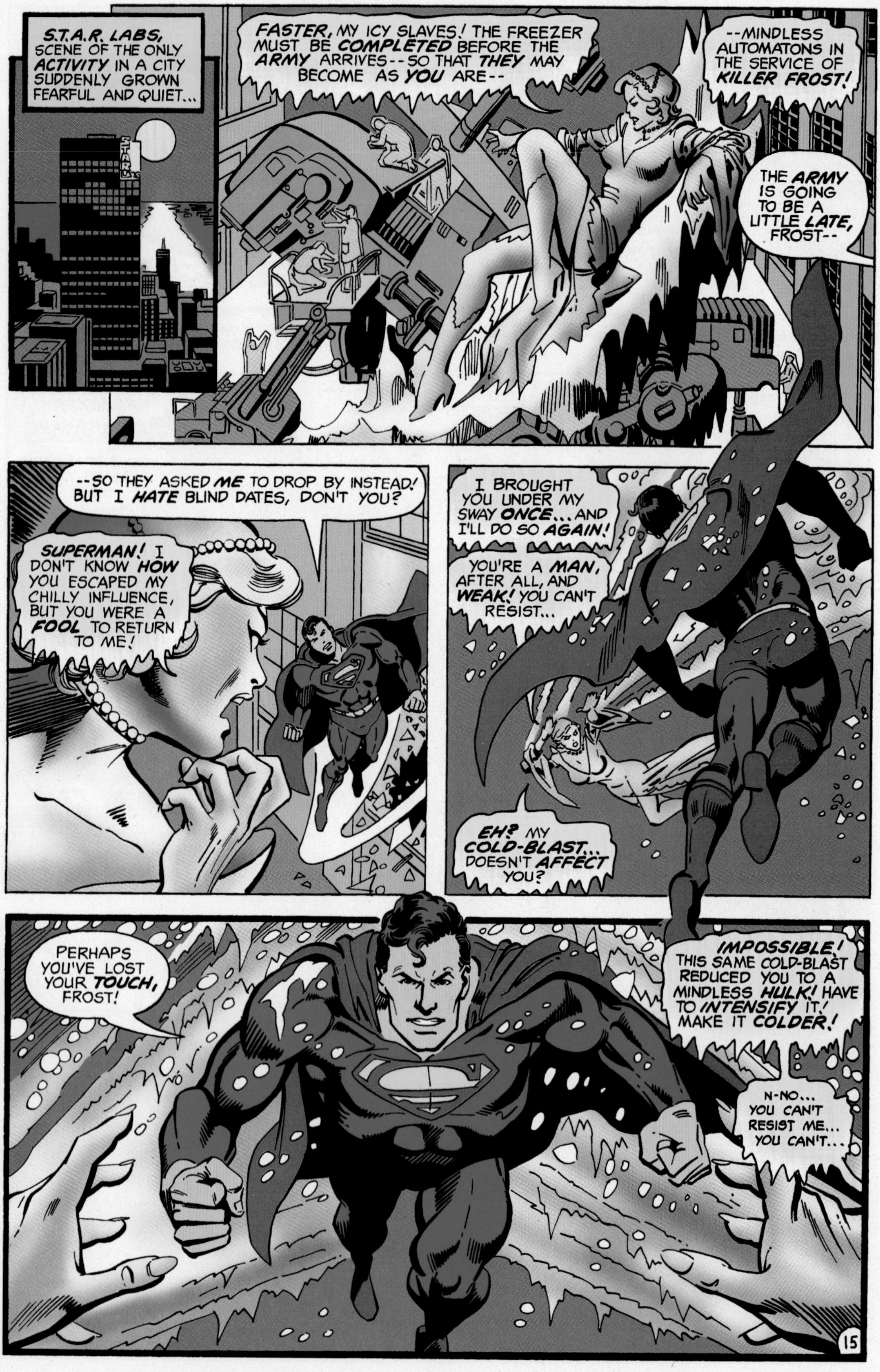
S.T.A.R. LABS, SCENE OF THE ONLY ACTIVITY IN A CITY SUDDENLY GROWN FEARFUL AND QUIET...
FASTER, MY ICY SLAVES! THE FREEZER MUST BE COMPLETED BEFORE THE ARMY ARRIVES--SO THAT THEY MAY BECOME AS YOU ARE--
--MINDLESS AUTOMATONS IN THE SERVICE OF KILLER FROST!
THE ARMY IS GOING TO BE A LITTLE LATE, FROST--
--SO THEY ASKED ME TO DROP BY INSTEAD! BUT I HATE BLIND DATES, DON'T YOU?
SUPERMAN! I DON'T KNOW HOW YOU ESCAPED MY CHILLY INFLUENCE, BUT YOU WERE A FOOL TO RETURN TO ME!
I BROUGHT YOU UNDER MY SWAY ONCE...AND I'LL DO SO AGAIN!
YOU'RE A MAN, AFTER ALL, AND WEAK! YOU CAN'T RESIST...
EH? MY COLD-BLAST... DOESN'T AFFECT YOU?
PERHAPS YOU'VE LOST YOUR TOUCH, FROST!
IMPOSSIBLE! THIS SAME COLD-BLAST REDUCED YOU TO A MINDLESS HULK! HAVE TO INTENSIFY IT! MAKE IT COLDER!
N-NO... YOU CAN'T RESIST ME... YOU CAN'T...
15

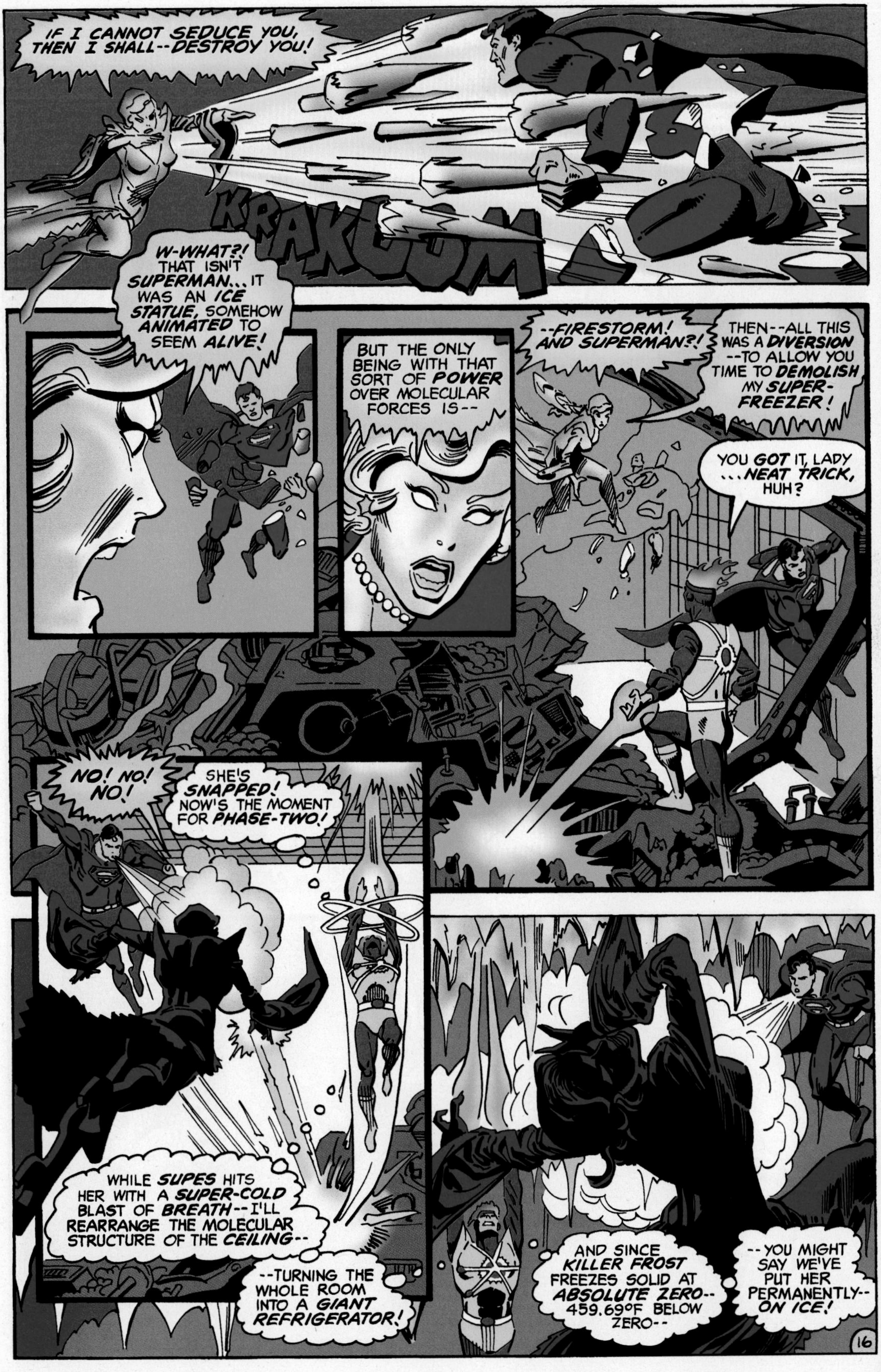
IF I CANNOT SEDUCE YOU, THEN I SHALL--DESTROY YOU!
KRAKOOM
W-WHAT?! THAT ISN'T SUPERMAN... IT WAS AN ICE STATUE, SOMEHOW ANIMATED TO SEEM ALIVE!
BUT THE ONLY BEING WITH THAT SORT OF POWER OVER MOLECULAR FORCES IS--
--FIRESTORM! AND SUPERMAN?!
THEN--ALL THIS WAS A DIVERSION --TO ALLOW YOU TIME TO DEMOLISH MY SUPER-FREEZER!
YOU GOT IT, LADY ...NEAT TRICK, HUH?
NO! NO! NO!
SHE'S SNAPPED! NOW'S THE MOMENT FOR PHASE-TWO!
WHILE SUPES HITS HER WITH A SUPER-COLD BLAST OF BREATH--I'LL REARRANGE THE MOLECULAR STRUCTURE OF THE CEILING--
--TURNING THE WHOLE ROOM INTO A GIANT REFRIGERATOR!
AND SINCE KILLER FROST FREEZES SOLID AT ABSOLUTE ZERO-- 459.69°F BELOW ZERO--
--YOU MIGHT SAY WE'VE PUT HER PERMANENTLY-- ON ICE!
16

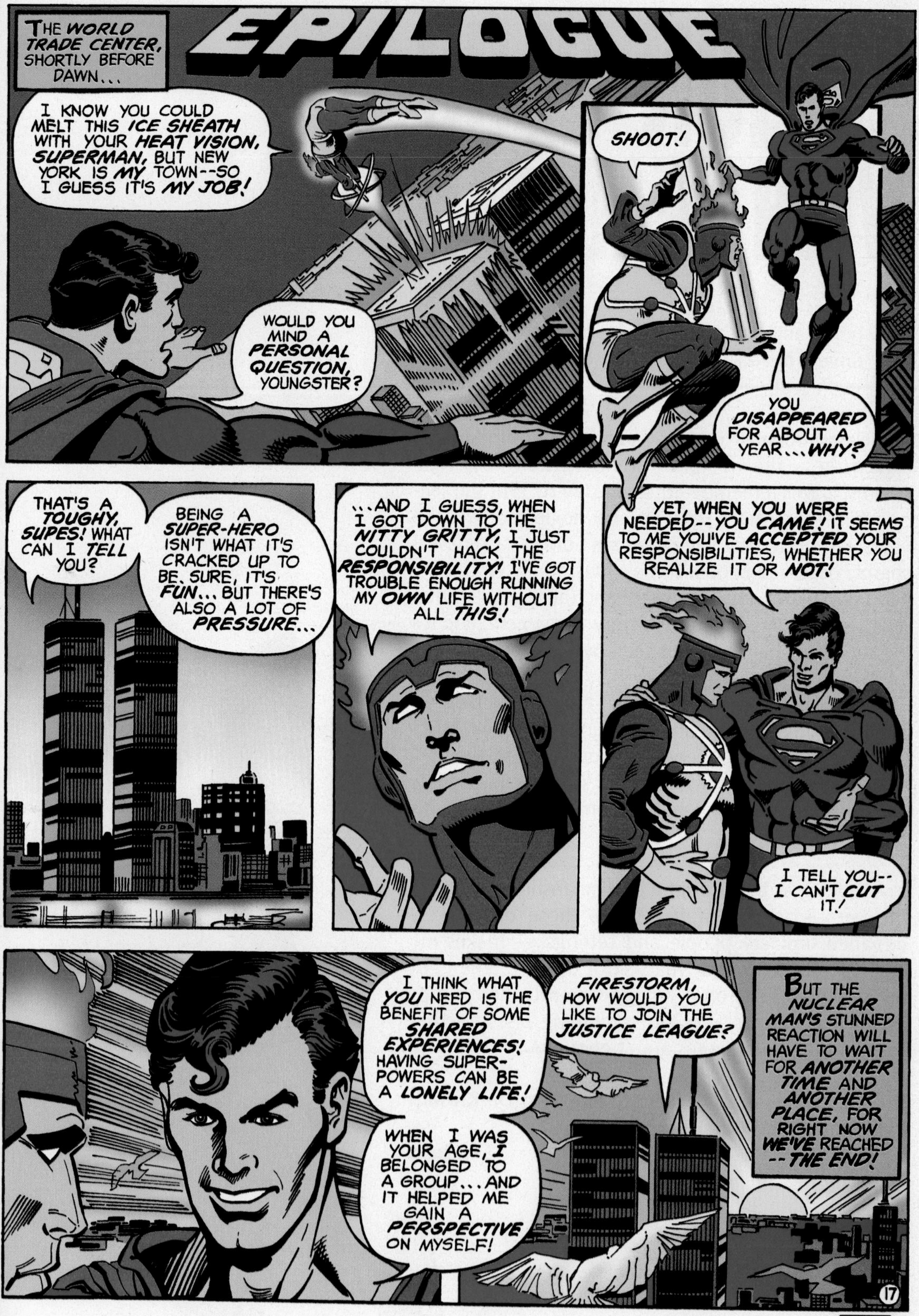
EPILOGUE
THE WORLD TRADE CENTER, SHORTLY BEFORE DAWN...
I KNOW YOU COULD MELT THIS ICE SHEATH WITH YOUR HEAT VISION, SUPERMAN, BUT NEW YORK IS MY TOWN--SO I GUESS IT'S MY JOB!
WOULD YOU MIND A PERSONAL QUESTION, YOUNGSTER?
SHOOT!
YOU DISAPPEARED FOR ABOUT A YEAR...WHY?
THAT'S A TOUGHY, SUPES! WHAT CAN I TELL YOU?
BEING A SUPER-HERO ISN'T WHAT IT'S CRACKED UP TO BE. SURE, IT'S FUN... BUT THERE'S ALSO A LOT OF PRESSURE...
...AND I GUESS, WHEN I GOT DOWN TO THE NITTY GRITTY, I JUST COULDN'T HACK THE RESPONSIBILITY! I'VE GOT TROUBLE ENOUGH RUNNING MY OWN LIFE WITHOUT ALL THIS!
YET, WHEN YOU WERE NEEDED--YOU CAME! IT SEEMS TO ME YOU'VE ACCEPTED YOUR RESPONSIBILITIES, WHETHER YOU REALIZE IT OR NOT!
I TELL YOU--I CAN'T CUT IT!
I THINK WHAT YOU NEED IS THE BENEFIT OF SOME SHARED EXPERIENCES! HAVING SUPER-POWERS CAN BE A LONELY LIFE!
WHEN I WAS YOUR AGE, I BELONGED TO A GROUP... AND IT HELPED ME GAIN A PERSPECTIVE ON MYSELF!
FIRESTORM, HOW WOULD YOU LIKE TO JOIN THE JUSTICE LEAGUE?
BUT THE NUCLEAR MAN'S STUNNED REACTION WILL HAVE TO WAIT FOR ANOTHER TIME AND ANOTHER PLACE, FOR RIGHT NOW WE'VE REACHED --THE END!
17

ACTION-PLUS WITH DEADMAN

DC COMICS PRESENTS #24

Now here's an offbeat team-up — a Superman adventure driven by and co-starring someone Superman can't even see!

The classic original run of Deadman stories in *Strange Adventures*, drawn (and often written) by Neal Adams, is well remembered, and justly so. But the second run — ah, that's been unfairly neglected over the years. It ran mostly in *Adventure Comics*, a series of sharply observed people stories, masterfully written by Len Wein with art by Jim Aparo and (all together now) José Luis García-López. Each story was a gem, and it's a shame they haven't been seen by more people.

This story is the grand finale of that run, picking up and tying off a few threads set up in those earlier tales. But don't worry — everything you need to know is recapped in the story itself, and it stands solidly on its own. And hey, there's Jenet Klyburn again! Maybe it's the black shirts…

Just looking at the beautiful draftsmanship — not just the hero-adventure stuff, but all those distinctively designed ordinary people and settings — makes me realize it's been twenty years since the one time I got to work with José, on a 7-page Green Lantern Corps story. Hey, José! Let's do something else together soon, huh? Seven pages aren't enough!

It doesn't even have to have Chemo and Dr. Klyburn in it, honest…

— **kdb**

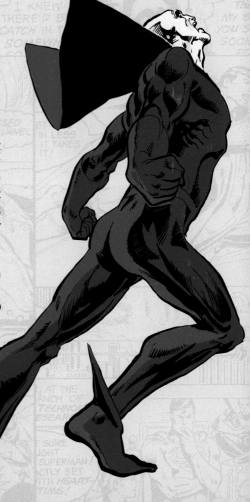

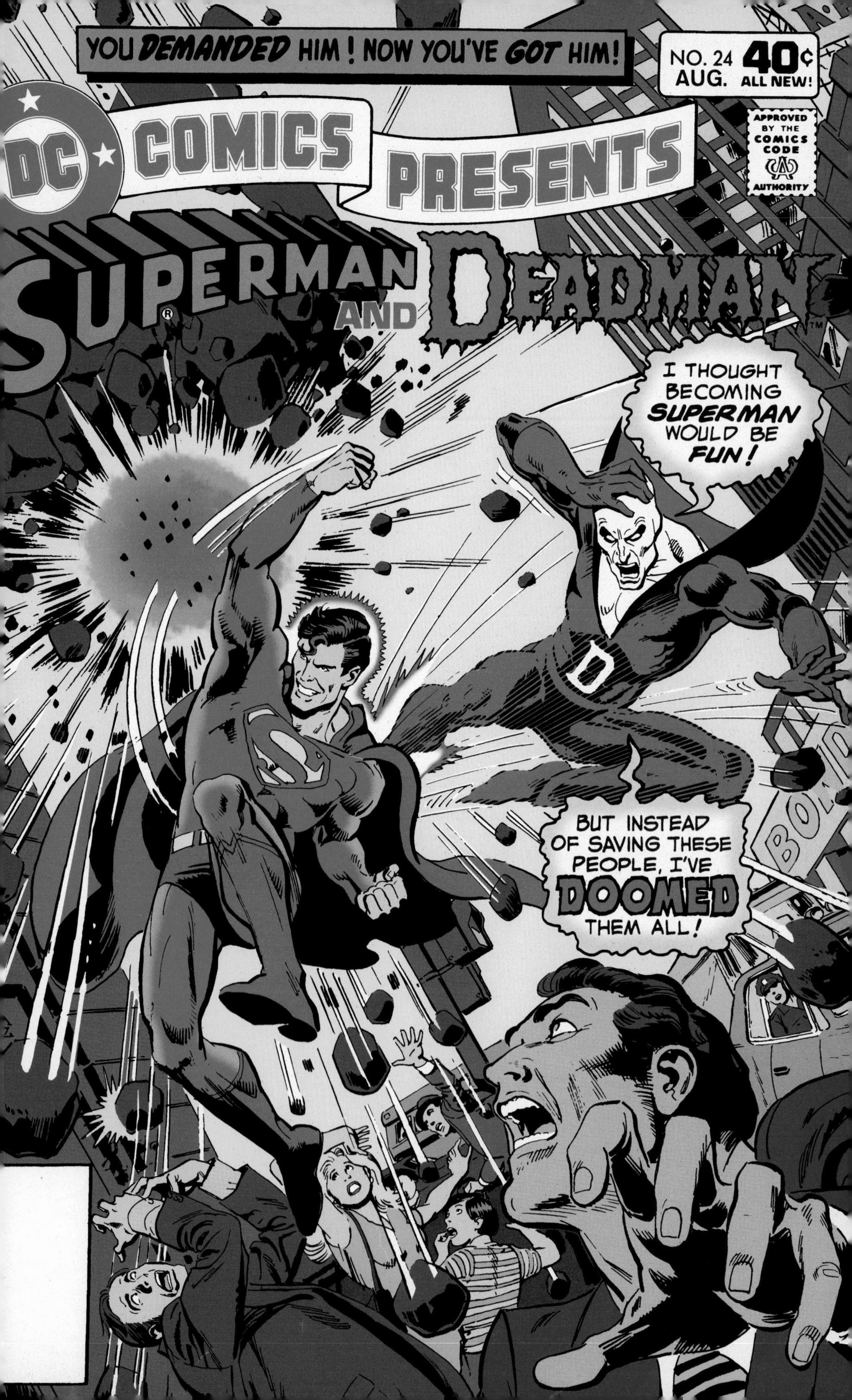

YOU DEMANDED HIM! NOW YOU'VE GOT HIM!
NO. 24 AUG. 40¢ ALL NEW!
DC
COMICS PRESENTS
APPROVED BY THE COMICS CODE AUTHORITY
SUPERMAN AND DEADMAN
I THOUGHT BECOMING SUPERMAN WOULD BE FUN!
BUT INSTEAD OF SAVING THESE PEOPLE, I'VE DOOMED THEM ALL!

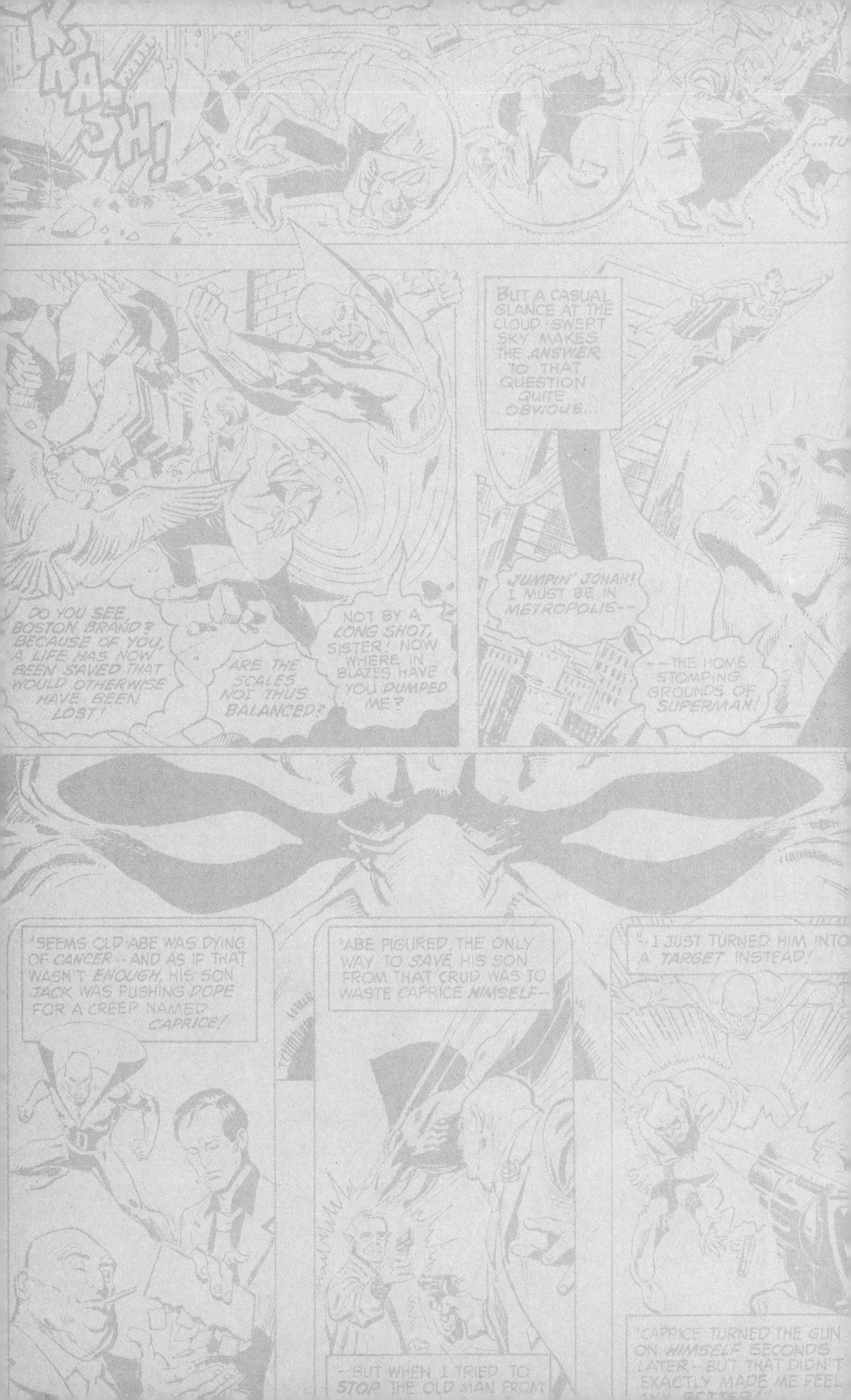
KA-ASH!
...TU
DO YOU SEE, BOSTON BRAND? BECAUSE OF YOU, A LIFE HAS NOW BEEN SAVED THAT WOULD OTHERWISE HAVE BEEN LOST!
ARE THE SCALES NOT THUS BALANCED?
NOT BY A LONG SHOT, SISTER! NOW WHERE IN BLAZES HAVE YOU DUMPED ME?
BUT A CASUAL GLANCE AT THE CLOUD-SWEPT SKY MAKES THE ANSWER TO THAT QUESTION QUITE OBVIOUS...
JUMPIN' JONAH! I MUST BE IN METROPOLIS--
--THE HOME STOMPING GROUNDS OF SUPERMAN!
"SEEMS OLD ABE WAS DYING OF CANCER--AND AS IF THAT WASN'T ENOUGH, HIS SON JACK WAS PUSHING DOPE FOR A CREEP NAMED CAPRICE!
"ABE FIGURED THE ONLY WAY TO SAVE HIS SON FROM THAT CRUD WAS TO WASTE CAPRICE HIMSELF--
"--BUT WHEN I TRIED TO STOP THE OLD MAN FROM
"--I JUST TURNED HIM INTO A TARGET INSTEAD!
"CAPRICE TURNED THE GUN ON HIMSELF SECONDS LATER--BUT THAT DIDN'T EXACTLY MADE ME FEEL

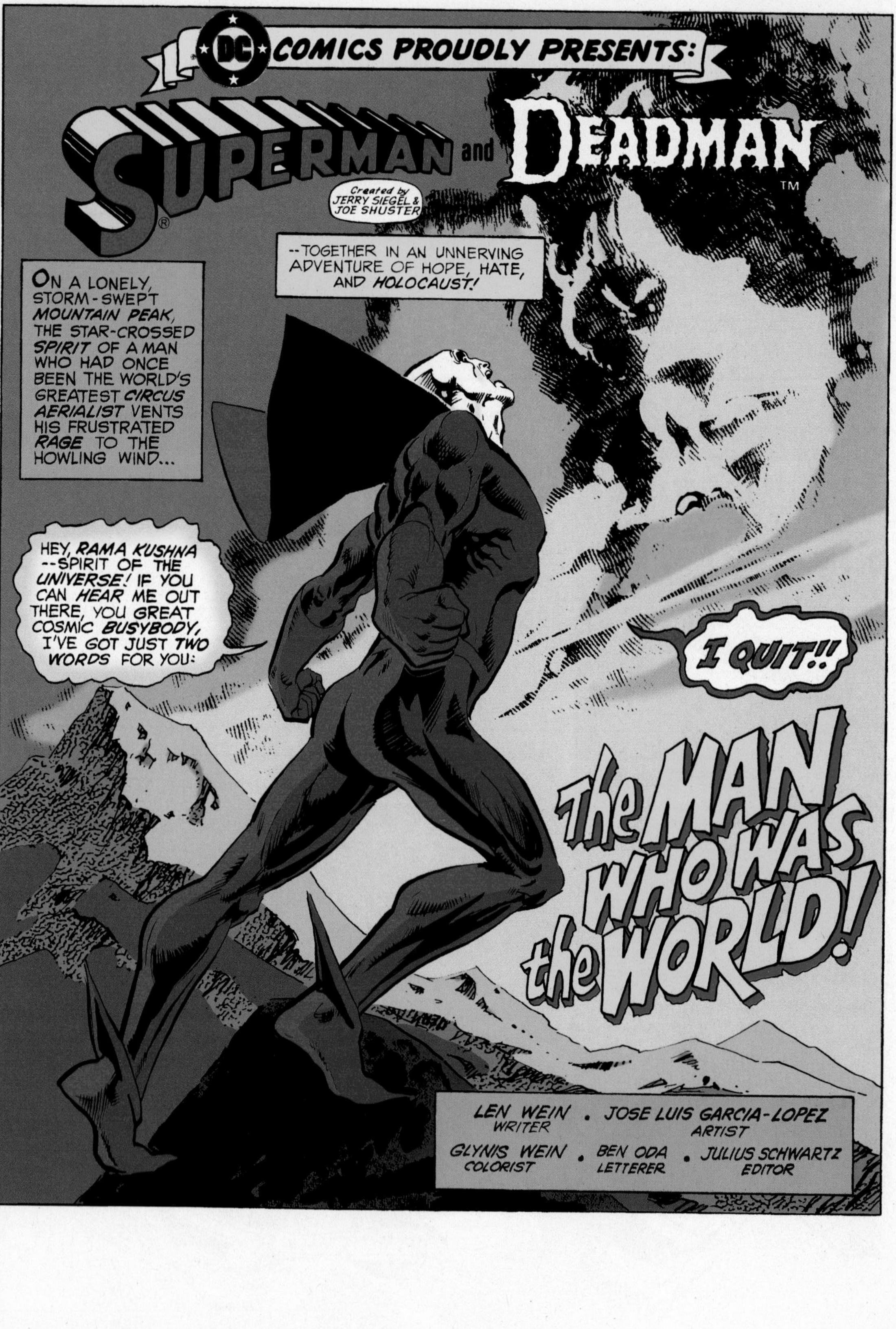
DC COMICS PROUDLY PRESENTS:
SUPERMAN and DEADMAN
Created by JERRY SIEGEL & JOE SHUSTER
--TOGETHER IN AN UNNERVING ADVENTURE OF HOPE, HATE, AND HOLOCAUST!
ON A LONELY, STORM-SWEPT MOUNTAIN PEAK, THE STAR-CROSSED SPIRIT OF A MAN WHO HAD ONCE BEEN THE WORLD'S GREATEST CIRCUS AERIALIST VENTS HIS FRUSTRATED RAGE TO THE HOWLING WIND...
HEY, RAMA KUSHNA --SPIRIT OF THE UNIVERSE! IF YOU CAN HEAR ME OUT THERE, YOU GREAT COSMIC BUSYBODY, I'VE GOT JUST TWO WORDS FOR YOU:
I QUIT!!
The MAN WHO WAS the WORLD!
LEN WEIN WRITER • JOSE LUIS GARCIA-LOPEZ ARTIST
GLYNIS WEIN COLORIST • BEN ODA LETTERER • JULIUS SCHWARTZ EDITOR

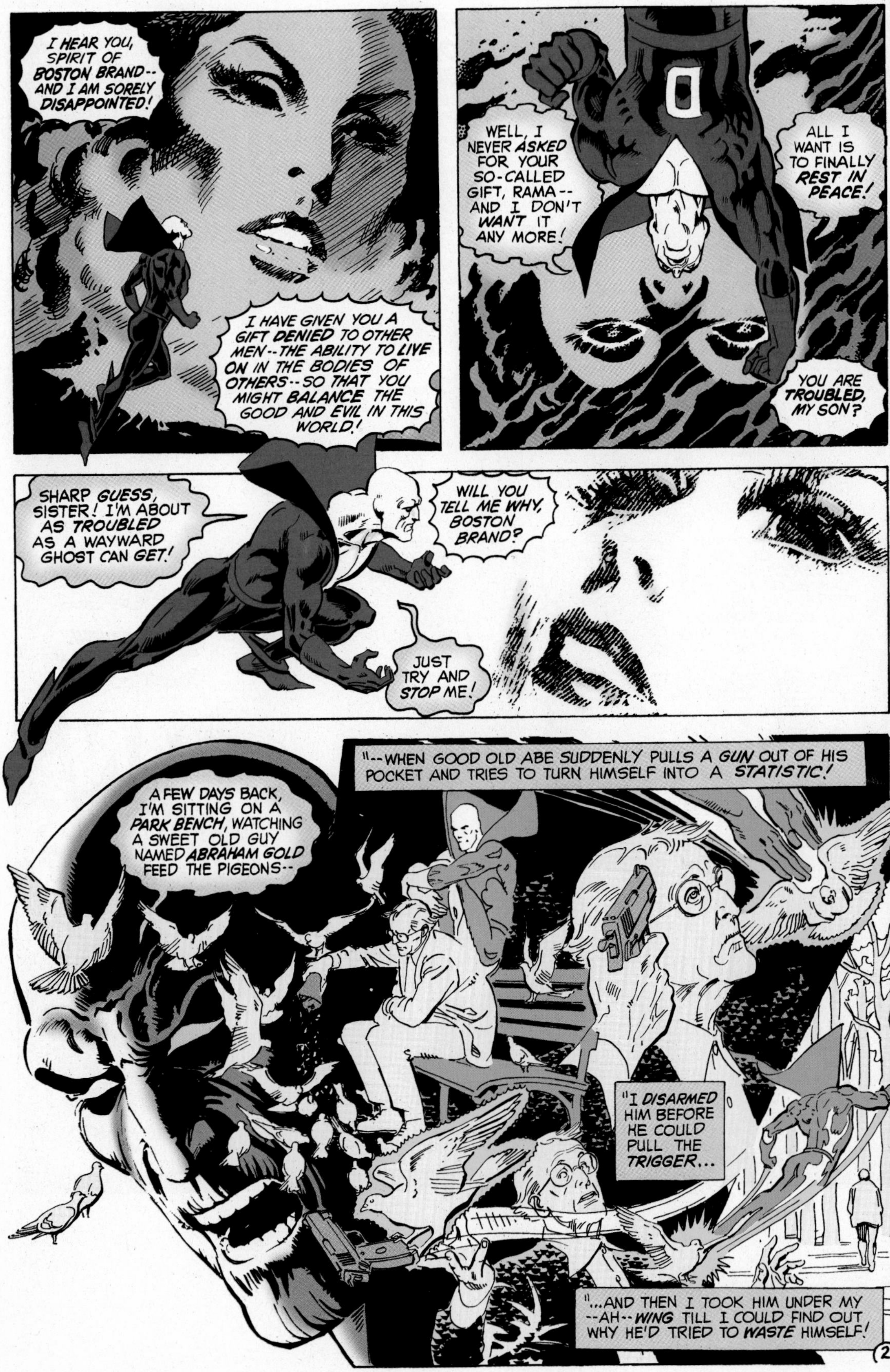

I HEAR YOU, SPIRIT OF BOSTON BRAND-- AND I AM SORELY DISAPPOINTED!
I HAVE GIVEN YOU A GIFT DENIED TO OTHER MEN--THE ABILITY TO LIVE ON IN THE BODIES OF OTHERS--SO THAT YOU MIGHT BALANCE THE GOOD AND EVIL IN THIS WORLD!
WELL, I NEVER ASKED FOR YOUR SO-CALLED GIFT, RAMA-- AND I DON'T WANT IT ANY MORE!
ALL I WANT IS TO FINALLY REST IN PEACE!
YOU ARE TROUBLED, MY SON?
SHARP GUESS, SISTER! I'M ABOUT AS TROUBLED AS A WAYWARD GHOST CAN GET!
WILL YOU TELL ME WHY, BOSTON BRAND?
JUST TRY AND STOP ME!
A FEW DAYS BACK, I'M SITTING ON A PARK BENCH, WATCHING A SWEET OLD GUY NAMED ABRAHAM GOLD FEED THE PIGEONS--
"--WHEN GOOD OLD ABE SUDDENLY PULLS A GUN OUT OF HIS POCKET AND TRIES TO TURN HIMSELF INTO A STATISTIC!
"I DISARMED HIM BEFORE HE COULD PULL THE TRIGGER...
"...AND THEN I TOOK HIM UNDER MY --AH--WING TILL I COULD FIND OUT WHY HE'D TRIED TO WASTE HIMSELF!
2

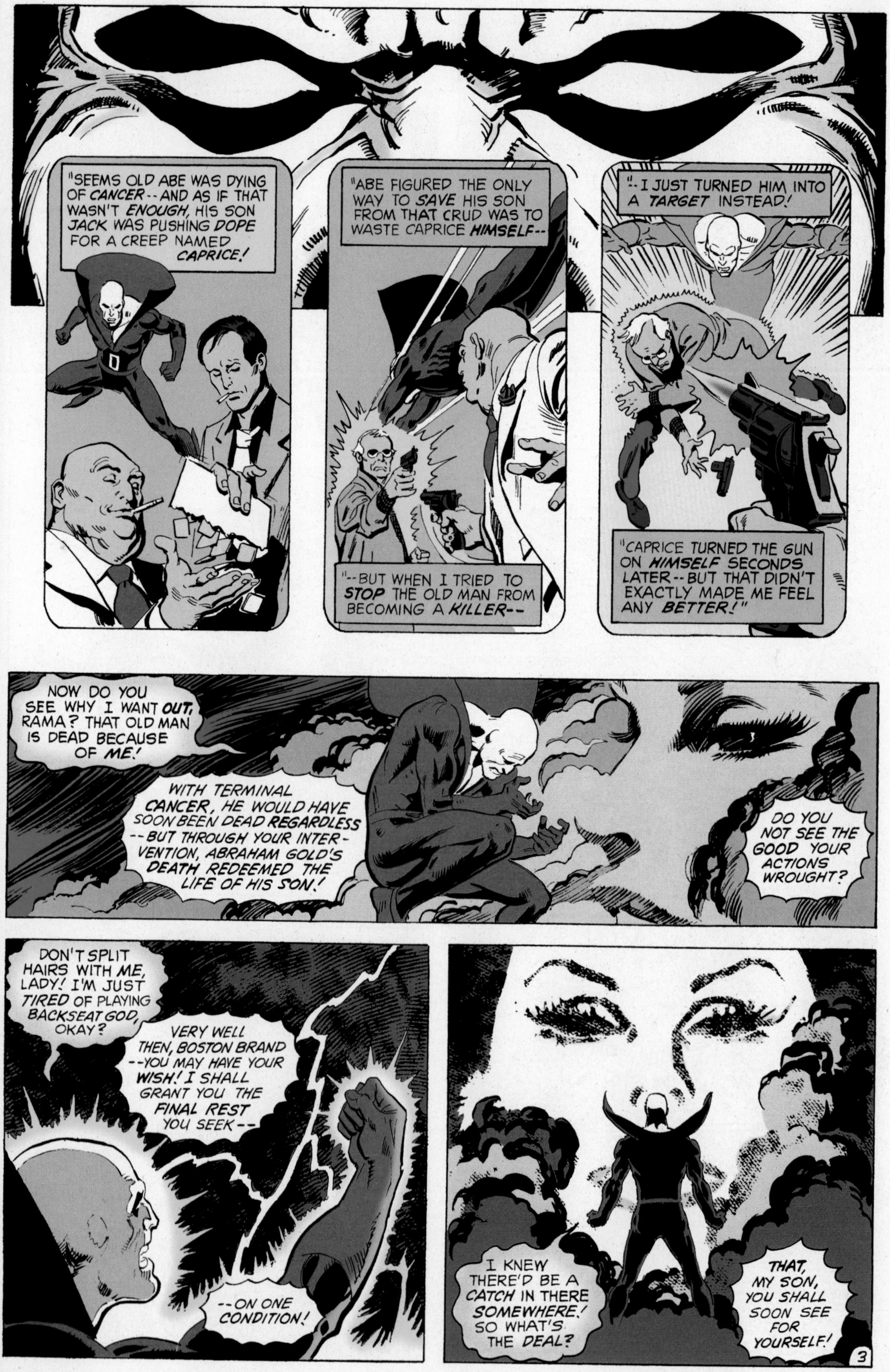
"SEEMS OLD ABE WAS DYING OF CANCER -- AND AS IF THAT WASN'T ENOUGH, HIS SON JACK WAS PUSHING DOPE FOR A CREEP NAMED CAPRICE!
"ABE FIGURED THE ONLY WAY TO SAVE HIS SON FROM THAT CRUD WAS TO WASTE CAPRICE HIMSELF--
"--BUT WHEN I TRIED TO STOP THE OLD MAN FROM BECOMING A KILLER--
"-- I JUST TURNED HIM INTO A TARGET INSTEAD!
"CAPRICE TURNED THE GUN ON HIMSELF SECONDS LATER -- BUT THAT DIDN'T EXACTLY MADE ME FEEL ANY BETTER!"
NOW DO YOU SEE WHY I WANT OUT, RAMA? THAT OLD MAN IS DEAD BECAUSE OF ME!
WITH TERMINAL CANCER, HE WOULD HAVE SOON BEEN DEAD REGARDLESS -- BUT THROUGH YOUR INTERVENTION, ABRAHAM GOLD'S DEATH REDEEMED THE LIFE OF HIS SON!
DO YOU NOT SEE THE GOOD YOUR ACTIONS WROUGHT?
DON'T SPLIT HAIRS WITH ME, LADY! I'M JUST TIRED OF PLAYING BACKSEAT GOD, OKAY?
VERY WELL THEN, BOSTON BRAND --YOU MAY HAVE YOUR WISH! I SHALL GRANT YOU THE FINAL REST YOU SEEK --
-- ON ONE CONDITION!
I KNEW THERE'D BE A CATCH IN THERE SOMEWHERE! SO WHAT'S THE DEAL?
THAT, MY SON, YOU SHALL SOON SEE FOR YOURSELF!
3

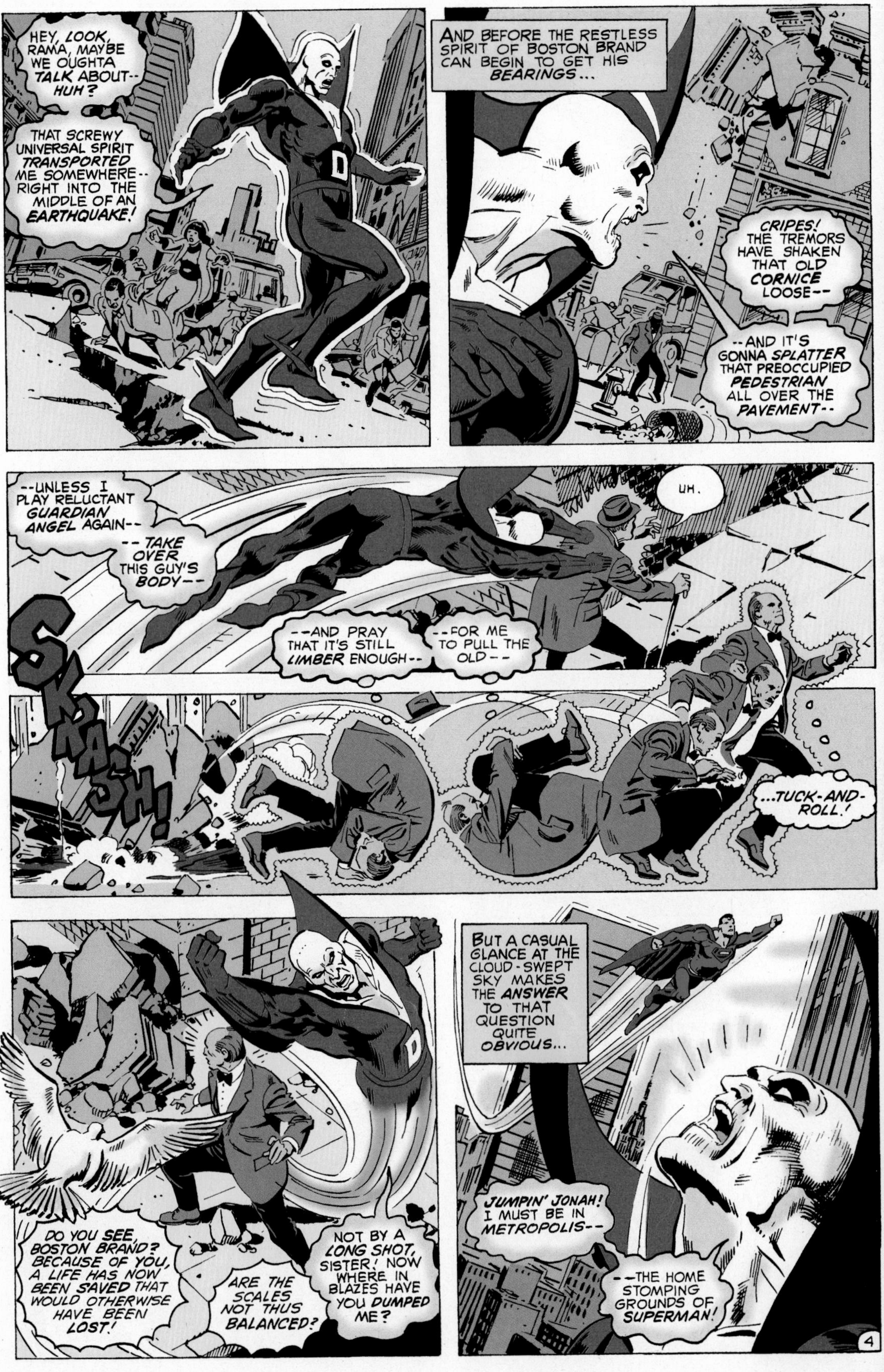
HEY, LOOK, RAMA, MAYBE WE OUGHTA TALK ABOUT-- HUH?
THAT SCREWY UNIVERSAL SPIRIT TRANSPORTED ME SOMEWHERE-- RIGHT INTO THE MIDDLE OF AN EARTHQUAKE!
AND BEFORE THE RESTLESS SPIRIT OF BOSTON BRAND CAN BEGIN TO GET HIS BEARINGS...
CRIPES! THE TREMORS HAVE SHAKEN THAT OLD CORNICE LOOSE--
--AND IT'S GONNA SPLATTER THAT PREOCCUPIED PEDESTRIAN ALL OVER THE PAVEMENT--
--UNLESS I PLAY RELUCTANT GUARDIAN ANGEL AGAIN--
--TAKE OVER THIS GUY'S BODY--
UH.
--AND PRAY THAT IT'S STILL LIMBER ENOUGH--
--FOR ME TO PULL THE OLD--
SKRASH!
...TUCK-AND-ROLL!
DO YOU SEE, BOSTON BRAND? BECAUSE OF YOU, A LIFE HAS NOW BEEN SAVED THAT WOULD OTHERWISE HAVE BEEN LOST!
ARE THE SCALES NOT THUS BALANCED?
NOT BY A LONG SHOT, SISTER! NOW WHERE IN BLAZES HAVE YOU DUMPED ME?
BUT A CASUAL GLANCE AT THE CLOUD-SWEPT SKY MAKES THE ANSWER TO THAT QUESTION QUITE OBVIOUS...
JUMPIN' JONAH! I MUST BE IN METROPOLIS--
--THE HOME STOMPING GROUNDS OF SUPERMAN!
4

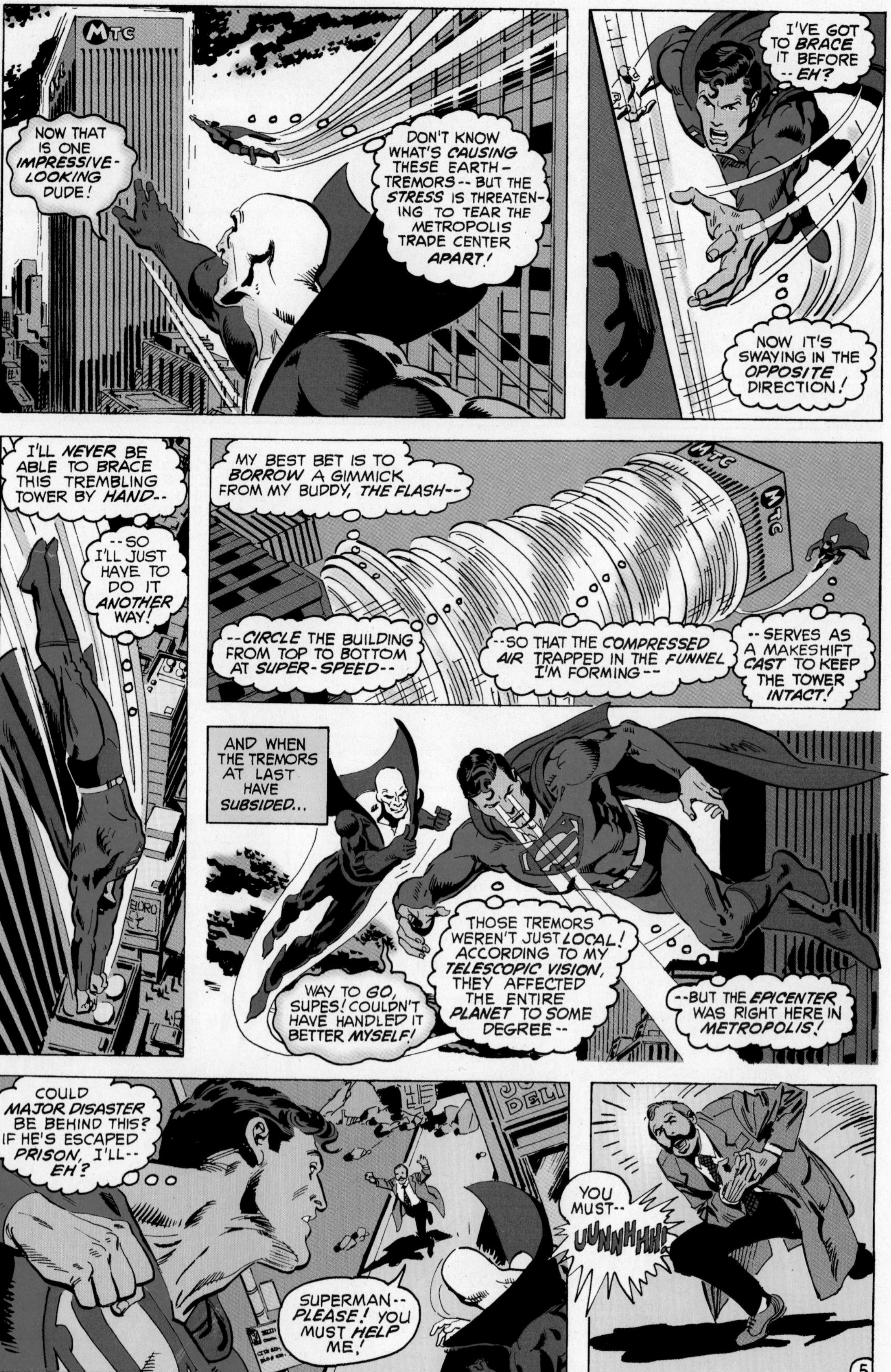
NOW THAT IS ONE IMPRESSIVE-LOOKING DUDE!
DON'T KNOW WHAT'S CAUSING THESE EARTH-TREMORS-- BUT THE STRESS IS THREATENING TO TEAR THE METROPOLIS TRADE CENTER APART!
I'VE GOT TO BRACE IT BEFORE --EH?
NOW IT'S SWAYING IN THE OPPOSITE DIRECTION!
I'LL NEVER BE ABLE TO BRACE THIS TREMBLING TOWER BY HAND--
--SO I'LL JUST HAVE TO DO IT ANOTHER WAY!
MY BEST BET IS TO BORROW A GIMMICK FROM MY BUDDY, THE FLASH--
--CIRCLE THE BUILDING FROM TOP TO BOTTOM AT SUPER-SPEED--
--SO THAT THE COMPRESSED AIR TRAPPED IN THE FUNNEL I'M FORMING--
--SERVES AS A MAKESHIFT CAST TO KEEP THE TOWER INTACT!
AND WHEN THE TREMORS AT LAST HAVE SUBSIDED...
THOSE TREMORS WEREN'T JUST LOCAL! ACCORDING TO MY TELESCOPIC VISION, THEY AFFECTED THE ENTIRE PLANET TO SOME DEGREE--
WAY TO GO, SUPES! COULDN'T HAVE HANDLED IT BETTER MYSELF!
--BUT THE EPICENTER WAS RIGHT HERE IN METROPOLIS!
COULD MAJOR DISASTER BE BEHIND THIS? IF HE'S ESCAPED PRISON, I'LL-- EH?
SUPERMAN-- PLEASE! YOU MUST HELP ME!
YOU MUST--
UUNNHHH!
5

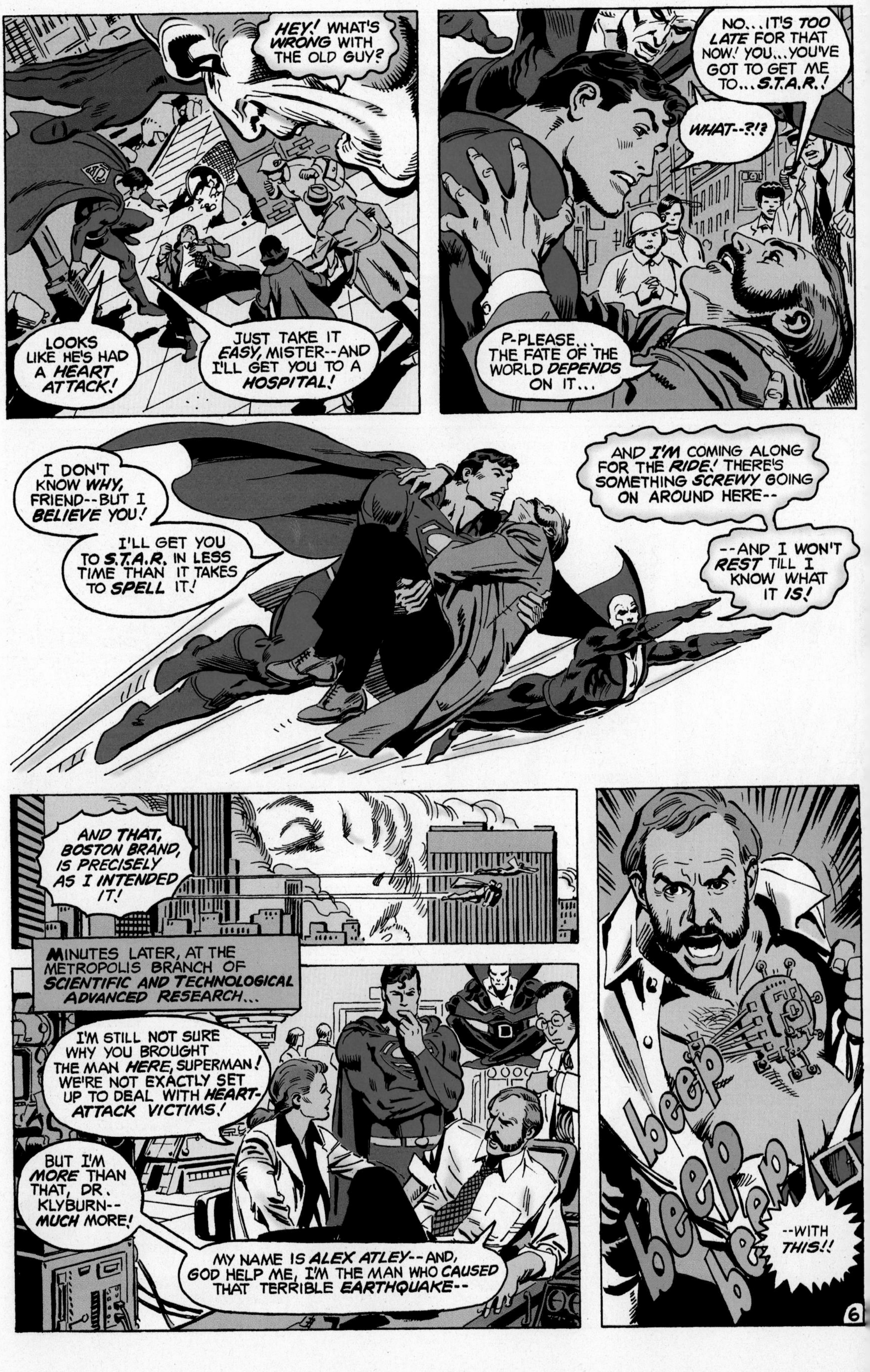

HEY! WHAT'S WRONG WITH THE OLD GUY?
LOOKS LIKE HE'S HAD A HEART ATTACK!
JUST TAKE IT EASY, MISTER--AND I'LL GET YOU TO A HOSPITAL!
NO... IT'S TOO LATE FOR THAT NOW! YOU... YOU'VE GOT TO GET ME TO... S.T.A.R.!
WHAT--?!?
P-PLEASE... THE FATE OF THE WORLD DEPENDS ON IT...
I DON'T KNOW WHY, FRIEND--BUT I BELIEVE YOU!
I'LL GET YOU TO S.T.A.R. IN LESS TIME THAN IT TAKES TO SPELL IT!
AND I'M COMING ALONG FOR THE RIDE! THERE'S SOMETHING SCREWY GOING ON AROUND HERE--
--AND I WON'T REST TILL I KNOW WHAT IT IS!
AND THAT, BOSTON BRAND, IS PRECISELY AS I INTENDED IT!
MINUTES LATER, AT THE METROPOLIS BRANCH OF SCIENTIFIC AND TECHNOLOGICAL ADVANCED RESEARCH...
I'M STILL NOT SURE WHY YOU BROUGHT THE MAN HERE, SUPERMAN! WE'RE NOT EXACTLY SET UP TO DEAL WITH HEART-ATTACK VICTIMS!
BUT I'M MORE THAN THAT, DR. KLYBURN-- MUCH MORE!
MY NAME IS ALEX ATLEY--AND, GOD HELP ME, I'M THE MAN WHO CAUSED THAT TERRIBLE EARTHQUAKE--
beep beep beep beep
--WITH THIS!!
6

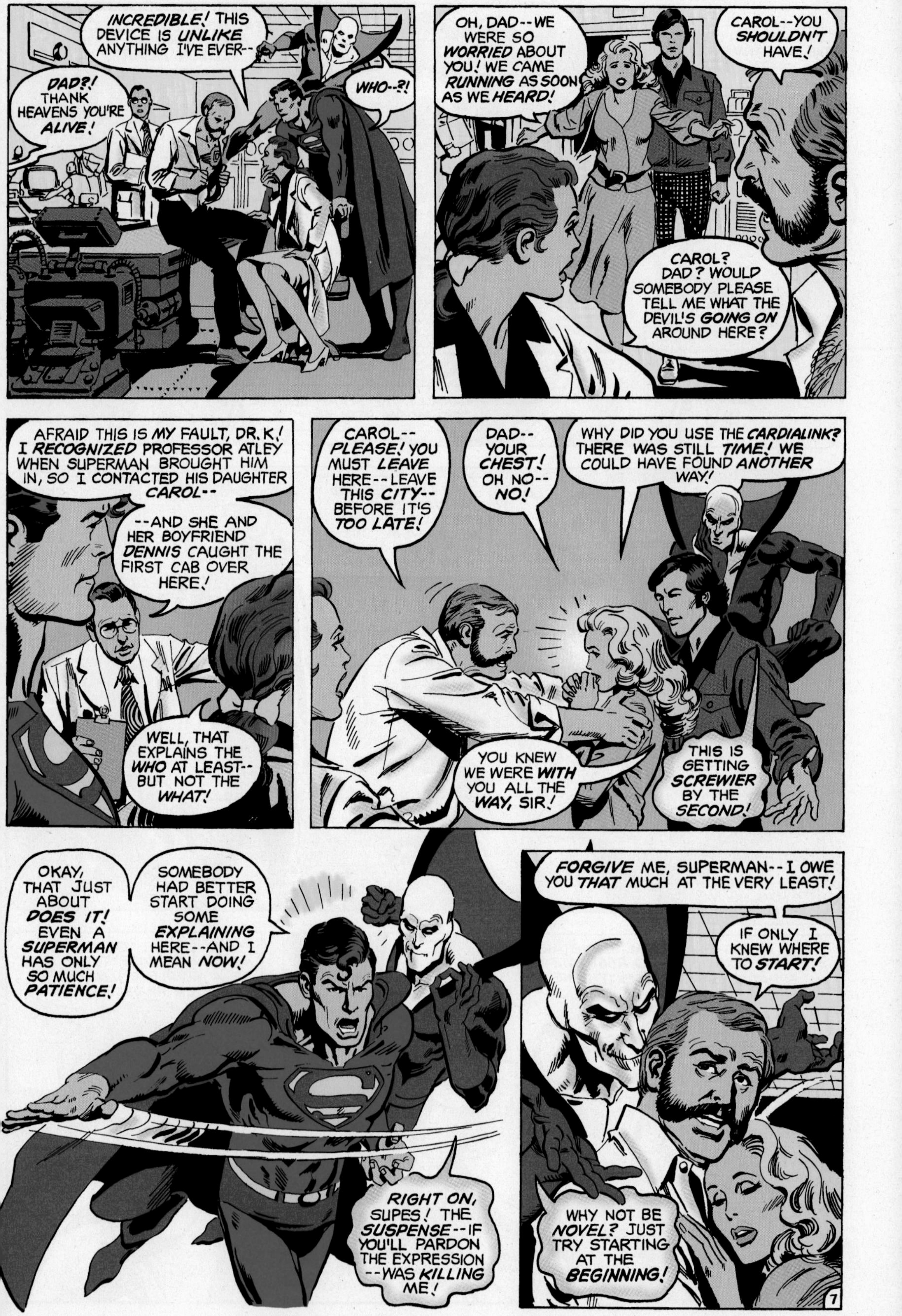
DAD?! THANK HEAVENS YOU'RE ALIVE!
INCREDIBLE! THIS DEVICE IS UNLIKE ANYTHING I'VE EVER--
WHO--?!
OH, DAD--WE WERE SO WORRIED ABOUT YOU! WE CAME RUNNING AS SOON AS WE HEARD!
CAROL--YOU SHOULDN'T HAVE!
CAROL? DAD? WOULD SOMEBODY PLEASE TELL ME WHAT THE DEVIL'S GOING ON AROUND HERE?
AFRAID THIS IS MY FAULT, DR. K! I RECOGNIZED PROFESSOR ATLEY WHEN SUPERMAN BROUGHT HIM IN, SO I CONTACTED HIS DAUGHTER CAROL--
--AND SHE AND HER BOYFRIEND DENNIS CAUGHT THE FIRST CAB OVER HERE!
WELL, THAT EXPLAINS THE WHO AT LEAST--BUT NOT THE WHAT!
CAROL--PLEASE! YOU MUST LEAVE HERE--LEAVE THIS CITY--BEFORE IT'S TOO LATE!
DAD--YOUR CHEST! OH NO--NO!
WHY DID YOU USE THE CARDIALINK? THERE WAS STILL TIME! WE COULD HAVE FOUND ANOTHER WAY!
YOU KNEW WE WERE WITH YOU ALL THE WAY, SIR!
THIS IS GETTING SCREWIER BY THE SECOND!
OKAY, THAT JUST ABOUT DOES IT! EVEN A SUPERMAN HAS ONLY SO MUCH PATIENCE!
SOMEBODY HAD BETTER START DOING SOME EXPLAINING HERE--AND I MEAN NOW!
RIGHT ON, SUPES! THE SUSPENSE--IF YOU'LL PARDON THE EXPRESSION--WAS KILLING ME!
FORGIVE ME, SUPERMAN--I OWE YOU THAT MUCH AT THE VERY LEAST!
IF ONLY I KNEW WHERE TO START!
WHY NOT BE NOVEL? JUST TRY STARTING AT THE BEGINNING!
7

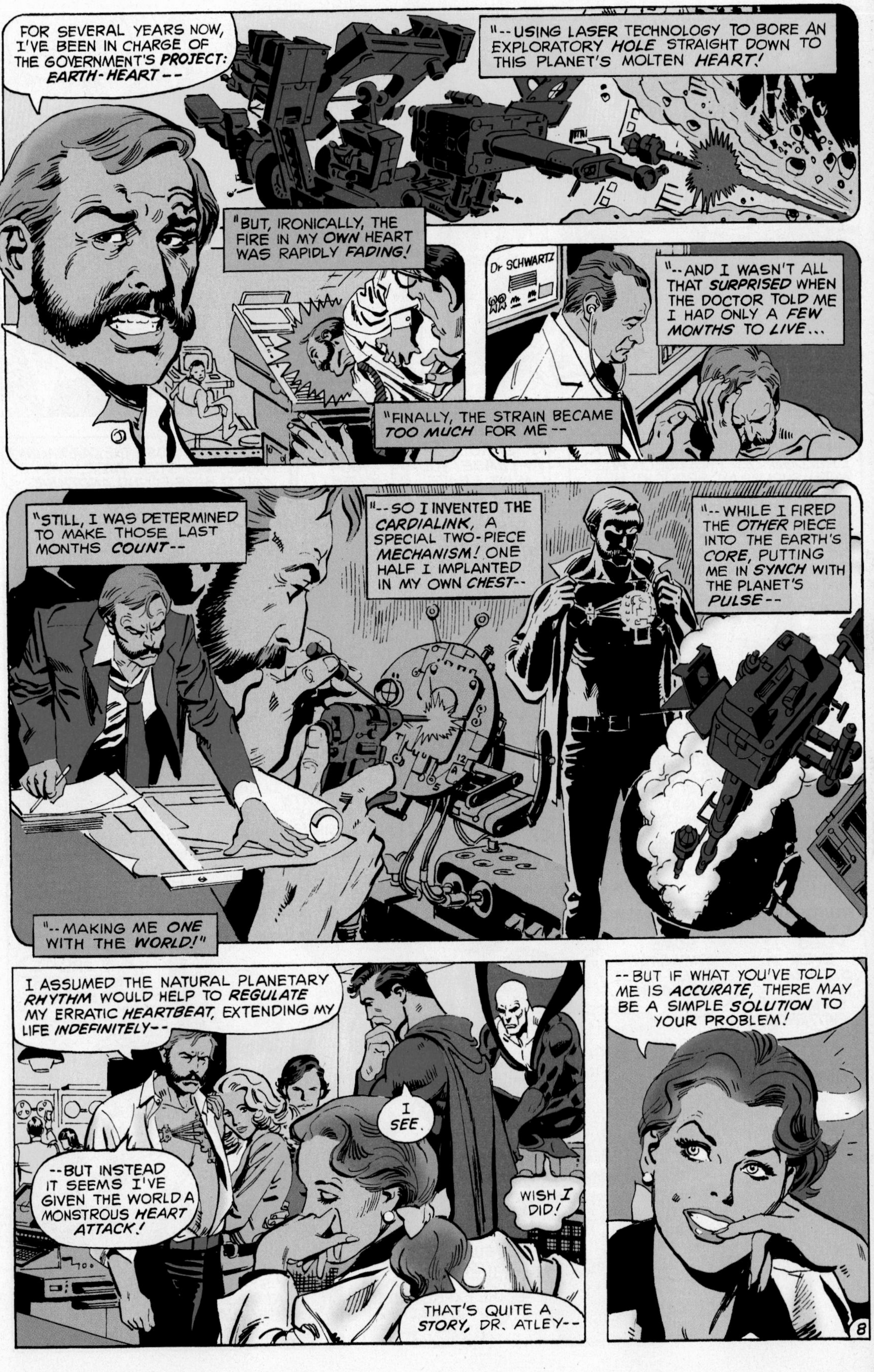
FOR SEVERAL YEARS NOW, I'VE BEEN IN CHARGE OF THE GOVERNMENT'S PROJECT: EARTH-HEART --
"--USING LASER TECHNOLOGY TO BORE AN EXPLORATORY HOLE STRAIGHT DOWN TO THIS PLANET'S MOLTEN HEART!
"BUT, IRONICALLY, THE FIRE IN MY OWN HEART WAS RAPIDLY FADING!
"FINALLY, THE STRAIN BECAME TOO MUCH FOR ME --
Dr SCHWARTZ
"--AND I WASN'T ALL THAT SURPRISED WHEN THE DOCTOR TOLD ME I HAD ONLY A FEW MONTHS TO LIVE...
"STILL, I WAS DETERMINED TO MAKE THOSE LAST MONTHS COUNT--
"--SO I INVENTED THE CARDIALINK, A SPECIAL TWO-PIECE MECHANISM! ONE HALF I IMPLANTED IN MY OWN CHEST--
"--WHILE I FIRED THE OTHER PIECE INTO THE EARTH'S CORE, PUTTING ME IN SYNCH WITH THE PLANET'S PULSE--
"--MAKING ME ONE WITH THE WORLD!"
I ASSUMED THE NATURAL PLANETARY RHYTHM WOULD HELP TO REGULATE MY ERRATIC HEARTBEAT, EXTENDING MY LIFE INDEFINITELY--
--BUT INSTEAD IT SEEMS I'VE GIVEN THE WORLD A MONSTROUS HEART ATTACK!
I SEE.
WISH I DID!
THAT'S QUITE A STORY, DR. ATLEY--
--BUT IF WHAT YOU'VE TOLD ME IS ACCURATE, THERE MAY BE A SIMPLE SOLUTION TO YOUR PROBLEM!
8

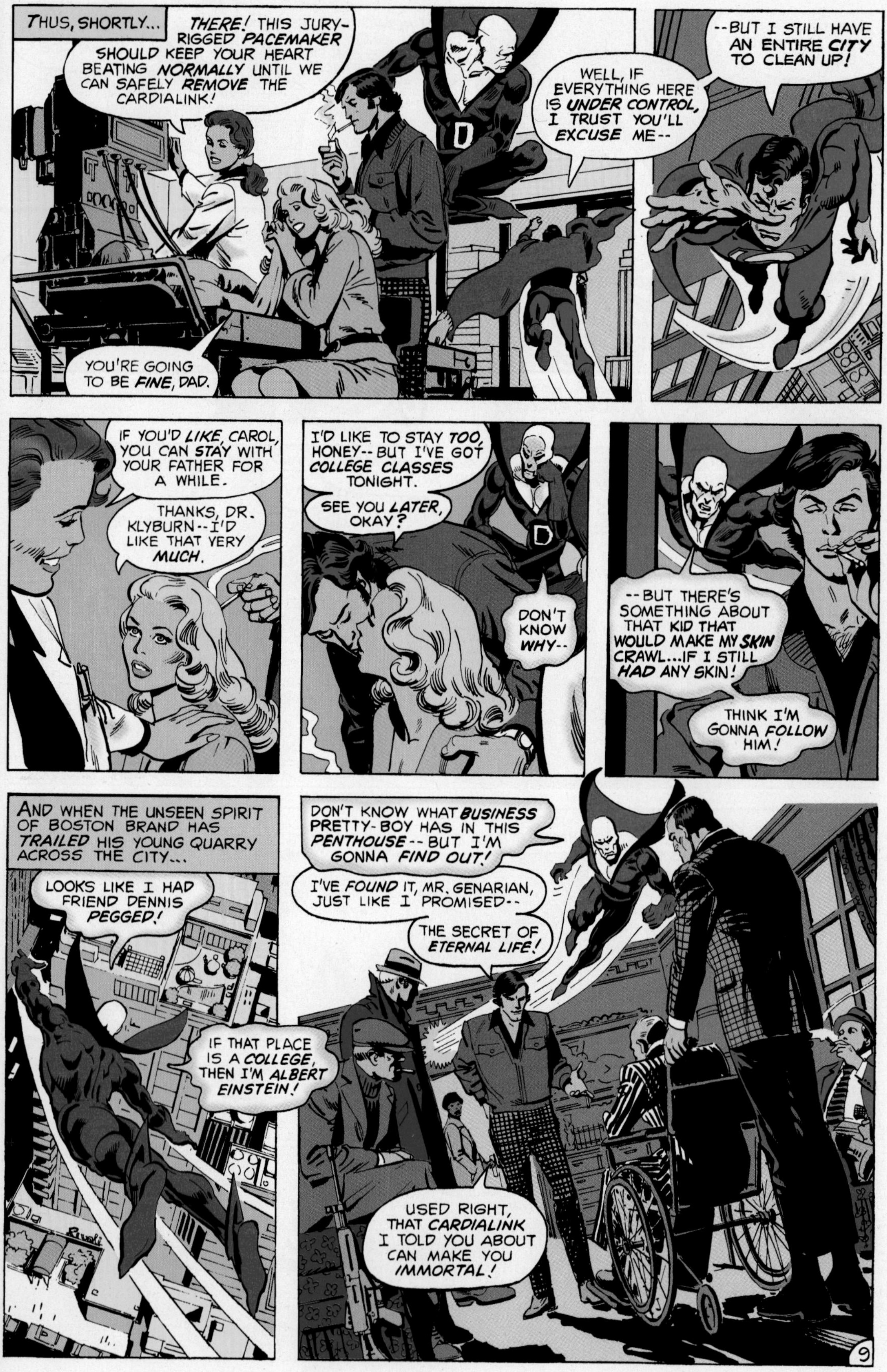
THUS, SHORTLY...
THERE! THIS JURY-RIGGED PACEMAKER SHOULD KEEP YOUR HEART BEATING NORMALLY UNTIL WE CAN SAFELY REMOVE THE CARDIALINK!
YOU'RE GOING TO BE FINE, DAD.
WELL, IF EVERYTHING HERE IS UNDER CONTROL, I TRUST YOU'LL EXCUSE ME--
--BUT I STILL HAVE AN ENTIRE CITY TO CLEAN UP!
IF YOU'D LIKE, CAROL, YOU CAN STAY WITH YOUR FATHER FOR A WHILE.
THANKS, DR. KLYBURN--I'D LIKE THAT VERY MUCH.
I'D LIKE TO STAY TOO, HONEY--BUT I'VE GOT COLLEGE CLASSES TONIGHT.
SEE YOU LATER, OKAY?
DON'T KNOW WHY--
--BUT THERE'S SOMETHING ABOUT THAT KID THAT WOULD MAKE MY SKIN CRAWL...IF I STILL HAD ANY SKIN!
THINK I'M GONNA FOLLOW HIM!
AND WHEN THE UNSEEN SPIRIT OF BOSTON BRAND HAS TRAILED HIS YOUNG QUARRY ACROSS THE CITY...
LOOKS LIKE I HAD FRIEND DENNIS PEGGED!
IF THAT PLACE IS A COLLEGE, THEN I'M ALBERT EINSTEIN!
DON'T KNOW WHAT BUSINESS PRETTY-BOY HAS IN THIS PENTHOUSE--BUT I'M GONNA FIND OUT!
I'VE FOUND IT, MR. GENARIAN, JUST LIKE I PROMISED--
THE SECRET OF ETERNAL LIFE!
USED RIGHT, THAT CARDIALINK I TOLD YOU ABOUT CAN MAKE YOU IMMORTAL!
9

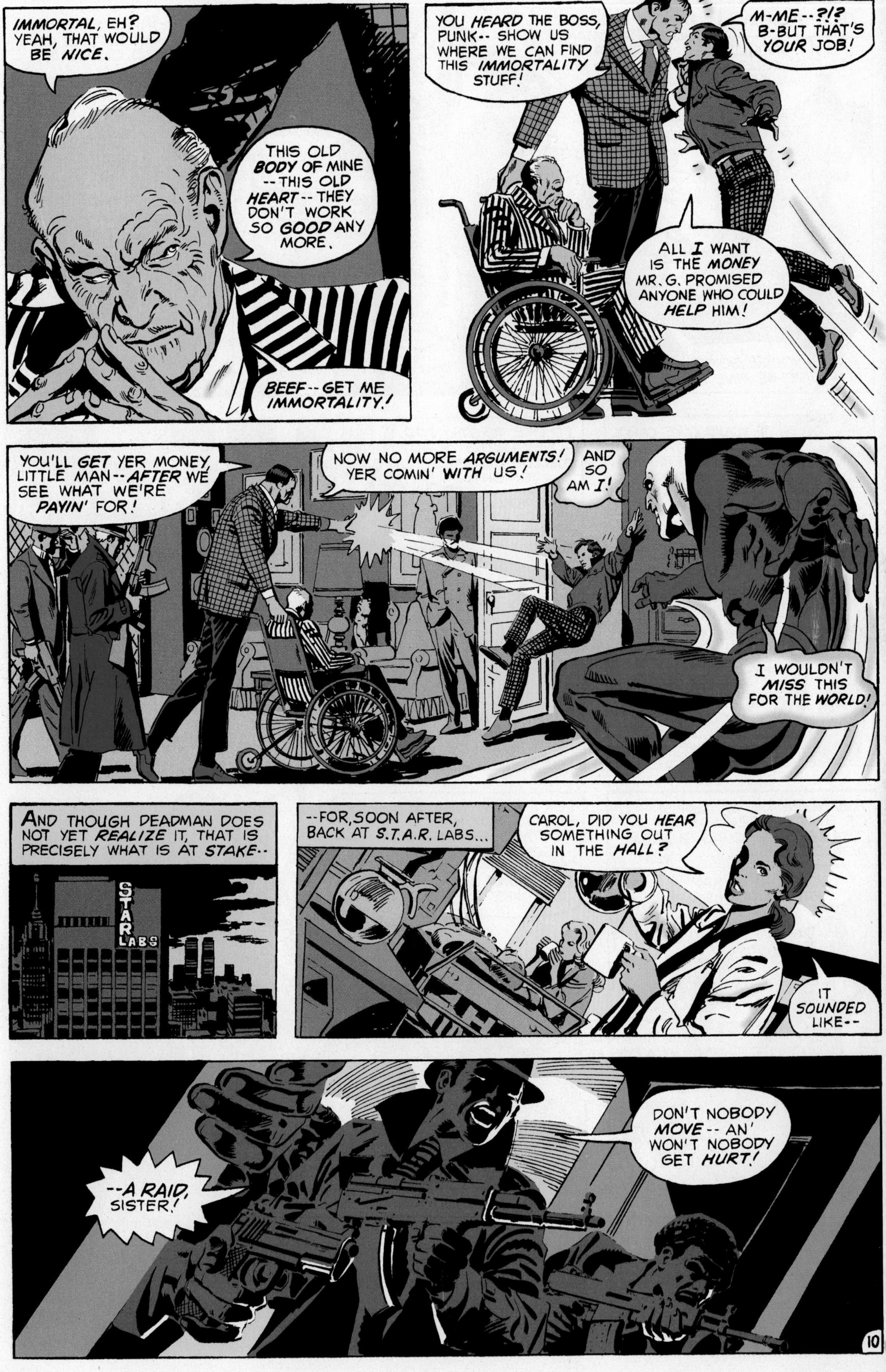
IMMORTAL, EH? YEAH, THAT WOULD BE NICE.
THIS OLD BODY OF MINE -- THIS OLD HEART -- THEY DON'T WORK SO GOOD ANY MORE.
BEEF -- GET ME IMMORTALITY!
YOU HEARD THE BOSS, PUNK -- SHOW US WHERE WE CAN FIND THIS IMMORTALITY STUFF!
M-ME--?!? B-BUT THAT'S YOUR JOB!
ALL I WANT IS THE MONEY MR. G. PROMISED ANYONE WHO COULD HELP HIM!
YOU'LL GET YER MONEY, LITTLE MAN -- AFTER WE SEE WHAT WE'RE PAYIN' FOR!
NOW NO MORE ARGUMENTS! YER COMIN' WITH US!
AND SO AM I!
I WOULDN'T MISS THIS FOR THE WORLD!
AND THOUGH DEADMAN DOES NOT YET REALIZE IT, THAT IS PRECISELY WHAT IS AT STAKE--
STAR LABS
--FOR, SOON AFTER, BACK AT S.T.A.R. LABS...
CAROL, DID YOU HEAR SOMETHING OUT IN THE HALL?
IT SOUNDED LIKE--
--A RAID, SISTER!
DON'T NOBODY MOVE -- AN' WON'T NOBODY GET HURT!
10

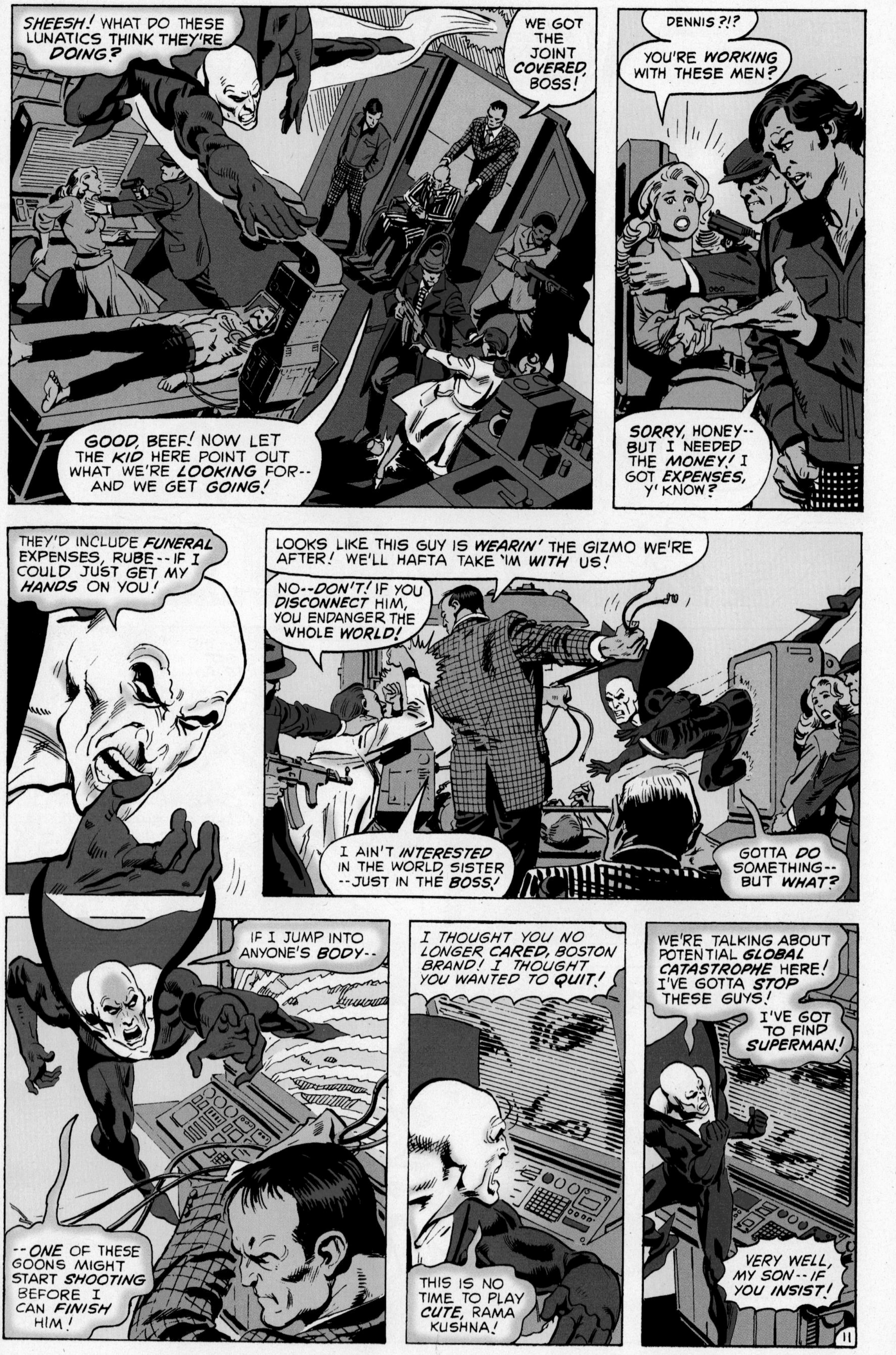
SHEESH! WHAT DO THESE LUNATICS THINK THEY'RE DOING?
WE GOT THE JOINT COVERED, BOSS!
GOOD, BEEF! NOW LET THE KID HERE POINT OUT WHAT WE'RE LOOKING FOR-- AND WE GET GOING!
DENNIS?!?
YOU'RE WORKING WITH THESE MEN?
SORRY, HONEY-- BUT I NEEDED THE MONEY! I GOT EXPENSES, Y'KNOW?
THEY'D INCLUDE FUNERAL EXPENSES, RUBE--IF I COULD JUST GET MY HANDS ON YOU!
LOOKS LIKE THIS GUY IS WEARIN' THE GIZMO WE'RE AFTER! WE'LL HAFTA TAKE 'IM WITH US!
NO--DON'T! IF YOU DISCONNECT HIM, YOU ENDANGER THE WHOLE WORLD!
I AIN'T INTERESTED IN THE WORLD, SISTER --JUST IN THE BOSS!
GOTTA DO SOMETHING-- BUT WHAT?
IF I JUMP INTO ANYONE'S BODY--
--ONE OF THESE GOONS MIGHT START SHOOTING BEFORE I CAN FINISH HIM!
I THOUGHT YOU NO LONGER CARED, BOSTON BRAND! I THOUGHT YOU WANTED TO QUIT!
THIS IS NO TIME TO PLAY CUTE, RAMA KUSHNA!
WE'RE TALKING ABOUT POTENTIAL GLOBAL CATASTROPHE HERE! I'VE GOTTA STOP THESE GUYS!
I'VE GOT TO FIND SUPERMAN!
VERY WELL, MY SON--IF YOU INSIST!
11

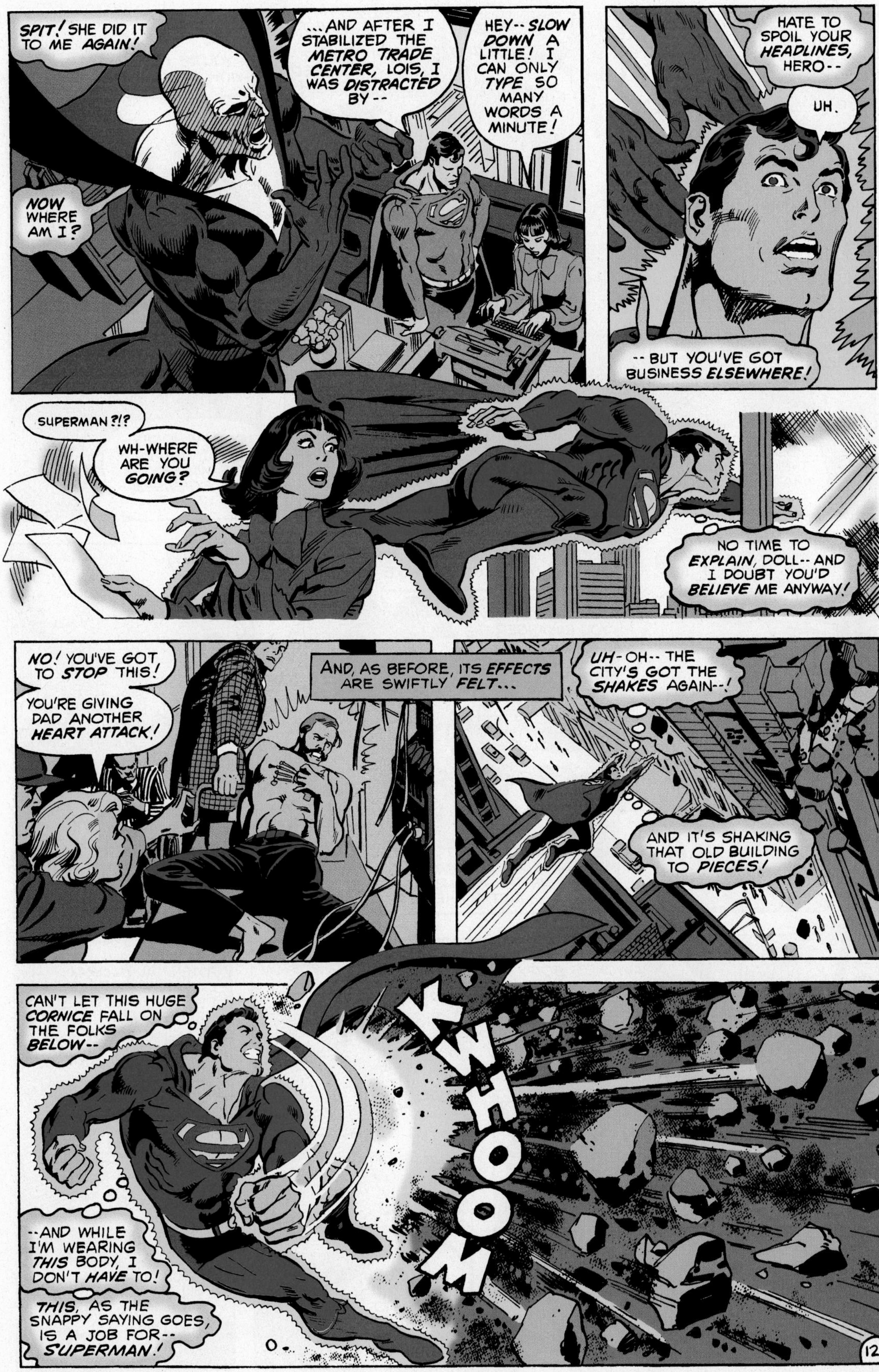
SPIT! SHE DID IT TO ME AGAIN!
NOW WHERE AM I?
...AND AFTER I STABILIZED THE METRO TRADE CENTER, LOIS, I WAS DISTRACTED BY--
HEY--SLOW DOWN A LITTLE! I CAN ONLY TYPE SO MANY WORDS A MINUTE!
HATE TO SPOIL YOUR HEADLINES, HERO--
UH.
--BUT YOU'VE GOT BUSINESS ELSEWHERE!
SUPERMAN?!?
WH-WHERE ARE YOU GOING?
NO TIME TO EXPLAIN, DOLL-- AND I DOUBT YOU'D BELIEVE ME ANYWAY!
NO! YOU'VE GOT TO STOP THIS!
YOU'RE GIVING DAD ANOTHER HEART ATTACK!
AND, AS BEFORE, ITS EFFECTS ARE SWIFTLY FELT...
UH-OH-- THE CITY'S GOT THE SHAKES AGAIN--!
AND IT'S SHAKING THAT OLD BUILDING TO PIECES!
CAN'T LET THIS HUGE CORNICE FALL ON THE FOLKS BELOW--
KWHOOOM
--AND WHILE I'M WEARING THIS BODY, I DON'T HAVE TO!
THIS, AS THE SNAPPY SAYING GOES, IS A JOB FOR-- SUPERMAN!
12

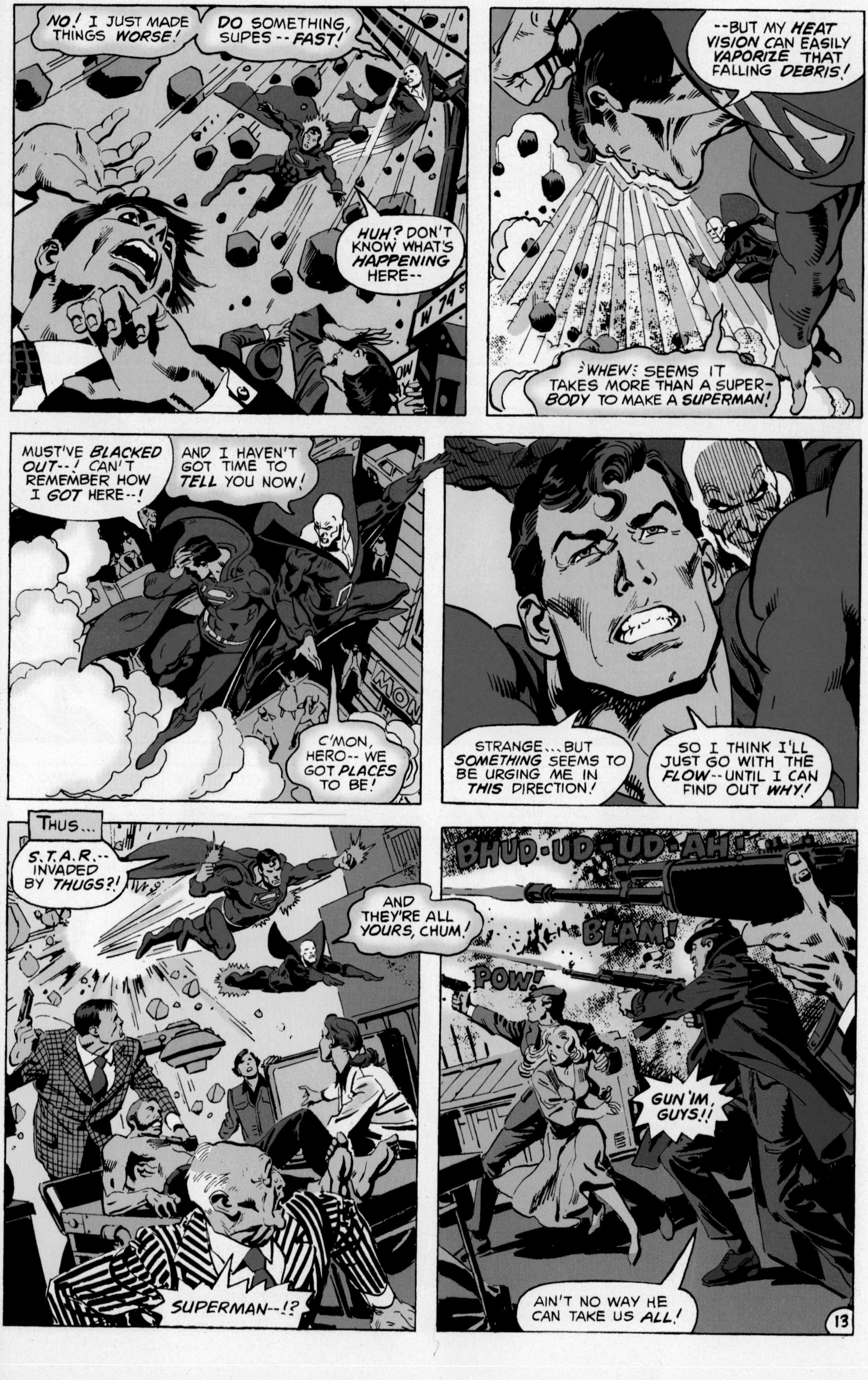

NO! I JUST MADE THINGS WORSE!
DO SOMETHING, SUPES -- FAST!
HUH? DON'T KNOW WHAT'S HAPPENING HERE--
--BUT MY HEAT VISION CAN EASILY VAPORIZE THAT FALLING DEBRIS!
WHEW! SEEMS IT TAKES MORE THAN A SUPER-BODY TO MAKE A SUPERMAN!
MUST'VE BLACKED OUT--! CAN'T REMEMBER HOW I GOT HERE--!
AND I HAVEN'T GOT TIME TO TELL YOU NOW!
C'MON, HERO-- WE GOT PLACES TO BE!
STRANGE... BUT SOMETHING SEEMS TO BE URGING ME IN THIS DIRECTION!
SO I THINK I'LL JUST GO WITH THE FLOW--UNTIL I CAN FIND OUT WHY!
THUS...
S.T.A.R.-- INVADED BY THUGS?!
AND THEY'RE ALL YOURS, CHUM!
SUPERMAN--!?
BHUD-UD-UD-AH!
BLAM!
POW!
GUN 'IM, GUYS!!
AIN'T NO WAY HE CAN TAKE US ALL!
13

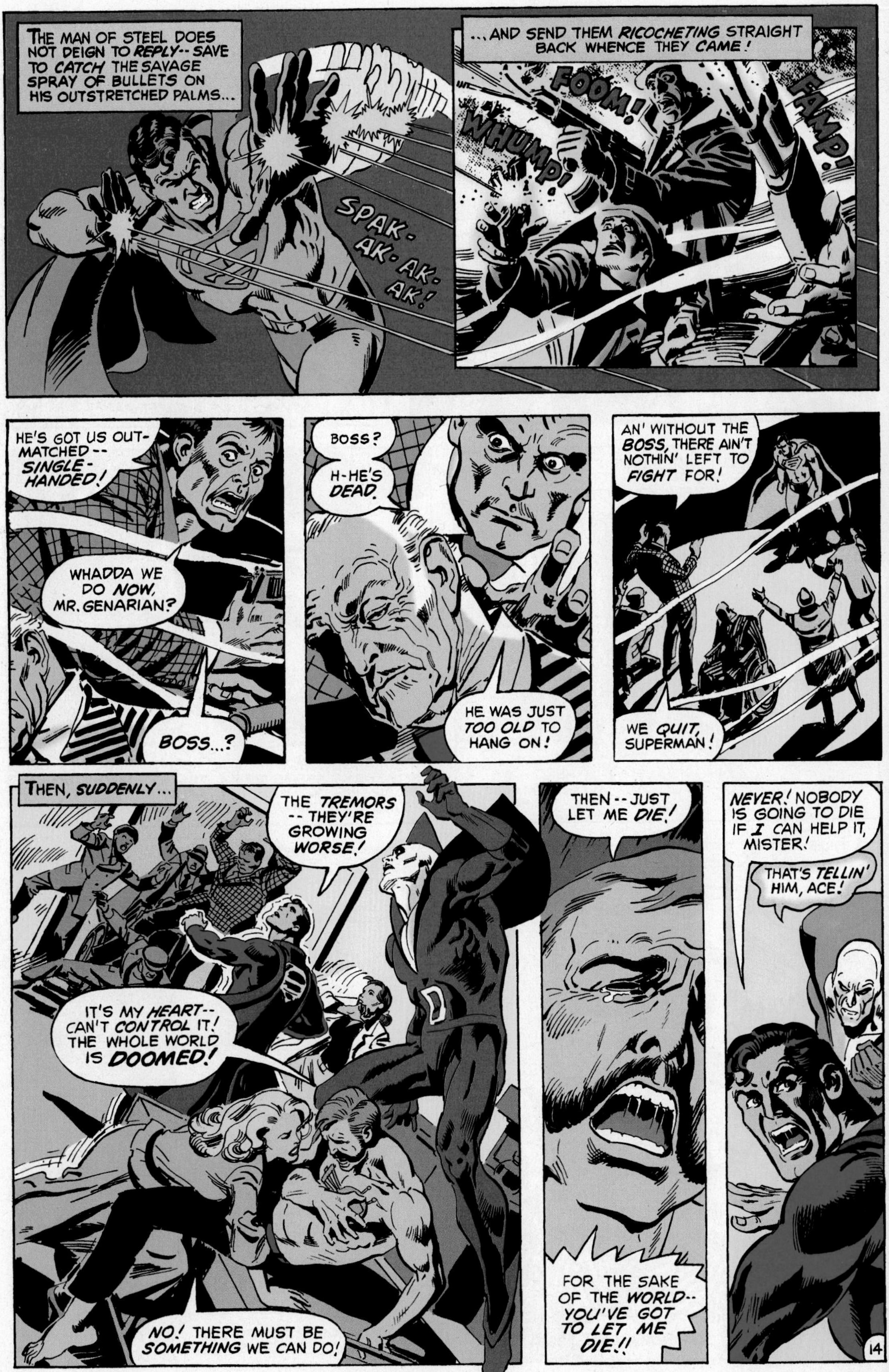
THE MAN OF STEEL DOES NOT DEIGN TO REPLY-- SAVE TO CATCH THE SAVAGE SPRAY OF BULLETS ON HIS OUTSTRETCHED PALMS...
SPAK-AK-AK-AK!
...AND SEND THEM RICOCHETING STRAIGHT BACK WHENCE THEY CAME!
FOOM!
WHUMP!
FAMP!
HE'S GOT US OUT-MATCHED -- SINGLE-HANDED!
WHADDA WE DO NOW, MR. GENARIAN?
BOSS...?
BOSS?
H-HE'S DEAD.
HE WAS JUST TOO OLD TO HANG ON!
AN' WITHOUT THE BOSS, THERE AIN'T NOTHIN' LEFT TO FIGHT FOR!
WE QUIT, SUPERMAN!
THEN, SUDDENLY...
THE TREMORS -- THEY'RE GROWING WORSE!
IT'S MY HEART-- CAN'T CONTROL IT! THE WHOLE WORLD IS DOOMED!
NO! THERE MUST BE SOMETHING WE CAN DO!
THEN -- JUST LET ME DIE!
FOR THE SAKE OF THE WORLD-- YOU'VE GOT TO LET ME DIE!!
NEVER! NOBODY IS GOING TO DIE IF I CAN HELP IT, MISTER!
THAT'S TELLIN' HIM, ACE!
14

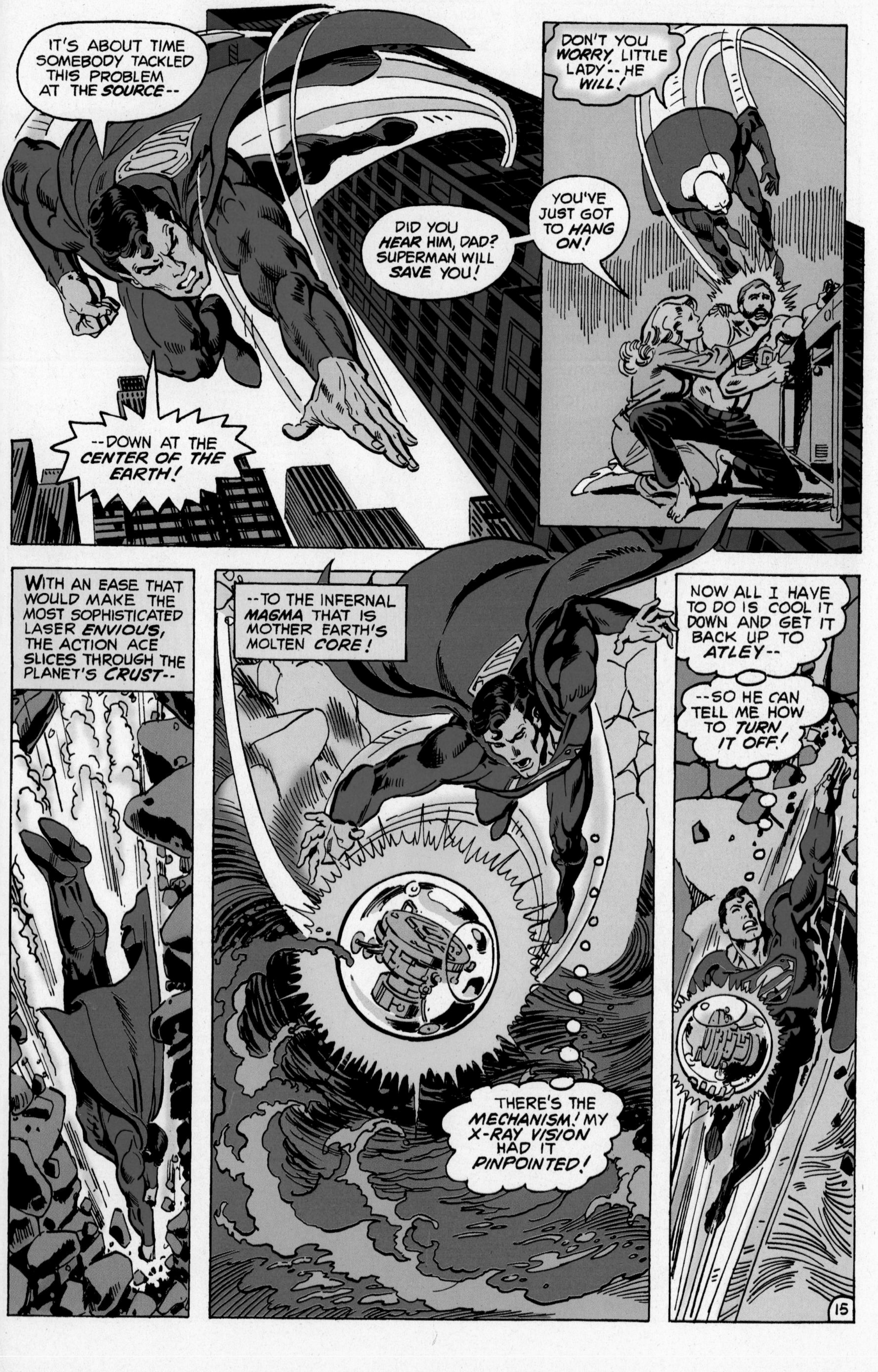
IT'S ABOUT TIME SOMEBODY TACKLED THIS PROBLEM AT THE SOURCE--
--DOWN AT THE CENTER OF THE EARTH!
DON'T YOU WORRY, LITTLE LADY--HE WILL!
DID YOU HEAR HIM, DAD? SUPERMAN WILL SAVE YOU!
YOU'VE JUST GOT TO HANG ON!
WITH AN EASE THAT WOULD MAKE THE MOST SOPHISTICATED LASER ENVIOUS, THE ACTION ACE SLICES THROUGH THE PLANET'S CRUST--
--TO THE INFERNAL MAGMA THAT IS MOTHER EARTH'S MOLTEN CORE!
THERE'S THE MECHANISM! MY X-RAY VISION HAD IT PINPOINTED!
NOW ALL I HAVE TO DO IS COOL IT DOWN AND GET IT BACK UP TO ATLEY--
--SO HE CAN TELL ME HOW TO TURN IT OFF!
15

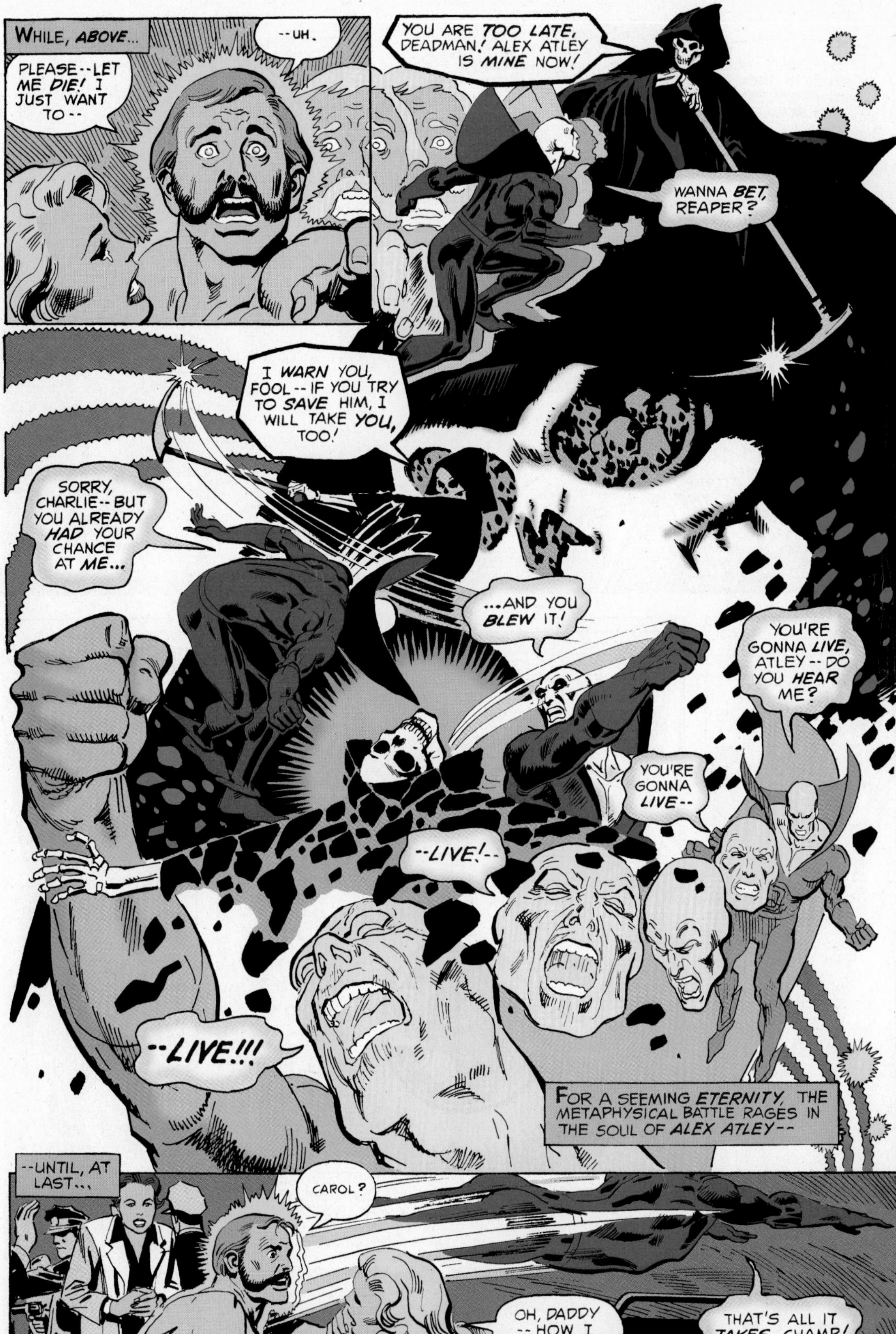
WHILE, ABOVE...
PLEASE--LET ME DIE! I JUST WANT TO--
--UH.
YOU ARE TOO LATE, DEADMAN! ALEX ATLEY IS MINE NOW!
WANNA BET, REAPER?
I WARN YOU, FOOL--IF YOU TRY TO SAVE HIM, I WILL TAKE YOU, TOO!
SORRY, CHARLIE--BUT YOU ALREADY HAD YOUR CHANCE AT ME...
...AND YOU BLEW IT!
YOU'RE GONNA LIVE, ATLEY--DO YOU HEAR ME?
YOU'RE GONNA LIVE--
--LIVE!--
--LIVE!!!
FOR A SEEMING ETERNITY, THE METAPHYSICAL BATTLE RAGES IN THE SOUL OF ALEX ATLEY--
--UNTIL, AT LAST...
CAROL?
PLEASE... HELP ME!
OH, DADDY--HOW I WANT TO!
THAT'S ALL IT TAKES, CHAMP! NOTHING CAN LICK YOU NOW!
16

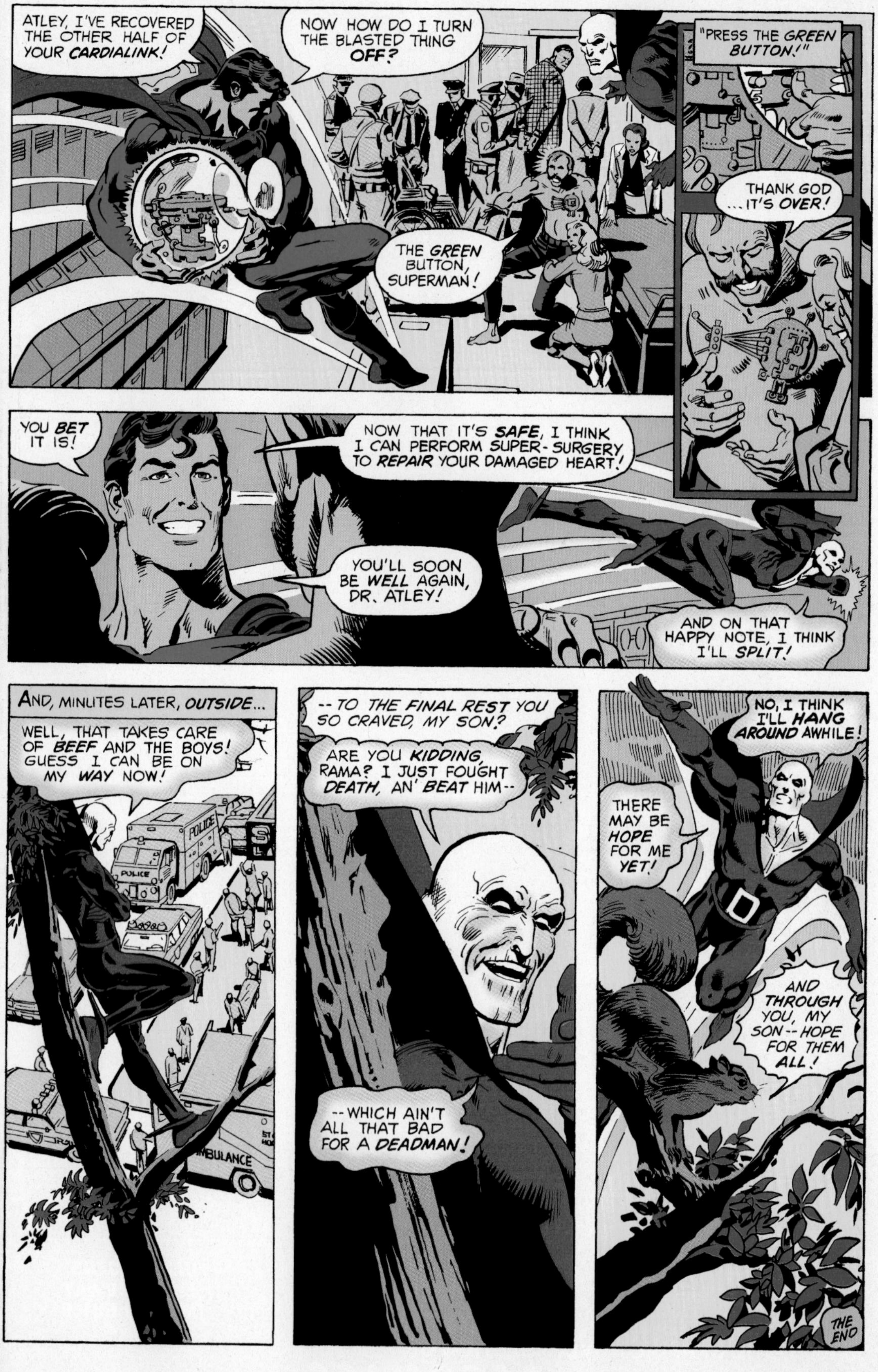
ATLEY, I'VE RECOVERED THE OTHER HALF OF YOUR CARDIALINK!
NOW HOW DO I TURN THE BLASTED THING OFF?
THE GREEN BUTTON, SUPERMAN!
"PRESS THE GREEN BUTTON!"
THANK GOD ...IT'S OVER!
YOU BET IT IS!
NOW THAT IT'S SAFE, I THINK I CAN PERFORM SUPER-SURGERY TO REPAIR YOUR DAMAGED HEART!
YOU'LL SOON BE WELL AGAIN, DR. ATLEY!
AND ON THAT HAPPY NOTE, I THINK I'LL SPLIT!
AND, MINUTES LATER, OUTSIDE...
WELL, THAT TAKES CARE OF BEEF AND THE BOYS! GUESS I CAN BE ON MY WAY NOW!
POLICE
AMBULANCE
--TO THE FINAL REST YOU SO CRAVED, MY SON?
ARE YOU KIDDING, RAMA? I JUST FOUGHT DEATH, AN' BEAT HIM--
--WHICH AIN'T ALL THAT BAD FOR A DEADMAN!
NO, I THINK I'LL HANG AROUND AWHILE!
THERE MAY BE HOPE FOR ME YET!
AND THROUGH YOU, MY SON--HOPE FOR THEM ALL!
THE END

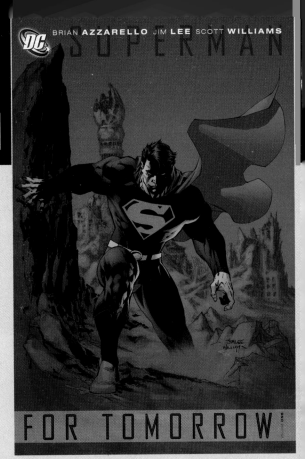
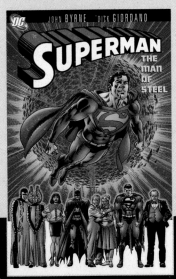
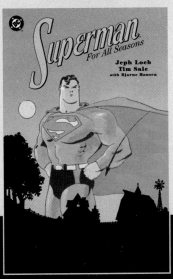
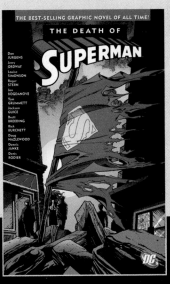

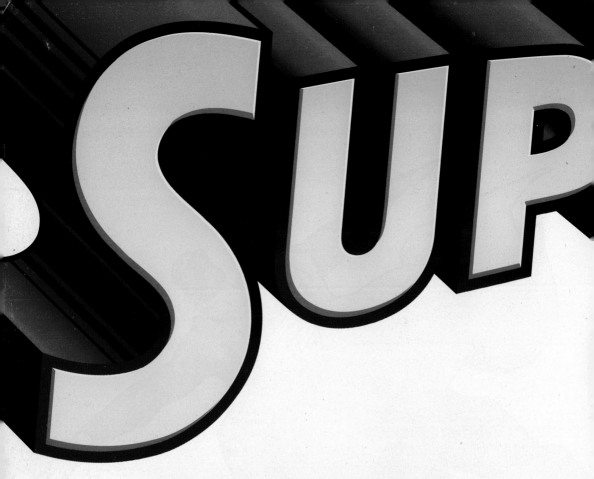

SUPERMAN CREATED BY **JERRY SIEGEL** AND **JOE SHUSTER**

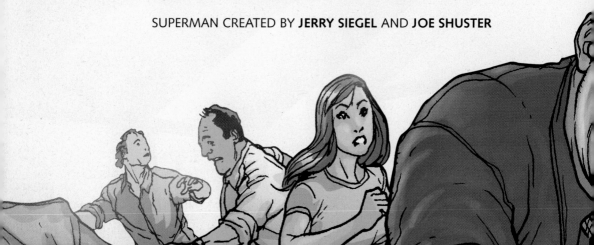

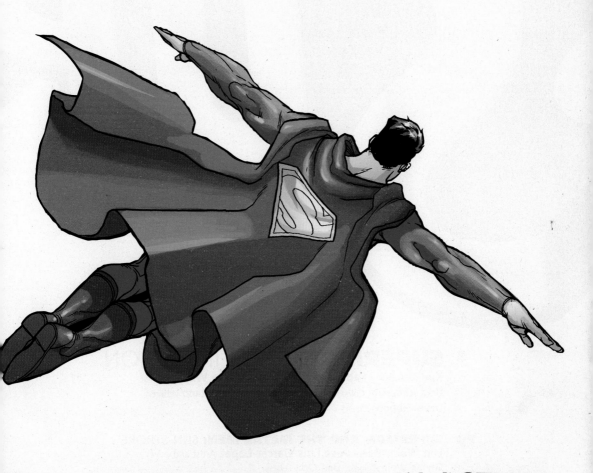

SUPERMAN: BACK IN ACTION